A POLITICAL HISTORY OF FOOD
From the Paleolithic to our days

Paul Ariès

A POLITICAL HISTORY OF FOOD
From the Paleolithic to our days

Max Milo

Max Milo Editions, Paris, 2023
www.maxmilo.com
ISBN : 978-2-315-01090-5

The fish we eat together has no bones.
Democritus

You don't have to look at what you eat so much as who you eat with [...].
There is no sweetness for me, nor sauce so appetizing
than the one that gets out of the company.
Montaigne

From the same author

La Fin des mangeurs, Éd. Desclée de Brouwer, 1997
Les Fils de McDo, Éd. L'Harmattan, 1997
Déni d'enfance, Éd. Golias, 1997
Scientology, laboratory of the future? The secrets of an infernal machine, Éd. Golias, 1998
Petit manuel anti-McDo à l'usage des petits et des grands, Éd. Golias, 1999
La Scientologie : une secte contre la République, Éd. Golias, 1999
José Bové, the revolt of a farmer. Interviews with Paul Ariès and Christian Terras, Éd. Golias, 2000
Le Goût (with Gong Gang), Éd. Desclée de Brouwer, 2000
Animal liberation or new terrorists? Éd. Golias, 2000
Les Sectes à l'assaut de la santé, Éd. Golias, 2000
Anthroposophy : investigation on an occult power, Éd. Golias, 2001
Disneyland, le royaume désenchanté, Éd. Golias, 2002
To save the earth: should the human species disappear? Éd. L'Harmattan, 2002
Harcèlement au travail ou Nouveau Management, Éd. Golias, 2002
Fucking your brand! Éd. Golias, 2003
Démarque-toi ! Petit manuel anti-pub, Éd. Golias, 2004
Satanisme et Vampirisme, Éd. Golias, 2004
Misère du sarkozysme. Cette droite qui n'aime pas la France, Éd. Parangon, 2005
Décroissance ou Barbarie, Éd. Golias, 2005
No conso. Manifesto for a general strike on consumption, Éd. Golias, 2006
Le Mésusage. Essay on hypercapitalism, Éd. Parangon, 2007
Learning to make the void (with Bernadette Costa-Prades), Éd. Milan, 2009
Disobey and grow, Les éditions écosociété, 2009

Cohn-Bendit, l'imposture, (with Florence Leray), Max Milo, 2010
La Simplicité volontaire contre le mythe de l'abondance, La Découverte, 2010
Le Socialisme gourmand, La Découverte, 2012
*Amoureux du bien vivre, Africa, Americas, Asia… What does the ecology of the
    poor teach us*, Éd. Golias, 2013
Nos rêves ne tiennent pas dans les urnes, Éd. Max Milo, 2013
Ecology and popular cultures, Éd. Utopia, 2015
La face cachée du pape François, Éd. Max Milo, 2016

For all contacts (conferences and press):
paul.aries@laposte.net

APPETIZERS

Many histories of food exist but no political history, as if our ways of forming society, of settling our conflicts, of choosing who are our friends and our enemies, of determining what we consider to be common to us, did not interfere with our conceptions of food and our ways of going or not going to the table, with our definitions, always changing, which make it possible to say who has the right to take part in the banquet, who must receive several shares, a full share, a half share, or even a bad share[1]. This journey will sometimes be anecdotal because it is necessary to say how, why, where, and with whom our ancestors ate and drank, but it does lead to a determining observation for the 21st century. If mankind has largely humanized itself by humanizing its table, it could well be that it dehumanizes itself by dint of dehumanizing it.

---

1. Our political history of food opens up a wide disciplinary field, but it intersects with many other well established histories. For a historical approach: Massimo MONTANARI and Jean-Louis Flandrin (eds), *Histoire de l'alimentation*, Fayard, 1996, reprinted 2014; Odile REDON, Sallmann LINE and Sylvie STEINBERG (eds), *Le Désir et le Goût, une autre histoire (XIIIe-XVIIIe siècle)*, international colloquium in memory of Jean-Louis Flandrin, Paris, Presses universitaires de Vincennes, 2005. For a moral and philosophical history: Jean-Pierre CORBEAU and Jean-Pierre Poulain, *Penser l'alimentation entre imaginaire et rationalité*, Toulouse, Privat, 2002; Maguelonne TOUSSAINT-SAMAT [1997], *Histoire naturelle et morale de la nourriture*, Toulouse, Le Périgrinateur, 2013; Saadi LAHLOU, *Penser, manger*, Paris, Presses universitaires de France, 1998. For a cultural approach: Massimo MONTANARI, *Le manger comme culture*, Brussels, Éditions de l'université de Bruxelles, 2010; Florent QUELLIER, *la Table des Français. Une histoire culturelle (XVe-XIXe siècle)*, Rennes, "Tables des hommes", Presses universitaires de Rennes/Presses universitaires François Rabelais, 2013. For a psychoanalytical approach: Gérard Haddad, *Manger le livre*, Paris, "Figures", Grasset, 1984, reedited under the title *Manger le livre. Rites alimentaires et fonction paternelle*, Paris, Fayard/Pluriel, 2012. For a sociological approach: Jean-Pierre Poulain, *Sociologies de l'alimentation : les mangeurs et l'espace social alimentaire*, Paris, Presses universitaires de France, 2013. For a religious approach: Aïda KANAFANI-ZAHAR, Séverine MATHIEU and Sophie Nizard (eds), *À croire et à manger. Religions et alimentation*, Paris, L'Harmattan, 2008. For an ecological approach: Jacques BARRAU, *Les hommes et leurs aliments. Esquisse d'une histoire écologique et ethnologique de l'alimentation humaine*, Paris, Messidor/Temps actuels, 1983.

Humanity has humanized itself through its table by interposing between itself and what it eats and drinks a whole series of choices (between what is consumable and what is not, between those who are entitled to the banquet and those who are not, between various cooking methods, etc.), of values (between those recognized for the various foods and the various ways of cooking, seasoning, eating), of objects (from the treading stick to the spit and the pot), and between the different types of food and the different ways of cooking.), of values (between those recognized to the various foodstuffs and to the various ways of cooking, of seasoning, of eating), of objects (from the treading stick to the spit and the pot), of knowledge and know-how (in hunting and gathering, in storage, in conservation, of seasoning, cooking), cultures (from popular cultures to aristocratic cultures through religious or scientific aspects), rituals (domestic, religious or political), thus transforming nutrients, which concern the biological body alone, into food. The history of food is therefore first and foremost that of this distancing, this ritualization and symbolization that contribute to living together.

Humanity could just as easily dehumanize itself by dehumanizing its table. We have still not learned, in several millennia, to guarantee the right to banquet to the whole of humanity, which would suppose to conceive a new symbolism, a new rituality, other practices. On the contrary, we eat more and more anything, anyhow, anytime, anywhere, with anyone and for any reason. We no longer accept that the community can have a say in the way we eat, and already waste, because we no longer know what eating means. We imagine, against all that the history of humanity teaches us, that the table would be an individual matter for which we would not have to account neither anthropologically, nor socially or culturally, nor, of course, politically.

Why a history of food?

Our century is no exception: its main challenge is not the conquest of space but how to feed 8 billion people without destroying ecosystems. In this respect, history should have inoculated us against a double illusion, which is unfortunately deadly. The one according to which today's table is necessarily better than yesterday's and necessarily worse than tomorrow's. The history of food belies this falsely progressive conception: people died less of hunger in the Egypt of the Pharaohs than under Louis XV, and prehistoric eaters had access to a more diversified diet than the French of the 19th century.

A political history of food. From the Pateolithic to our days

The history of food is not the history of a long triumphant march towards something better, but the history of conflicts of use, with the alternative of pooling stocks or letting a minority appropriate them, or the choice between destroying chestnut groves to favor potatoes or wheat, and letting the people live well, in their own way. Indeed, the powerful have only been able to impose their conception of agriculture and food by forbidding to the majority, often brutally, other ways of eating and therefore also of living. We are not able to say what the history of food would have been if these other popular choices had been respected. The powerful (tribal chiefs, lords, kings, aristocrats, capitalist bourgeois) only achieved their ends with the support of religions, and in particular, as far as we are concerned, with the support of the Catholic Church, always ready to denounce the claims of the poor to want to eat as well as the rich... The sin of *gula* ("gluttony") is first and foremost a weapon of war against the poor and not against the rich.

Another illusion that we should mourn is the idea that "technical progress" and innovations in agriculture would be able to meet hopes. Our ancestors were lulled into such illusions from the great reforms of Antiquity to the absolute monarchy and the Revolution. The republican potato has not emancipated humanity any more than the medieval bread or, tomorrow, food biotechnologies. It is not by chance that the "progressive" 19th century, of which the collective memory only retains the golden legend of the great gastronomes, was a particularly dark century in terms of popular food with its immoral projects to feed the people using all the scraps of industry. Even in ancient Greece, slaves were entitled to the delights of sweet wine and to banquets (rarely, though) to honor their dead! Commensality had for a long time the consequence of reminding humans that they must all, obligatorily, eat and drink. Capitalism having invented, with its specific functioning of money, another general equivalence between things, Comus and Bacchus found themselves belittled, not to say simply desacralized.

To make a history of food is therefore, already, to bear witness to this profanation of the living when societies (and the powerful) no longer think of themselves as nourishing, when the rich no longer even perceive what is immoral in their excesses and in the excess of their food wastage (estimated by the UN at 40% of production), when the leaders no longer imagine what food policies could be, whereas the Ancients had known how to deploy *sumptuary* laws for centuries so that the excesses of some would not deprive others, and *annuity* laws to guarantee the supply of each and everyone. The French Revolution was not born of a bad harvest, but of the abandonment by the powerful of this "moral economy" that the people had never ceased to call for and that they sometimes applied by force during grain requisitions and sales at the right price.

Why a political history of food?

Food was one of the fields where this human dimension was forged, to which we will give the name of politics much later. Indeed, politics existed long before Greek democracy and its famous banquets. I would like to convince the reader that we can talk about food politics since prehistoric times and that the choices made were not less interested and passionate than ours. Politics was not born with the first city-states, like Babylon, but with the great hunts, with the storage of foodstuffs, with the first vegetable banquets. This history bears witness to a tinkering process, sometimes with lightning advances, but also with lasting setbacks. This tinkering has made it possible to bring to life something that goes beyond the framework of family, tribal and simple neighborhood relations. One will always make something new out of something old in this field, and one tinkers with what is already there.

Commensality, which has a precise meaning in the family context, takes on another meaning here. From being a private matter, the mastery of fire becomes one of the foundations of a political community that is invented, tightly knit around a common home. It is not so much the community that closes around its fire as this common hearth that creates the community, just as it is not the community that shares a banquet, but this banquet that creates the community as a political body. At the same time, politics is the constitution of this common space, removed from the only privative logics, and the development of particular modalities to manage it. Politics was at first a banal matter of food before becoming this abstract thing which excludes the greatest number.

Political, the learning of cooperation, perhaps already at the level of gathering, and, certainly, with the great hunts. Political, the definition of gathering and hunting territories to be defended against other tribes or against predators. Politics, the learning of collective security with the constitution of reserves and the invention of varied and efficient methods of managing food stocks. Politics, the mastery of fire as the foundation of future common goods and future cities. Political, the invention of the commensality because it supposes to make choices in terms of distribution of the pieces, but also in terms of feeding (or not) the weakest. Political, the first hospitable meals with a certain diplomatic function as well as

A political history of food. From the Pateolithic to our days

the first funeral or bloody banquets. That politics was invented with table affairs, in particular, is not so surprising since the table is, like politics, a matter of mixing (of peoples, values, customs in one case, of aromas, spices in the other). The ancient Greeks were well aware of this, as they always had to mix their wine with water.

Why a national food history?

Of course, the history of food is universal, but it can only be understood if we accept to circumscribe it in specific territories, whether climatically, geographically, culturally, socially or politically. France, in its history, has a specific relationship with its table because it is, more than others, a political nation. To study the French political history of the table is to give oneself the maximum chance of understanding this intertwining of politics and food, as it affects all societies, each in its own way. It is therefore necessary to look at the long term, and even the very long term, since the French table remains dependent on ancient tables well beyond the famous bread-wine-oil triangle and the tradition of banquets. What characterizes the French table is this relationship, always continued and renewed, between the contents of the plate and politics, between table manners and politics, between (counter-)utopias and politics, and this, from the Gallo-Roman era to that of the Carolingian empire, from feudalism to absolute monarchy, from the humanism of the Renaissance to that of the philosophy of the Enlightenment, from the Revolution of 1789 to the 19th century, the "dark century". The danger would have been to make the political history of the food of the powerful alone, thus evacuating the point of view, also political, of the people on the affairs of the table. The people, far from being silent, have even been rather stubborn over the centuries, always looking in the same directions for solutions to food issues... This popular history of the table has however always been depreciated, to the point of retaining only the point of view of the powerful (and of the scholars), including on measures desired and demanded by the people. Ordinary people did not mainly wish to eat the same and in the same way as the powerful, it will take a lot of suffering to make them give up their own conceptions and practices of table. The hatred of free food distributions, always repeated since ancient Rome, is another good symptom.

I invite my readers to a long gastronomic journey that I hope will be gourmet. I present this book in the manner of the old French table by proposing, by way of chapters, 13 successive services, but from which each one can draw at will (which the eater could not do at the time): prehistoric

---

tables, the Mesopotamian table, the Egyptian table, the Greek table, the Roman table, the Gallic table, the Merovingian table, the Carolingian table, the clerical-feudal table, the table of the absolute monarchy, the republican table, the bourgeois table and finally the industrial tables of the 20th century and the beginning of the 20th century.

First service: Prehistoric tables

The reader may be surprised at a journey so far back in history to understand how we eat and drink today. This is because anyone curious about food must begin by deconstructing images of how our distant ancestors were known to eat[2]. We imagine them as "savages" discovered in the 19th and 20th centuries. We accept them as carnivores or herbivores as long as they spend their short lives finding a few meager nutrients, without any concern for others, nor pleasure. We will never know exactly how hominids ate two million years ago, or even in the Upper Paleolithic, but we do know enough thanks to the work of prehistorians and recent scientific discoveries to deconstruct some preconceived ideas. Our distant ancestors were curious, greedy and perhaps gourmets; they knew how to organize themselves collectively and acquire the necessary technologies, particularly in terms of storage and preservation, to guarantee their subsistence[3].

An explosive table

We imagine that talking about prehistoric food would be safe, but this is a controversial area because it has religious and political implications.

How to admit the humanity of the most ancient hominids without questioning certain beliefs that justify our illusions and our ways of being.

---

2. Raymond DUMAY, *Le Rat et l'Abeille, court traité de gastronomie préhistorique*, Paris, Phébus, 1997. We also have some monographs, such as that of Lucie MARTIN, *Premiers paysans des Alpes. Alimentation végétale et agriculture au Néolithique*, Rennes, Presses universitaires de Rennes, 2014.
3. Catherine PERLÈS, "Les stratégies alimentaires dans les temps préhistoriques" *in* Massimo MONTANARI et Jean-Louis Flandrin (dirs), *Histoire de l'alimentation, op. cit.* p. 29-46 ; Catherine PERLÈS, "Les origines de la cuisine. L'acte alimentaire dans l'histoire de l'homme" in *Communications*, vol. 31, 1979, thematic number: *La nourriture. For a biocultural anthropology of food*, p. 4-14.

For a long time, the Churches could not admit that humanity was much older than the Bible tells us, nor even that "man descended from the ape".

For a long time, science sought what it wanted to find, rejecting everything else. Thus, when Jacques Boucher de Perthes, a simple customs official, demonstrated, in 1846, the contemporaneity of flint tools carved by man and bones of large animals (in *Celtic and Antediluvian Antiquities*), his words on the existence of a man "before the Flood" provoked the joint wrath of the Church and the Academy of Sciences, which would take ten years to admit the facts, thanks to the English scientists. To maintain that Neanderthal man or the oldest *Homo sapiens* already knew what eating and drinking meant upsets our established certainties. In 1879, the discovery of the Altamira cave in Santander, with its painted ceiling of about twenty bison, provoked a new controversy because of a stone lamp in the shape of a cup that proved the existence of lighting and therefore the possibility of painting at the bottom of dark caves. The great master of prehistory, Emile Cartailhac (1845-1921), published, in 1902, his "Mea culpa of a skeptic" (in *L'Anthropologie*, volume 13, 1902, p. 348-354) officially recognizing the cave art. If the scientists do not cease to move back the great dates of the food humanization (control of the fire, constitution of the stocks, division of the society), it is enough to consult the textbooks to note that we continue to cling to a history more ideological than objective.

How can we admit the humanity of the most ancient hominids without noting that the great invariants that structure our relationship to food have changed little and that we have still not resolved the free access to the banquet for all. The questions posed undeniably intersect with our own: what are the food choices to be made to guarantee everyone's right to food? Should animals be considered as meat reserves or partners? How does a minority seize food stocks or make the table a vector of inequality?

Determinism and food choice

Prehistoric diet is the product of the tension between a series of determinisms creating possibilities among which choices exist. Our food practices are not so far from those of other animals in some respects: individual or group collection, personal or collective hunting, transport of food to the lodge, modalities of transformation of the physical state (cutting, grinding, premastication), of the physico-chemical state (drying, rotting, cooking, combination of basic foodstuffs). We will see that one of the first causes of our differentiation is political, insofar as the history of the table crosses that of inequalities. The diet is, of course, largely dependent on the climate.

Thus, in the Paleolithic period, because of the ice ages, vegetation was scarce, so the diet was mainly meat. The climatic change of the Mesolithic will allow a reorientation of the diet towards plants. However, prehistorians are convinced that since the dawn of time, eating habits have also been the result of constructed choices. The prehistorian Catherine Perlès has shown that, from that time, food is marked by cultural choices and that the food options, and even culinary, of man have played an important role in the formation of human society, so : "The human species is the only one to cook its food, on the one hand, to combine the ingredients, on the other hand [...] The food act was as much a factor of homonization as a criterion of homonization"[4].

The history of food is not understood as long as we accept the binary opposition constructed *a posteriori* between the Paleolithic and the Neolithic. This reading closes the possibility of glimpsing what other evolutions could have been, with other techniques, other diets, etc. We must therefore distinguish between three major periods and the most important one, in terms of the table, is neither the Paleolithic nor the Neolithic, but the Mesolithic. However, we must accept to momentarily share the table of the first hominids, to better understand the choices made.

Food in the Paleolithic

The Paleolithic can be divided into four periods: Archaic (before 2 million years and up to 600,000 years BP[5]), Lower (from 600,000 years BP to 300,000 years BP), Middle (from 300,000 years BP to 35,000 years BP) and Upper (from 35,000 years BP to 9,000 years BP). We speak of epipaleolithic from 9000 years BP to 7000 years BP and mesolithic from 7000 years BP to 5000 years BP. The expression "prehistoric man" there-fore necessarily covers very different food realities. About twenty species of hominids succeed each other between 2 and 2.8 million years BP. Our most distant ancestor was vegetarian like all the great anthropoids, but a little over three million years ago, bipedal primates (australopithecines,

---

4. Catherine PERLÈS, "Les origines de la cuisine" in *Communications*, vol. 31, 1979, thematic issue: *La nourriture. For a biocultural anthropology of the food*, p. 4-14.
5. "BP": English abbreviation for *Before Present*, or, in French, "avant le présent" (abbreviated as AP). This abbreviation is used in various fields (anthropology, archaeology, climatology...) to designate the ages expressed in number of years counted backwards from the year 1950 of the Gregorian calendar. This date was arbitrarily fixed as a reference year and corresponds to the first attempts at dating by carbon 14. The dating before Christ (BC), after Christ (AD), to name years, centuries and millennia according to the supposed year of the birth of Jesus Christ as it was estimated in the 6th century, will be used in the following chapters as the usual standard.

Homo habilis) appeared with omnivorous dentition, which indicates an increased consumption of meat. They used sticks and carved pebbles for cutting. However, Juan Luis Arsuaga explains that although *Homo habilis* (2.5 million to 1.5 million years old) is perfectly adapted physiologically to a herbaceous ecosystem, a predominantly vegetarian diet is doubtful given the low number of apes in Europe - a sign of a scarcity of plant resources. The products of gathering are abundant, indeed, only during the autumn[6]. Marc Groenen qualifies this thesis, because if *Homo ergaster* (about two million years ago) is a great consumer of game, he also eats fruits, berries, roots or tubers[7]. Its food behaviors already include preferences, some animals are mainly exploited for their meat (deer), others for their fur (bear). S. Boyd Eaton reminds us that around 40,000 years ago BP three species coexisted: Neandertal in the process of becoming extinct, Flores man already condemned, and *Homo sapiens*, our distant ancestor, the last to arrive[8]. These hominids share many things but eat differently. Neanderthals have a mainly meaty diet, but we do not know if this diet is due to the climate or to the behavioral signature of this species. *Homo sapiens*, who arrived in Europe around 30000 years BP, immediately had a diversified diet, mainly meat but with lots of fish. The biological signature of *Homo sapiens* is to be an omnivore. Claude Fischler therefore plays nicely with words by speaking of "homnivore"[9].

The first ages of the Paleolithic

Compared to Neanderthal man, *Homo sapiens* has a thinner bone structure and narrower hips, so it needs much less energy. Paradoxically, this fragility becomes an asset, especially in terms of food strategies. Eating less but thinking a lot, *Homo sapiens* can organize his vegetal and meat supplies differently, create stocks, imagine sophisticated preservation techniques, learn to play with fire, make mixtures and seasonings ever more precise. Food is not only the satisfaction of a physiological need, but one of the main occasions for the use of the hands and the coordination of movements. Thus, it leads to the invention of the first tools, starting with the digging stick and the club, and then the first containers, in the form of holes dug in the earth; it also implies an awakening of

---

6. Juan Luis Arsuaga, *Le Collier de Neandertal. Nos ancêtres à l'ère glaciaire*, Paris, Odile Jacob, 2001, reprinted in Paris, "Poches Odile Jacob", Odile Jacob, 2004.
7. Marc Groenen, *Introduction à la préhistoire*, Paris, Ellipses, 2009.
8. Stanley Boyd Eaton, Marjorie Shostak and Melvin Konner, *The Paleolithic Prescription: A Program of Diet and Exercise and a Design for Living* (New York: Harper & Row, 1988).
9. Claude Fischler, *L'Homnivore*, Paris, "Poches Odile Jacob", Odile Jacob, 2001.

the capacities of observation and analysis, the memorization of edible or indigestible products, of the best times and the best places for gathering or hunting; finally, it implies the development of collective strategies of gathering or hunting, and soon of storage... and, naturally, it is at the origin of the conflicts.

The Upper Paleolithic

Homo sapiens, who is anatomically identical to us, was at first a carnivore because the climate was too cold to allow him a vegetable diet. This long period is that of the development of hunting (especially that of large herds of herbivores: oxen, bison, horses, reindeer), which implies a great familiarity with the herds exploited by man and, already, a kind of semi-domestication for the reindeer and the horse. These hunters therefore cooperate to organize "large collective hunts". The rule of sharing fundamentally governs this world of hunters, because "a hunter does not consume his own game" (Pierre Clastres)[10]. Margaret Conkey has hypothesized that large gatherings of many communities were held in central sites for hunting and that during these episodes, religious rituals were organized based on the abundance of game but also great feasts, because we could not otherwise explain the very large quantities of meat that were stored there, with dense accumulations of bones, remains of feasts, with objects, such as spoons made of animal wood, or ivory or bone[11]. Alain Testart adds that if the access to the food does not indeed pose a problem, on the other hand, the question of its conservation is much more thorny. The solution imagined is that of gift... and counter-gift between groups. It is a matter of giving when there is too much and receiving, in return, when there is not enough[12]. Marshall Sahlins had calculated that food stocks had become so large, as early as the time of the nomadic hunter-gatherers, that they represented at least one year's food consumption, in addition to that of the current year[13].

---

10. Pierre Clastres, "L'arc et le panier" in *L'Homme*, vol. 6, n° 2, 1966, p. 13-31.

11. Margaret W. Conkey, *Beyond Art: Pleistocene Image and Symbol* (edited with Olga Soffer *et al.*), California Academy of Sciences/University of California Press, 1997.

12. Alain Testart, *Les chasseurs-cueilleurs ou l'origine des inégalités*, Paris, Société d'ethnographie (university Paris X-Nanterre), 1982, reprinted under the title *Le communisme primitif : économie et idéologie*, Paris, Maison des Sciences de l'Homme, 1985.

13. Marshall Sahlins, *Stone Age, Age of Plenty. L'économie des sociétés primitives* ["Stone Age Economics"], trans. (English) Tina Jolas, preface by Pierre Clastres, Paris, "Bibliothèque des Sciences humaines", Gallimard, 1976.

A diversified diet

This period is also the time of great fishing activity in sea and fresh water, shellfish harvesting, birds and eggs consumption. The climate also allows the gathering of wild plants, such as mosses, lichens, fruits, but also some wild cereals[14]. It is agreed that the communities already had a very high degree of control over food resources, thanks to an excellent knowledge of the surrounding fauna and flora and an efficient plant technology. This period of the Upper Paleolithic is considered as a kind of golden age, before the very difficult period of the beginning of the post-glacial (8000 and 7000 years BP) which presents difficulties in the supply of meat, because the forests now cover the former bare lands (steppes) and cause the disappearance of reindeer as well as a strong decrease in oxen and horses. It is true that instead of wild boar, deer are hunted, i.e. animals that like the forest, but they are more solitary and reduce the supply by making the "big hunts" such as Solutré more often unproductive. Human groups are therefore smaller in number because of these new food constraints, but they remain in constant interaction, exchanging what they cannot store.

Eating symbols

I share the view that these men are already fully human. These communities, which already form a society because of their level of organization, live centered on food and sexual questions. We usually prefer to talk about the sophisticated tools of prehistoric men and their great achievements, such as the megaliths, forgetting, however, other cultural forms more insignificant and become invisible. Thus, Juan Luis Arsuaga has shown that the question of identity (ethnicity, to use his formula) is already present because of the importance given to the adornment that says a lot about the place of each person within the society. This means that belonging to the group went far beyond the purely biological aspect and was organized around shared symbols. Precisely, prehistoric food fulfilled these two conditions: to eat is to feed oneself biologically, but also anthropologically, because humans, as far as our knowledge allows us to go back in time, always eat symbols. Indeed, eating symbols is not the monopoly of modern times. Certainly, we lack tangible proofs, but it took a very long history before all religions started at about the same time to cobble together systems of food representation. How else to explain the

---

14. Maria Luisa MIGLIARI and Alida AZZOLA, *La gastronomie de la préhistoire à nos jours*, Paris, Éditions Atlas, 1979; Marylène PATOU-MATHIS, *Mangeurs de viande de la préhistoire à nos jours*, Paris, Perrin, 2009; Gilles DELLUC, Brigitte DELLUC et Martine ROQUES, *La nutrition préhistorique*, Périgueux, Éditions Pilote 24, 1995.

universality (in an extreme diversity) of the systems of food prohibitions, except to postulate a divine intervention? I will rely more on what is shown in cave or parietal art.

Hunters or scavengers?

According to Juan Luis Arsuaga, man has always been more of a hunter than a scavenger, even if modern man likes to think the opposite, as a way of denying his prehistoric ancestors their humanity and ensuring that he has the monopoly. This additional scavenging is not so "stupid and nasty", because it is based on a fine observation of the predators' behaviors, such as the movement of the birds of prey in the sky, in order to intervene at the right moment to steal the animal (still warm and sometimes even alive) from the beasts of prey. The importance of the scavenger activity can be seen by the simultaneous presence of human cut marks and animal bite marks. It is also known that when the fossil is complete, it is because man has taken over the whole body of the animal; but when certain bones are missing, we can assume an involuntary commensality with the animals. This scavenging is done in three ways: by the chance discovery of a naturally dead animal; by the snatching of a game animal from its predators before they finish it off; by the consumption of the remains of an animal feast. It is also known that if predators first attack weakened animals, humans will always hunt, with a strange preference, adult animals. The development of hunting techniques (javelin and bow propulsion) will transform the human/game balance and reinforce the place of hunting. Its efficiency caused the disappearance of many species (among the big game). Horses had the chance to have a status other than only food.

Is gathering feminine and hunting masculine?

Why, in hunter-gatherer societies, is it generally the woman who gathers and the man who hunts? The traditional answer is well known: hunting requires a lot of mobility whereas the reproductive function of women requires more immobility. Alain Testart has shown that this argument does not hold since women participate in certain forms of hunting for game that can be dug up with a digging stick, knocked out with an axe or smoked. The women also participate in hunting, while the man is on the lookout, thus immobile. As a result, Testart maintains the thesis that it is not from hunting that women are excluded, but from the use of a certain type of weapon (edged or thrown).

There is therefore a masculine pole, that of percussion, linear throwing (axe, adze), ponctiform thrown percussion (javelin, arrow, dagger), and a feminine pole, that of diffused and posed percussion (grinder, grindstone, etc.). The mixed gestures are also feminine: ponctiforme percussion but posed (digging stick, sewing needle), thrown percussion but diffuse (pestle, beater), linear percussion posed (scraper, scraper, knife). According to Alain Testart, it is the "ideology of blood" which prohibits the use by women of throwing weapons or sharp tools, because there would be incompatibility between menstrual blood and animal blood[15]. Preventing any contact between these two substances would be the foundation of the sexual division of work among the hunter-gatherers.

Store

Storage appeared to be the only way to ensure the gap between two periods of hunting and gathering and thus to face the fear of lack. Not having the capacity to overwinter like other animals, man invented non-biological solutions to winter, thus of a political nature. The storage of plant and animal foodstuffs is one of the major issues of prehistory. Progress began well before sedentarization (even if it was temporary), because nomadic hunter-gatherers stored in places that they knew they would use again later. How can we not be admiring of their ingenuity? Desiccation by drying in the sun, freezing in earth or frozen water, salting, coating with fat, clay, honey, juices from various trees, use of herbs with fungicidal and antibacterial functions, etc. These methods show a good knowledge of the mechanisms of food decay and the ways to prevent it. The Paleolithic people are also specialists in acid fermentation (food products preserved in pits dug in the ground): these solutions are consumed in the form of soups, porridges or patties. However, the belly will remain for a long time the main storage container, explaining the alternation between periods of frugality and bombast.

Season

Seasoning fundamentally changes the status of food. It transforms ingredients into food and establishes cooking, understood precisely as the art of mixing and composing opposites. The seasoning testifies to a search for good taste, and therefore for pleasure. Prehistoric man made great use of condiments and other seasonings, but also of fats and animal blood. Anticipating the analysis of the Mesopotamian tables, let us underline that the preparations always remain very simple within the societies of

---

15. Alain TESTART, *Essai sur les fondements de la division sexuelle du travail chez les chasseurs-cue-illeurs*, Paris, "Cahiers de l'homme", Éditions de l'École des Hautes Études en Sciences Sociales (EHESS), 1986.

A political history of food. From the Pateolithic to our days

hunter-gatherers. This is probably because, as we shall see, great cooking presupposes, even before technical means, an unequal division of society. However, I insist on the fact that the technologies of food preparation are as important as the technologies of breeding or agriculture. Before going any further, I would like to address the question of vessels, because it is often believed that the lack of knowledge of pottery and ceramics slowed down the invention of cooking. Man did not need to master pottery: he used rock hollows, shells, animal skins, holes dug in the earth, tree bark. He used skulls and bones. Later, he used animal intestines and made leather bags. He constantly improved these technologies, learning to work with bones, making his containers ever more watertight and inaccessible to rodents, coating the holes in the earth with clay, and later, when he mastered fire, sanitizing them by burning wood inside. These "archaic" storage techniques will continue to be used alongside other more sophisticated ones (pottery/ceramic).

This very ancient use of containers (born of the human imagination) explains the place that the symbolism of the cauldron (one of the first myths) will take. Let's think about the cauldron of abundance and the cauldron of immortality... The cauldron is what allows cooking, and thus access to the good life. It is associated with the mother's womb, where man returns to be reborn. Later, the magician Medea, having demonstrated to the daughters of Pelias that a goat could be made young again by boiling it, incited them, out of revenge, to do the same with their old father, whom they then plunged into the boiling water of a cauldron, a bath that did not make Pelias young again, but killed him! In many cultures, the cauldron will become the ancestor of the coffin only because it was previously the sign of commensality.

The love of fat

Paleolithic man particularly savored fat, well beyond the physiological need to compensate for a diet that was too meaty. Undoubtedly they already knew that the fat is the support of the taste, therefore of the pleasure. Thierry Tillet is a specialist of the fatty food of the hunter-gatherers. After having listed the sources of fat (of which the use of the brains and the fracturing of the bones), he wonders about the famous "fatty broth" that many prehistorians qualify as a distant ancestor of the kitchen[16]. If the

---

16. Thierry TILLET, "Les bouillons gras du Paléolithique : un exemple de comparatisme ethnographique critiquable" *in* Sophie ARCHAMBAULT DE BEAUNE, *Chasseurs-cueilleurs : comment vivaient les hommes du Paléolithique supérieur - méthodes d'analyse et d'interprétation en préhistoire*, CNRS Éditions, 2007, p. 89-96.

fracturing of bones is a certainty, the fatty broth is only probable. Some authors, such as Adam Maurizio (University of Warsaw, 1931), maintain that acid-lactic fermentation was the first dish to be invented, from which all other culinary preparations were later born[17]. From acid-lactic fermentation to bread, it would only be a matter of time.

However, why fracture bones to extract marrow when only 6 or 7% of the fat is in the bones, compared to 93 to 94% in the soft tissues? The only answer lies in the need not to lose any fat. Everything was a pretext to use fat either to better preserve food (some people wrapped seeds in animal fat) or to better appreciate them (they were coated just before eating them).

Cook

Man did not need fire to eat hot (or lukewarm) food: he was able, thanks to his scavenging activity, to consume still warm flesh; he also used stones heated by the sun to warm and cook his food. Old myths, such as that of the Chilouk people, tell us that men reserved the top of the food heated by the sun for themselves, leaving the bottom to women (the Roman kitchen will sometimes reserve the hot food for the good society)[18].

Prehistorians keep advancing the date of the mastery of fire (around 600,000 years BP). Some even think that it goes back beyond a million years. What is certain, is that our images of epinal in this field are sad in the face of a history infinitely richer and often particularly surprising. If we are certain of the antiquity of the mastery of fire, it is however very difficult to know what it was used for, because it was not necessarily first for heating and cooking, but perhaps for various rituals. In any case, fire was perfectly mastered around 350,000 years BP. The work of Isabelle Théry-Parisot has enabled us to better understand this question and to specify which fuels were used to light the various fires[19]. Indeed, there were different fireplaces depending on whether they were used to cook food or to smoke meat; some fireplaces were equipped with ventilation ducts allowing for oxygen intake, and therefore faster combustion. Jacques Collina-Girard[20] insists on the technologies of fire production: there are only two ways of proceeding, by percussion or by friction, but in both

---

17. Adam MAURIZIO, *Histoire de l'alimentation végétale depuis la préhistoire jusqu'à nos jours*, Paris, Payot, 1932. On the same theme, Philippe MARINVAL, *l'alimentation végétale en France du Mésolithique jusqu'à l'âge de fer*, center régional de publication de Toulouse, CNRS, 1988.
18. Catherine PERLÈS, *Préhistoire du feu*, Paris, Masson, 1977.
19. Isabelle THÉRY-PARISOT, *L'économie des combustibles au Paléolithique*, CEPAM, *Dossiers de documentation archéologique*, n° 20, Paris, CNRS Éditions, 2001.
20. Jacques COLLINA-GIRARD, "Feu par percussion, feu par friction. Les données de l'expérimentation" in *Bulletin de la Société préhistorique française*, vol. 90, n° 2, 1993, p. 159-176.

---

cases the spark must fall on a very flammable product: the prehistoric men used tinder from a mushroom. The specialists incite to prudence and not to sink in a utilitarian and simplistic interpretation, because the techniques are not limited to their utilitarian function and make system with all the other aspects of the life. It is thus probable that the production of fire was symbolically assimilated to a ritualized sexual act, as attested to by the choice of persons of the opposite sex according to the manner chosen to make the fire, or that of different techniques according to whether men or women were in charge of the production of fire (Marcel Otte[21]). The Catholic Church will not be mistaken there: it prohibited, still in the 8th century, to light wild fires by rubbed wood (the *Indiculus superstitionum et paganiarum*), after the council of Leptines in 743, convened by the uncle of Charlemagne. The very idea of rubbing had something to dislike... as we shall see. One also used, as of the paleolithic, lighters of pyrite or marcasite. Prehistorians insist on the fact that the mastery of fire does not only mean knowing how to produce it, but also knowing how to control it according to its objectives. Not only can we distinguish between fires that were collected, preserved, transported and manufactured, but the fireplaces attest to a good knowledge of how to improve combustion and draught, by playing on the fuel or ventilation.

We must not have a miserable vision of cooking: grilling on charred stones, roasting (green wooden spit), heated water with burning stones thrown into a hole dug and coated with clay, leather pouch (intestines ancestors of the cauldron), steam cooking obtained by dropping water, drop by drop, on burning stones, etc. This mastery of fire was not only used to cook meat but also to make soups, porridges, purees, cakes... This mastery of fire was not only used to cook meat but also to make soups, porridges, purées, pancakes... These prehistoric "soups", made with various ingredients, ranged from acidic to sweet soups. Adam Maurizio used to rave about them: "And what a wealth we find in these ancient times of gathering, what an abundance of species, what a variety in the preparation of dishes. With the controlled use of cooking a whole culinary technology develops: food with a hard crust and a softer interior is cooked.

As much as I am suspicious of the thesis that explains the birth of commensality by the sole mastery of fire, I am convinced that it played an essential role in the evolution and specialization of religious forms. Homer explains how the first men knew how to transport fire into caves where it

---

21. Marcel OTTE, *L'évolution des gestes techniques de la Préhistoire*, Brussels, Éditions De Boeck, (with the contribution of Pierre NOIRET), 2010.

was much easier to keep it. It was also kept in the hollows of shrubs or by means of certain plants, such as ferulas, whose stems contain a consumable pith. During all Antiquity, these stems will be used to transport it (*"ferula"* in Latin, from *fero*, verb meaning "to carry"). The cult of fire very quickly had its rites, its priests and priestesses. During Antiquity, this "sacred fire" was kept in the temples.

The loss of fire is an anguish common to all peoples. Terrible punishments were reserved for negligent vestals by peoples who had mastered the production of fire and for whom its loss was no longer of material importance, but who continued to condemn to death, in memory of the time when the extinction of fire was an evil. The eternal lamp called "of the holy sacrament", which still burns in churches today, is all that remains of this primitive institution.

Establishing a common property

The practice of commensality is generally referred to the control of fire. The already existing communities would have gathered around the hearth. Before even evoking the hypothesis of cold vegetable banquets, which were much earlier, I think that another reading of the link between fire and community is possible, since we can think that it is precisely the foundation of a hearth (common and permanent) that will crystallize the abstract notion of community and make humanity pass from the stage of the pack to that of society. Indeed, the notion of civic (or political) community could only be elaborated from very concrete practices, such as the organization of great hunts, the storage of foodstuffs, their redistribution, the maintenance of the fire, the commensality.

In the same way that fire has played an essential role in the evolution and specialization of religious forms, the hearth has played a similar role in the evolution and specialization of political forms of group organization. We can therefore admit the importance of the hearth as a materialization of the abstract notion of community, without recognizing it as an exclusive dimension. It is probable that language, tattoos, common houses, secret societies also participate in this political function of aggregation. It must however be recognized that this common home has the great merit of representing all the homes (those of the various families) without assimilating to any of them. Specialists note that its management will soon require functional specialization. It does not matter that this function, initially shared, became the monopoly of a staff leaning more to the religious side. This staff, charged with a collective mission, a public service, was almost always women, priestesses, religious and feminine specifications. Not only did our distant ancestors eat and not just eat, but they did so in a political way, in the sense that they discovered very quickly the need to recognize "friends" and "enemies" by choosing with whom to accept or refuse to eat (as we like to define today, sadly, politics), but also, on this occasion, by building among themselves a "something" that they knew was common to them and that they had to share. Cooking was therefore an institutional act as much as a culinary one, especially since commensality did not go without the invention of other collective uses. Marcel Otte notes that from the Upper Paleolithic onwards, musical instruments abounded: stringed instruments, percussion instruments, wind instruments (bone flutes)[22], most of which were made of vegetable matter. As no human society is known to practice music without dancing or singing, we can also admit that fire does not go without these instruments and activities. The Mesolithic period will thus see the development of the dance as a source of fertility, because its movements, assimilated to those of the universe, awaken the buried forces.

Food in the Mesolithic

This second period benefited from a much milder climate, and resources diversified, with the diet becoming more plant-based. However, isotopic studies show that the Mesolithic men of the Atlantic coast continued to eat mainly fish, shellfish and game. It is these Mesolithic *Homo sapiens* who will develop Neolithization over a period of four thousand years (from 8000 years BP). The unequal character of the communities is certainly reinforced, but the rule of sharing still governs the relations until the Neolithic. These *Homo sapiens* of the Mesolithic are in fact the last hunter-gatherers. (Semi-)sedentary villages gradually replaced the camps. The first silos and granaries appeared alongside the pits.

Animal domestication

Jacques Cauvin distinguishes two major phases in domestication[23]. Everything begins with animal domestication, which first concerns the dog around 10,000 years BP, then 3,000 years later, the goat and the sheep, then much later, the ox, the pig, the horse and the donkey. The explanatory theories of animal domestication are multiple: there would have

---

22. Marcel OTTE, *La Préhistoire*, Bruxelles, "Université", Éditions De Boeck, 2009 ; Marcel OTTE and Marylène PATOU-MATHIS, "Comportements de subsistance au Paléolithique moyen en Europe" in *Paléo*, vol. 4, n° 1, 1992, p. 29-34.
23. Jacques CAUVIN, *Naissance de l'agriculture*, Paris, CNRS Éditions, 1998.

been a long time cooperation/commensalism between the wolf and men, since the wolf killed and man consumed the remains, then the wolf (dog) would have been integrated into the community of men, until becoming part of it. These dogs (then other animals) would thus have been initially goods of prestige, i.e. goods allowing some to establish their power on the others. The domestication of the cat, much later, would also have had two objectives: to limit the presence of rodents and birds, which were harmful to crops, and to become a new prestige/companion animal to complement the dog. Jean-Denis Vigne notes that this animal domestication, which extends over several centuries, even several millennia, was not systematic[24]. Some peoples have never gone beyond the domestication of the dog alone. Jean-Pierre Digard puts forward an explanation: domestication was only made possible on a larger scale by the change in the conception of humans of their place within nature, since by producing animals, they also produced domestication, and therefore power over the animal[25]. Daniel Helmer adds that this desire to distinguish oneself from the natural environment is attested by the absence of domestic/wildlife crossbreeding, as if this practice had suddenly become infamous, like that of scavenging[26].

The domestication of animals, although causing a proto-farming, does not modify the semi-nomadic life, but it has on the other hand important effects on the techniques of cutting (thus cooking) and the size of the animals, as a consequence of a selection of the least dangerous animals and the confinement of the herds. Thus, the consumption of meat will come for a long time from breeding and hunting, of variable importance depending on the place and the time. However, the ways of cooking meat are not the same, symptomatic of this need to differentiate more and more the two domains. Semi-nomadic animals are treated (cut and cooked) in the same way as farmed animals, without there being anything in their animal characteristics to justify this. We can already see the opposition between game and livestock that will mark our history, without knowing what meaning was attached to it. This proto-farming has two other

---

24. Jean-Denis VIGNE, "Exploitation des animaux et néolithisation en Méditerranée nord-occidentale" *in* Jean GUILAINE, Claire MANEN and Jean-Denis VIGNE (dirs), *Pont de Roque-Haute (Portiragnes, Hérault). Nouveaux regards sur la néolithisation de la France méditerranéenne*, Toulouse, Centre d'anthropologie (Archives d'Écologie préhistorique), 2007, p. 221-301.
25. Jean-Pierre DIGARD, *L'Homme et les animaux domestiques. Anthropologie d'une passion,* "Le temps des sciences", Paris, Fayard, 1990, reprinted 2009.
26. Pierre BONTE, Anne-Marie BRISEBARRE, Daniel HELMER and Sidi MAAMAR (eds), *Anthropozoologica - Domestications animales : dimensions sociales et symboliques* - Hommage à Jacques Cauvin, Publications scientifiques du Muséum, Paris, vol. 39 (1), 2004.

A political history of food. From the Pateolithic to our days

consequences: an over-consumption of young animals to benefit from their mothers' milk, and of males to ensure the survival of female breeders.

Shellfish harvesting

The gathering of shellfish and mollusks from rocks (periwinkles, limpets, barnacles, mussels) or from sand (clams, razor clams) is done intensively thanks to simple but sufficient tools, such as pebbles cut to detach the shellfish from the rocks and cut them in two. River and sea fishing is now done with small boats. New fishing techniques appeared, such as the poisoning of rivers with oleander, fern, weed, whitebait, etc., or the fishing of large fish with harpoons made from deer horns.

Plant domestication

The domestication of some plant varieties follows that of animals, but without this leading to a complete sedentarization. Indeed, these first cultivators chose to continue to be gatherers, just as the first breeders continued to be hunters. Agriculture is not therefore immediately preferred, especially as gathering techniques continue to progress: gathering is no longer merely opportunistic but becomes intensive in view of the quantities of wild grasses stored in silos and granaries, and man never ceases to discover new edible "herbs" or to learn how to make them more edible or better.

We will see further on, thanks to the work of prehistorians such as Jacques Cauvin, that the effective passage to the Neolithic period was not the work of these indigenous hunter-gatherers, but of settlers who brought with them not only the sedentary way of life but also their own animal and plant species, which they cultivated[27].

Plant commensality

The Mesolithic table is therefore still a hunter-gatherer table, but one in which the plant dimension takes on greater importance. This protoagriculture is sufficient to modify the interpretation of fertility. What becomes primary is no longer the opposition between animals and humans, but between them and the earth. The pattern of fecundity, from animal and sexual, is going to be more associated with fertility, therefore with seeds. Gathering constitutes par excellence a means of ecological production. It is both an economic and a political activity, because it implies the transformation of a space into a territory, in short, the definition of gathering zones and collective ownership modalities and, consequently, the establishment

---

27. Cf. *below* the developments on what prehistorians call "the great exodus".

of rules of good use - gathering presupposes reflection in order to choose the right places and times. Maurice Godelier reminds us that it is not necessarily experienced as work, since in many of these peoples' languages the word "work" and the representations linked to it simply do not exist.

We are unfortunately blind to what was the vegetable civilization. Already because it left very little material for the prehistorians. Then because it is the most distant from our schemas of functioning. It is thus very likely that we underestimate the knowledge related to the vegetable world as well as the vegetable tools that these men had to invent. The historian and biologist Adam Maurizio will again be our guide. Numerous clues lead us to believe that the gatherer is hardly more individualistic than the hunter: firstly, because human beings are social beings in all their activities; secondly, because evidence has been found of the existence of stocks of seeds that a single individual could not have constituted and of which he would have had no use; and thirdly, because the civilization of the plant world took place between two periods of meat eating, due to climatic fluctuations. How could the habit of hunting collectively not have influenced the modes of intensive collection of vegetable foodstuffs? A cultural tropism spontaneously considers the vegetable civilization as inferior and prevents from accepting the thesis of a collective gathering followed by an equally collective consumption, especially since the plants are worked either to make them edible when they are not directly - by prolonged washings with running water in order to eliminate toxic substances or to hydrolise the starch if the product is too bitter -, or to make them easier to consume thanks to techniques such as slicing, drying, roasting, fermenting, or to make them better thanks to mixtures, seasonings, cooking more or less strong or fast.

The existence of a vegetable banquet is thus much more than a hypothesis, because the sharing is initially a necessity with regard to the children, the sick, the handicapped, the old people, before being a pleasure or an obligation. I speak well of banquet, because not only there is exchange (the cereals which will make the continuation of the history of food are all imported), but these plants are almost never consumed in their raw state, but crushed, crushed, dried, grilled, chewed, mixed between them, in short, cooked. These mixtures mean that we are trying to make real vegetable dishes. How not to think, with Adam Maurizio, that this vegetable food is the context of the invention of the porridge, mother of all the cuisines to come: "The porridge makes pass completely in the background the roasting. The roasted vegetable food has no descendants, while the porridge, as it came out of the soups of cereals practiced with the hot stone, leads straight to the bread. With it appears in the cultivation of the soil a modification extremely rich in consequences: the cultivation with the hoe. The man for whom porridge has become a regular and daily food ceases to be a collector of plants. He makes his porridge with plants which, cultivated with the hoe, were the predecessors of the cereals provided later by our agriculture"[28].

Jacques Barrau and Alice Peeters have built a whole grammar of plant food. First principle: the wilder the plant, the more complex the method of preparation, because it is necessary to eliminate what is toxic or unpleasant[29]. These preparations are consumed in soup, porridge, puree and cake. On the *contrary* with agriculture: cultivated plants do not require such learned and complex preparations. Second principle: technological progress in the preparation of plants has preceded by far those in domestication/production. This civilization of the plant finally includes biodegradable tools, often of single use: thorny plants are used as graters, others as sieves or containers.

The feasts of the Mesolithic

This long period is that of the invention of new types of feasts. To the banquets of hunter-gatherers gathered for "great hunts" or on the occasion of food exchanges between different communities, succeeded, with the development of inequalities, competition feasts and, with the birth of the cult of the ancestors, the first funeral feasts. These two types of feast are emblematic of trans-egalitarian societies in which the principle of private property is gradually recognized.

The competition feasts of the transnational companies

The trans-egalitarian societies are born within the richest communities of hunter-gatherers. Brian Hayden[30] (from whom I borrow this concept) lists the factors that favoured this mutation: the abundance of food resources, the storage of these foodstuffs, the existence of prestige goods, especially food, the beginning of sedentarisation with cattle breeding and agriculture, the existence of "secret societies" linked to the invention of agriculture, the organisation of competition and funeral

---

28. Adam MAURIZIO, *Histoire de l'alimentation végétale depuis la préhistoire jusqu'à nos jours, op. cit.*
29. Jacques BARRAU and Alice PEETERS, "Histoire et préhistoire de la préparation des aliments d'origine végétale, les techniques d'utilisation de ces aliments chez les cueilleurs et les cultivateurs archaïques de l'Australasie" in *Journal de la Société des océanistes*, vol. 28, no. 35, 1972, pp. 141-152.
30. Brian HAYDEN, *Man and Inequality. L'invention de la hiérarchie dans la Préhistoire*, Paris, "Le passé recomposé", CNRS Éditions, 2008.

feasts, etc. Among the first markers of social hierarchy, we find many kitchen objects, such as wooden spoons, ivory, bone, all honorific utensils that are not preserved with care, but voluntarily broken during meals of a new type: "The destruction of prestigious objects is attested in the feasts of competition [...] during which the participants outbid each other in the display of gifts of wealth, which could give rise to the breakage or voluntary destruction of valuable objects such as wrought copper plates, covers and other symbols of wealth."

We also witness the invention of discriminatory banquets, open only to a fraction of the members of the group. Brian Hayden makes the most richly decorated caves meeting places of secret societies gathering a privileged part of the community (the richest? the best hunters? the first to master the seeds?). It seems that this mutation of commensal practices can be linked to the passage from hunting to breeding and from gathering to agriculture, with the need for initiation, that is to say, the transmission of knowledge and know-how. These secret societies, of a shamanic type, indeed borrow the theme of rebirth, characteristic of a society centered on the vegetable world.

What to do with food stocks?

In recent decades, prehistorians have developed a new understanding of the development of inequalities within prehistoric societies. Brian Hayden's work reinforces the intuition that the division of society was organized around food issues. They allow us to contrast simple hunter-gatherer societies, in which there is no accumulation of wealth and no hierarchy, and complex societies which, having the capacity to draw a surplus from their environment and making this choice, create food stocks: "The major cause of the intensification of food production in trans-egalitarian societies is neither the lack of food nor demographic pressure, but rather the gene-ration of more surplus to obtain power, wealth and survival advantages."

We cross-reference Alain Testart's analysis of the storage of large quan-tities of food which, when it becomes the property of a few families, is transformed into a sign of wealth and a source of division: one of the most universal strategies for obtaining power is, in fact, according to anthropo-logists, the conversion of any surplus into "prestige goods". These prestige goods are not only an opportunity to identify a chieftaincy but to say who within the group has the right to take part in the banquet. These two phenomena are linked, however, because it is these new chiefs who will make the possession of these prestige goods an indispensable factor for being admitted on an equal footing within this divided society that is being invented. The poor families are obliged to go into heavy debt in order to remain politically viable, in Hayden's words, to exist: "Using surplus food to create reciprocal contractual debts and to forge powerful alliances was one of the most universal means of acquiring political and economic advantage in trans-egalitarian societies, and even in more complex societies. Feasts provide security and show the extent of power, but they are very costly and labor intensive, perhaps one of their most interesting features for ambitious leaders. Like the use of gifts by the simplest hunter-gatherer societies to forge social bonds and alliances, feasts (which were surely initially only manifestations of collective exchange) could be easily transformed by bold leaders into a means of appropriating the surplus goods of participants by deception and of establishing, in the right situations, hierarchies based on debt"[31]. These theses are confirmed by the work of Michel Dietler and Ingrid Herbich, who have established that those who cannot dispose of surpluses find themselves excluded from collective events, such as large feasts, and thus marginalized.

Why accept to be excluded from the feast?

Two conditions are necessary for this transition to trans-egalitarian societies: that the majority agrees to work more to build up a surplus; and that it also agrees to cede control (of part) of the surplus to a minority. How did fraternal banquets gradually become discriminatory? How did the majority accept to be dispossessed? Several theses have been proposed, and we will examine them successively.

The majority would have accepted to be discriminated against in exchange for a protection that would have been first of a magical (then religious) nature before being warlike. Brian Hayden thus puts forward the hypothesis of a "structural deception" on the part of the chiefs, who would have abused the other members: it is by monopolizing the consumption of the first fermented beverages, a condition for privileged access to the supernatural, that one ends up taking the best pieces. Everything is good for establishing division and marking one's superiority over the others: "The chiefs also fight to see who will have the largest fruits and vegetables to demonstrate the superiority of their magical abilities"[32]. The food taboos, gradually instituted, are also used to reinforce the power of the chieftain-cies, since transgression of the prohibitions is punished by fines, payable to the village chiefs, and, if they are unable to pay, the poor are reduced

---

31. Brian Hayden, *Man and Inequality. The Invention of Hierarchy in Prehistory, op. cit. loc. cit.* p. 60.
32. *Id., ibid.,* p. 66.

to slavery and at the mercy of the chiefs. Brian Hayden thus insists on the fact that the "progress" brought about by animal and plant domestication was diverted to the benefit of the chiefs: "All the major developmental activities of the elites or proto-elites were based on the production and use of surpluses, whether they were destined to give feasts, presents, dowries, to conclude alliances, exchanges, to acquire objects of prestige or any other activity"[33]. Banquets were therefore not made possible by the increase in stocks and the development of inequalities, they directly contributed to the development of inequalities and thus to the increase in stocks.

Lindsay Falvey breaks another trail by speaking of an inverted socio-economic pyramid. Those who were not initially entitled to the feast must have been a tiny minority (captives, too poor...), otherwise the social division would never have been accepted.

Others point out that it would have taken a long time for the vast majority, who were initially part of the elite, to be excluded from the feast.

Mary Douglas makes this first movement of exclusion the origin of modern poverty.

Antonio Gilman explains this consent to spoliation by the heavy investments made by the first (semi)sedentary farmers. The latter were henceforth tied to their land, and therefore more vulnerable, and they were prevented from fleeing from these chieftainships. A small minority would thus have taken advantage of the weakness linked to sedentarization.

Kim Tremaine explains the emergence of inequality by the fact that food surpluses would have been used to establish institutional hierarchies (of a political, warlike or religious nature). This thesis is also that of Jeanne Arnold, who explains that it is political control over people outside the nuclear family that is at issue, because mastering or controlling food resources, or exchanging objects of prestige, is the best way to exercise domination over others.

All these theses have in common that they sweep aside the functionalist model to make the existence of the surplus not the consequence but the cause of the development of human inequalities and the division of society. Among these functionalists, the proponents of the demographic thesis explain that inequality would be the consequence of too much demographic pressure that would have made it impossible to continue moving around and would have forced people to settle down, and thus to accept new techniques, including plant and animal domestication, and finally - as a necessary evil - political domination. Others put forward the

---

33. *Id., ibid.*, p. 32.

          A political history of food. From the Pateolithic to our days

thesis of an acceptance of the division by the need for a rapid response to threats of invasion from other peoples or following natural disasters. In these two cases, the community would have finally invested certain individuals with a hierarchical power in order to be able to act more effectively. These theories are not tenable, because, on the one hand, there is no critical population threshold above which sedentarization would be inevitable, and, on the other hand, the African population, although just as large, only experienced the development of inequality much later...

I prefer to stick to the idea that humans, who had not diverged much from the rest of the animal world in their feeding behavior during the first two million years, developed at the end of the Paleolithic period the capacity to transform surplus food into a source of political division. What is new is not so much the existence of surpluses, because we have seen the importance of storage operations in previous periods, as the use of surpluses as objects of prestige, that is to say of power. What is new is the conversion of food surpluses into a debt system. I must admit that Brian Hayden's "triple A" thesis seems enlightening to me. "This type of pathological personality would exist in all societies, and, as Hayden points out, 90% of the problems come from those 10% of humans who follow their own interests to the detriment of the community.

The agricultural production of foodstuffs, which succeeds gathering, does not disrupt this pattern, but in the long run allows for the production of ever greater surpluses, thus creating the opportunity - other compromises would have been possible - to develop inequalities, chieftaincies and soon proto-states and the first states as in Mesopotamia. The birth of unequal societies is not the consequence of transformations in the way of production but a choice of society among others. The stocks could have continued to be managed collectively, the banquets could have remained fraternal instead of becoming discriminatory. The birth of unequal societies is therefore a choice that humanity has long refused, even though the techniques that would be used to divide groups already existed. These techniques were simply left fallow, because it was not seen as useful to exploit them further in the context of egalitarian societies. They will therefore only be used in earnest as inequality increases. The political factor (of the history of food) takes precedence here over the natural or technical factor. The decisive factor has not been the production of food through breeding or agriculture, but the appropriation of stocks by a minority. If Brian Hayden is right, it is understandable that he would conclude: "I see the emergence of trans-egalitarian societies in general (and complex hunter-gatherer societies in particular) as the most important change between the first appearance of human hunter-gathe-rers two million years ago and the advent of industrial and nuclear technology. The production of food through agriculture and animal husbandry, in which it was thought to be the major development of human prehistory, should rather be seen as a mere by-product of a more fundamental development related to trans-egalitarian societies, i.e., the emergence of regular surpluses that led to competition and advantages based on economics and socioeconomic hierarchies."

Funeral feasts

Humans live in colonies for different reasons than other species of social animals, because they worship the dead and believe in the need for burial grounds. According to Lewis Mumford[34] , the cities of the dead are at least as old as those of the living, and Jacques Cauvin[35] has established a link between the making of the first tombs - those of the chiefs - and the hereditary appropriation of plots. The gradual shift from hunter to herder and from gatherer to farmer fundamentally altered the relationship of Mesolithic man to death. The farmer no longer deals with death in a constant way like the hunter and gets closer to the vegetal cycle, which is that of eternal renewal. Mircea Eliade established a link between this vegetal cycle (that of the annual resurrection) and the emerging religious speculations on the human resurrection. Mesolithic man began to think about his survival, first under the protection of the "great mother" (a female deity), then under that of other deities. Still according to Eliade, the cult of the ancestors is also to be put in connection with the lengthening of the lineages, thus with the increase in the life expectancy. Once all this has been established, we can better understand the birth of the first funerary feasts: they are to be placed on the same level as the deformations of the skull reserved for the chiefs alone, or even for their children, a sign not only of a hierarchy but of a hereditary hierarchy. The cult of the ancestors is thus to be linked to these particular forms of division of society, which are the restricted access to the supernatural (which is notably translated by the advent of a religious caste) and the restricted - and even costly, accor-ding to Brian Hayden - access to the secret societies of the trans-egalitarian societies. This period is the one of gigantic feasts, as shown by the size of the homes and also by the importance of faunal remains of all kinds.

---

34. Lewis MUMFORD, *The City in History* (1961), Marseille, Agone, 2011.
35. Jacques CAUVIN, *Naissance de l'agriculture, op. cit*; Jacques CAUVIN, *Naissance des divinités. Naissance de l'agriculture. La révolution des symboles au Néolithique*, Paris, "Empreintes", CNRS Éditions, 1994, reedition Paris, Champs/Flammarion, 1998.

          A political history of food. From the Pateolithic to our days

These feasts are the occasion for new specific behaviors, for example, bones crushed in a special way, concentrations of boar's teeth, human heads cooked in fireplaces, sacrifices (especially of dogs, and also probably of humans, slaves and women) and cannibalism.

The evolution of representations, prelude to food transformations
Between 200,000 and 150,000 years ago, the painted or engraved tablets over-represent animal (and human) figures and totally ignore the plant world. This long period is emblematic of a period of meat eating. However, the same tablets opened up to plant representations just before humanity changed its diet. The marginalization of animals in the diet is therefore accompanied by the marginalization of zoomorphic representations in parietal and sculpted art: specialists note that although animals still appear, their status changes: the bull is no longer represented for its concrete utility, but as a virile power and it is for this reason that it is still sacrificed. The Mesolithic period thus upset the relationship between humans and animals. It seems that the accompaniment prevails over the systematic killing: the dog is a companion and a guardian before being a prey or a hunter, the pig is as much an auxiliary of salubrity as an animal of butchery. This tension, perceptible from that time on, runs through the history of Antiquity: is the animal first and foremost a partner who provides guarding, hygiene, clothing, transport, traction, fertilizer, or a meat reserve?

Jacques Cauvin has overturned traditional analyses by explaining that the transition to agriculture was not the response to a situation of scarcity linked to climatic change, nor, of course, the consequence of a demographic explosion, but the result of what he called "the revolution of symbols", a phenomenon that predates domestication by a long time[36]. It is this mutation, situated between 10000 and 9500 years BP, which would explain domestication and not the reverse: thus the domestication of the goat, then of the sheep, does not result from food choices but from a desire of domination. The art of the hunter-gatherers, which is especially zoomorphic and rests on a bipartition of the animal kingdom with a classification in two sexual classes, does not show (and for good reason) any beginning of hierarchization between deities. The new cave art, which retains almost exclusively female representations, includes a hierarchy of which the mother-goddess becomes the keystone. These Venuses, always represented with a hypertrophy of the pelvis, the breasts

---

36. Jacques Cauvin, *Naissance des divinités, naissance de l'agriculture. la révolution des symboles au Néolithique, op. cit.*

and the genitals, are more on the side of the celebration of fecundity (thus of rebirth) than of human/animal sexuality. The transformation of mental images is also very clear with the representation of the hands, since they are always women's hands, left hands, four-fingered hands, the very symbol of industrious humanity, that of the beginning of breeding and agriculture. This thesis means that when humanity began to eat, preferably farmed meat, it was not for efficiency, nor even for ease, let alone for taste, but because it allowed them to satisfy their desire for domination. This thesis also means that when humanity began to eat, preferably cultivated cereals, it was not for the sake of efficiency, nor even for ease or taste, but because it also allowed them to bring another representation of the living to life. Thus, the importance given to the mother-goddesses, at the dawn of protoagriculture, refers to Lewis Mumford's theses on the matrilineal dimension of these communities. Mumford notes that the first villages of the Mesolithic are placed under the double sign of the hearth (of the fire) and the mother, with, in particular, the thematic of the protective enclosure and the direction of the hospitality (to accomodate, protect, nourish). The emblems of these villages have a feminine symbolism, with a preference for rounded forms (house, oven, silo, cistern, attic, tombs, etc.) as a reminder of the theme of fertility. A Greek myth, much later, tells that the first mold for making bread would have been made from the imprint taken from the breast of Aphrodite. Mumford follows the same evolution of techniques in the Mesolithic: the tools of hunters have sharp edges (picks, arrows, axes), while those of the first pastoralists/farmers have rounded shapes (polished stones, stone troughs, pottery, pits, houses, granaries, etc.). However, Lewis Mumford qualifies by noting that daily life remains centered on food and sex, subsistence and procreation. I would gladly add speech.

The development of agriculture, and therefore of a vegetable diet, coincides with the assimilation of women to the earth and then to food. This perception, specific to the Neolithic period, contrasts with what women represented in the Paleolithic period. At that time, the woman was identified, according to Pierre Lévêque, with a forest populated with game, which is why hunting was seen as a sexual possession, hence the assimilation of the wound to the vulva, hence also the fact of considering the death of a woman, during an animal attack, as a sexual possession, with as an extreme consequence the belief that the sacrifice of women made it possible to appease the wild beasts[37]. The Neolithic woman is identified

---

37. Pierre LÉVÊQUE, "Contribution à une théorie historique de la production de la pensée religieuse dans les sociétés du Paléolithique et du Néolithique", *Dialogues d'histoire ancienne*, vol. 7, n° 1, 1981, p. 53-92.

with the earth (and thus with its rhythms). Prehistorians have drawn a parallel between the invention of animal husbandry and agriculture and, on the one hand, the development of liturgies and rituals and, on the other hand, the emergence of a new, specialized body of priests and priestesses. It is notably from this period that the myth of the "first inventor" dates: the Greek pantheon says which god, or which goddess, gave men wheat, the olive tree, the fig tree, the horse, wine, fire. These great myths date back to the Neolithic period.

Sacrifices and offerings

The vegetation of the Mesolithic period is translated into new rites - offerings - supposed to ensure the renewal of nature. Humanity will never cease to offer food and drink not only to other humans, but to deities. How can we not see a disturbing parallel between the advent of this generosity towards the gods and that of the increasingly discriminatory banquets between humans? As if humans were losing in sharing what they give to the gods. Some authors have noted that the offering establishes a deferred time corresponding to that of the farmer and the shepherd, and not to that of the hunter-gatherer. The principle of offerings changes the meaning of the sacred since they are no longer part of the logic of gift and counter-gift, but of submission. Polemics between prehistorians have not lacked on the meaning of offerings: self-destructive form or promise of abundance. This pattern will be reproduced with the powerful to whom the villages will concede an important part of the food surplus, in exchange for their protection.

The Neolithic table

In 1925, Gordon Gilde proposed the concept of a Neolithic revolution: sedentarization would have made it possible to develop agriculture and livestock. The cause of this rupture would have been climatic changes which, notably because of drought, would have forced the use of seedlings[38]. Since then, this classical explanation of the Neolithic revolution has been questioned. This linear vision of the evolution of ways of eating, with the passage from hunting and gathering to animal husbandry and agriculture, does not correspond to history but is in conformity with the great dogmas of industrial society.

---

38. Jean ZAMMIT, "Les conséquences écologiques de la néolithisation dans l'histoire humaine", in *Bulletin de la Société préhistorique française*, vol. 102, n° 2, 2005, p. 371-379.

We owe it to Alain Testart to have proposed, in 1982, a new vision in which the Neolithic revolution is neither a revolution nor a Neolithic revolution, because sedentary hunter-gatherer societies already existed, because these societies practiced significant food storage, and finally, because these non-agricultural societies mastered techniques (such as pottery or transplanting) that would not be mobilized until much later. Marc Groenen has established the proof that this sedentarization existed from the end of the Paleolithic period by studying certain pathologies of the spinal column, but also by identifying habitat structures that were too impressive for nomads, such as houses made from 150 mammoth skeletons. Testart estimates that these hunter-gatherers, sedentary and stockpilers, represent more than half of the known societies, in short, the revolution of the stockpiling techniques was as important as that of agriculture. Wild cereal harvesters only became cereal farmers because they mastered the techniques of harvesting, transporting, drying, storing, and grinding wild grasses. Similarly, hunters only became ranchers because they mastered the techniques necessary to manage their herds.

The great exodus
Man has lived for almost all of his history by hunting and gathering. Agriculture has only existed for 10,000 years, or 500 generations. This transition to agriculture was therefore not compulsory and it was implemented, mainly by groups coming from the east of the continent. Jacques Cauvin describes as "great exodus" the phase of diffusion, from the Near East, of lifestyles related to the domestication of plant and animal species. This term of exodus is very accurate because it is indeed a displacement of populations that came to colonize the indigenous human communities. We know today that it was not these groups that converted to agriculture. This is why neither the first cultivated cereals nor the first livestock resulted from the domestication of local varieties or breeds. A long period of cohabitation between these two cultures and these two types of food will be set up with reciprocal influences. However, the indigenous population, which remained attached to hunting and gathering, was gradually marginalized economically and politically. Testart gives as a sign the disappearance of the small houses of hunter-gatherers to the benefit of the large houses of farmers and breeders. Cauvin also shows that this "great exodus" is accompanied by the development of rectangular houses, while rounded forms are no longer reserved for community houses and religious sanctuaries. The offerings no longer come from hunting products but from livestock. Hunting still exists, but first as a prestige good, as shown

A political history of food. From the Pateolithic to our days

by the deposits of objects made from materials from wild animals, and in particular deer, the animal already most valued. Isabelle Sidéra[39] warns us, however, that "this transfer of the hunting universe from the material to the ideal constitutes the peripheralization of this activity in time and in the minds", in other words, the exaltation of the hunt does not mean the return to the hunt and to the hunters, because "this exaltation is rather the construction of the breeders" than of the hunters. We will find this phenomenon during millennia with the king hunter: "The generalized adoption of the attributes stemming from the wild sphere would sign a double phenomenon of appropriation by the stockbreeders, of symbols, of virtues, of values exalted by a culture partly foreign to theirs, at the same time as a first fusion of the mesolithic and neolithic cultures." This observation means that this period is that of a progressive integration of the hunter-gatherers within the pastoral civilization. They will indeed fulfill a function of mediation and protection towards other tribes, in short, the ex-hunters begin to metamorphose into warriors. Isabelle Sidéra notes that there is no dissolution of this old world not only because this process of acculturation is spread over several centuries, but because at the same time as they metamorphose to fulfill a new function, these former hunters who have become warriors preserve different habitats and a different diet.

On the breeding side

The animals consumed by the newcomers are now systematically domesticated, such as pigs, goats, sheep and dogs. The study of faunal remains shows that they perfectly mastered the demography of their herds, preferring to slaughter males rather than females and deciding on slaughter choices according to age and species. Goats have a consumption peak between zero and 2 months. Why kill suckling kids if not to be able to use their mothers' milk? The second consumption peak concerns cull goats. Jean-Denis Vigne[40] formulates the hypothesis according to which the exploitation of dairies was perhaps the first objective of the first breeders, because in terms of meat, breeding brings no advantage over hunting, which is more diversified and simpler. This iconoclastic hypothesis is based on undeniable technical arguments: curds can be

---

39. Isabelle SIDÉRA (dir), with the collaboration of Emmanuelle VILA and Philippe ERIKSON, *La chasse. Pratiques sociales et symboliques*. Paris, "Colloques de la Maison Archéologie & Ethnologie René-Ginouvès", Éditions de Boccard, 2006.
40. Jean-Denis VIGNE, "Préhistoire du Cap Corse : les abris de Torre d'Aquila, Pietracorbara (Haute-Corse). La Faune" in *Bulletin de la Société préhistorique française*, vol. 92, n° 3, 1995, p. 381-389.

drained without pottery, with basketry or simple cloth. As the researcher points out, milk was exploited in the Ardèche as early as 5000 BP, that is to say, well before the pseudo-revolution of secondary production... The prehistorian also shows that from that time onwards, butchering techniques were skilful: the animals were cut into four large quarters: the head, the front limbs, the back and the rear. The head is then re-cut to separate the throat from the head. The forelegs are also trimmed to separate the hams and legs and to remove the terminal phalanges. The back is re-cut to remove the two loins, to cut the backbone and to recover the ribs. If the cutting of the large quarters is coarse, the cutting of the half-cuts is much finer, it is not done with the same tools, nor perhaps by the same people. The cooking methods are varied: grilling, roasting, stone oven, heated stones thrown in water contained in containers, such as skin bags, etc. Some pieces are systematically grilled or roasted (head, throat, legs) while others are never. As Vigne notes, we are therefore in the presence of structured culinary habits and that, without doubt, do not date from the Neolithic but are very previous to it.

In view of the importance of the tools and ordinary objects taken from the animal world (punches, scrapers, adze handles, sledgehammers, pendulum rings, made from long bones, teeth, ribs, deer antlers, etc.), and therefore the complexity of the technologies used to process bovid and suidae bone materials, it is not possible to exclude that for some areas the consumption of meat was only a by-product and not the primary purpose. This hypothesis would explain the questioning of the hierarchy of animals: cattle and sheep lose the quality of privileged resources. It seems that we can date from this period the fact that the pig becomes the meat food par excellence, while the other animals are used for everything else. The sheep is thus destined, at first, for the bone industry and for textiles. The value of the animal gradually changes, it is alive that it is valued because of the work it can accomplish and the dairy products of which it is the source.

One of the consequences of this multiform exploitation of the animal world is that man no longer appears as an element among the others, contrary to the characteristic representation of hunter-gatherers. This period is that of the beginning of hierarchical representations of the world: humanity is closer to the divinity than the (other) animals, the animals are above the plants and the mineral world is at the bottom of the scale. Man thus gives himself the right to dominate and appropriate animals. Hunting, which had declined at the beginning of the Neolithic period, returns in force not for a food reason, but as a sign of power that testifies to the existence of social inequalities. These inequalities are also expressed through the methods of preparation: indirect cooking, which allows for more refined preparations, will soon be preferred to direct cooking, and certain cuts will become more noble.

On the agricultural side

Agriculture is not a way to continue gathering by other means. It fundamentally changes the way people eat. Among the last hunter-gatherers, gathering was sufficiently organized and learned to have allowed access to the "secrets" of fertility cycles. The gatherer knows, better than the hunter, that plants are subject to seasonal cycles, to the eternal restarting (except bad year). The plant world is thanked for its gifts as much as the animal kingdom, and the plant eater sacrifices seeds and herbs just as the meat eater sacrifices fat, viscera and bones.

The first crops came from Anatolia, they crossed the Dardanelles Strait, the Aegean Sea, the Balkans, before reaching Gaul. The eight plants at the origin of agriculture are all from the Near East: einkorn (small spelt), starch, barley, lentils, peas, flax and chickpeas. Conservation techniques adapted to the new mode of production: grains were dried or roasted in ovens before being stored, terracotta jars were used in addition to granaries and silos, or simply holes dug in the ground and coated with clay and then subjected to fire in order to maintain a good defense against humidity, rodents and certain insects. Landscapes are transformed, an open vegetation environment is created, many hedges are planted to protect the plots from the wind, which also allows to eat more berries and birds. The retreat of the forest, by means of an important clearing by fire, leads to the removal of an important part of the game, in particular of the biggest. These first changes in food practices will call for another: while the hunter consumes enough salt by eating meat, just like the shepherd by drinking the blood of animals or their milk (cheese), the cooking of plants removes salt from food and therefore endangers health. So the farmer uses sea salt, rock salt, salt efflorescences, etc., thus learning to season better. Certain new pathologies, such as dental caries, are the result of an increase in the consumption of sugar and a decrease in fats. A new grammar of taste is put in place, facilitated by the importance of exchanges, as shown by the importance of the groups of huts, the numerous roads and the existence of important artisanal stations. The villages that developed did not yet exceed 200 inhabitants, but they were in contact with each other and exchanged their know-how. Of course, the techniques were still rudimentary but perfectly adapted: a digging stick (a straight stick cut to a point, sometimes burned and provided with a hook), a deer or tree wood hoe, a wooden spider, a flint pick, etc. The plough came a little later, first without wheels and then with, first without an iron share and then with.

The feasts of the Neolithic

These first villages had collective institutions such as common houses with rounded shapes, streets, squares, wells, community granaries, altars, etc. The councils of elders exist everywhere, an obligatory form of power and transmission of knowledge in societies that are still totally oral. We have an idea of the customs of the chiefdoms through, for example, the representations of the banquets of the divinities that are beginning to appear. Large feasts, lasting several days, continue to develop, but we are no longer in an egalitarian logic because, as Testart points out, gift and exchange are as clearly opposed as free acts and paid acts[41]. Testart shows that the potlatch begins to undermine the mechanisms of sharing. It presupposes the individual or group appropriation of goods for the accumulation of wealth intended to be exchanged within this framework. The potlatch, by reducing exchange to a struggle between chiefs, gives rise to a hierarchy and divides society in a more or less lasting and important way. The potlatch, according to Testart, is a transformation of the principle of dispossession through sharing into a principle of dispossession through private appropriation. Claude Lefort joins this thesis by showing that the potlatch is linked to a power of constraint through the mechanism of the recognition of the other by his other.

The food balance sheet of neolithization is finally quite contradictory. Already, humanity is on the verge of extinction due to pandemics whose propagation is facilitated by the sedentarization of large villages; food diversity is reduced, both on the animal and plant side, since as soon as communities master breeding and agriculture, they quickly "unlearn" everything that allowed them to live from hunting and gathering, not only the edible products or the way to make them so, but also the technologies, especially plant technologies, that were theirs. Humans will discover with the Neolithic that one can spend one's life working, because the productivity of hunting and gathering is much better, and that not everyone will automatically have a place at the banquet. As Jacques Rancière would say, the non-participants will become the majority.

---

41. Alain Testart, *Critique du don. Études sur la circulation non marchande*, Paris, Syllepse, 2007 ; Alain Testart, "Échange marchand, échange non marchand" in *Revue française de sociologie*, vol. 42, n° 4, 2001, p. 719-748.

Towards the protohistoric societies

This overview of prehistoric tables should cure us against any perception of a linear evolution: the Paleolithic table interpenetrates with the Neolithic one, which itself will continue until our days: hunting and gathering did not disappear with animal and plant domestication! We can think with Lewis Mumford and Brian Hayden that the ancient hunters, marginalized for a time, ended up prevailing over the first peasants by becoming the basis of the new royal and religious power. This change marks the transition from matrilineal to patriarchal societies, through what the historian calls "manly strength. Lewis Mumford specifies that the hunters are not warriors and that the invention of the warrior figure is specific to the agricultural and pastoral way of life. The ancient hunters became the armed protectors of the first villages of farmers and herders against the great beasts, then against other humans. They built fortresses near the villages and developed weapons. From protectors of the villages, they will become their masters. This hunter, who became king, is the one who will invent haute cuisine in his palaces. In the same way that the hunters will make the future warriors, it is probable that a fraction of the gatherers (with the medicinal and religious dimension) and of the stockbreeders (with the pastoral activity) will give the specialized clergy, prelude to the birth of religions much more formalized, centralized, hierarchical. Mumford insists on the mental predispositions that pastoral activity gives rise to and that will be mobilized, much later, by the priestly caste. The image of the shepherd and his flock is still remembered today. The family god will, of course, take a long time to disappear, but he will eventually give way to a god that will be appropriated by a polytheistic, then monotheistic, caste. For his part, the shepherd, who had become a priest, developed the "cuisine of sacrifice".

This period is the one of the return to the male figures, to the cult of the bull as a virile element, to the taste for the armament, first in connection with the hunting, then without connection with it, but in a warlike atmosphere, it is finally, the great time of the development of the secret brotherhoods. Hunting, which had regressed a lot, made a comeback at the end of the Neolithic period. It is now the emblem of a nascent aristocracy which will soon reserve for itself the monopoly of weapons and, at least, that of the big game. The meat diet will take, for a long time, its dimension of strength.

SECOND SERVICE: THE MESOPOTAMIAN TABLE

The traveler who has accompanied me throughout these hundreds of thousands of years already has in his cauldrons some reference points on the way our distant ancestors conceived food and on what they ate. The overview of Mesopotamian tables will have a different status, because we know much more about the customs and mores of this period. In view of the accounts that have come down to us, we must admit that the Mesopotamian civilizations knew what eating could mean. This civilization will last three millennia (around 3400 years BC to 200 AD). The food question crosses that of the creation of city-states, from the IVe millennium BC, with the birth of new political ideologies on food. It seems to me that we have not yet cooked this period enough to make it give back all its juice in terms of relations between food and politics. Sargon, founding sovereign of the Akkadian empire (around 2779-2334 BC), was made king, while he was the great cupbearer of Zabata, king of Ur, thanks to a crisis of regime around a reform of the rituals of food offerings.

Undeniably, the Babylonian table constitutes a great leap forward, not because the Mesopotamians suddenly became more gourmet, not even because they had more resources, but because this period seals the appearance of absolute power. The Mesopotamian table is first of all politics made of cooking and vice versa. We know the famous formula of Samuel Noah Kramer: "History begins in Sumer". I would add: the food separatism of the powerful begins in Sumer.

The establishment of the first city-states

Admittedly, this period is much shorter than the previous one, but rich enough for a traveler in much less of a hurry than ourselves to establish tasty variations from one city-state to another. There are notable food differences between the Akkadian empire, the dynasties of Ur, Sumer, Babylon, and Egypt, which will be tasted in the next chapter. How was the transition from the power of the assemblies of family heads to a very quickly centralized and authoritarian monarchy possible? It is commonly explained as the consequence of the constitution of a league of the first city-states, with delegation of powers to a single individual, called the "great man", who would then have passed from the designation by the assembly of notables to direct election by the gods (thus the clergy). The hypothesis of a "King-Priest" initially combining the two functions has now been abandoned, and it is better to think in terms of a distinction of functions and therefore of powers, even if our secular criteria are inoperative. Of course, the dosage of powers is different according to the city-states, but everywhere we see a physical separation of the palace and the temple, and we note then that only the temples and the tombs are built in stone, whereas the palaces will continue to be built in wood, less prestigious. While the city-state puts an end to food self-sufficiency, the princes and the clergy will appropriate respectively the granaries and the distribution markets. The appropriation of the goods concerned initially the common goods... Thus the granaries, collective property, became property of State, then, with the appropriation of the State by the sovereigns, they will be the personal goods of the sovereigns. The constitution of the first city-states also led to a reinforcement and a transformation of the traditional role of the temples and their personnel, which in fact appropriated the food distribution circuits. The market was first physically integrated into the temples, and then their personnel took direct charge of the supply, storage and distribution of foodstuffs in exchange for a rather lucrative tax. The temples thus functioned as a sort of department store. The increase of the population leads to a transfer of these activities to a secular staff, and thus to the development of corporations linked to trade. This period also saw the appearance of public squares dedicated to the food market and now integrated into the popular districts.

We will go to the essential, by seeking to establish in what the establishment of the first city-states allowed to develop a food separatism.

What do we know about the Mesopotamian table?

Four authors will be our guides to taste the Mesopotamian tables. We owe to Jean Bottéro a good knowledge of the culinary techniques that marked the third millennium of the Mesopotamian civilization. The historian insists on the passage to wet indirect cooking, that is to say on the generalization of the fatty broth, a culinary technology which, because it implies a preliminary preparation of the food, allows to develop a true gastronomy, especially as it integrates many ingredients[42]. Our other guide is Francis Joannès, who insisted above all on the analogies between the food of the elites, that of the kings, and the food of the gods[43]. Royal or sacred banquets testify to the same desire to demarcate themselves from the cuisine of the people, moving from a feminine to a masculine cuisine. Our third guide is naturally Jack Goody, because the English anthropologist is the first to have thought so intimately the relation between the birth of a "high cuisine" and the development of social inequalities. The more a society is divided, the more the arts of the table develop within the framework of a real staging, a sign of the relations of power[44]. It does not matter whether this power is essentially political or religious, economic or cultural, because the grammar remains the same. Our last guide will be Liliane Plouvier, historian of gastronomy, for her analysis of the tablets of the Yale Babylonian Collection, which contain the first known culinary recipes dating back to the court of Hammurabi[45].

I wanted to cross-reference the recipes of these four guides to see how far this cross-fertilization could lead us in terms of the history of food. I insist on the fact that this history is not univocal, since other policies, which are less talked about, such as the system of rations or "food fields", respond to the magnificence at the top. The palatial table thus concerns the powerful as much as their servants. Moreover, we note that the first kings hesitated between a discourse on the good king who nourished his people and the qualities of a warrior and hunter king. This nourishing and protective function is shared with the temples, because the high level of offerings and sacrifices makes it possible to constitute a second particularly well organized food distribution network. Indeed, after the rituals, the offerings are distributed according to very strict rules between the temple staff and the

---

42. Jean Bottéro, *La plus vieille cuisine du monde*, Paris, Louis Audibert éditeur, 2002.

43. Francis Joannès, "L'alimentation des élites mésopotamiennes : nourriture du roi, nourriture des dieux" in *Pratiques et discours alimentaires en Méditerranée de l'Antiquité à la Renaissance*. Actes du 18ᵉ colloque de la Villa Kérylos à Beaulieu-sur-Mer, les 4, 5 & 6 octobre 2007, "Cahiers de la Villa Kérylos", vol. 19, n° 1, Paris, Académie des Inscriptions et Belles Lettres, 2008, p. 23-38. For a global approach of the period see Françis Joannès, *Les premières civilisations du Proche-Orient*, Paris, "Atouts Histoire", Belin, 2006.

44. Jack Goody, *Kitchens, Cooking and Classes*, trans. (English) Jeanne Bouniort, Paris, Centre Georges Pompidou, Centre de création industrielle 1985.

45. Liliane Plouvier, "À la table du roi Hammurabi de Babylone d'après les tablettes de la Yale Babylonian Collection" in *Proceedings of the 15th World Congress of the International Union of Prehistoric and Protohistoric Sciences (IUPPS)*, Oxford, Archeopress, vol. 34, 2010, read at: http://www.oldcook.com/histoire-cuisine_mesopotamie

palace administration. The little people also regularly benefited from these redistributions. Paradoxically, to increase the volume of the offerings (one knows that they depend on each god even if the divinities always eat much more than the humans), is to increase the capacities of redistribution. Jean Bottéro insists on the risk of anachronism to speak about a clergy, because all is religious, that is why better to stick to a functional distinction being able to mobilize the same notables, with the palate or the temple. This religious dimension is already expressed by the importance of prophecies and divinations: the liver of sacrificed animals is observed before each major political decision, such as during declarations of war or alliances. Its importance also appears in the inventory of the lands belonging to the temples, either from the king's gifts or from purchases from their resources.

A palatial economy, a palatial diet

The political regime of Babylon is a very particular system of divine right. Although the king was a member of a royal lineage, he nevertheless had to be elected by the gods (which attests to the essential role of the clergy), and then accepted by the people (thanks to amnesties for maintenance debts). The government of the kingdom was based on the notion of the "royal house", which obviously attests to a patrimonial conception of the state since (almost) everything was supposed to belong to the king, but also marks the beginning of more abstract notions, such as the service of the king or the service of the state and the general interest. Each king is not defined by himself but in relation to his capital city (for example, the king of Babylon). The essential decisions are taken in a Council described as "secret". The government staff includes the royal family, then the "great servants" of the king, his ministers (viziers) accompanied by "scribes of the secret" (hence the name of secretary). Each king had various palaces, even within his own capital. It is also customary to call any place the king lives a palace. It seems to me that there is a kind of contrast between the reality that makes (still) largely of the king a nurturing king and his official representations that show him as a warrior or, as a simple variant of the same motif, as a hunter... If (almost) the entire economy is of the palatial type, its organization rests, in the first place, on what I would call "food policies".

A debate divides the specialists on the effective place of the private property, at the sides of the "great organizations" (that are the temples and the palaces), but Jean-Pierre Vernant seems to me convincing, when he explains: "The social life appears centered around the palace whose role is at the same time religious, political, military, administrative, economic.

In this system of palatial economy, the king concentrates and unifies in his person all the elements of power, all aspects of sovereignty. Through the intermediary of scribes, forming a professional class fixed in tradition, thanks to a complex hierarchy of palace dignitaries and royal inspectors, he controls and meticulously regulates all sectors of economic life, all areas of social activity [...] One cannot see that there is any place, in an economy of this type, for private commerce"[46].

The people's table

Mesopotamian civilization, with the birth of city-states, introduced (widened and made commonplace) a division that still exists today between the food of the powerful and the rest of the population. This separatism of the powerful is organized materially and legitimized ideologically: indeed, a significant part of the population works for the benefit of the temples and the palaces or within the framework of the great works carried out by the elites. These workers were paid in kind, with monthly rations of barley and oil, the amount of which depended on their sex, age, and function. These rations were sufficient for food but politically divisive. The people also benefited from more diversified redistributions made by the temples.

The system of rations and food fields
The economy is more and more administered from the IInd millennium B.C. with large agricultural domains belonging either to the palaces or to the temples. An important part of the food thus depends on the powerful. The latter also progressively took control of storage structures, including grain silos which were already large enough to ensure the feeding of more than 20,000 people during a year. The available agricultural production came either from land owned by the palace and entrusted to "private" entrepreneurs in exchange for a fixed fee called *biltum* (payable partly in kind and partly in money), or from another system which consisted of the king allocating plots of land ("food fields") to private individuals in exchange for a service called *Ilkum* (military service, craft work, etc.) or sukussum ("food").) or *sukussum* ("subsistence fields")[47], a designation that can be explained by reference to the other possible mode of remuneration

---

46. Jean-Pierre VERNANT, *Les origines de la pensée grecque*, Paris, Presses universitaires de France, 1962.
47. See *Le système palatial en Orient, en Grèce et à Rome*. Actes du colloque de Strasbourg (19-22 juin 1985), Edmond Lévy (éd.), "Travaux du center de recherche sur le Proche-Orient et la Grèce antique", université des sciences humaines de Strasbourg, 1987.

by the palace, namely the granting of rations. The city-states thus had two ways of providing for the needs of the various categories of population (especially urban) that they employed: either the system of rations or the more innovative system of food fields.

Rations were given to soldiers, of course, but also to administrative, technical and domestic staff of the palaces and temples. These rations depend on the function, the sex and the age of each servant. At the end of the third millennium the barley ration was 2 liters per day for a man, 1 liter for a woman and 0.3 and 0.6 liter for a child or an old man. Bowls of three types of capacity were used for standard distributions. Specialists have identified many conflicts over the allocation of these rations, especially during the most distant military operations. Thus, during the siege of the city of Larsa, the soldiers protested, because they did not receive oil, the power offered them instead of sesame, which they refused.

Does the system of food fields respond to these dysfunctions? What is certain is that the bulk of the troops were soon paid, like the other servants, according to this system in return for the military service they performed. A whole administration composed of surveyors and scribes was in charge of managing these "food fields": the allocated surfaces oscillated between 6 and 36 hectares, according to the nature of the services rendered (worker or high dignitary). The beneficiaries of these fields can cultivate them themselves or have them cultivated by a farmer in exchange for a rent (in kind and in money). These food fields cannot be sold, and, in the event of illegal transfer, the tablet that materializes the legal act is simply broken, the plot returned to its original owner, and the money lost by the purchaser. These "food fields" include land, orchards and houses. It is forbidden to dismember them in order to endow one's daughter or to make a dower for the surviving wife to enjoy.

A diversified diet

Jean Bottéro and Cécile Michel[48] remind us that managing to feed the people in sufficient quantity and quality is a sign of good power. The popular diet is quite diversified even if it is based, as we shall see, on the duo of breaded food/water, then breaded food/beer. We know the Mesopotamian table quite well thanks to the numerous tales that have come down to us and to the gourmet literature. We learn that misery

---

48. Cécile MICHEL, "L'alimentation au Proche-Orient ancien : les sources et leur exploitation" in *Dialogues d'histoire ancienne*, Supplément n° 7, 2012, p. 17-45, numéro thématique : *L'histoire de l'alimentation dans l'Antiquité. Bilan historiographique* - Journée de printemps de la SOPHAU, 21 mai 2011.

consists in lacking bread, beer and meat. Contrary to the rich merchants and notables, the people ate, in principle, kneeling in front of a large dish from which each one helped himself by hand. They had a variety of dishes (spoons, knives, dishes, pots, trays held on a tripod, etc.) made of wood, reed, clay, metal, etc. The Mesopotamians of the people used different varieties of cereals (especially barley, but also wheat and spelt) to make flour, semolina, porridge, pastry, beer, and, of course, bread. There are up to 200 types of breads, if you believe the richness of the vocabulary. Some breads contain leaven, spices, fruits, honey, etc. We also eat oil, millet, beans, sesame seeds, onions, garlic, vegetables like leeks, and fruits (dates, pomegranates, apples, figs, pistachios, grapes, etc.). We also eat "pastries" such as cakes, gingerbread, cakes filled with dates, apples, figs, honey, etc. Meat and fish are rarer, even if it is necessary to differentiate according to the times. Beef, mutton, geese, ducks, pigeons, turtle doves are consumed, but also, especially the poorest, pork. It is in this context that a progressive demonization of the pig appears, first associated with bad omens in divinatory literature, then considered by the clergy as "dirty, stupid and a symbol of ritual impurity" - a condemnation that will continue until the Old Testament. These herds of pigs, consumed by the people, belong to the palace.

The bread and water duo

I have already said that the Mesopotamian table, although very varied, is based on the couple breaded food/water, then, later, breaded food/beer. The same Sumerian ideogram (as in Egyptian) means bread and food. I preferred not to attribute directly to Mesopotamia the couple bread/beer considering the place that water still holds in writing and in the imagination. The sign that indicates the fact of drinking is the pictogram of water and not that of beer, which refers more to the side of joy, of civilization. The water can be flavored, which allows us to propose "infusions", "decoctions" and "water moistened with fruit juice" (pomegranates, grapes). Two types of beverages are thus opposed, those called "natural" and those fermented; but among the "natural" beverages, we come up against the status of milk, considered as much as a food as a drink. The Mesopotamians, especially the Babylonians, drank a lot of beer, but with (still) the feeling of accessing an exceptional drink. The basic beer is also called "intoxicating liquid", which seems to testify to its specific and probably quite exceptional status. These beers are made from a variety of cereals, resulting in a wide range of products (red, black, white, "sweet", "very sweet", "good quality", "superior quality", etc.). There are even beers that are cut with water (half, third or quarter), which corresponds to an extension of consumption throughout the day, rather than a by-product for the poorest. At the beginning, beers were domestic preparations whose surplus was marketed. Soon the first "Houses of the tavernière" appear, sign of the still domestic character of the drink, which will be transformed, later, into "Houses of the taverniers", sign of its dedomestication. The consumption is made there by means of a blowtorch (i.e. a large straw) which makes it possible to draw the drink in a large tank, located at the center of the room. Jean Bottéro allows us to approach the status of this drink in Mesopotamia when he writes that "beer could offer the ancient population [...] a kind of ideal of mouth, a source of pure pleasure, within the reach of (almost) all".

Natural or artificial feeding

The Mesopotamians do not classify food in our way and when they seem to approach it, it is the moment when they are farthest from it. Thus the true opposition, as Bottéro reminds us about *The Epic of Gilgamesh*, is between a natural food, produced without any human intervention, and an artificial food elaborated by the man. This second food is preferred because corresponding to the civilized life. I think that this is why bread and beer have become inseparable, because they are "the result of human intervention and effort".

The Mesopotamians use a comparison with sexuality to better understand what distinguishes food from nutrients by opposing bestial mating, therefore natural, with a female, and true love with a woman of the city, expert and lustful (*sic*). Beer, contrary to water, is not a natural production; it is thus on this account and not, as it is often written, because of its thick consistency that it is more a question of eating (thus of making) than of drinking. The first principle of the Mesopotamian table is, in fact, to make its food, and consequently to cook it, because cooking is a fabrication, except for some raw vegetables (but perhaps they are already cooked by the sun?). In reality, cooking is the big issue, because incorporating uncooked food is pointless. For lack of wood, the Mesopotamians use naphtha (oil outcrop found in this region of the world) and charcoal. Jean Bottéro, after having recalled the opposition of principle between direct cooking (by roasting, grilling or roasting for seeds) and indirect cooking, makes the invention of indirect cooking with water (or wet) the great specificity. This indirect cooking means that the real cooking, for a Mesopotamian, is done in a pot, with fatty water, possibly after a quick pre-cooking in a cauldron. This fatty broth is most often made with sheep fat (probably also with pork). Bottéro has identified 36 additives that allow to play on the tastes

     A political history of food. From the Pateolithic to our days

and substances, "which implies a rather astonishing refinement of the taste and militates in favor of a sought-after cooking, and, consequently, of an authentic gastronomy". Salted and dried meat is cooked in this type of broth. The Mesopotamians also consume a kind of brine made of fish and locusts, extremely salty and partly decomposed (we will see later the place of *garum* in the Roman table). Finally, Bottéro evokes the use of an indirect dry cooking, in ovens, thanks to the use of ceramic dishes, which makes it possible to obtain a cooked and moulded food of which the Mesopotamians are fond.

There is no shortage of occasions for banqueting… even for the people, whether it is the wedding banquets in which the bride and her family eat the food offered by the groom and his relatives who seal the union, or the feasts offered by the kings or the notables.

The table of the gods

Men were created to serve the gods, so they had to build them houses (temples), furniture (sacred), weave them clothes and ornaments and, of course, give them food and drink. Each god has his own temples, his own statues, which multiplies the volume of daily or exceptional offerings. Four daily meals are offered to the deities, including dairy products (butter, cheese), bread, semolina, oatmeal, grilled or roasted meat, accompanied by oil and spices, condiments, fruits (dates, pistachios, pomegranates), pastries, fermented drinks, etc.

At least five types of barley beer are produced by the temple brewers. Each statue consumes the equivalent of several hundred people. Only what is considered the best is offered to the gods, so no pork or goat. Each god has his own prohibitions, one the sheep, the other the ox. The sacrificial butcher, in charge of slaughtering animals for the preparation of meals, was one of the most important members of the religious staff. He carried out the killing - as soon as the blood was collected, it was sprayed on the doors of the temples -, cut the animal into pieces and threw them into a stew pot, and cooked them while reciting prayers. The deities receive real meals, thus allowing their redistribution. We already know that the remuneration of the temple personnel (an important fraction of the urban population) is done in three ways, either a maintenance ration, or a share on the distribution of offerings, or a "food field". This staff therefore eats, more or less, like the statues of the deities. As a small bonus, the butcher is entitled to the skins that he scrapes with his knife. Big bonus, the most noble religious functions are generally hereditary, the others are often sold in the form of lucrative prebends... The distinction between religious and secular functions does not correspond to our criteria: thus the sweepers are religious, because they purify the premises.

This table of deities tells us a lot about ordinary food. Firstly, because the food offered to the gods constitutes real meals which feed the personnel of the temples, since the offerings are not burned, as during the sacrifices in the form of holocausts, but distributed. Then, because these divine meals obey the same protocol rules as those used for the sovereign, his court and the notables, so much so that Bottéro qualifies the service of the gods of "sublimated transfer of the etiquette of the court, itself generous amplification of the ordinary *modus vivendi*". However, I would insist on the shift which exists between the preparations. The table of the gods is much less refined/cooked than that of the powerful... One could get away with explaining that the gods appreciate grilled food, because they like the smell, whereas civilized men have to eat boiled food, but I believe rather in a lowly material explanation: the divinities not consuming the preparations, they must remain simple to facilitate the redistribution, which can moreover take place later and elsewhere... I add especially that the texts organizing the offerings envisage that these must be adapted to the wealth of the individual and to the agricultural situation, in particular in the event of dearth: in this case, the gods are put automatically on the diet, with 1 liter of beer and bread... The temples have, finally, an obligation of assistance between them in the event of difficulty of provisioning. They even have an obligation towards the palace.

The table of the powerful

Mesopotamia is famous for the magnificence of its banquets. I cannot resist the greed of repeating the description of the famous banquet offered by the king of Assyria for the inauguration of his new palace: "The most gigantic of these banquets was the one offered by Assurnarsipal II (883-859 B.C.) after the completion of the palace of Kalhu by inviting 69,574 people to a feast which lasted ten days. The list of the food consumed covers several tens of lines and enumerates gigantic quantities: 1,000 fat oxen, 14,000 sheep, 1,000 lambs, several hundreds of various kinds of deer, poultry, including 20,000 pigeons, 10,000 fish, 10,000 sheafs, 10,000 eggs, not to mention thousands of jugs of beer and wineskins. Huge quantities of bread, baskets of vegetables and fruit, and condiments are also cited and carefully detailed, showing that all the resources of the empire had been put to use"[49]. Experts argue about the realism of such banquets. Eva Miller of Oxford University, for example, believes that "such a high number seems impossible and was certainly a grandiloquent exaggeration typical of the king. However, she adds: "Even so, it is a good indication that luxurious public feasts for crowds were a possible feature of royal events"[50]. The main point is therefore elsewhere.

These descriptions show enough that if these first city-states undoubtedly do something new, they do it with old. Nothing comparable would have been possible without the achievements of the preceding periods. It was necessary that forms of political commensality had already been experimented so that they could (so quickly) reach such a perfection. Moreover, the extravagant character of this banquet should not occult the regularity of the feasts. As Jean Bottéro writes, what counts, it is "the assumption of responsibility by the king on this festive occasion of the eating and drinking of his people"; the historian points out that these feasts had something of institutional, they do not concern a liberality of the monarch. They are necessary in the normal exercise of its office for any good sovereign.

The life of the palaces is thus punctuated by the organization of banquets either to commemorate events or to celebrate legendary dates, or on the occasion of the visits that the princes and dignitaries regularly make to each other, or even on the occasion of diplomatic dinners between delegates of the city-states. The chronicles are particularly verbose concerning

---

49. Francis JOANNÈS, "La fonction sociale du banquet dans les premières civilisations", in Jean-Louis FLANDRIN et Massimo MONTANARI (dirs), *Histoire de l'alimentation, op. cit*, p. 55.

50. *The Banquet Stele of Assurnasirpal II records the 9th century Neo-Assyrian king's renovation of the city of Kalhu (modern-day Nimrud), which he made his capital. It boasts of the lavish palace and gardens he built, the restoration of temples, and the resettlement and rejuvenation of surrounding towns. The 'banquet' moniker derives from its most unique claim: that in 879 BC, Assurnasirpal II celebrated his new capital with a lavish feast at which he served 69574 people - male and female, local and foreign envoy -with an obscene amount of meat, poultry, vegetables, and alcohol. This number seems impossibly high, and was likely a typically bombastic royal exaggeration. All the same, this is good evidence that luxurious mass public feasting was one possible feature of royal events. (Eva Miller, University of Oxford).* "The banquet stele of Ashurnasirpal II bears witness to the 9th century Neo-Assyrian king's renovation of the city of Kalhu (now Nimrud) as his capital. It praises the sumptuous palace and gardens he built, the restoration of the temples, and the relocation and rejuvenation of the surrounding towns. The nickname "banquet" comes from his most remarkable claim: in 879 B.C., Assurnasirpal II is said to have celebrated his new capital with a sumptuous feast that he served to 69,574 people, men and women, local and foreign representatives, with an obscene amount of meat, poultry, vegetables, and alcohol. Such a high number seems impossible and was certainly a typical grandiloquent exaggeration of the king. Even so, it is a good clue that luxurious public feasts for the crowd were among the possible features of royal events." (Eva Miller - cdli.ox.ac.uk/wiki/doku.php?id=banquet_stela_assurnasirpal_ii, translation by Ariane Bischoff Batma).

---

the visits of ambassadors, first itinerant, then remaining on site until their mission was fully accomplished, and finally more and more in residence. The protocol was very strict: reception at the gates of the city, initial presentation of gifts which was equivalent to accreditation by the king, accommodation in guest houses, transfer to the palace, introduction to the king, further exchange of gifts, participation in the banquet according to the rank and/or importance of the king. The palace of Mari, with its 3,000 rooms on a surface of 25,000 square meters and its hundreds of cooks, cupbearers and waiters, was designed for these rituals. The specialists like Joannes agree on the fact that the banquets already abundant in third millennium will become plethoric in IInd millennium.

The city-state, it is initially the organization of banquets intended for the elites. However, this commensality is not sufficient to itself, it was necessary that it takes place in the respect of strict rules, but also in the "good mood". Then, the city-state, it is the organization of big banquets for the people. The one who holds and is legitimate to exercise the power is the one who distributes. The banquets last days and feed tens of thousands of subjects. This table of the powerful ones will rest on the writing of a new grammar concerning its design, its receipts, its accounts of banquets, finally its rituals.

A kitchen that creates separatism

Historians have made the most of the famous tablets of the Yale Babylonian Collection, translated by Bottéro and analyzed by Liliane Plouvier. One can, of course, be satisfied with admiringly listing all the dishes mentioned, but the essential point is that such a cuisine would never have been possible without a real raid on the food resources of the whole region and without the organization of a vast system of imports. Thousands of servants were thus charged only with supplying the table of the great king whose subjects were obliged to give him, during his travels, very large sums of money which enabled him to organize, in return, grandiose banquets. Such a cuisine would never have been possible without a highly qualified staff, without real specialists of the table: cooks (maîtres queux), bakers, butchers, meal planners, waiters, servants, etc. These maîtres queux are looked upon, as if they were a part of the king's family. These maîtres queux are considered, says Plouvier, as possessing a particular gift. They are out of the ordinary because they fulfill an out of the ordinary function. One becomes cook at the end of a long initiation with the greatest. Bottéro quotes certain contracts of training of fifteen months and points out that the profession of cook is among the most

    A political history of food. From the Pateolithic to our days

honourable, which justifies that the representatives of this trade have the status of priests. In the "Queen's house", in the 8th and 7th centuries BC, there were 400 cooks, 400 pastry cooks, 220 cupbearers, 300 servants, etc. This system allowed for the creation of a cuisine which, even before being better, had to be different from the ordinary cuisine of commoners. One will eat different dishes, served differently, consumed in another way, and all this is put at the service of a social separatism. Thus, if the ordinary kitchen is the lot of women, that of the king is made by men. The only exception, even in the palace, the making of bread and beer remains a female activity, because the products are too common to be male (grinding grain is an activity of women or prisoners). Food is therefore feminine when it is simply a matter of feeding, it becomes masculine when it serves to say and produce social separatism. Gastronomy is placed at the heart of the palatial universe, not only because it serves to glorify the sovereign, but as a modality of his power.

A gourmet literature in the service of power

Mesopotamia, because it pushes much further than the previous transegalitarian societies the social division and the separatism of the powerful, invents with the table of the powerful a whole new discourse on the table. This discourse will be a milestone since it continues to run for millennia. The ideal is that of a frugal and simple but regular and sufficient diet. The soldier in the field *(sic) is* praised... a significant metaphor, even though this model corresponds to that of the first permanent armies. This new figure of the soldier (archer and horseman) brings a new aesthetic and leads to a new way of conceiving the body, thus also to a new way of feeding it. This ideal of frugal and simple food is however compensated by the valorization of excesses during exceptional events. I do not think, contrary to the usual theses, that this system of alternation is mainly explained by the fear of lack. This strategy of excess goes hand in hand, in this case, with the division of society. It is not only a question of overindulgence, but of developing a refinement of the dishes and paying the king so that he finances, in return, these excesses. We have enough descriptions of the great banquets of this time to have a fairly accurate idea of the practices and political issues. This first marriage of the words and the dishes serves above all to say the power. This language passes by rituals, codes, ways of sitting, of being served, of eating, etc., but also by a first gourmet literature. Liliane Plouvier, historian of gastronomy, has seen that it was not until the golden age of ancient Greece that such culinary literature flourished. So why this lasting exception in the Mediterranean environment? I don't think that this particularity is a matter of interest or greed, more or less important depending on the people or the times. This gourmet literature was reborn, in Greece, at the moment when the banquet became a way, not only to say but to do citizenship, as the Babylonian food festivities were also a way, not only to say, but to do absolute power.

A kitchen of mixtures

This royal table, with its claimed social separatism, with its specialized male staff, with its new food discourse, is also a different cuisine, a more refined cuisine, a much more expensive cuisine that takes on an emblem: being a cuisine based on mixtures. The mixture of liquid and solid elements (more than solid elements between them, or, with spices, condiments or aromatics) creates a cuisine made of soups and porridges more or less thick. The royal *mu* (or *me*) ("soup") does not refer so much to a culinary specialty, nor even to a separate episode of the meal, as to a vision of the cosmos (according to Liliane Plouvier). The status of the mixture does not say the same thing as in Greece. While in Greece the mixing of wine and water is a reminder of the political gesture, here it testifies to the dimension of the duality of the monarch, for if all sovereignty belongs to a divinity who delegates it to a king, this one, although he is (still) human, is his representative on earth, he acts in his name. Liliane Plouvier reminds us that the word *mu*, which is used in almost all royal recipes, is an abbreviation of *muhaldim*, which means "queux". The *mu* is therefore a dish which, because it is the result of a mixture - an important gesture that is sufficiently complicated to be reserved for men only (the queux masters) - makes the royal table a totally unique table. This royal cuisine is also inseparable from an extreme obsession with hygiene: foodstuffs are washed several times, dishes are constantly scrubbed, hands must be clean, clothes changed, etc. Liliane Plouvier insists on the fact that this constraint of cleanliness serves to say and to make an element (clothing, person, food) become noble.

The last Babylonian tablet is largely devoted to the description of spectacular preparations, these "pastries" which prefigure, says Liliane Plouvier, the "pièces montées" of the Middle Ages and the "vol-au-vent" of Lent, so called "because they set out to conquer the air, like the tower of Babel". Babylon is the inventor of the multi-storey tower, a symbol of power. The Babylonian "pastry" thus combines the two dimensions of power: the religious dimension, since sweet cakes were first exceptional offerings before being sweets for humans; the political dimension, since the multi-storey tower is the very emblem of power.

A political history of food. From the Pateolithic to our days

Table rituals

The Mesopotamians usually ate seated on the ground, placing the dishes on small portable trays, themselves placed on low tripods. The royal table therefore distinguished itself from this ordinary way of doing things by inventing other devices: the most important people were entitled to a chair, sometimes an armchair, and the others ate seated on stools or on the ground. The ritual provides for the way of dressing, of washing the hands, each guest receives a vial with perfumed oil with which he anoints himself at the beginning and at the end of the meal, etc. Perfume burners are placed between the tables to remind us of the religious character of any banquet, since they are used to smoke food and odorants in the temples. The ritual also foresees who can speak and the number of times that it is obligatory to bow when entering and leaving the table during each meeting. The guests, divided into groups according to their status, are collectively given a certain number of victuals that they must share. These victuals vary in quantity and quality according to the hierarchical position of each group. The meal always includes grilled and stewed meat accompanied by bread cakes, vegetables, semolina, fruit and pastries. The meals are washed down with beer (very exceptionally with wine). These banquets will become more and more luxurious during the Ier millennium BC, with an increase in the number of guests and dishes prepared, with increasingly abundant and expensive crockery... The king eats alone, separated from the other nobles. A demarcation is sometimes drawn with flour, in order to separate him, and thus to distinguish him, from the other guests. This process will have its extension in the religious field with the custom of hiding the divinity behind a cloth veil when eating. The king will eat for a long time seated on an armchair (throne) in front of a table. The practice of the reclining banquet develops however, from the 7th century B.C. This new ritual could be easily imposed, because all the furniture already existed. The bed is indeed a symbol of power in many cultures. The royal archives of Mari have two words to designate "the bed for sleeping" and "the day bed". This "day bed" carries the king during his activities. Eating while lying down is a sign of absolute power, so much so that if the king eats while lying down, the queen kneels at his feet, but cannot lie down. The royal ritual places great importance on the holding of cups. The king usually holds a cup in his hands during audiences. At banquets, he drinks to the health of each of his guests to whom he offers a cup. Possessing as many cups as possible is a sign of power. Finally, the ritual gives great importance to the possession of carpets. Some carpets can only be walked on by royal feet...

The Babylonian period

The so-called "Babylonian" period (1792-1595 BC) corresponds to the domination of the city of Babylon and the state constituted around it over Sumer and Akkad. Hammurabi, the main architect of this Babylonian power, operates from his palace in Mari and creates the first great military power of the time. His army consisted of several tens of thousands of peasant soldiers. Hammurabi's successors continued his work (including the destruction of rival cities) and took up the Sumerian-Akkadian image of the "good king" who guaranteed the supplies and well-being of his people. Babylon inherited the Sumerian-Akkadian state forms but strengthened several elements, which intersect with our political history of food, both through the practice of banquets at the top and through innovative policies of food distribution, the famous rations and the "food fields" whose mechanism made it possible to maintain an army of peasant-soldiers who were obliged to train militarily. The remuneration of other compulsory chores was also done in kind: 10 liters of barley per day, and up to double for some heavier chores.

In exchange for its submission, the people will benefit from the protection of the palace. Thus, in the Code of Hammurabi, the notion of exclusive belonging to a territory, that of a city, that of a city-state, is established. Each individual not taken in charge by the dense network of family solidarities is helped by the temples and other palatine institutions. The population which does not benefit from sufficient rations is often in difficult situations at the time of the welding between two harvests. They were then forced to ask for subsistence loans in barley (or sometimes in money) and had to repay the capital with an interest rate. The temples were not the last to lend grain to the poorest on the basis of a reference rate of interest called the "Samias rate", named after the god of Justice, a rate fixed however at... 33% per year of barley in addition! This rapacity of the rich led to an explosion of cases of debt bondage. The phenomenon was significant enough to justify measures to cancel debts, taken by the kings at the time of their appointment. These cancellation edicts even provided for sanctions for recalcitrant lenders, such as the payment of compensatory indemnities to slaves for debts, up to six times the amount, or even the death penalty against the rich.

The temples were among the largest landowners, because of royal donations to the various gods to benefit from their protection, but also because they bought a lot of land with their own funds, worked by slaves (especially for debts) and "free" peasants, but legally attached to the land acquired by the temples.

Mesopotamia deserved this detour in the framework of a political history of food, because it is the first region to have experienced, as early as 9000 BC, neolithization, urbanization, statehood and the birth of imperialism. Mesopotamia is, for all these reasons, the region which, the first, will push the farthest the food separatism of the richest and will thus give birth not only to a "high cuisine", characteristic of the unequal societies, but a political food ideology which will defend the principle of a simple and frugal food for the people, compensated either by the excesses of the powerful, or by the excesses that the powerful offer to the humble, thanks to the monopolization of the resources, and sometimes even to the systems of taxes. Mesopotamia is also the region that, while destroying certain old food policies through, among other things, the privatization of granaries, will invent new instruments such as rations and food fields, and will also give birth to the figure of the peasant-soldier, which will mark history.

Third service: The Egyptian table

Egypt is the first civilization to have conceived its table as a language. The same hieroglyph means "eat" and "speak": "I eat" means "I speak". Thus the table is structured as a language, but if "eating" means "speaking", then "eating" also means "knowing", given the importance of magical thinking ("when saying is doing") in Egypt. Egyptologists have said enough that in ancient Egypt everything is a symbol not to take seriously the fact that its table is more full of symbolism than those before. However, it will not be a question of finding a secret meaning to these symbols, but of noting their existence and trying to understand the reason for their existence[51].

The Egyptian table is of course dependent on the Mesopotamian tables. There is no need to choose here between the two competing theses, i.e. between a network of Mesopotamian trading posts and colonies established in indigenous lands within the framework of an economic proto-empire, and a colonization of agrarian settlement, with exchange circuits between the center and the periphery.

A table dependent on power

Egypt is characterized by its state dirigisme: the pharaoh is master of the country and of everything in it but he claims to be responsible for its prosperity. In the Old Kingdom, the pharaoh was the owner of all the land (even if private property gradually came into being), which implied an important system of chores to maintain this property and also an important administration to count and manage it. The herds were thus counted

---

51. We refer to the works of Pierre TALLET, *La Cuisine des pharaons*, Arles, "L'Orient gourmand", Sindbad Actes Sud, 2003, and Madeleine PETERS-DESTÉRACT, *Pain, bière et toutes bonnes choses... L'alimentation dans l'Égypte ancienne*, Monaco, "Champollion", Éditions du Rocher, 2005.

every two years, and the pharaoh had numerous granaries and grain silos built and inspected.

This deeply unequal civilization even saw the development of a real social separatism on the part of its elites, both in terms of religion (since the religion of the elite was monotheistic and that of the people polytheistic) and in terms of its food, which was conceived as a language expressing, in particular, the superiority of the elites and the respect due to them by the people. The latter is caught between caning, which is the most frequent punishment, and the perception of a food ration, bread and beer, in sufficient quantity: there is no famine and little undernourishment, except in bad periods. However, the fear of scarcity is structural, as the Bible testifies (Ge. 41. 28-36): "Thus, as I have just told Pharaoh, God has shown him what he will do. Behold, there come seven years of great plenty in all the land of Egypt. And seven years of famine shall follow them; and all this abundance shall be forgotten in the land of Egypt: the famine shall reduce the land to nothing. After that, no one will be able to notice anything of the abundance in the land, so overwhelming will be this famine. If the dream was repeated twice to Pharaoh, it means that the thing is decided by God, and that God will hasten to execute it. Now let Pharaoh find a man of understanding and wisdom and establish him over the land of Egypt. Let Pharaoh act and appoint officials over the land, to raise a fifth (of the crops) of Egypt during the seven years of plenty. Let them gather all the food of these good years that are to come; let them make, under the authority of Pharaoh, stores of wheat and food in the cities, and let them keep them. And they shall store them for the land, for the seven years of famine which shall come upon the land of Egypt, that the land be not consumed by famine."

We will see how the Egyptian government invented different policies to curb the programmed prospect of leaner times. We shall see, in particular, how it developed a system of food rations to compensate for its appropriation of (almost) all goods.

A centralized state at the service of a predatory caste

Ancient Egypt, with a population of between 3 and 7 million, was an exception: while the other city-states remained at this stage of organization, the Egyptian state was built according to a unitary and centralized system[52]. To the divestment of the people answers, progressively, that

---

52. Joseph G. MANNING, "Irrigation et État en Égypte antique" in *Annales. Histoire, Sciences Sociales*, 57ᵉ année, n° 3, 2002, p. 611-623.

　A political history of food. From the Pateolithic to our days

of the principalities to the profit of a more and more personal power. Understanding this evolution is essential for understanding the food situation of the country[53].

The term pharaoh comes from an expression which means "big house". It designates, first, the palace, then the person of the pharaoh himself since the palace is supposed to be where the king is, including during his travels. The pharaoh is not a god, but the representative of the gods on earth, he is the incarnation of Horus and the son of the solar god Ra... The pharaoh is no longer only a representative of the divine authority, he represents the whole community. He appropriates the whole of the common goods which he manages as personal goods, hence the foundation of new capitals according to his own interests, hence his reserved domains, his lands, but also the personal appropriation of sectors such as taxes or the management of granaries.

The whole Egyptian society constitutes the property of the pharaoh: 100 000 people thus take part in the construction of the great pyramid. One perceives the extent of this parasitic economy with regard to the speed of realization of these great works taking into account the existing technical means. The pyramids and the capitals are realized during the pharaoh's lifetime, whereas it will take centuries to complete the cathedrals, a few millennia later.

The whole society is conceived in the unique interest of the ruling classes. Egypt did not initially know a landed nobility but only a nobility of functions: religious leaders, military leaders and high officials. Officially, these groups are not hereditary, but they reproduce. It is not an exaggeration to speak of a real social separatism[54].

Of course, this functioning requires a reinforcement of centralization. The power is thus endowed with new structures such as the office of vizier, from the 4th dynasty, in charge of justice, finances and archives. He also bears the name of "mayor of the palace" (which we will find again in Gaul), because he ensures the military command of the citadel. The pharaoh was in fact in charge of the military and the religious, relegating the day-to-day administration to the vizier, his officials and the nomarchs (heads of the provinces). The regime evolves at first towards more religious forms, to the point of recognizing the pharaoh as an (almost) god holding the monopoly of immortality. The distribution systems (not only

---

53. Ciro F. Cardoso, "Village Communities in Ancient Egypt" in *Dialogues of Ancient History*, vol. 12, no. 1, 1986, pp. 9-31.
54. Bernadette Menu, *Recherches sur l'histoire juridique, économique et sociale de l'ancienne Égypte* preface by Joseph Mélèze-Modrzejewski, Versailles, 1982.

food) then progressively came under the control of the temple, i.e. of the religious, and it was only later that public squares dedicated to the market came into being. In the primitive cities, the supply, storage and distribution were done in the temples with the participation of their religious personnel. The priests, who thus ensured a monopoly of this service, collected a tax. The palace reserved for itself the police, the prison, the barracks and the tax administration. One understands from then on the importance that will take the food prohibitions. We can also understand this explosive mixture of religion and socio-politics. Of course, pork is not forbidden to be eaten, but simply to be eaten in the temple, i.e. it cannot be sacrificed. The pig is not perceived as a repulsive animal, but it is linked like other species to the god Set, murderer of Osiris, and as such guilty of having wounded the eye of the god Horus; moreover, its consumption remains too popular to be legitimate...

The Egyptian ideology

The Egyptians were "great ideologists", authors of numerous chronicles, true biolegends to the glory of the pharaoh and of the main notables. Having said that, and because it is necessary to limit the subject, only the pharaonic period will be really approached, and little the Greco-Roman period. This civilization flourished for three thousand years, under three successive Empires: the Old Kingdom (2700-2190 B.C., 3rd to 6th Dynasty) the Middle Kingdom (around 2060-1785 B.C., end of the 11th dynasty and 12th dynasty) and the New Kingdom (around 1580-1085 B.C., 18th to 20th dynasty), interspersed by long periods of instability (called "intermediate periods"), crises of power and divisions of territory.

Egypt remains a country above all agricultural, thanks to the floods of the Nile and the power will always grant a great importance to the exploitation of the subsoil, which does not prevent from considering the peasants and the cooks as beasts of burden. Agriculture is irrigated, but irrigation remains natural for the most part. Barley is the cereal of the flooded lands, wheat of the drier lands. One of the specificities of Egypt is the importance of the funerary domains, these foundations whose production is used for the funerary cult of the king or the nobles.

Each of the 38 (then 42) regions (nomes) was placed under the authority of an officer delegated by the central power (the nomarch), a function that was both civil and religious. Although this office is not hereditary, historians note the presence of large family dynasties. Little by little, they were replaced by civil servants, directly subject to the authority of the vizier, who administered territories much smaller than the nomes.

A political history of food. From the Pateolithic to our days

The pharaoh speaks (and only he) to the goddess Maat, the great regulator of the cosmic order, who makes the sun rise every morning and disappear behind the horizon every evening; it is also she who, every year, makes the Nile overflow so that it gives a fertile land. The pharaoh communicates with her through his dreams, thanks to the intercession of the priests, but also by respecting the rules of life[55]. The food must be in conformity with what the custom and the rite dictate. Everything is prescribed: the number of meals, the possible dishes, the way of eating. The pharaoh cannot deviate from the rules, otherwise the displeased gods could inflict curses on the country. He is thus the guarantor of normality, that is to say of an Egyptianization of the ways of life, in particular food. This Egyptianization is obligatory and vital for any foreigner, whether captive or passing through. The prisoners of war, while being branded with a red iron, received an Egyptian name. The children of foreign notables taken hostage were placed in royal nurseries and educated to become civil servants. Still under the heading of Egyptianization, the temple of the Jews on the island of Elephantine was destroyed because the Jews were carrying out sheep sacrifices, a prohibition for the Egyptians because of the place of the ram in their religion.

A compensation system with predatory power

This predatory power will set up a system of compensation, not out of kindness or generosity as its official ideology would have us believe, but because no regime can live without social compromise. The pharaoh is defined as the one who multiplies goods, the one who knows how to give. He distributes land to dignitaries, royal officials, members of his family, friends, etc. He makes considerable donations to the temples and to the people. He made considerable donations to the temples, he granted land to his soldiers, he allowed the peasants cultivating the land for the benefit of the State or the temples to own small livestock, small equipment and a fraction of the harvests, he multiplied the food distributions, during the great festivals in his honor and the religious ceremonies whose calendar gives rhythm to the year. The chronicles tell that Ramses III (1186-1154 BC)[56] distributed 441,000 fish and 126,250 poultry during a great festival that lasted several days. Pharaoh Niouserre (around 2420 to 2389 B.C., 5th dynasty) organized, around 2400 B.C., a meal for 1600 guests[57].

---

55. Max GUILMOT, "L'espoir en l'immortalité dans l'Égypte ancienne du Moyen Empire à la basse époque" in *Revue de l'histoire des religions*, vol. 166, n° 1, 1964, p. 1-20.
56. When dates follow the names of pharaohs, they are those of their reign.
57. Marie-Ange BONHÊME and Annie FORGEAU, *Pharaon, les secrets du pouvoir*, preface by Jean Leclant, professor at the Collège de France, Paris, Armand Colin, 1988, reprinted 1997.

But to compensate for the dispossession of land and to face the "great fear" that remains that of lack, the pharaohs and nomarchs had to go even further and take charge of the feeding of a large part of the working population by guaranteeing it a stable food ration. The expropriating and monopolizing king was thus metamorphosed into a nourishing king. The pharaoh master of wheat becomes responsible for the construction of silos. He is shown inspecting the temple stores accompanied by the priests. Pharaoh Amenemhat III (1843 or 1842 to 1797 B.C., 12th dynasty) will want to be a model of the good nourishing king: "There was nobody hungry in my time. When the years of famine came, I plowed all the fields [...] keeping my people alive and providing them with enough food [...] I gave to the widow as much as to the one who had a husband. I did not favor the great over the small in all that I gave." Pharaoh Keti explains to his son the reason for this generosity: "A poor man can become an enemy, a man who lives in need can become a rebel. A rebellious crowd is calmed with food; when the multitude is angry, let them be directed to the granary."

If the figure of the good nurturing king can be useful to keep the people quiet, the Egyptian elites prefer the image of a warrior king and even a hunter. His physical strength was exalted and he had to prove his endurance regularly. His education is sporty because it is above all warlike since the pharaoh has a double mission: that of ensuring the respect of the cult of the gods, and that of constantly extending the territory of Egypt while preserving it from chaos. The Egyptians think of themselves as the guarantors of the order of the world (Maat is the goddess of Order, of the Balance of the world, of Equity, of Peace, of Truth and of Justice). The foreigner is not only a Barbarian (in the Greco-Roman sense) that should be contained, but a vital danger that should be fought and annihilated. This imperialist aim has economic, but first of all political aims. Making war is the only way to maintain order against the forces of evil. This is evidenced by the gradual rise in power of the theme of the nine bows, i.e. the populations subjected to the absolute power of the king. Exterminating one's enemies is a necessity, which is why Egyptian thought is easily pessimistic, and not only during the intermediate periods. Faced with this structural pessimism, the Egyptians cobbled together two systems of defense: banquets were an opportunity to display a joie de vivre and monumental construction allowed the pharaohs to defy time. A pharaoh is thus a builder, but a builder of tombs (the famous pyramids), then a builder of solar temples, when the god Ra will take more and more importance within the pantheon and the policy.

The political principle of the food ration

Ancient Egypt pushed the principle of the food ration very far: it increased the number of entitled persons while increasing its volume. This supply first concerned civil servants, soldiers and all those who performed chores in the service of the pharaoh or the nomes. It extended, progressively, beyond the differences in the legal status of the workforce (independent, domestic, compulsory, contractual work), for all the subjects of the king were in some way at one time his employees. The principle of compulsory corvée for all and remunerated by a system of rations is the direct consequence of the policies of "great works" (irrigation, agrarian planning, urbanization, construction of monuments). This ration system was perfectly codified according to the social status of each person. The daily ration for a laborer working for the pharaoh's great constructions is 10 loaves of bread (1 kilo) and 1 measure of beer, for a deputy foreman 100 loaves of bread and 3 measures of beer and for a chief 200 loaves of bread and 5 measures of beer. In addition, they receive vegetables, fish, oil, fat and even wood. There are also standard rations for civil servants, soldiers, temple staff and palace staff. I call this system of rations "political", in the sense that it is the counterpart of the very organization of Egyptian society. This ration, composed of bread and beer, does not constitute a vital minimum. It is not a matter of taste, but a matter of state!

This system extends the tradition of the ration developed in Mesopotamia. But the Egyptian table being conceived, from start to finish, as a language, this "bread-beer" must also be a discourse, that of submission to the system. The food ration, the bread-beer, is structuring a political relationship. It creates a debt from the fed to the one who feeds him, a debt that is not food, economic, social, but literally anthropological. The fed depends on his feeder, the latter thus hiding the fact that he first dispossessed him. The Egyptian food ration has therefore nothing in common with the distribution systems that will be set up in Greece, but especially in Rome. The food ration is not a right of the citizen, but a duty of the dominant. It is true that ancient Egypt knew almost no slavery, but this was because it had its own mechanism of subjection, of which bread/ beer was the counterpart. The fact that this ration system corresponds to an economy that has not yet been monetized, in which exchange is often measured in grains, does not exhaust its own logic, just as the present-day wage is not only the counterpart of a job done, but also the form that a bond of subordination takes. The ration system is designed to irrigate (almost) the whole of society, because insofar as it is too important to be totally consumed by the beneficiary and his family, it will end up, in part, on the market, where it will supply the category of the unfed, although subjugated. This system is much more structuring than the regular food distributions carried out by the temples and, sometimes, the palace. This is why it is against delays in the distribution of the ration and not against beatings that the people invented what we call the strike.

The chronicles evoke several episodes of social crisis under Ramses III. The scenario is always the same: the population leaves its work, but also its villages in which it must in principle remain locked up, and goes with women and children to the temples where all are accommodated and fed. The resolution of the conflict requires an additional distribution of food. Things are therefore never as univocal as the powerful would like. The very principle of the ration (by its intrinsically collective character) creates a political body, with its system of *ad hoc* institutions and the prenotion of rights, not individual, i.e. based on relations of subjection, but collective, whose transgression provokes a collective reaction. The workers call upon the pharaoh and the vizier as political and not moral authorities. The scribe Amennakht writes: "Year 29, second month of winter, day 10. On this day the team passed the five checkpoints of the necropolis saying: 'We are hungry! 18 days have already passed in this month", and the men went to sit at the back of the funerary temple of Menkhéperrê [Thoutmosis III]"[58]. Conciliation having failed, the workers maintained their strike and had the scribe write a new statement: "If we have come to this point, it is because of hunger and thirst; there is no more clothing, nor ointments, nor fish, nor vegetables; write to the pharaoh, our good lord, about this, and write to the vizier, our superior, so that provisions may be given to us!"

The choice of the elites against the "bread and beer
The notables are always trying to distinguish themselves from the popular bread and beer. This tradition is so important to the Egyptians that they wish each other "bread and beer" as a word of welcome. Two strategies were developed. Wine begins to be valued among the elites to the detriment of beer, just as later wheat (thus wheat bread) and rice (thus rice bread) will replace the ordinary barley bread. The Pharaohs took advantage of the military conquests to deport vine specialists from the conquered territories, and then they introduced the cultivation of durum wheat (*Triticum durum*) instead of barley. Historian Joseph G. Hanning

---

58. Quoted by Robert Paris, "Egypt: the first known strike in history," Matter and Revolution website, February 3, 2011, read at: http://matierevolution.fr/spip.php?article1901

 A political history of food. From the Pateolithic to our days

notes that "the scale of the enterprise is on a par (or close to it) with the construction of the pyramids, nearly two thousand years earlier, but for an entirely different purpose. This wheat, first planted in the "model" domains of the 2nd century B.C., that is to say in lands allocated by the pharaoh to settlers, ex-military, in exchange for services rendered, was then generalized to such an extent that Egypt became the granary of Greco-Roman antiquity. However, these wheats (probably imported from Ethiopia) do not allow, because of their varieties (hard and dressed), to make a bread corresponding to our criteria, but rather flat cakes.

The land of bread

Ancient Egypt has remained famous for having developed the culture of bread. Bread is symbolized by Akhet which designates the first season of the milotic calendar (the first day of which corresponds to the flooding of the Nile - thus Akhet symbolizes floods and fertility). The bread corresponds to the first day of the year, emblematic of the new beginning. The conical bread is the very image of giving, giving meaning here "sharing", with an idea of division, of portions. The Negro-Egyptian also gives meaning to white bread, purity and the baby (childbirth). White pyramid-shaped breads were already used in rituals of the Old Kingdom to signify the rebirth of the monarch as a god. This bread called "bnbn" with its elongated conical shape is the sign of transmission. Bread is considered to be the symbol of eternal life and resurrection. The "house of bread" is synonymous with the vagina. The texts emphasize the white bread as an instrument to ensure the place of the deceased at the side of Ra. Egypt gave birth, with the soft wheat, to the real leavened bread (bread-making). The cereals stored in silos were under the supervision of scribes. The "director of the granaries" was responsible for supplying grain to the bakers on a daily basis for the production of bread and beer (or "beer bread"). Breads were mainly made from barley and sometimes from wheat (starch). The breads have very varied shapes (flat, round, square, oval, conical), with or without a deliberate fingerprint, with a central cavity serving as a bowl for the filling (eggs for example, or vegetables), with several compartments for the elaborate meals of festivities. Some are spicy, stuffed with dates, figs, lotus seeds, honey. First made in the form of patties and then shaped by hand in the form of cylinders (fingers?), they are baked in molds that are broken to extract the bread. The containers are used only once.

The beer

Herodotus defines the Egyptians as beer drinkers who ignored wine. In reality, this is not the case, but it cannot be denied that beer is the common drink, so much so that the same word is used to designate beer and any liquid[59]. Its consumption is not or hardly ritualized, which does not mean that it does not have a symbolic charge, since it has a sacred dimension. It was invented by the god Ra to save men from the anger of the lioness goddess Sekhmet. Ra had 7000 jugs of beer poured on the ground that the bloodthirsty goddess took for blood and drank until she became drunk... According to other traditions, it is a gift from Osiris, a compound of barley and water.

Beer is consumed on a daily basis, as it is made in a domestic way. It is drunk at any time of the day, at work, as well as in the taverns. These "breweries" were very closely watched by the pharaoh's police, and the beer was drunk by drawing it directly from the vat with a blowtorch.

There are dozens of varieties of beer, such as *heneket* beer, which is made in every household, or *seremet* beer, which is made from a mixture of barley, wheat and dates. The beer jugs are coated with clay, not to ensure that they are watertight (as the beer cannot be preserved), but to allow it to become clearer. The common beer is the brown beer. Blonde beer is more reserved for celebrations. The Egyptians, beer drinkers, were mocked by the Greeks and Romans. Pliny the Elder was offended: "Beer is not soaked in water like wine", and he added: "Foul industry of vice! We have found a way to make water intoxicating...". It is true that there are beers with a high alcohol content, but drunkenness is commonly admitted only among the elderly.

Wine versus beer

The Egyptians consumed a wide variety of drinks: water, beer, fruit juices (pomegranate, grape, carob, aniseed), mead (water and honey), liqueurs (pomegranate), etc. However, wine will take the place of the noble drink, as soon as it becomes the drink for the elites (Pierre Tallet). The perception of beer, however national drink, becomes negative. The Egyptologist specifies: "It is not by chance that the place of depravity, where one drinks badly and in bad company, is regularly called the "house of beer", [whereas] wine, on the contrary, is inserted in numerous metaphors

---

59. Pierre Tallet, "Une boisson destinée aux élites : le vin en Égypte ancienne" in *Pratiques et discours alimentaires en Méditerranée de l'Antiquité à la Renaissance*. Actes du 18ᵉ colloque de la Villa Kérylos à Beaulieu-sur-Mer, les 4, 5 & 6 octobre 2007, "Cahiers de la Villa Kérylos", vol. 19, n° 1, Paris, Académie des Inscriptions et Belles Lettres, 2008, p. 39-51.

     A political history of food. From the Pateolithic to our days

transmitted by the contemporary corpus of love songs [...] proceeding to a true ritualization of desire"[60]. Wine is thus sung in all the love poetry of ancient Egypt: "Take, drink and make a happy day"; "Wine comes and unites with gold, it overwhelms your house with joy! Drink day and night and never cease to do so, be happy without a care while the singers and songstresses rejoice and dance to make you a beautiful day of celebration."

The Egyptians distinguished wines not according to their terroir but according to their production techniques: red wine, white wine, black wine, sweet wine, *paour* wine (piquette obtained by re-soaking the must after a first pressing and intended for domestic staff), wine flavored with dried figs, cooked wine, etc. Herodotus specifies that there is a wine made from barley. The name of the vineyard, the name of the master winemaker, the date of manufacture, the quality: good wine, very good, mixed, double good wine, etc. are also indicated. Specialists maintain that the processes of wine making were known since 4500 BC, but that the drink was then reserved for the priests, even if everyone could drink it at will during the full moon festivals. Wine is thus associated with the sacred domain. Each temple has vine plants. The temple of Amun-Ra under Ramses III has more than 500 different vineyards.

Pierre Tallet recalls that wine was initially a drink for funerals and notes the presence of wine jars on the funerary material of the princely tombs of the Nagada III period (last period of formation of the Egyptian state around 3300 BC). In more recent tombs, up to 7,000 jars of imported wine (4,500 liters) have been found. This wine culture is encouraged as a marker of power. The areas of vine cultivation follow the location of the pharaoh: first on the western branch of the delta, as long as Memphis is the capital, then on the eastern branch after the successive changes of capital: "The vine was thus planted there by the will of the king to satisfy the greatest consumers of this product, the pharaoh and his entourage, as well as the principal cultic foundations established in the city" (Pierre Tallet). The seals on the clay stoppers closing the amphorae are the property mark of several pharaohs, the main wine owners. The Egyptologist also gives the example of a high official of the Second Dynasty whose tomb lists the possession of abundant vineyards. He notes that scenes of wine making appear about a hundred times on the pharaonic tombs against only two times for scenes of brewing. The vine, symbol of renewal, is associated with the gods, in particular with Osiris, god of human resurrection, for a long time the privilege of the pharaoh alone. The production of wine

---

60. *Id., ibid.*

also makes it possible to differentiate between "good drunkenness" (that of wine, that of the notables): "Bring me 18 cups of wine, see, I want to get drunk, my insides are as dry as straw", and "bad drunkenness" (that of beer, that of the people), as this account denigrating the drunkenness provoked by beer testifies: "I am told that you are neglecting the practice of writing and that you are giving yourself over to pleasure. You hang around from tavern to tavern. Beer takes away all human respect; it leads your mind astray. You are like a broken rudder, which is useless. You are like a chapel deprived of the god, like a house without bread. You have been found jumping over a wall. People flee from your dangerous blows [...] You are taught to sing to the sound of the flute, to say poems to the sound of the double oboe, to sing "sharp" to the sound of the harps, to recite to the sound of the zither! Here you are sitting in the tavern, surrounded by the girls of joy. You wish to pour out your heart and follow your pleasure [...] Here you are in front of a girl, flooded with perfume, a garland of flowers around your neck, drumming on your stomach. You wobble and fall to the ground, all covered in filth."

The drunkenness of the elites is assimilated to a possession, to an initiation rite allowing to communicate with the gods. The color of wine reminds us of blood, unlike beer, which is decidedly vulgar. The "twice good wine of the oasis" allows to reach the divinity, better than the prayer. This is why, during the great festival of Hathor, goddess of Beauty, Music and Love, everyone could freely succumb to drunkenness. However, here again, one opposes the "good drunkenness", close to the sacred drunkenness known in the temples, accompanied by dreams and visions, to the "bad drunkenness", that of the popular beer, that of the drunkard, useless, because without dreams. Other fermented beverages such as the popular date wine (dates macerated in water) or palm wine allow one to reach intoxication, all the more so as their sugar content is reinforced without it being known if it was to guarantee a better preservation or a higher alcohol content. These drinks correspond to a festive use including music and dance. Specialists note that women drank as much as men. The wine is drunk through a straw and a filter to remove herbs and spices. Drunkenness, initially the prerogative of the priests, then associated with funerals, gradually changed its meaning by being associated with joy. Good drunkenness" is thus, in the Egyptian context, a sign of power and might: showing one's joy is part of the prerogatives of the powerful.

Feed the gods, feed the dead, feed the living

Egypt, more than any other civilization, is based on a triple obligation: feeding the gods, feeding the dead, feeding humans. One could be tempted (many authors are) to understand this centrality of food as a legacy of a past (not so distant) where eating was uncertain. I believe that other explanations are possible, such as the particular place occupied by food in its relationship to language, a particularity that can perhaps be linked to the place of writing, which was for a long time the monopoly of the State. I recall that if the Egyptians like the table and like to talk about the table, the notables show a great contempt for the gardeners, the peasants and the cooks: "As for the gardener who carries the big pole, his shoulders are burdened as if by old age; his neck presents an enormous purulent swelling, he spends the morning watering the vegetables, in the evening they are [other] plants, after that, at noon, he has worked in the orchard; when the time of the rest comes, he is dead. The reputation of this profession is that it is the most difficult of all [...] The worker in the field [the peasant] complains more than the guinea fowl, and his cries are louder than those of the crow. His fingers are swollen with an excessive stench. He tires near the marshes, so that he is broken. He feels as well as a man can feel among the lions; suffering is his lot, for the drudgery is often tripled. When he returns home in the evening, the march has broken him [...] A peasant is not called a man...".[61]

While Greece is the cradle of philosophy (without underestimating the richness of the older Negro-Egyptian thought), because this new form of thought corresponds to the needs of scholars acquired to democracy who seized this discipline to fight irrationality, Egypt appears as the paragon of magical thought: Thus, magic is considered a divine

---

61. The passages extracted from the *Teaching of Khety*, known under the modern title of *Satire of the trades*, concern first Meskhenet, the goddess of births: she predestines the child to a literary profession. Then, after a short excerpt from the *Hymn to the Nile*, comes the series of different professions with a commentary on their disadvantages. "The mat maker in the workshop is more miserable than a woman, he has his knees in his stomach, without air to breathe. If he loses a day without weaving, he is beaten with 50 strokes of the thongs, he bribes the doorman to let him go out in the daylight [...] The caravan driver goes abroad after bequeathing his possessions to his children, for fear of the lion and the Asiatic [...] He returns home in despair after his journey has broken him. His house is only cloth and bricks, he will not relax..." This discouraging enumeration ends with the praise of the scribe's profession, which evokes the unquestionable superiority of this profession "[...] for it is he who commands. If you know how to write, this is more useful for you than [all] the other jobs I have placed before you. See!..." (trans. Piankoff) - The *Satire of the Professions* is a text dating from the Middle Kingdom (12th dynasty), see about it and the tablet where it is found on the site of the Louvre museum: http://www.louvre.fr/oeuvre-notices/tablette-d-eleve-scribe

heritage and the pharaoh as the supreme magician capable of mobilizing divine forces through speech and image and through the ingestion of certain foods/drinks (as well as through other processes). Thus, there are magical formulas for (almost) everything: to guard against snakes, to drive away diseases, to cure infirmities, to procure food and drink, to ward off hunger and thirst.

Feeding the gods

In its relationship to religion, food occupies a unique place in Egypt, just as it will have a unique place in Greece in its relationship to politics. It is indeed an essential means of being heard by the gods. Everything is therefore prescribed, from the number of meals to the types of consumption. The food must be in conformity with what the custom and the rite dictate. Herodotus judges that the Egyptians have morals contrary to the other men. Plutarch expresses the same opinion, adding that only the inhabitants of Lycopolis eat sheep, since the wolf, considered by them as a god, eats them. The prohibitions change according to time and place, but, above all, some prohibitions are valid only at one time of the year and not for everyone.

The temple, thanks to its rituals, managed to get its hands on an important part of the foodstuffs, just as the palace got its hands on the land. These powerful people, who have secured for themselves the monopoly of the dialogue with the gods (the temples are not places of recollection for the faithful but places of habituation of the gods that the religious alone accompany in their life), have the conviction to hold a knowledge superior to that of the common people, since if the people are maintained in polytheism, the elites are monotheistic in the sense that they believe in a single god who would appear under various aspects.

Food is sacred in the heart of the temples (but also in the palace). Each meal is considered a divine offering. The priest, shaved and circumcised, is subject to an obligation of purity: ablutions twice a day and twice a night, respect of very strict food obligations, etc. There are many dietary taboos, such as the prohibition of eating the animal in which the main deity of the region is incarnated (more than forty species including sheep, ewes, dogs, cats, bulls, crocodiles, baboons, cattle, lions, gazelles, various birds and fish, etc.). Some fish are not eaten because of their harmful role in the cycle of Osiris (the virile member devoured by fish). Things are more complex, however, because some foods that are forbidden in certain religious contexts are allowed in ordinary life. Thus, while there may not even be representations of the pig in a funerary context, its meat

A political history of food. From the Pateolithic to our days

is widely consumed by the people. Herodotus notes that this animal is so impure that if an Egyptian is touched by a pig, he must immediately purify himself by bathing in the Nile. Pigs are simply forbidden to enter the sacred precincts of the temples. The consumption of cattle is in principle forbidden, but in reality, it is mainly the head of the cow or ox that must be thrown into the Nile, pronouncing ritual formulas to attract misfortune upon it. Herodotus indicates that by analogy a mistrust of the head of all animals will develop. According to specialists, this prohibition on the cow is a late borrowing from other religions. The goddess Hathor is thus adored in the form of a cow and symbolizes love and joy and, by extension, procreation. Isis, the mother-goddess, is also represented by a white cow... totally taboo, of course, but during certain rituals, its meat is distributed to the people. Sheep, like pork, is forbidden for the priests, but its consumption is possible once a year, during the sacrifices offered to the moon and to Osiris. Certain species of fish were, during certain periods, forbidden, and in any case the notables rejected this food which was considered too popular. On the ninth day of each month, the people eat a fish in front of their door, while the priests make a holocaust (fish consumed by fire). Onions are forbidden for the priests, because this plant is still growing while the moon (eye of Horus) is weakening. Beans are sometimes forbidden, as well as the pink lotus, a sacred plant that adorns the headdress of the god Nefertum and served as the cradle of the young Horus, the rising sun. At the time of the death of the pharaoh or his dogs, the priests are also forbidden grains and wheat.

Feeding the dead

The question of death haunts the Egyptian civilization more than any other. One of the last ceremonies performed by the priest on the mummy of the deceased consists in symbolically giving him back the use of his senses by touching his face with an adze. This rite, called "opening the mouth", allows the dead person to speak, eat and drink. Otherwise, death, normally considered as a simple stage, would be definitive[62]. The survival of the dead does not depend only on embalming and mummification. In addition to the word symbolically restored according to the ritual, it is also necessary that the descendants remember the deceased by pronouncing

---

62. Max GUILMOT, "Les lettres aux morts dans l'Égypte ancienne", in *Revue de l'histoire des religions*, vol. 170, n°1, 1966, p. 1-27.

his name and by bringing him food and drink[63]. For this reason, a great deal of food is placed in the grave or tomb: jugs of wine or beer, bread and cakes, poultry, etc. This ritual took two main successive forms: firstly, a classic funeral offering service, at the end of which the food was consumed by the temple staff and/or redistributed to the people; then this offering service became symbolic, in the sense that thousands of small miniature containers replaced the thousands of real dishes. During the ritual of the opening of the mouth, all the necessary foods are listed, thus offering tens of thousands of virtual foods... This magic is based on the idea that the word possesses a creative power. It also relies on the power of images, with the use of signs (tables of food left in tombs alongside the figurines). These same devices function within family funeral temples, called "castles of millions of years", with displays of food.

I see two dangers in the interpretation of these mortuary rituals. The first is to consider the meals of the living in the image of these offerings: one does not commonly eat as one feeds the dead, especially since figurines and then signs have replaced the real food. The second danger would be to underestimate the impact of these rituals on the table. It is certainly not possible, with regard to Egypt, to speak of a "cuisine of sacrifices", as Vernant and Detienne will do for Greece, but this cuisine of mortuary offerings will have impacts on ordinary life. Thus, the simple fact of replacing food with its representation, first in the form of figurines (made of wood or stone) and then of lists of offerings, undeniably reinforces the conception of the table as an act of language. The Egyptians push very far what is called a performing speech. Mortuary cooking is based on the principle of "when saying is doing". The idea that the cuisine of the dead must be sufficient, diversified and good ends up reflecting on the very conception of the food of the living, who will end up eating like the dead, the dead eating like the living. Let us not underestimate either the know-how of the cooks attached to the temples and the repercussions on the profane diet. These reciprocal influences are all the stronger since the Egyptians themselves claim these constant passages from the sacred to the profane. The mortuary dimension also appears in the use of reminding one's self of the mortal nature of humans during good meals: this is done by means of statuettes, speeches, games (such as the ancestor of the game of checkers): "At gatherings among the wealthy Egyptians, after the meal is over, a man carries around a wooden figurine in a coffin, painted and

---

63. *Id.* "La signification des métamorphoses du défunt en Égypte ancienne" [d'après les Textes des Sarcophages, un corpus de textes funéraires s'échelonnant de 2200 av. J.-C. environ à 1800 av. J.-C] in *Revue de l'histoire des religions*, vol. 175, n° 1, 1969, p. 5-16.

A political history of food. From the Pateolithic to our days

carved in very exact imitation of a dead man, measuring in all about a cubit or two; he shows this figurine to each of the guests, saying, "Look at this one, and then drink and enjoy yourself, for once you are dead, you will be with him"[64].

Feeding the living

Humans were created to take care of the gods and the dead, so it is logical that they should also eat to be able to provide for their tasks. This principle is not so far from that of the political ration. But from this principle, one could envisage an austere, frugal, vegetarian table, and the Egyptian is said to be a big eater and lover of good things. In *The Tale of the Eloquent Peasant* (9th dynasty), Khoun-Inpou, the scorned man, receives in compensation 10 loaves of bread and 2 jugs of beer per day. Before evoking the symbolic dimension of the Egyptian table and the question of the royal feasts, it is essential to recall that the daily food is not reduced to the famous "bread and beer" of the political ration. The Egyptians ate three meals a day: the breakfast called the "washing of the mouth", then a meal around noon, and the main meal in the evening. They first ate sitting or squatting in front of a rush mat as a sign of humility and respect before the table (the most respectful position was to squat on one heel, with one knee raised in front of you); then sitting on a chair in front of a high table.

The complements to "beer bread"

In reality, Egyptians eat much more diversified than the "bread and beer". They already eat a lot of fish, but also products from the vegetable garden. Before describing the food diversity in more detail, let us note that for the Egyptian, eating is "bread and beer", everything else is something else! Eating depends on the state, other foods are more personal. The "bread and beer" of the poorest is usually supplemented with garlic and onion. Salt is distributed to the population, quite regularly, in the form of bread and is mainly used as a means of preserving food in jars. The main problem is the lack of sufficient wood for cooking. To overcome this, policies of importing wood were implemented via the maritime routes of the Levant, hence the invention of charcoal for stoves and braziers. Vegetable waste and cow dung were used as fuel. Dung deposits have been found in some tombs of notables. Stones exposed to the sun or the direct heat of the

---

64. Quoted by Bertrand Pinçon, *The Enigma of Happiness. A Study on the Subject of Good in the Book of Qohelet*, Leiden, "Supplements to Vetus Testamentum" [119], Brill Academic Publishers, 2008.

sun were used, as a result of which the Egyptians often ate raw, except of course for bread and meat.

The vegetable garden

Legend has it that the god Osiris taught agriculture to the Egyptians in order to make them lose the habit of eating each other. Isis would have given the use of wheat and barley by distinguishing them from other wild plants.

The Egyptian wants to be, first of all, an eater of herbs says Madeleine Peters-Destéract[65]. The agrostis, herbaceous plant, has the reputation to be able to provide a sufficient food to feed all the Egyptian population. Sometimes, Egyptians hold a clump of these herbs in their hands when they approach the altars. The harvest scenes are always described in a happy way, with the presence of music and songs. This predilection for plants is really about barley and wheat. Barley is the basic cereal (because it is resistant to salinization during the Nile floods), even if the Egyptians cultivated two varieties of wheat (einkorn and starch). It was offered in large quantities to the gods and distributed free to the people, notably under Horemheb (last pharaoh of the 18th dynasty, around 1323-1295 BC). It seems however, according to the specialists who quote Herodotus, that the Egyptians make a great use of wild plants, in particular of the plants of the marshes, like the lotus (very diversified plants) of which all the parts are edible, all year long, without requiring much work. Herodotus speaks of "lotus bread" but also of "papyrus bread". One consumes a lot of soups and porridges (with ground cereals or grains).

The Egyptians are also fond of vegetable farming based on a division of the plots into very small squares in order to allow controlled irrigation. In addition to onions, a popular food par excellence, the list of vegetables is very rich: cucumbers, zucchini, onions, beans, leeks, chickpeas, lentils, broad beans, lettuce, asparagus, celery, cabbage, turnips, radishes, artichokes, lettuce, parsley, watercress, endives, gourds, eggplants, etc., but also aromatic and condiment plants: dill, anise, cinnamon, coriander, cumin, juniper, bay, marjoram, mint, etc. Access to fruits is more reserved for the elite: palm nuts, dates, jujube, sycamore fruits, *Persea*, figs, grapes, carobs, pomegranates, melons, watermelons, etc. Only dates and figs (dried or fresh) are consumed throughout society, they are also used to preserve meats and to flavour drinks.

---

65. Madeleine PETERS-DESTÉRACT, *Bread, beer and all good things... L'alimentation dans l'Égypte ancienne, op.cit.*

　　　　A political history of food. From the Pateolithic to our days

The importance of fat and sugar

Historians have noted the importance of fat and sweetness in ancient Egypt. The Egyptians overconsumed fat and never ceased to diversify their sources of supply (animal fats, butter, vegetable oils, olives, etc.). These fats are used as a preservation process as well as a taste enhancer. Eating fat is first and foremost a way to enjoy food. It is therefore to affirm one's human quality, to show off one's social success. The distribution of oil (and probably other sources of fat) is sometimes part of the political ration. The "bread-beer", supplemented with fat, constitutes the ideal ration that the nourishing king should ensure to all his subjects. Unquestionably, oils were part of the basic rations of part of the population: scribes were entitled to oil, messengers and standard bearers received a precious ration of olive oil... The State therefore set up systems for collecting and storing fats. The oils used are numerous (sesame, radish, olive, coloquint, *moringa* nut, castor oil). Some are a state monopoly (coloquint oil). Not all these oils are socially equivalent, so olive oil (also used for lighting) is considered the most noble.

Sugars are part of the complements to the "bread and beer". A lot of sugar is consumed from certain fruits (dates, figs, grapes, carobs, etc.). Honey production is strictly regulated by the royal administration. Fruit juices and grape juice (heated fruit juice) are consumed. Sugar refers to gluttony, but through a religious mediation. The sweet is first what pleases the gods, for example cakes: cakes are offerings, they will become gifts.

Fish consumption

Fish is naturally an extremely consumed resource because of the presence of the Nile, but also because of the importance of the marshes. This resource is sufficiently abundant to be assimilated by the notables to a popular consumption, therefore vulgar, unless it is because its consumption is strictly forbidden to any sacralized individual. The Egyptians mastered many fishing techniques: fish trapped in pots, by means of test tubes, with collective nets, hooks (invention of the fishing rod probably in the Middle Kingdom), river fish poisoned with certain poisonous herbs, etc. Fish (carp, perch, mullet, catfish, tilapia, etc.) could be eaten fresh, sometimes even raw, but more often than not, they were dried (the fish was cut open at the back, emptied of its entrails, sometimes heavily salted, then dried in the sun). The scribes keep a careful account of the fish caught, as the proceeds are shared between the officials, the owner and the fishermen.

Meat consumption

The consumption of meat is quite massive in Egypt, where it does not have the status of sacrificial meat that it will take in the Greco-Roman context[66], but not everyone can eat any animal or any piece.

Meat consumption is reduced for the poor by the lack of resources. It is also regulated by an extremely complex system of prohibitions. We have already mentioned the specific case of pork which, although declared impure, is consumed by the people, but not by the rich who do not stoop to eating camel or even beef. Camel is the last meat that can be bought when one is very poor. Beef is the popular meat par excellence, since it is neglected by the elite. In principle, neither the horse, nor the donkey, nor the dog, appear on the Egyptian table. On the other hand, wild animals were captured and fattened in enclosures (gazelles, oryx, antelopes, hyenas, hares, hedgehogs, mice). The farmyard is particularly appreciated: geese, ducks, cranes, hens and roosters, pigeons, etc. The Egyptians force-feed geese and cranes, but it is not known whether they made foie gras. Important bird farms are established for the production of eggs. The Egyptians also eat water birds (teal, ducks, quails, cranes).

The slaughter of large animals is ceremonial. The butcher's first act is to cut off the front leg, the piece of choice for funeral meals, then the head is cut off and kept with its skin and horns to appear on the offering tables. The butcher then cuts the other pieces (legs, chops, shanks, giblets, etc.). After the slaughter, a procession brings the choice pieces to the temple (one priest carries the head, another the heart and the ribs, and another the *khepesh*, the front leg). The meat is eaten by first boiling it in water, often flavored, and then preparing it with a sauce. While poultry is always roasted, other meats never seem to be grilled, except in religious and therefore mortuary contexts. Meat is preserved in amphorae with animal fat, or dried, salted, spiced, smoked, it can be put in brine or honey. Very finely cut strips are put to dry in the sun or in ovens. These preserved meats have the reputation of being particularly spicy, but it is likely that the purpose is as hygienic as dietetic since the Egyptians, using certain aromatics for mummification, have acquired excellent knowledge of their antiseptic and bactericidal properties.

Less common than in Mesopotamia, meat consumption became a luxury good, but also a political commodity used during food distributions carried out by the temples and the palace. The government very

---

66. Youri VOLOKHINE, *Pork in ancient Egypt: myths and history at the origin of dietary prohibitions*, Liege, Presses universitaires de Liège, 2014.

A political history of food. From the Pateolithic to our days

quickly set up an accounting system, essentially for fiscal purposes, first on large livestock, then on small livestock. This lower consumption of meat is compensated by the access to fish resources. Meat and fish are always accompanied by vegetables, eaten raw or simmered in oil, butter or goose and veal fat. The cuisine is very spicy (salt, sesame, juniper, coriander, fenugreek, black cumin, pepper, savory, poppy, peppermint, other aromatic herbs), but the religious and medical aspects are not absent from this choice of taste, since the spices used for mummification have a sacred dimension and the Egyptians also attribute medicinal and sexual virtues to them.

Dairy products are also widely consumed: milk is kept in earthenware jugs, closed with earthen or grass stoppers. Milk (cow's, sheep's, goat's, donkey's) is used by adults and children alike. It is also preserved in the form of butter, cream and cheese. Curdled milk is common in the diet of the people. It appears in the tombs, because it is supposed to make the flesh of the deceased healthier.

The Egyptians have the reputation of not having developed a high cuisine: they ate a lot but simply... This judgment seems to me to be hasty. It is true that Egypt was characterized by a reduction in cooking methods: little grilling, a large refusal of frying (except for pastries), but there is a great use of roasting or wet cooking, which allows one to play with aromatics and condiments and to add fat. I also believe that this thesis underestimates the importance of table manners and the symbolic dimension in favor of the content of the plate alone. How else to explain that butchers, with their precise and fine cutting techniques, with a well-established vocabulary of meat, form, alongside priests, a rather closed and apparently well-organized corporation, benefiting from social recognition.

A kitchen of symbols

Much emphasis is placed on the place occupied by the scribes within Egyptian power, firstly through their mastery of numbering and accounting, and secondly and above all through their quasi-monopoly of writing obtained by means of a coup de force which consisted in imposing a learned and complex script. For this reason, the Egyptian civilization remains a civilization based on orality (which the Greek and Roman civilizations will not be). I have already said that the Egyptians were great ideologists seeking to surpass other civilizations in the construction of biolegends to their own glory.

This attraction could explain, in part, the place given to symbolism. I will take just one example: while our symbolism is largely ternary in nature, the

Egyptians developed a symbolism of duality, with Upper and Lower Egypt, with the white and red crowns of the pharaoh, with the public treasury called "the double house of money", with the creation of the "double granary", with the opposition of "black earth" (alluvial valley) and "red earth" (Sahara), with the binomial of bread/beer, etc. This binary symbolism can be found throughout the grammar of the table, with a series of oppositions, raw and cooked, hot and cold, ration and non-ration, etc. Egypt certainly did not invent the symbolic dimension of the table but, more than elsewhere, it made it an instrument of theocratic domination. It would be wrong to think of this symbolic production in a controlled way, firstly because the religiosity of the powerful is not that of the people, and secondly because their food will never (and even less and less) be identical. We know much more about the symbolic production of the powerful than that of ordinary people, but nothing authorizes us to think that it did not exist.

This symbolic dimension of the table (of which Egypt is not the origin) is one of the characteristics of human food: we also eat signifiers. We can think that there were more food symbols than we are able to know today. The choice of products, the cutting, the cooking method, the presentation, the types of aromatization, the way of eating, all this meant something, including for the people who knew how to read their table (and in part that of others) as easily as they "read" the Nile or interpreted their dreams. One difficulty lies in their management, different from ours, of the relationship between the sacred and the profane. Thus the lotus, a major emblem of ancient Egypt and the object of absolute veneration, is nevertheless consumed, in several ways, in a desacralized manner. This consumption concerns each of its elements: rhizome, stem, seeds. Lotus flowers are also used in the context of feasts, with the aim of embalming and flowering the room, and to sacralize the guests and the meal.

Let us take seriously the fact that the same hieroglyph means "to eat" and "to speak". If "to eat is to say", therefore to do, eating takes on a completely different meaning. One can advance that the Egyptians have sensed the link between the two oralities a few millennia before the fathers of psychoanalysis. The Egyptian meal is in this respect a particularly talk-ative meal... It speaks about the situation of each one, it also speaks about the society and the relations of power. It is impossible to establish a diffe-rence between a religious and a political symbolism, already because of the double character of the pharaoh, also because of the economic power of the temple, finally because the symbols themselves are ambivalent: half-sacred, half-profane, half-religious, half-political... To eat is to speak; it is thus to know. One eats the law, one incorporates it. This ardent obligation extends

                            A political history of food. From the Pateolithic to our days

to the person of the pharaoh, obliged to eat certain pieces, awakened in the middle of the night to eat and be well.

The Egyptians invented many food symbols: bread as a symbol of eternal life and wine as a symbol of humanization. The Egyptian eater is not a free consumer on a free market. He eats what he has to eat according to his status, according to his function, according to the events, according to the context, according to the calendar, probably according to his sex. Thus, there are dozens of different breads in terms of shape, taste, color, etc. This diversity expresses something other than the fact that the breads are made in different ways. This diversity expresses something other than a choice. These breads cannot be eaten at any time, in any way, anywhere, nor even by anyone or with anyone. This coding of the table is, in the cultural context of ancient Egypt, much more structuring and imperative as one rises within the social hierarchy, as one gets closer to the person of the monarch. The pharaoh is probably not the most "free" in his diet.

The feast is not a banquet

The extreme social inequality will allow the development of a sophisticated cuisine (abundance and rarity of dishes and specialized personnel). The staff in charge of the preparation of the pharaoh's meals is composed of civil servants: butchers, pastry cooks, brewers, bakers, scribe-intendant, etc. The concern for perfection exists as much in the dining room as in the kitchen. It is difficult to distinguish what is aesthetic and what is symbolic. For example, lotus flowers, which are used for embalming, are often used as a tablecloth, but they also represent a promise of rejuvenation after death. How do we interpret the garlands of flowers around the wine jars? How do we understand the predilection for boiled food and the place of the pot, at once a feminine symbol (the pot was originally a hole dug in the ground) and the first coffin? The very opulence of the Egyptian table is one of the emblems of power. The table of the sovereign must be the best... but this must be understood in several ways, taking into account the magical character of food.

Festive meals are an opportunity to play, but, like food, these games are coded, not only expressing something, but they can achieve it. The game of semet (ancestor of our checkers game) symbolizes the crossing of the underworld. The one who wins the game would succeed in the weighing of the heart and would thus overcome all obstacles to be reborn in the afterlife. The ball games are numerous but the ball represents the eye of Apophis, snake-demon that the king hits with a bat assimilated to the eye of Ra... it is thus a question of chasing away the evil forces...

However, the Egyptian feast has very little political function, even when the pharaohs themselves organize large meals. The Egyptian table ensures that everyone has something to eat and drink, but it never puts the political question of sharing at the heart of its reflection or its practice. First, because the feast is not a banquet, since the guests are not (and for good reason) citizens. Secondly, because the table should not say equality (not even equality in difference), but hierarchy. Finally, because it is never to the political body (to the political dimension), but to the biological body, to the religious body, to the hedonistic rigor, that the feast is addressed.

The feast or the staging of the celebration

The Egyptians do not share a sacrificial and sorrowful ideology: there is nothing to atone for, so there is no necessary redemption based on privation. This taste for celebrations also has a much more political basis. The pharaoh and all the powerful must have a good time, because the joy of living is the very sign of their success and their divine election. The apparent happiness speaks much more than the mere display of wealth. The table must then be not only tasty, beautiful, but joyful. It would be wrong to take literally the calls for frugality in certain papyri: "If you are a guest at a banquet of someone more important than you, accept what he gives you when it is placed before your nose. You should only look at what is in front of you [...]"; "If you sit in society, hate the bread you desire, it is a short time to control yourself. Gluttony is baseness, one points the finger because of it. A bowl of water quenches the thirst. A mouthful of greenery strengthens the heart [...]"[67]. If you sit with a glutton, eat only after his hunger has passed. If you drink with a drunkard, do not drink until his craving is satisfied. Do not clutch the meat next to the greedy one. Accept when he gives you"[68].

This discourse should not be confused with any kind of slimming diet, but as a condemnation of a debauchery of which we no longer have any idea: the feast is the occasion for a display of wealth, of which the famous episode of the pearls that Cleopatra melts in vinegar is only a symptom. The search for moderation in all things is the sign of a constant game of the elites with excess (as the construction of the pyramids testifies).

---

67. *Instructions for Kagemni*. This instruction composes the first two plates of the Prisse Papyrus. This text from the Middle Kingdom (11th dynasty?) is attributed to the vizier Kagemni (see Bibliothèque nationale de France, Cabinet des médailles [02/071]).
68. *Id.*

I believe that it is Madeleine Peters-Destéract who uses the most accurate term by speaking about social gatherings, because it is above all a question of meeting between people of the good society and of dazzling (in the respect of the hierarchy). This social gathering is a discourse, and already a discourse of power because the arrangement is designed to show off (the respect due to) the hierarchy; it is also a discourse on power, with the joy of living that befits the powerful. Banqueting is a whole art: "Holding the table was obviously a complex art, governed by very rigid social conventions, marked by a great respect for hierarchy, and in which the whole social system of ancient Egypt was embodied"[69].

The division is expressed by the different dishes but above all by the way of sitting. The participation in the social gathering is the occasion of a staging: there are those who sit on the ground, those who have a stool, those who sit on a chair, those who have the right to an armchair, those whose armchair is covered with a feline skin, those who have the right to cushions, etc. The pharaoh eats separately. The vizier also. There are men's meals and women's meals, although they can eat together. The codes to be respected are precise: the care of the body is obligatory before the meal, this obligation is more a constraint of purification than a hygienic concern, even if the Egyptians are famous, then, for their extreme cleanliness. A meal must always be associated with rejoicing, putting on a show of joy of living is an obligation which is not a matter of propriety but of a political status. These social gatherings are made with music with a typical orchestra of three instruments (harp, double flute, tambourine). The guests participate in the show by clapping their hands in rhythm.

This staging of happiness is much more sophisticated than one might suppose: it is not, for example, a matter of appearing happier than a superior. The celebrations and their manifestations must be adjusted to the social status. The presence of a superior obliges one to make do, that of an inferior to overplay. The powerful "sad" person is somehow not worthy of being a chief/king. The cheerful servant does not hold his place and does not show respect. The first sign of rejoicing is the mandatory wearing of the floral necklace. The men abandon the dress related to other activities to put on a loincloth covered with a long transparent skirt. The women wear long dresses with straps and wigs held at the level of the forehead by a crown decorated with flowers. Their ears are pierced with large rings. Their make-up is particularly elaborate and careful, as well as their perfumes. The

---

69. Pierre TALLET, *La Cuisine des pharaons, op. cit.*

body is constrained in its movements by the obligation to stand as it should (according to its rank), by the obligation to dress appropriately, by the tradition which wants that one holds, with the right hand, a lotus flower, that one gets drunk of its soft perfume, the left hand posed on the chest.

This hymn to the lotus can be understood in two ways simultaneously. First of all, the lotus is the symbol of the daily rebirth of the sacred star: indeed, it hides under the water during the night to blossom at each sunrise; it is thus the promise of an eternal restart, of a long life. The presence of the lotus flower thus expresses this constraint of rejoicing, it mobilizes all the senses: it is beautiful, it embalms, it is held in the hand, it could even be eaten. Then, the lotus is the emblem, much more profane, of the nymphaeaceae, these aquatic plants whose different varieties are widely consumed. The lotus inherits this double contradictory status: It is the emblem of the vegetable garden (thus of neolithization) while it refers more to the period of gathering. The lettuce will finally be preferred as a symbol of virility. It is also (unlike the lotus) the product of human labor... Pierre Tallet recalls that many of these banquets retain a funerary character since the deceased remains present, through his statue, with a table abundantly stocked with victuals placed in front of him...

These mundane gatherings are never an excuse to philosophize. The Egyptians have a common sense that could be described as practical. For example, their knowledge of astronomy is much more limited than that of the Babylonians, because they have kept only what is useful to them. They don't care about having an encyclopedic knowledge of natural sciences, but they are, on the other hand, excellent agronomists. They are little interested in metaphysics, contrary to the ancient civilizations. Egypt had few (or no) philosophers, but moralists, such as the vizier Ptahhotep or the pharaoh Amenemope (991- ? BC, 21st dynasty): the ideal of life that they gave was that of balance, of moderation in all things, food of course, but also sexual. The table of the powerful thus oscillates between an obligation of frugality and a constraint of rejoicing, while the table of the poor invents, with the political mechanism of the ration, a system of distribution which owes nothing to the benevolence of the rich.

These characteristics, more political than religious, create a table that makes Herodotus say that the Egyptians love everything that other peoples hate. This feeling of strangeness must be taken seriously, whether it is a question of "bread and beer", the question of pork, the absence of sharing in the Greek sense, a symbolic dimension where the symbols concern the food itself and not the sharing of food, and, in particular, the Greek circulation of wine and speech. Food concerns the gods, the relationship of each one to the gods, the relationship of each one to oneself, but very little the relationship of each one with the others, if it is not, of course, to express the relationships of power and submission. The food is indeed a vector of power in all that it can have of brutal, with an overabundant cooking, sophisticated, voluntarily magic...

The time had come to leave Egypt but its history continues. Its Hellenistic period was characterized by a decline in the cultivation of barley, which was then used as fodder and no longer primarily to feed the people. Egypt will then become the granary of the Roman Empire. This predominance of wheat bread will be characteristic of the Orientals. Maimonides explains that wheat bread should be baked when it is fully ripe, but long before it begins to spoil. One should not use refined flour, but sift it to remove the particles that produce sourness. Ibn Kutaiba quotes the 9th century philosopher Al-Asmaa (828) as saying, "White rice with melted butter and white sugar is not a food of this world."

Fourth Service: The Greek Table

The Greek table is not reduced to the banquet, but *deipnon* (meal) and *symposion* (which designates the moment when one drinks together) are at the heart of the political production of society. Politics, in the Greek sense, appears realized only in the Athenian democracy of the 5th century, which establishes a radical innovation in the history of humanity: the individual identifies himself completely, for the first time, with his status of citizen. His participation in the political body is sufficient to define his personal and community identity and subordinates all other forms of representation. What are the consequences in terms of food policies? This innovation will allow a renewal of the frumentary policies on the basis in particular of another interpretation of the food crises: famine is no longer a divine punishment of an individual or collective fault requiring the expulsion of the guilty ones as a condition of the appeasement of the gods, but the sign of unjust behaviors subjected to a collective moral appreciation.

The table as sharing

Ancient Greece is a confederation of city-states whose history spans several centuries: there are therefore variations and breaks in its conception of the table but, essentially, its grammar remains the same. If we owe the conception of the table as a language to the Egyptian civilization, Greece will generalize the conception of the table as sharing. In the same way that the same hieroglyph means "to eat" and "to speak", the same word, *dais*, means "to eat" and "to share" with a connotation of obligation. There was also a term, *monophagein*, to mean "to eat alone". To eat alone is to fail in one's dimension of *zoon politikon* ("civic animal"), it is not to be fully civilized and... not to really eat. It doesn't matter what we share, since the essential thing is the sharing itself. The vocabulary of many languages testifies to the almost universal character of this conception of the table: buddy or companion, the one with whom I share the bread; friend, the one with whom I share the salt (the spirit).

The table of the zoon politikon

The table must therefore be shared, but there are several ways of sharing. We know the importance of this question in Greek philosophy, with Aristotle's opposition between redistributive justice and commutative justice. The Greek meal is always a language, but a language of sharing, before being a language made of food symbols (like bread or wine). The Greek table is much poorer in culinary terms than the Mesopotamian and, of course, Roman tables, because its purpose is elsewhere. The food of ancient Greece is already well known to the public, thanks to the work of many historians including Jean-Pierre Vernant and Marcel Detienne[70]. We also owe to Pauline Schmitt Pantel a copious analysis of the banquet[71]. However, we will devote a first approach to the ordinary meal, because the Greek food question could not be reduced to that of the banquets. Obviously, because not everyone is at a banquet and, except in exceptional cases, women, children and slaves are excluded; then, because two of the three daily meals are taken in another form than the banquet.

The importance of meals, for the Greeks, is not only physiological, dietetic, gastronomic, philosophical, but it is also political. The importance they attached to their table can be seen by comparing the richness of their vocabulary in this field with the great poverty of ours: dozens of specific terms differentiate the types of banquets: *dais* is the shared meal, *xenia* is the meal given or received as part of hospitality, *eranos* is the meal where each person brings his or her own contribution, *euochia* is the meal that brings joy[72] , etc. It should be noted, moreover, that this richness expresses much more the diversity of the ways of practicing commensality than that of the contents of the plate, undoubtedly because the table is above all for the Greeks a political instrument, but no longer only for the chiefs (as in the Mesopotamian or Egyptian tables), but also for the *demos*, since to take part in the banquet is to become a citizen; it is worthwhile, in a way, as an

---

70. Jean-Pierre Vernant and Marcel Detienne, *La Cuisine du sacrifice en pays grec*, Paris, Gallimard, 1979.

71. Pauline Schmitt Pantel, *La Cité au banquet*, Paris-Rome, Publications de l'École française de Rome, 1992. Read also her inventory of the existing historiography: Pauline Schmitt Pantel, "Les banquets dans les cités grecques : bilan historiographique" in *Dialogues d'histoire ancienne*, Supplement n° 7, 2012, p. 73-93, thematic issue : *L'histoire de l'alimentation dans l'Antiquité. Bilan historiographique* - Journée de printemps de la SOPHAU, 21 mai 2011.

72. Pauline Schmitt Pantel, *La Cité au banquet, op. cit.*

     A political history of food. From the Pateolithic to our days

identity and voter card. The Greek food is thus, from part to part, that of the *zoon politikon*. The first two principles aim at ensuring the (re)production of society by enacting sumptuary laws and by organizing distributions.

Sumptuary laws

Ancient Greece, like all the great civilizations, adopted sumptuary laws aiming to curb the display of luxury, especially food. These ostentatious practices date from the first transegalitarian societies. We have already evoked these feasts of competition and the ancient evergetism. Two kinds of measures will be taken in history to curb these competitions: either laws aiming at reinforcing the homogeneity of the aristocratic group, or even at forbidding some rich people to be more rich than the king, or laws taken against the aristocracy to answer a concern for sharing or to avoid an excessive clientelism which could threaten democracy. Periander, tyrant of Corinth, prohibited all pleasures in a general way. Solon, legislator of Athens, will take measures against the excessive taste of the luxury: it prohibits to immolate an ox at the time of the funerals, it prohibits to the women to leave from the house with more than three clothing, to carry food and drinks for more than one obole and in a basket large of more than one cubit, in order to restrict the abundance at the time of the banquets by ecots...

Food distributions

The question of wheat was the major concern of most governments, to the point that the Greek political system would never abandon the responsibility of supply to private initiative. To the traditional means of transport and conservation are added policies of financing stocks by the rich, first in an exceptional way, then permanently. The Greek cities thus got into the habit of distributing food free of charge in times of abundance, then in times of famine, and finally in an almost systematic way. Thus laws forbid the sale of wheat outside the territory of the cities to avoid speculation. After the famine of 329 B.C., which saw the price of cereals soar, Athens decided on a subscription intended to finance the acquisition of wheat on a regular basis ; in Samos, after 246 B.C., the rich citizens were given the mission of acquiring wheat in a sustainable manner in order to be able to finance, if necessary, free distributions.

The survival kitchen of Philo of Byzantium

The so-called "survival kitchen" is of course the paragon of community intervention in the field of food. It allows us to understand certain political issues. Philo of Byzantium, a Greek architect of the 1st century B.C., is the author of a treatise on poliorcetics, consisting of five titles, the last of which concerns food in a situation of extreme crisis when a strong city is attacked and besieged[73].

First principle: food and drink are defined as public goods. "It is proper to deposit public goods in private houses, but [only] for articles not likely to be corrupted, e.g. roasted barley, bundled wheat, chickpeas, lupins, ers (a kind of lentil), sesame, hippak or mare's milk cheese, poppies for the composition of medicines, millet, red wheat loaves." It is also useful to deposit in private houses sea onions and others, and to cultivate them around the city, all along the walls, so that, employing the recipe of Epimenides, the citizens do not suffer in times of famine: "After having cooked the onions and cut them very small, one mixes with them one fifth of sesame, about one fifteenth of poppy, and grinds the whole together, adding honey of the best quality, then one makes pellets of it the size of strong olives. If one takes a dose of this composition at about 2 o'clock in the morning and another at about 10 o'clock in the morning, one need not fear to suffer much from hunger.

Second principle: it is necessary to multiply the techniques of conservation. Philo of Byzantium cites the preservation of roasted vetch or vetch kneaded with olives, because by this means it becomes incorruptible, of livers preserved with gall (except those of pigs), salted and dried in the shade. He also recommends to preserve, for the well-to-do citizens, meats stored in suspension, some in wine lees, others in salt...

Third principle: Philo recommends requisitioning professionals by decree, including cooks. He also recommends digging silos four fingers deep and covering them with a coating of clay mixed with olive pomace and chopped straw, which "will be excellent stores for the above-mentioned provisions, once they have dried out completely. Once the wheat has been introduced, a bottle of the most acidic vinegar must be inserted in the central part and brought up to the neck, and then a cover made of bricks covered with a plaster will be placed over the whole. In this way, the provisions will be safe from putrefaction". Philo indicates yet another means of preserving wheat from corruption: it is, after having made a kind of litter with straw, to spread it all around the silos, then to cover it with

---

73. Charles-Émile RUELLE, "L'alimentation en temps de siège chez les anciens" in *Comptes rendus des séances de l'Académie des Inscriptions et Belles-Lettres*, 14ᵉ année, 1870. p. 307-315.

   A political history of food. From the Pateolithic to our days

a clay bed, to put the supplies there and finally to throw in dried deer's liver cut into small pieces " [...] When one wants to supply a city, it is necessary that it is at least for one year. One must make the purchases at the time when the foodstuffs are at their lowest price, then, after a certain lapse of time, one consumes the old provisions, and one stores again as a precaution against the cases of siege or dearth..."

Mandatory group meals

Many Greek cities went much further than the traditional sumptuary laws or the regular organization of food distributions, free or not, by establishing the principle of a collective meal. The modalities differed from one place and time to another but remained similar. These obligatory banquets constitute, in the eyes of the Greeks, a particular form of political organization of the city, one of the forms of the *politeia*. The daily presence at the common meals, the *andreion* in Crete, the *syssition* in Sparta, is registered in the obligations required to reach the citizenship and to preserve it. According to Ephorus (historian of the 4th century B.C.), to frequent for the young boy, son of citizen, what the Cretans call the *ageles*, is a sign of integration in the group of the citizens, as testifies the gifts which the young Cretan receives at the end of the adolescence: beside a panoply which confirms his new statute of defender of the city, an ox and a cup devotees him as banker[74].

The Spartan banquets

The situation of Sparta is the best known: one allots to Lycurgue, mythical legislator, the decision to have imposed obligatory daily banquets: "It obliged the citizens to eat all in common, and to nourish themselves of the same meats, the same dishes regulated by the law. He forbade them to take their meals at home, on sumptuous beds and in front of magnificent tables; to put themselves at the mercy of pastry cooks and cooks; and to fatten up in the darkness, like gluttonous animals. It is, indeed, to corrupt both one's mind and one's body, to let go of all sensuality and debauchery, and, consequently, to make oneself a need for long sleeps, hot baths, continual idleness, and, as it were, a daily treatment of the sick. This was a great point; but an even greater result was to have put wealth beyond the reach of theft..." (Plutarch).

---

74. Ephorus *in* Strabo, *Geography*, X, 4, 21, quoted by Pauline Schmitt Pantel, "Les repas grecs, un rituel civique" *in* Jean-Louis Flandrin and Massimo Montanari (dirs), *Histoire de l'alimentation, op. cit.*, p. 159.

These common meals have two objectives: first, they are public meals, that is to say, meals taken in the eyes of all, so that this publicity is the condition for a real sharing and a transparency of the ways of life. The opacity of the table is seen as a failure of any society worthy of the name. These common meals are also, necessarily, simple and frugal meals. This refusal of abundance and luxury is the condition of a good education. This frugality is also considered as sufficient by many. These Spartan banquets constitute the prototype of the aristocratic banquet, since they are reserved to the only adult males and members of the elite. To be admitted there, the young Spartan, 20 years old, must pass the tests of the *krupteía* ("cryptie"), i.e. to live alone, in full countryside, without external assistance. The selection does not stop there, since to be admitted, it is still necessary that the young man is accepted by those with whom he will have to share the table: each of the members of the *syssition*, which includes about fifteen (according to Plutarch, in his *Life of Lycurgus*), votes with a pellet of bread deposited solemnly in an urn carried on his head by a slave. If only one of these pellets is crushed, the candidature is ruthlessly rejected. This system combines, under the features of the fraternal circle, political and friendly dimensions, but also warlike since the tents used during the military campaigns also gathered 15 soldiers.

The Spartan table chooses to mix the ages, so that the younger ones are educated by the experience of their elders. The meal is frugal in order to be more talkative. The banquets are moments of eloquence: one tells beautiful actions. The texts fix the exact quantity of food and drink per guest. Each person brings his or her monthly share, called *phidite*, consisting of 77 liters of barley, 39 liters of wine, 3 kilograms of cheese, 1.5 kilograms of figs and 10 obols to buy the meat that is shared after the sacrifice. The main dish served is a black broth made of pork, salt, vinegar and blood. Everyone drinks moderately and goes home without light, because "one must get used to walking boldly and without fear of the darkness of the night". The portion of land allotted to each Spartan and cultivated by the hilots was to allow each one to be able to bring his share, without concern of wealth. Let us add that it is interdict to eat at home before coming to the banquet. This institution will provoke the revolt of the rich and a series of demonstrations. One knows the famous scene which sees Lycurgus obliged to flee from the public place. This organization refers to the oligarchic functioning of the city, since only the members of the aristocracy over 60 years old exercise a real power through what is called "the Gerousia", Spartan equivalent of the Senate.

Cretan banquets

The Cretan situation is different, since even the children eat. They eat among themselves, sitting on the floor, and serve the adults. They are fed at the expense of the state. Each adult brings one tenth of his or her harvest. A woman is in charge of each group of guests and, according to the texts, must award the best pieces to those who have distinguished themselves in war or by their wisdom. These banquets are held in two buildings: one reserved for the Cretans, the other for the foreigners, and when there is only one building, the tables must be necessarily distinct. Everyone gets an equal share, the youngest receive a half share of meat. Orphans are entitled to a full share, excluding spicy food. On each table is a cup filled with wine previously cut with water. After the meal, each person drinks another cup of wine, again cut with water. The children have their own crater[75]. Once the meal is over, it is time for deliberations and decisions on common affairs.

Plutarch, follower of the geometrical distribution, praises Lycurgue for having established it in Sparta and condemns Solon, partisan of the arithmetical distribution. In other cities of Laconia, of which Sparta is the capital, each one brings what to eat, but by respecting the quantities fixed by the law (barley, wine, cheeses and figs). Aristotle criticizes, in his book *The Politics*, the Spartan system because, according to him, the expenses should be entirely taken in charge by the public Treasury. For Aristotle, the political purpose of the banquet must be to allow more democracy, but the system by ecot generates less democracy, since the one who cannot pay cannot banquet, thus is deprived of his citizenship. This political purpose does not go without influencing the culinary choices themselves: the typical dish of the *syssities* (obligatory common meals) is the *cyceon*, an intermediate preparation between drink and food, made of barley gruel lengthened with water and wine, and added with herbs and aromatics; it is, also, sometimes, carried out with grated goat cheese and onion.

Sacred food versus ordinary food?

How to present the Greek table without falling into the usual pitfalls? The first risk is to oppose too quickly the sacred meals to the ordinary meals, in the manner of the great historian of the 19th century Fustel de Coulanges. Jean-Pierre Vernant explains that this opposition has no

---

75. In ancient Greece, the crater was a container in which wine and water were mixed. See *below* the developments about the crater whose symbolic meaning made it much more than a simple container.

meaning (and cannot have any) in the Greek city where different forms and degrees of sacredness exist, rather than a polarity between the sacred and what would be profane. Each meal, even if it is ordinary, is already sacred by the simple commensality. Let's extend this clarification of Vernant by the warning of Paul Veyne who called to relativize the religious dimension of the Greek banquets, since one sacrificed and banqueted in the temples, as one went, just as banal, to the sports games, however they were also dedicated to the deities. As Veyne writes, the religious dimension is so intimately interwoven with everyday life that it can be so without fail, but also without intensity. Friends buy together an animal (most often a pig) that they will sacrifice at the temple, leaving of course the right leg to the priests. They can then take the meat home to eat at one of their homes, or choose to eat there, in a room available within the temples. The banquet is conceived to pay homage to the gods without expecting anything from them. First, because the golden age of commensality between gods and men is definitively over; then, because "the gods are powerful strangers who live their lives, have their own lives, live for themselves and are more or less interested in humanity. It is the case with them as it is with the great ones of this world: one addresses them to honor them, to thank them or to ask them for something"[76].

The question of frugality
The Greek table is thought to be at odds with Mesopotamian civilization. Gluttony is judged as one of the main causes of decadence. The Persian table constitutes a repellent, a counter-model, but also a heritage that the Greeks will pass on *nolens volens* to the Romans, who will appreciate it. This rupture must be well understood, because if the Greek table shares with the Mesopotamian and Egyptian tables the same basic ingredients, it makes them work in a completely different way, within the framework of another grammar. The Greek table uses the same dishes, but its triad is different since it establishes the primacy of bread, olive oil and wine. It adopts, in the same way, the form of the lying down banquet, but by giving him another direction. The Greek table is frugal in order to be more political. Thus Plato feeds his ideal republic with a few simple foods: "They will have salt of course, olives, cheese, onions and those cooked vegetables that one prepares in the country. For dessert we will even serve them figs, peas and beans" (*The Republic*, 372c). This frugality

---

76. Paul Veyne, *Le pain et le cirque. Sociologie historique d'un pluralisme politique*, Paris, "L'Univers historique", Éditions du Seuil, 1976.

          A political history of food. From the Pateolithic to our days

is not primarily the consequence of climatic conditions, but of political and philosophical choices that lead to the exclusion of luxury. Gluttony is considered as a sign of oriental softness.

The Roman Plutarch, in *The Symposia*, expresses a sharp criticism of the political modalities of the sharing within the Greek banquet by opposing between them the principles of pooling of the food and of equal sharing. He settles his fate, quickly, with the first formula because, with the setting in common, "the glutton makes an enemy of which cannot follow and remains behind". Equal sharing is certainly a pledge of justice and simplicity, but the division of the meat with the drawing of lots for portions destroys the community: there would be as many diners as there are dinners, but no guests (*sic*). Plutarch also contests the fact of giving the same quantity to each one, because this measure for who needs little is too big, and for who needs more, too small (*sic*). This arithmetical equality, dear to the Greeks, would thus be that of the soldiers' meals: "One dies of hunger and thirst there…" Plutarch chooses the geometrical reason, but this less rough sharing would not be possible any more because of the development of the taste of the luxury: "It is with the luxury that the egalitarian sharing was lost because impossible to divide cakes, soufflés, sauces and all these juices and spices"; "One yielded thus to the greed, to the search for the voluptuousness, therefore one abandoned the egalitarian sharing of the dishes"; "That which restores the use of the distribution makes revive at the same time frugality." A Greek could not have said it better: sharing, whatever its form, implies staying at a simple table.

Table manners

The Greeks eat three times a day: a breakfast consisting of bread soaked in pure wine with, sometimes, figs, cheese and olives. A second meal, at the beginning of the afternoon, in principle frugal and cold. This obligation to eat cold and, in principle, only leftovers, is explained by the fact that this snack eaten alone should not be a source of pleasure. It should only satisfy the needs of the biological body. The *zoon politikon* (social being) is therefore not (or hardly) concerned by this midday meal. The third meal is essential since it is shared as soon as the night falls. It alone benefits from the name of *deipnon* because it satisfies the political dimension of the humans. The men eat first, then the women and the children. The slaves serve the men, otherwise it is the women and children. A Greek usually eats sitting down, except for banquets where he eats lying down. The dishes are abundant: clay and metal bowls, even if bread cakes are used as plates. The Greeks eat with their fingers, but have a knife and a spoon. Pre-cut pieces of bread are used to grip the food. Pieces of bread are used to wipe fingers and lips.

Barley flour versus wheat bread

Demeter, goddess of the harvests, is one of the most beloved goddesses, because she is the mother of food. Cereals are the basis of the diet (barley, spelt, durum wheat)[77]. The Greeks present themselves as bread eaters, but the reality is different. For a long time, wheat remained more of a political symbol than a reality, and it is barley, sometimes mixed with wheat, eaten in the form of *maza* ("flat cake") and not bread, that really constitutes the basic food. The Greeks were barley eaters, while the Romans ate porridge. Barley is reduced to gruel, and therefore ground into a coarse flour. Homer thus defines humans as "flour eaters" (of barley). Plato wants to make it, in *The Republic,* the basis of human nutrition. The oath of loyalty to the homeland of the young Athenians is however carried to the land where "wheat, vine and olive tree grow". Cereals are served with vegetables (cabbage, spinach, onions, lettuce, radishes, lentils, beans, etc.). This obligatory complementarity between "bread" (barley) and its complements allows us to better understand the status reserved for luxury. If only the "bread" (even if it is a barley cake) constitutes the essential food, this sends its complements (vegetables, legumes) to the side of luxury; but beware, this does not mean that this luxury is superfluous, insofar as it allows us to eat the necessary which, without it, would be insipid. This luxury is therefore a good insofar as it strengthens the necessary. The search for food pleasure is thus (re)legitimized, immediately excluded. We always eat for and with pleasure, not only because we do not eat alone and we choose our guests, but because we eat vegetables.

The status of meat

The new food triad (wheat, olive oil and wine) excludes meat. This does not mean that it is less important than in the Mesopotamian tables, but that its political and legal status is different. Massimo Montanari explains that meat is even more inseparable from the logic of sacrifice in the Greek world than in the Roman world[78]. The consumption of meat is thus weak, because linked to the bloody sacrifices. Historians estimate the annual consumption of a Greek at two kilos. In the eyes of the Greeks,

---

77. Marie-Claire Amouretti, *Le pain et l'huile d'olive dans la Grèce antique. De l'araire au moulin,* Annales littéraires de l'université de Besançon, Paris, Les Belles Lettres, 1986.
78. Massimo Montanari, *La Faim et l'Abondance. History of Food in Europe,* Paris, Éditions du Seuil, 1998.

          A political history of food. From the Pateolithic to our days

a meat-eater is a Barbarian, as is a milk-drinker. I am not forgetting the Pythagorean and Orphic sects who refused to eat meat because of their belief in metempsychosis and, above all, because of their refusal of distribution as the basis of society.

Eating meat is complex

The consumption of meat is a complex thing for a Greek. In the first place, because it is necessary to differentiate the types of meat according to whether it is meat of sacrifice or butchery, of not sacrificed or not sacrificable animals. Secondly, because the butchers who intervene are not the same (*mageiros, opsopoios* and *deipnopoios*) and do not make the same gestures. The *mageiros* is the only one to be sacrificer, butcher and cook. He intervenes thus mainly within the framework of the public sacrifices. His activity is highly ritualized and requires very precise gestures. The animals that remain outside the circuit of the sacrifice (recognized as unfit after the immolation, or dead naturally and, in principle, not consumable), land in another circuit, with its own butchers, its own rules.

The animal sacrifice remains exceptional and its vocation is first of all to tighten the links of the community with the gods but also with the institutions. The cuisine of the sacrifice is based on a double prohibition: that of sacrificing the ox, man's working companion, and the sheep, because of its wool. Moreover, bovicides are condemned as severely as homicides. The ox is indeed considered as a more or less human animal. When a bovicide is necessary, it is surrounded by purification rituals. The Greeks can, on the other hand, sacrifice (and thus consume) the cow. It can be seen that this system of prohibitions is contrary to that in force in Egypt, since the Egyptians prohibited the sacrifice of the cow, but made possible that of the ox and calves. Herodotus notes that no Egyptian would have ever kissed a Greek on the lips because of the consumption of the sacred cow. The second prohibition, concerning the consumption of any meat from an animal not killed by humans, says the impossible commensality with animals. The sharing of meat is therefore only possible between (civilized) humans. These animals killed in other ways receive different names. Man cannot become a scavenger without calling into question his humanity. The question of hygiene (that of the transmission of diseases through commensality) is very secondary to this anthropological concern.

The sacrifice is also a political act

To sacrifice, explains Vernant, is a religious act, but also political because it rests on a division between the gods and the men, then between the men. This thesis is verified at the level of the techniques of butchery which serve to say the type of political society to which one aspires. The sacrifice is political because it serves to express the society and, consequently, its divisions. It is indeed followed by sharing, and therefore depends on the choices of sharing made: egalitarian or unequal sharing, equality while respecting differences or not. Several (political) regimes of division have existed simultaneously. The equality in the difference can be said by the system of the chosen pieces or by that of the double or triple rations granted to certain magistrates. The egalitarian ideal leads to the drawing of lots for the pieces, or better, to the fricassee, which relies on pieces (made) interchangeable by cutting. This predilection for the democratic ideal of fricassee is reinforced by the fact that its preparation goes well with the use of boiling, more civilized in the eyes of the Greeks than roasting itself, more than grilling. The fricassee thus satisfies both the constraints of democratization and humanization.

The sacrifice is political because it imposes the redistribution of the remains, it does not only say equality/inequality but also founds food policies. The remains are in fact, except for the exceptional ritual of the hecatomb, much more important than the share of the gods. For ordinary sacrifices, this divine share can be a few hairs; for great sacrifices, it includes viscera, blood, bones, fat. The sacrifices give food to the people. Conservative currents will never cease to want to keep them within narrow limits by denouncing the possibility thus offered to the people to access, thanks to this generosity, illegitimate and dangerous pleasures. Some specialists, like Michael H. Jameson, qualify these sacrifices as "anti-economic", because it would have been much less costly for Greek society to feed the people only with cereals. This thesis should be taken seriously, even if this "anti-economism" is probably the price to pay for the invention of democracy. To say that the people have the right to eat meat is to defend the people's right to the benefits of sacrifice. The economic question is however reinscribed in the heart of the sacrifices because if, for the private sacrifices, pigs (the cheapest animal) are used above all, if, for those of the temples, sheep are used above all, it is only for the royal sacrifices that cattle are used.

The status of cheese

The ancient Greeks are often presented as cheese eaters. This people of stockbreeders, more than farmers, would have developed this way of consuming milk, in order to be able to store it and preserve it despite the climate. The Greeks made large round and compact cheeses with sheep's, cow's, mare's, donkey's, buffalo's and goat's milk. There are many prohibitions on

A political history of food. From the Pateolithic to our days

goat cheese, because while the sacrifice of goats is possible in Sparta, it is forbidden everywhere else. The ordinary rites of purification often include, in addition to sexual abstinence, the consumption of goat meat and goat cheese. Quebec professor Janick Auberger, a specialist in milk in ancient Greece, would add that the Greeks were shameful cheese eaters, because, even if cheese making appears to be a first step in making milk, this uncivilized product, just good for children, a semi-civilized food, it nevertheless retains something of its origin[79]. Milk is certainly not bad in itself, since it was, until the definitive loss of the golden age, the divine food par excellence (along with honey), but since humans no longer eat with the gods, since they have been living off the product of their work, milk has become animal and barbaric. Janick Auberger explains that milk, associated with honey as long as the golden age lasted, is now linked to blood. According to Aristotle, if sperm is blood cooked by the man, milk is blood not cooked by the woman, because she is not hot enough. Milk is therefore responsible for soft and effeminate temperaments. Janick Auberger reminds us that the analogy between blood and milk also means that the coagulation of milk into cheese is equivalent to the birth of human flesh. Christianity will take up this analogy in its own way by thinking of cheese as the product of childbirth, as the mystery of the incarnation. Janick Auberger thus maintains that the only thing that makes cheese worthy of a Greek is that it must be mixed with something else in a ritual way: "It is the recipe, the elaborated product and the ritual [...] that transforms the vulgar food into a refined dish [...] To eat fresh cheese with no other accompaniment than raw milk is to live in a primitive state, like a lazy nomad, regardless of the quality of the product that is dried on the racks.

Cheese is therefore the food of civilized man only if it is accompanied by rituals and, among them, the indispensable mixture with other foods. Thus, it is used in the composition of *cyceon*, a liquid porridge made of wine, flour and grated goat's cheese. It is eaten with bread or olives. Breads and cakes are made with cheese. Cheese can also be given as a gift as long as it is associated with another food. It can be an offering, but only if it is fresh and pure; it is then sacrificed with honey and flour in the initiation rites of children.

Janick Auberger goes on to note that not only is cheese sought after as a substitute for meat, but that the Greeks posited a true "general equivalence" between meat and cheese. We discover here a final functionality of cheese

---

79. Janick AUBERGER, "Le lait des Grecs : boisson divine ou barbare ?" in *Dialogues d'histoire ancienne*, vol. 27, n° 1, 2001, p. 131-157.

accompanied by something else, since it becomes "the very symbol of a satisfied frugality" (Auberger). As it is mostly used grated, the cheese grater has become for this reason the instrument of frugality, thus of self-control. Janick Auberger notes however that cheese and cheese makers will always constitute a rather constant comic spring among the Greeks: a way of ridiculing the Athenian democracy, sign of a generalized lack of ambition. Aristophanes thus mocks a democracy of small cheese merchants (*sic*).

The status of the pastry shop

Greece provides another opportunity to question the status of pastry. Homer puts on the table of the heroes only meat, which is suitable to keep body and mind in good condition, but he totally excludes fine pastry. Plutarch perhaps provides an explanation by making cakes, but also soufflés, sauces and spices, the sign of the forgetfulness of frugality. The Greeks are however lovers of cakes and not only during sacrifices. Cakes are not a matter of greed, but of discourse. Cakes are both divine, i.e. offerings to the gods, and "royal", i.e. emblems of political power and its might. The cakes have always served, also, to develop sexual symbolism. The first cakes seem to have been simple icons in paste: cakes with protuberances representing the sexual parts, with genitals for the cult of Priape; and cakes of circular form, therefore of female sex. Among the offerings, the Greeks grant a particular place to the cakes since they took again the custom to substitute some to the real victims. Athenaeus evokes the filiation of ancient Egypt with rituals that consist, during human sacrifices, in covering the victims with pastries and chicks. Pastry making is not a culinary field comparable to the others, that is why it escapes the competence of the cooks to be devolved exclusively to women called *deemiourgoi*. They use the symbolism of flavors (honey, cheese, various cereals) and shapes. The vocabulary used changes according to the nature and function of each cake. As a cake is always cooked, it is immediately on the side of civilization. As such, the offering of a cake does not have the same meaning as that of seeds. A cake flatters the greediness as much by the eyes, the nose as by the mouth. Food of the gods, symbol of wealth and power, it will become, progressively, food of the powerful, sign of their power.

Banquets, the main source of pleasure

The *symposion* constitutes the main source of pleasure of the Greek citizens. Pauline Schmitt Pantel will be our main guide to present the banquets: "Any meal is *symposion*, therefore any banquet has a religious dimension." The fact of eating certain food and drinking certain drinks

A political history of food. From the Pateolithic to our days

puts in play the relations between the men and the gods, but also between the men. We already know that there are two successive shares for the meats: a first share between men and the gods (bones and fat burned on the altar) then a second share between men, which is carried out according to various political methods bringing into play at the same time the principles of hierarchy and equality. Any meal thus recalls, on the one hand, the time when men and gods lived and ate together and, on the other hand, the definitive separation between the worlds of gods and humans. As a consequence, men are now the only ones who must reproduce and therefore die, and therefore also consume food. Each meal thus recalls the respective place of the divine, the human and the bestial. As Pauline Schmitt Pantel analyzes, eating and drinking are acts which, in themselves, are of little interest to the Greeks, since what is important according to them is the type of relationship that is established around the food and drink taken in common. Here we come across Jean-Pierre Vernant's thesis: commensality is almost always the foundation of the community. If Pauline Schmitt Pantel makes it possible to understand that the Greek banquets are neither a tribal survival nor a borrowing from the military model, but a widening and an institutionalization of the aristocratic practices, the Greeks of the first centuries of our era will not understand any more the shared meal like the base of the civic life and will make of it a simple private matter. The iconography says a lot about the political stakes that accompanied the generalization of the food uses of the aristocratic elites. By democratizing, the banquets gradually lost the emblems of the aristocratic life as the horse (an equestrian statue testified to a high social position) and the dog (of hunting). The disappearance of these emblems could have been a sign of softening, which is why the Greeks invented other devices to maintain their values. The banquet is too serious a matter to be left to the initiative of each one. Aristippus, philosopher of pleasure, was reproached for liking to party too much. To which he replied: "We do it well in honor of the gods": in other words, it is because the gods take pleasure in seeing men feasting in their honor that it is not a question of opposing the serious and the futile, but of distinguishing between different ways of celebrating, while remaining serious. The refusal of softness condemns any slackening of the bodies and the debates.

Opposition of the deipnon *and the* symposion

Pauline Schmitt Pantel showed that the banquet took several different forms since it is not any more a modality of the aristocratic sociability. The principal characteristic, it is that one cannot oppose the private, religious and political banquets because all is at the same time political, religious and friendly. The banquet generally serves to say the citizenship, that is to say the participation. The citizens banquet, certainly, with pleasure, but they always banquet according to precise rules, and except the presence of the non-citizens, who can be invited to a meal called *xenia*, but never with the *deipnon*. Indeed, the hospitality is not that of a meal, but of a sacrifice of hospitality which creates a new bond: one becomes guest of the city or of a person. These different types of banquets have in common that they are based on the structuring opposition of the *deipnon*, a moment dedicated to the consumption of food, and the *symposion*, destined to the circulation of the word thanks to the wine. This grammar of the banquet has no meaning unless carried over to the very conception of humanity since its separation from the world of the gods. The *deipnon* is more a constraint which corresponds to the food needs. The *symposion* appears as a consolation of the human condition.

Who attends the banquet?

The first great question is to determine who takes part in the banquet. It is advisable here to distinguish the aristocratic banquets which, pertaining to the private life, gather people sharing the same way of life. These aristocratic banquets thus gather, in a certain equivalence, adult men carrying the beard, young people without beards and some women. The guests are lying, alone or in pairs, on beds furnished with blankets and cushions.

The democratized banquets, on the contrary, mobilize a heterogeneous public, individuals who have of common only their citizenship but who differ by their ways of life, their wealth. These democratized banquets usually gather three types of guests: the host and his close relations, his friends, and characters named "parasites". Many banquets are held without women, even if they make sometimes an appearance. Those who appear lying on the beds with the male guests, dressed in a simple *chiton* or a *himation* or even completely naked are hetaera.

Parasites

Parasitein is a usual gesture within the religious sanctuaries, well before Solon extends the device to the banquets: it creates a turn of role and specifies that a citizen should not take part too often (sign of greed) nor refuse to go to the banquet (contempt of the community). This system will gradually become important in other contexts: citizens must take turns to be *parasitein* and cities send *parasitoi* ("parasites") for one year to represent them to other cities. However, the Greeks soon learned to

A political history of food. From the Pateolithic to our days

distinguish between parasites. The *adoxos* parasite is the one who has no *doxa*, the one who parasites without glory. The valued parasite, according to Pauline Schmitt Pantel, is the one who is more familiar with the smoke of the altars than with the smell of the kitchens. The *parasitoi* are official figures: they are chosen, their mandate lasts one year. It is necessary to have a double Athenian ancestry, to have goods and to have an honorable life. They are thus magistrates who have initially religious functions: they take part in the sacrifices, but especially, they eat "beside..." Pauline Schmitt Pantel argues that this establishment of commensality by delegation constitutes the birth of the representative system itself: "We are touching the beginning of the process that will increasingly abstract the definition of citizenship from the practice of eating in common."

The adoption of the semi-recumbent banquet

The oldest banquets were held seated by granting a great importance to the nature of the seat (simple stool, chair, armchair, throne, etc.). We owe to Jean-Marc Dentzer a tasty history of the *motive of the recumbent banquet in the Near East and the Greek world from the 7th to the 9th century B.C.*[80] The recumbent banquet appears in the Greek and Etruscan world at the turn of the SIXTH to the 5th century: it becomes, like hunting, a manifestation of royal power. The reclining position is first considered a privilege of kings: the bed is an emblem of power, like the throne, and the king receives lying down. Alexander the Great deals with business either on his throne or on his silver bed. Greece, by borrowing this oriental device, however, gradually gave it another meaning, since all the guests were to bank lying down, a sign of their general equivalence. This adoption does not go without causing many negative reactions: the cynics refuse to lie down and eat standing, as a sign of simplicity and frugality. Athenaeus sees in the lying down banquet a sign of softness, thus of decadence, in short a poisoned gift of the Orientals to the Greeks. The seated banquet is therefore considered spontaneously more noble; eating lying down is in principle forbidden to women, children and slaves, that is to say to all those that their identity already leads naturally to softness. Thus, at the court of Macedonia: a young man, to eat lying down, must first kill a boar with a stake without using a net.

---

80. Jean-Marc DENTZER, *Le motif du banquet couché dans le Proche-Orient et le monde grec du VIIe au IVe siècle avant J.-C.*, Paris-Rome, "Bibliothèque des écoles françaises d'Athènes et de Rome", n° 246, Publications de l'École française de Rome, 1982.

The deipnon

Luciana Romeri explains that, for the Greeks, the need for food prevents any aspiration to a state of divine perfection, since the gods do not eat bread, nor drink wine[81]. Men can only replace the nectar and ambrosia of the gods. Food is therefore what binds man to his state of eternal hunger. The mouth is not only on the side of evil, for it can also do good. What does most harm is the man of need (food); what does most good is the man of speech: "The point of the question is not so much that speech is good or bad, but that the tongue is good insofar as it serves speech and bad insofar as it serves food"[82]. Food, because it refers to the order of need, would be the political dimension, whereas speech, because it serves the order of good, would be the philosophical dimension. The digestive apparatus is itself double: the first part, located between the diaphragm and the neck (thus closer to the divine) is the source of courage; the second part, located below the diaphragm, corresponds to the desiring part of the mortal soul, that of appetite. The Greek banquet would thus have as a great stake to "cheat one's hunger", that is to say, explains Luciana Romeri, to arrange the need for food in the most limited time possible, to temper this need at the time of its satisfaction, to forsake solid foods that are too nourishing, to prefer to meat less fatty foods, such as soups, vegetables, fish, etc. These prescriptions update the principles of frugality and simplicity. Many banquets were held without meat because animal sacrifice was exceptional. Athenaeus relativizes this double constraint by pointing out that fish and pastries constitute the apogee of the banquet, because they allow the amphitryons to show their know-how and that of their servants in culinary matter.

The personnel in charge of the banquets is important. In addition to the symposiarch, Athenaeus evokes the function of the *trapezopoioi*, different from that of the cooks: they hold the lamps ready, arrange the beds of table, supervise the good course of the meal. However, they have no power over the kitchen. Eating is certainly of little importance, but the Greeks nevertheless pay some attention to this satisfaction of (too) human needs. Thus Athenaeus makes talk about cooks in his book on banquets: one wants to have the list of the guests to adapt the meal to the tastes of each people. To the Rhodians, one must give a large catfish on a very hot sauce and cooked in a court-bouillon. To the Byzantines, everything must be sprinkled with wormwood, salted heavily and garnished with garlic to

---

81. Luciana ROMERI, "Philosophes entre mots et mets. Plutarch, Lucian and Athenaeus around Plato's table" in *L'Antiquité classique*, vol. 75, n° 1, 2006, p. 420-422.
82. *Id., ibid.*

compensate for the large quantity of fish they eat, which fills them with "slimy sabre and pituitary". The ancients need a specific food that opens the appetite, such as cicadas or raves macerated in vinegar with mustard.

The symposion

The *symposion* is dedicated to the circulation of drink and speech. A series of rituals marks a firm separation from the time of the *deipnon*. The servants clean the tables and the floor while the guests gird their heads with garlands, wreaths of flowers or leaves. The *symposion* begins with a libation of pure wine (the only case where pure wine can be served) and a pean to Apollo that all the guests sing. The *symposion* obeys strict rules, including the choice of a game leader, called the "symposiarch". Plato explains that it is advisable to choose a symposiarch who is resistant to outbursts and thus capable of ensuring the preservation of friendship. Wine is reserved for men and, according to Plato, for those who are no longer young. As Pierre Boyancé writes in his study of Plato and wine[83] , for the Greeks, to say that wine contains fire is not a simple metaphor but the expression of a physical reality with which it is appropriate to compromise. Young people, up to the age of 18, must not "make fire flow over fire", young adults, up to the age of 40, may taste wine with reservation, drunkenness is therefore reserved for men over 40. The wine is obligatorily cut with water in a large crater (container). A law of Zaleukos (mythical legislator of Locres) punishes of death who drinks pure wine... except medical prescription.

The political status of the mixture

This compulsory mixture is made with two thirds or three fifths of water. Pierre Boyancé insists on the fact that it is not because the wine is strongly alcoholic that it is mixed with water, but because a mixture is necessary, since it always presides over the alliance of the gods with the city and men. The mixture of wine and water is thus related to a myth relating to Dionysus, that of his education by the Nymphs. Dionysos, it is the wine; the Nymphs, it is the water. The wine tempered by water is Dionysus corrected by his nurses. Plato also explains that the soul of the world is constituted by a mixture, that of the same and the other. Hephaestus, the god of blacksmiths, the god of fire, is the one who presides over the alloying of metals in fusion, thus over their mixing. However, Pierre Boyancé assigns an openly political status to the mixture: "It is not

---

83. Pierre BOYANCÉ, "Platon et le vin" in *Bulletin de l'Association Guillaume Budé*, n° 4, *Lettres d'humanité*, vol. 10, December 1951, p. 3-19.

easy to conceive that the State must be a mixture similar to that which is made in the crater, where the drinkers will fill their cups. The madness of the wine poured into it bubbles up, but when it has been corrected by the sobriety of another god than one's own, then thanks to this happy alliance, it gives rise to an excellent and well-tempered beverage." We know the importance of this category of mixture in philosophy.

The symposiarch determines the mixture, but also the number of cups to be emptied. The principle is that three craters are brought successively: the first is drunk in honor of the gods, the second in honor of the heroes, the last in honor of the humans. Each crater fills a large number of cups. The wine is thus a sense of measure, a sense of mixture, the very symbol of politics.

The political status of the crater

The crater is at the same time the new urn for mortuary ashes, since about the 6th century B.C., and the ritual object of wine consumption. The cauldron, which was formerly used as a coffin, became the sign of the common meal based on meat, thus of sacrificial banquet for a long time privilege of the warrior aristocracy holding the political, military, religious power. The crater is therefore not simply a vase allowing to realize a mixture water/wine, because taking into account the politico-philosophical statute of the mixture and the democratization of the banquet, it became the emblem of a political regime, that of the *civitas*, of the *polis*, that of the democracy (even limited), whereas it was initially the symbol of a simple meeting between familiar and friends. The crater became the sign of a society reconciled with itself, the sign of the search for the appeasement of passions, of harmony in the group. It is thus the symbol of the good functioning of the banquet and thus of the city. The banquet is a substitute for aggressiveness and an act of friendship and love. The *symposion*, like the banquet, will then have to answer the political question par excellence which is that of the nature of sharing and equality. The symposiarch will have to take into account that each one does not support the wine in the same way, consequently the mixture, in other words the sharing, will depend on each one. The principle of the banquet, of the common pot, does not impose absolute sharing. The Greeks will answer in their way, by recalling that the lover is not shared, even within the banquet. The private is thus what is not shared. Each one has right to his place at the banquet (equality) and to his courtesan (inequality).

A political history of food. From the Pateolithic to our days

The *symposion* is the opportunity to console mere mortals with the word. I like very much the definition that Luciana Romeri gives of wine as "pro-logue", as a foretaste of the word understood in the broadest sense. Thus, to drink without singing or to say nothing while raising the cup is rude. In Plato too, wine is always associated with speech. The *symposion* is not, however, a place for useless chatter, for light words. Each guest can take the floor to evoke more or less serious subjects, even if one speaks, in principle, about serious matters, like philosophical and political questions, but also poetic, because nothing is more serious for a Greek than poetry. It is indeed the poet who, by granting or not the praise, decides the value of a feat, preferably warlike, and thus recognizes the status of hero, of great man. Poetry is thus a political art since a man is worth what his *logos* is worth, a *logos* which must be said, sung or recited in front of the group of equals. Jean Defradas wonders then about the divinities which it is advisable to convene according to the nature of the merits: military, sporting, intellectual, diplomatic exploit, etc. Dionysus, the god of wine, who for the Greeks is really present during agape, is obviously present at all banquets, at all tributes. Pierre Boyancé, questioning the status of drunkenness during banquets, recalls that "the Greeks hardly knew any other artificial paradise than this one". Wine is thus the beverage of freedom and the reduction of control. We should not understand this intoxication in the modern way: it is not a question of losing self-control in order to forget our problems and reality. Plato puts us on the way by relating wine to the dances of the Bacchae: "Any dance of a Bacchic character mimics characters in a state of intoxication"; "wine was therefore given by Dionysus to arouse the ecstatic dances of the mysteries." The wine is thus well a divine phenomenon. Drinking wine is done under the sign of Dionysus, therefore of the values that this god promotes. In Plato, Dionysus is at the same time the symbol of wine and enthusiasm[84].

The Greek table, not only the banquets, carries very high the conviction that cooking, like politics, is the art of the composition of the opposites. This is why wine, mixed with water, was historically a more political drink than beer. It was therefore considered the democratic drink par excellence. That's why also the ancient Greek national dish is this soup, semi-liquid, which takes different names, like *cyceon*, according to the cities and the times. The cheese is therefore good only accompanied always by something

---

84. Roland MAY, "Les jeux de table en Grèce et à Rome" in *Bulletin de l'Association Guillaume Budé*, n° 1, mars 1995, p. 51-61.

else. The Greek table, not only the banquets, also carries very high the conviction that cooking as well as politics is the art of sharing, therefore of equality. This is why one does not necessarily choose one's guests, because sharing with relatives, with friends, is less powerful than sharing with parasites. This is why the cutting of the meat is also important, because fricassee, by making all the pieces equivalent, makes all the men equivalent. This principle of equivalence is however never absolute, in the same way that Aristotle differentiates arithmetical and geometrical equality, the symposiarchs mix water and wine in the respect of the differences. An anxious question remains: does the maximum of equality between the guests require, always, to remain at a necessarily simple and frugal table? The Romans, who were already obsessed with the table, thought that if they had to share, they might as well share good things... but this is another page in the political history of food, and therefore a new service.

Fifth service: The Roman table

The Roman table is the heir of the Egyptian and Greek tables insofar as it is largely structured as a language and a sharing, even if it gives a radically different meaning to these founding notions[85]. The essential thing is still to share, because the human being is a social being, and to eat alone would be to miss this anthropological dimension, but this commensalism is made from now on between friends and not between citizens. Friendship does not have a political function as the Greeks wished. The Roman *convivium* remains a private matter, contrary to the Greek banquet, because the Romans do not share the Greek conception of politics. The Greek citizen is that man included in structures of civic, civil and military participation. The Roman citizenship will never be that of an accomplished and self-sufficient community according to the formula of Aristotle. The *civitas* according to the Roman conception is thus not the equivalent of the Greek *zoon politikon*. The Romans did not eat like the Egyptians and the Greeks, the hierarchy of dishes was different and if the Roman table was as talkative as the Greek one, it said nothing about the power relationships that were established around the meals but spoke much more about the specificities of the products. The Romans were more obsessed with food than with what was exchanged at the table.

---

85. Even if I am responsible for possible blunders, I am indebted to the approach developed by Florence Dupont, "Grammaire de l'alimentation et des repas romains", and by Mireille Corbier, "La fève et la murène : hiérarchies sociales des nourritures à Rome", two articles that can be found *in* Jean-Louis Flandrin and Massimo Montanari (eds), *Histoire de l'alimentation, op. cit.* For a general vision of the Roman table, see: Inês de Ornellas e Castro and Joël Thomas, *De la table des dieux à la table des hommes. La symbolique de l'alimentation dans l'Antiquité romaine*, Paris, L'Harmattan, 2011; Nicole Blanc and Anne Nercessian, *La Cuisine romaine antique*, Grenoble, Éditions Glénat, 1992; Jacques André, *L'Alimentation et la cuisine à Rome*, Paris, Éditions C. Klincksieck, 1961, reed. 1981; and, *in* Jérôme Carcopino [1939], *La vie quotidienne à Rome à l'apogée de l'Empire*, Paris, Hachette, 1963 (one hundred and seventeenth mile), the now classic pages devoted to the *cena*, pp. 304-318.

The table and the secession on the Aventine

This relative "chosification" and privatization of the table did not prevent Rome from developing food policies in order to defend the supply of the *Urbs* and also a conception of the table. Roman policies in this field were based on four principles that the Latin legal spirit transformed into laws: sumptuary and frumentary laws, texts concerning free distribution or the setting of maximum prices.

One cannot understand what was at stake during several centuries under these great principles, if one does not go back to the beginning of the Republic. This period is marked by the struggle of the plebeians against the patricians, when it was a question of questioning the discriminations of which the people were victim, until the moment when the plebs decided to make secession and to withdraw on the hill of the Aventine. The result of the secession was the creation of tribunes of the plebs in charge of defending their interests (around 494-471 B.C.) and the adoption of the Law of the Twelve Tables which recognized the equality of all before the law. This social corpus also marks a beginning of secularization. Practitioners and priests never acknowledged defeat and used jurisprudence to defend an inegalitarian system which, over time, became increasingly oligarchic, until the Empire. They were helped in this by wars that enriched the richest and impoverished the poor. To the quasi-disappearance of the middle classes within the plebs answers the increase of the number of slaves because of the military conquests. The Gracchi, Tiberius and Caius, tried to rebuild a middle class of peasants, in order to save the Republic and to avoid that the plebs became the stake of ambitious demagogic consuls, like Pompey or Caesar.

The Roman conception of the table

Rome constantly needs to reinvent itself as a table that distinguishes its civilization from barbarian peoples and from other civilizations that it respects, such as Egypt and especially Greece.

The pulmentarium

The Romans inaugurated a new food triangle: the Hellenic "bread, olive oil and wine" was succeeded by the trilogy "bread, complements to bread and wine". This notion of bread complements, the *pulmentarium,*

A political history of food. From the Pateolithic to our days

is central and complex[86]. It is central because these complements to bread make up the essential part of the meal, from the caloric point of view, but also in terms of satisfaction. It is complex because it is the *pulmentarium* that, in the eyes of the Romans, makes bread pleasant, and therefore edible. Part of the debate is about its content, because not everyone can claim the same *pulmentarium* according to their social status. The *pulmentarium* of the free man is not the same as that of the slave or the soldier, nor is it the same as that of the worker, especially the worker on the land. However, the base is always more or less the same: vegetables, oil, salt, vinegar, sometimes olives, and *hallec* (or *allec*), which is a residue of fish flesh from the manufacture of *garum* (which we will discuss later). With the *pulmentarium* we find the principle of the ration emblematic of ancient societies.

With this principle, Romans, rich or poor, will eat for a long time globally the same products, only in different quantities. The dualisation of society will however lead to the dualisation of the table. Not only in terms of content but also in terms of practices and rituals. The *convivium* becomes the focus of aristocratic sociability, which leads to a refinement of the table, while the *popina* ("tavern") becomes the den of the working classes because it allows them to eat cooked and hot: "a sow's vulva in a hot tavern", writes Juvenal (*Sat.* , XI, 79-81). The cauldron, in which the stew that accompanies the bread simmers, thus becomes the emblem of the plebs' good pleasure. The enriched ones will never assume completely this divorce because they want to be a people of peasants and soldiers. They will develop a whole ideology centered on the frugality and the simplicity, this is why they will always look at the *prandium*, this simpler meal of midday "so quickly dispatched that it was not need, neither to draw up the table before (*sine mensa*), nor to wash one's hands afterwards (*post quod non sunt lavandae manus*)[87]", as preferable to the *cena*, this evening meal which, because it is taken among friends, certainly becomes *convivium*[88], but which has the disadvantage on the moral level of being often much

---

86. The very etymology of the word *pulmentarium* is a matter of debate. On reading Mireille Corbier's article "La fève et la murène…", one understands that if Pliny the Elder and Varron trace the word back to the time when cereals were consumed as porridge and propose an etymology based on the word *puls* ("flour porridge"), modern philologists (e.g. Isidore of Seville, 6th century AD) derive pulmentarium from pulpa, i.e. "meat", Modern philologists (e.g. Isidore of Seville, 6th century AD) derive *pulmentarium* from *pulpa*, i.e. the "meat" that goes into the preparation of a dish, as noted by N. Blanc and A. Nercessian, in *La Cuisine romaine antique* (see page 224 of the *Histoire de l'alimentation*).
87. Jérôme Carcopino, *La vie quotidienne à Rome à l'apogée de l'Empire, op. cit. loc. cit.* , p. 305.
88. Ancient authors had invented an etymology linking *convivium*, or "dinner among friends" (Cicero defines it as "taking a seat at the table among friends, because they have a community of life"), to the Greek *koinon* which means "in common".

too copious). The Roman table was not only based on this new triangle (bread, wine and *pulmentarium*) but on a series of binary oppositions. The Romans, unlike other peoples, are convinced that we think better through pairs than through ternary distinctions or even gradations. Hot/cold is easier to think about than variations in lukewarm, and cooked and raw is easier to implement than different degrees of cooking.

Pecks and fruges

The Roman table is based on the opposition of *fruges* and *pecudes*[89]. The *fruges* are not so much the products of the earth as those of the cultivated earth, with green vegetables, turnips, cabbages, cardoons, salads, leeks, turnips, carrots, bulbs, garlic, onions, etc. The pecudes group together the various meats. The *pecudes* include the different meats.

Our opposition of vegetal and meat is of little help in understanding this classification. The historian Mireille Corbier has established that the stakes are primarily political[90]. The *fruges* are indeed on the side of civilization because they depend on the modalities of occupation of the land and the types of activity. Livestock farming is devalued in comparison with agriculture, because it is wilder. However, things are never so simple with the Roman classifications. Not only did they differentiate politically and philosophically between plants and meat products, but not all meats were equal, and not all plants either, some were indeed worth more than others: the Romans distinguished between the fruits of the earth, depending on whether they came from gardens or ploughed land.

The garden (vegetable garden, vineyards, orchards) constitutes the most civilized land, because it has been definitively conquered from the wild lands: its products can therefore be consumed raw, that is to say in reality "cooked" by the sun (*cocta*), partially or completely. Thus, vegetables and fruits are never considered raw when they are harvested.

The ploughed lands (*arua*) are less civilized, since they are reclaimed every year by ploughing, so their products - cereals (*frumentum*), legumes (*legumina*) - are more raw than vegetables and fruits, so they must be cooked.

The *pecudes*, which initially concerned the only meats of breeding, indicate by extension all the meats, because the Romans never made a great difference between breeding and hunting, to the point of constituting

---

89. Florence Dupont, "Grammaire de l'alimentation et des repas romains", art. cit. *in* Jean-Louis Flandrin and Massimo Montanari (dirs), *Histoire de l'alimentation, op cit.*
90. Mireille Corbier, "Le statut ambigu de la viande à Rome" in *Dialogues d'histoire ancienne*, vol. 15, n° 2, 1989, p. 107-158 ; *id.* "La fève et la murène : hiérarchies sociales des nourritures à Rome", art. cit. *in* Jean-Louis Flandrin and Massimo Montanari (dirs), *Histoire de l'alimentation, op. cit.*

reserves of wild animals. The *pecudes* are on the side of the forests, of the uncultivated lands, i.e. of the savagery (including the necessary savagery). This savagery is not to be banished but to be framed, to be socialized. The *pecudes* are besides necessary since they are at the base of the bloody sacrifices, therefore of the religious, but also of the *cena* and particularly of the banquets.

The raw and the cooked

Much has been said about the Romans' hatred of raw food, without sufficiently emphasizing the fact that the opposition between cooked and raw food does not coincide with our own[91]. The issue is not dietary or culinary but cultural and political. The raw refers to the savage, sometimes even to barbarism. Cooked food is everything that is civilized. A salad is always cooked, not only because it is cooked (*cocta*) by the sun but because it is the result of agricultural work. Jean-Pierre Vernant summarizes the matter with his sense of synthesis: "Bread is to the standing plant (the living wheat) and to the flour (dead but still raw) what a dish of cooked meat is to the standing beast (the living animal) and to a piece of bloody flesh (dead but not yet cooked). In this state of transition between nature and culture (flour, raw meat) remains an impurity that makes untouchable that from which life has been taken, that which has been killed, without giving it its full form of human food." So raw is not bad in itself, especially in terms of taste, it may even be necessary for the soldier. It is more in the head that it has bad taste since it moves away from the civilized. We can therefore understand the Roman preference for boiled food, because boiled food is more cooked than roasted food, which is itself more cooked than grilled food. We remember the condemnation of the Huns by the Roman poet and military Ammianus Marcellinus (330-v. 395) because they eat their meat barely heated under the saddle of their horses.

Hot and cold

The Romans prefer *fruges* to *pecudes* and cooked food to raw food, but they also prefer cold food to hot food. Eating cold refers to two virtues. The cold is already the status of the *prandium* and therefore the meal of the active man. The cold is also the refusal of any softening, thus of the decadence. Eating cold is also very well suited to eating standing up, quickly, and if possible only leftovers from the previous day's meal. Roman

---

91. Florence Dupont, "Grammaire de l'alimentation et des repas romains", art. cit. *in* Jean-Louis Flandrin and Massimo Montanari (dirs), *Histoire de l'alimentation, op cit.*

legislation sometimes forbids eating hot food. This is the case of soldiers, during military campaigns, who lose the right to cut their wine with hot water; it is also the case of the ordinary citizen who, during certain events such as public mourning, no longer has the right to buy hot food. Caligula forbade the sale of hot water on certain occasions. Society sometimes needs to forbid itself anything that might weaken it.

The soft and the hard

The oppositions of raw and cooked, of hot and cold, intersect with that of soft and hard. The savage is represented by the *pecudes*, and the savage is soft. One must understand, by these two terms - the hard and the soft - "less a sensitive consistency to the touch than an internal cohesion more or less strong. Indeed, it is difficult to understand why a boiled turnip or lettuce would be harder than a boar's leg. What is hard is that which does not risk coming apart, that which is compact; what is soft is that which is imminently threatened by a disintegration into heterogeneous elements, like a sauce that turns. Culture hardens; savagery softens"[92]. The savage is thus naturally linked to the *cena*, that is to say to the luxury and the waste. The *pecudes* moreover do not nourish the body but purge it, soften it. Yves Roman explains that *mollitia* ("softness") is a major concept in Roman civilization, which is found in two important issues: that of food and that of sex and eroticism[93]. His approach is fruitful because far from reducing the opposition to organoleptic preferences (as is often done), he shows the political basis of this opposition. Moreover, this classification does not refer to our own taxonomy since we know that, for a Roman, a meat is always softer than a salad. Soft is, by extension, everything that is not autonomous, and therefore also everything that can make one dependent: women, passive homosexuality, amorous passion, but also the situation of dependent workers (those whose lives depend on a salary or the collection of a commercial turnover). The hard, it is all that makes the autonomy, it is thus the proper of the aristocrat. Also, "the citizen, because he was a male, because he was a Roman, could not abandon himself to softness. To do so was to become dependent on his pleasures, whatever they were, a Greek in short [...] No one could or should, if he intended to be a statesman, depend

---

92. *Id., ibid.*, p. 208-209.
93. Yves ROMAN, "Le mou, les mous et la mollesse ou les systèmes taxinomiques de l'aristocratie romaine" in *Pratiques et discours alimentaires en Méditerranée de l'Antiquité à la Renaissance*. Actes du 18ᵉ colloque de la Villa Kérylos à Beaulieu-sur-Mer, les 4, 5 & 6 octobre 2007, "Cahiers de la Villa Kérylos", vol. 19, n° 1, Paris, Académie des Inscriptions et Belles Lettres, 2008 p. 171-186.

        A political history of food. From the Pateolithic to our days

on his stomach, his wife, his sexual partners, his pleasures. By the negative, by the refusal of the softness, the Roman aristocracy meant its ideals"[94]. We can understand the choice of Curius Dentatus, consul in 290 B.C., who, when receiving guests, ate barely cooked root vegetables from his garden, a sign of their hardness and therefore of his own hardness. One can understand the resistance to the passage from porridge to bread, since a ground cereal necessarily changes status: by becoming dead, it automatically passes from hard to soft, thus from Roman to less Roman. We find here the exception of lard which, already hard when the pig was alive, still hardens during its preparation (desiccation and salting) whereas the wild boar, which became soft a first time when it died, is also soft because of its cooking. Any cooking is therefore dangerous since it is softening. We can still follow Yves Roman when he establishes a link between the love of hard work and the political ideology of self-sufficiency based on the garden and the small agricultural property: the Romans call this ideal state *paupertas*, a situation of poverty that has nothing in common with misery (*inopia*) that weakens, since, on the contrary, by making self-sufficient, it reinforces the power of the citizen-owner, able thanks to his field or his garden to feed his family daily. Its main virtue is moreover to prevent from sinking into excess. This constant fight against softness explains why the legionnaires are big consumers of pork, which they eat in their rations, because the hardness that lard gives should allow them to resist effort, pain and temptation. We will let Yves Roman conclude by maintaining that "the *mollitia* was thus linked to the easy life, to Greece, to luxury. It was initially a lack of "social masculinity", including all at the same time the passive homosexuals, the amateurs of all these Greek things pertaining or not of the sex, the *gula*. Their *mollitia*, proceeding from a deregulated abuse of pleasures, having definitively made them lose their status of Roman male, of responsible man"[95].

To each according to his social status

This grammar of the table explains that everyone has the obligation to eat according to their social status. The exclusion of meat certainly characterizes the popular meal, but other restrictions concern fat, cooked and hot food. The plebs usually ate lean, raw and cold food. These restrictions are not explained by medical considerations related to the personality of the eater, as will be done later with the system of humours[96]. The Roman who changes

94. *Id., ibid.*
95. *Id., ibid.*
96. Éric BIRLOUEZ, *La santé par l'alimentation de l'Antiquité au Moyen Âge*, Rennes, Éditions Ouest-France, 2013.

his status gains access to a different diet. The peasant who became a soldier could no longer be satisfied with servile food, which is why his ration necessarily included pork. The Roman soldier is subject to other prohibitions such as buying cooked dishes, cutting his wine with hot water, possessing as kitchen utensils something other than a spit, a copper pot and a cup.

Roman food policies

The Roman State recognized its right to intervene in food matters, a sign that it knew that people did not eat with impunity and that every meal involved society. One can think that if the Republic and then the Empire had to invent so many food policies, it is already because of the urban gigantism of Rome. The city, with its 800,000 to 1.2 million inhabitants, could not live in self-sufficiency and had to import massively from Egypt and North Africa[97]. The challenge is to protect the capital from food crises by inventing policies and institutions that are equal to the difficulty. These food policies concern production, raiding, storage, distribution, control, and even consumption and the organization of meals. Mireille Corbier notes that this intervention of the political power was strong enough to unify the modes of food, at least at the level of the plebeian citizens, domiciled in Rome and within the army, because these two categories depended directly on the State for their supplies. It is worth noting that the treatises on agronomy that flourished at the time devoted lengthy developments to the issues of conservation and storage of foodstuffs, since there would be no point in knowing how to cultivate if the crops were massively lost. The Romans naturally inherited techniques that were often ancient, but they made a virtue of this necessity by consuming mainly canned food, i.e. products whose color, texture and taste were no longer natural. Vegetables are preserved in vinegar or brine, meats are salted and smoked, fruits are stored in wine, honey, etc. Eating a natural food is less valued than a denatured product.

Sumptuary laws

It is difficult to understand the reason for and the scope of the sumptuary laws because it is not so much a question of restricting luxury as of

---

97. "From Spain came the brines with which eggs were seasoned; from Gaul the cold meats; from the East, the spices; and from all the regions of Italy and the universe, the wines and fruits; apples and pears, figs from Chio, lemons and pomegranates from Africa, dates from the oases, plums from Damascus" (*in* Jérôme CARCOPINO, *La vie quotidienne à Rome à l'apogée de l'Empire, op. cit., loc. cit.* , p. 314).

　　A political history of food. From the Pateolithic to our days

defending a conception of the table. For several centuries, Rome was to make two principles triumph: the refusal of ostentatious over-consumption of products, especially meat, and the defense of the free consumption of products from cultivated land. The Flavius law of 161 B.C., which limits the expenses per banquet, does not actually concern spelt or vegetables. A Roman can therefore eat a lot but only if he eats in the Roman way (vegetables and cereals). The first texts aimed at restricting excesses date from the law of the Twelve Tables, so it is indeed a law obtained under pressure from the mobilized plebs. A dozen other laws were progressively enacted during the Republic and the Empire, not to mention numerous specific texts. It has often been said that this succession of texts was either proof of the ineffectiveness of these laws, or the sign that these laws had an incantatory and not a real dimension. Marianne Coudry's work allows us to make a different judgment: these texts follow one another, certainly, but with an ever greater territorial competence, since they initially concerned only the citizens of Rome and eventually extended to the whole of Italy; these texts also widened the sanctions to include the persons invited and no longer only those who received them, and finally they increased the scope of the prohibitions. Thus, while the first laws simply limited the number of guests, the following ones modulated the expenses, according to the ordinary or festive days, restricting or forbidding certain dishes on certain occasions more than on others. Other texts set the principle of the so-called "centennial" meal, because it did not exceed 100 aces, others still determined a maximum price for a series of rare foods or limited the participation of magistrates in private banquets, etc. The poulardes, the goats, and, especially, the exotic birds, are prohibited. Rome also did not allow the consumption of unfertilized chickens and limited the purchase of smoked meat for a festive meal to 20 talents, etc.

These sumptuary laws were not adopted or applied without great controversy. It is interesting to note that many were the result of plebiscites. Some proposals were rejected by the legislator, such as the obligation to eat with the door open or the prohibition to use gold dishes. The inspiration for these laws is undoubtedly Greek, with the example of Solon's texts limiting the number of guests for funeral banquets, but whereas the Greeks speak mainly about clothes, the Romans devote most of their legislation to repressing the luxury of the table, more because (it seems to me) of the importance they give to it than because of excesses.

Since 1981, historians have agreed with Guido Clemente that the objective of these sumptuary laws was political and not moral, since it was a question of inventing legislation to regulate the aristocracy. The aim was first of all to prevent the development of clientelism: thus, in case of transgression, a ban on running for a magistrate's post for up to ten years could be pronounced, and, in case of buying votes, the guilty party could be banished for life. A censor, in charge of the application of these texts, has a police force that can check the contents of the tables, especially during banquets. The list of offenders is published and sometimes fines are imposed. Marianne Coudry was able to show that, contrary to the assertions of many, these laws were the result of a meticulous legislative work since the maximum authorized expenses followed the evolution of prices[98]. The historian notes that the opponents of these laws changed their arguments: at first, they criticized the very principle of these laws, then they questioned their effectiveness before arguing that, unfortunately (?), it would no longer be possible to oppose the now inevitable character of the development of luxury. This last argument will be that of the emperor Tiberius explaining that one cannot go against the refinements of the palace born of the imagination and the intelligence. These laws will fall into disuse under the Empire in spite of Julian's attempt.

The kitchen of subterfuges and metamorphoses

The rich Romans never stopped cheating with the sumptuary laws. One could oppose, on the one hand, the cuisine of metamorphoses, whose objective is to play with the forbidden, since it proposes authorized dishes by giving them the appearance, the form, the taste, of (temporarily) forbidden foods, and, on the other hand, the cuisine of deception, which gives the appearance and the taste of authorized dishes to forbidden products. One suspects that neither the motivations nor the sanctions are identical, but these two strategies nevertheless allowed for considerable progress in the field of culinary technology[99]. Oysters, for example, were replaced by mushroom-based compositions, and lamb's liver, poultry or artichokes were substituted for fish flesh. Petronius describes a beautiful deception: "However, to cut the boar, one did not see the "Cutter" who had torn the poultry to pieces, but a huge bearded man [...]; he took out his hunting knife and struck the boar's belly strongly: from the opening thrushes flew out. There were some birders there, ready with their reeds coated with glue, who quickly caught the birds flying through the dining room" (Petronius, *Satiricon*, 40, trans. by Pierre Grimal). Athenaeus recalls the feat of a cook who presented a whole pig, half

---

98. Marianne Coudry, "Loi et société : la singularité des lois somptuaires de Rome", *Cahiers du Centre Gustave Glotz*, vol. 15, n° 1, 2004, p. 135-171.
99. Nicole BLANC and Anne NERCESSIAN, *La Cuisine romaine antique, op. cit.* and Pierre DRACHLINE (with Claude PETIT-CASTELLI), *À table avec César*, Paris, Éditions Sand, 1984.

          A political history of food. From the Pateolithic to our days

boiled, half roasted and, moreover, stuffed. Apicius explains that this cuisine of metamorphoses transforms food in such a way that "at the table, no one will recognize what one is eating". Trimalcion's cook turns a sow's vulva into a fish, bacon into a wood pigeon (Petronius, *Satiricon*, 70), and a ham into a turtledove. The Romans liked to play with the codes, mixing domestic and wild animals, cooked animals, therefore dead, and live birds. Thus, during the wedding meal of the young emperor Caracalla with Plautille, daughter of the prefect of the Pretorium, in 202, dishes were served in two ways: *basilikôs* and *barbarikôs*, in the Roman way (cooked meat) and in the barbarian way (raw meat and live animals).

The Roman cuisine of mixtures, unlike the Greek, is based on an excellent knowledge of flavors, consistencies, in short, of taste. The Romans differentiated seven flavors, two more than we do today: salty, sweet, sour, bitter, pungent, watery and aromatic. The watery flavor is that of cucumbers, the aromatic one that of celery. The Romans are well aware of the distinction between the perception at the level of the papillae and the retronasal perception, and even if they favor the latter, they know how to satisfy the former. The sensations of the palate are never neglected even if they are fleeting. The good cook is the one who knows how to play with the complementarities, or on the contrary, the oppositions between all these notes. Seneca takes a stand against mixtures, signs, according to him, of softness and decadence. The Stoic philosopher denounces the long march towards the unique flavor resulting from these constant mixtures which make that all will end up having the same taste.

The cuisines of subterfuge and metamorphosis are cuisines of mixtures. One might therefore be tempted to make them variants of the Greek principle, but this would be to fail to see everything that fundamentally differentiates them. Roman cuisine certainly accentuates the mixture of opposites, but by giving it a culinary, even artistic, if not ostentatious dimension, but absolutely not a political one.

Food distributions

It is necessary to bend the antiphon about the perversity that would have introduced the food distributions, first paying and then free, vilified under the expression of *panem et circenses* ("bread and games") taken from the satire of Juvenal. Paul Veyne has rehabilitated these practices, noting that far from feeding populism and demagoguery, they correspond to the highest possible degree of politicization[100]. In an economy that has not yet

---

100. Paul VEYNE, *Le pain et le cirque, op. cit.*

been fully monetized and with a State that does not benefit from the current infrastructure, distributing in kind what is needed to live is indeed the shortest way to enable everyone to live. More interesting would be to note that these distributions (free or not), the near disappearance of famines, the opulence of aristocrats, are based on the plundering of conquered territories, on wheat imported to Rome from North Africa. We would be wrong to think that these distributions would be the continuation of evergetism: the rich "patrons" certainly had the habit of distributing food (*sportules*) to their "clients" in the form of money or meal baskets. These distributions are also going to be totally emancipated from the religious. It was only on this double condition that they became systematic, since, no longer falling under the heading of alms, they changed their legal-political status to become part of a logic of rights.

The rich Romans did not cease to resist the assumption of responsibility for supply by the cities and to express their preference for evergetism "which designates the generosity shown by individuals for the good of the community"[101]. Moreover, this system does not regress with the system of distributions. It was necessary for Rome to establish rules to curb the (false) generosity of the rich, for example by instituting a rotation of roles to allow each aristocrat to prove his generosity without maintaining the suspicion of clientelism. The introduction of the great frumentary law of Caius Gracchus in 123-122 B.C. was therefore above all a bad blow against the aristocracy. The brothers Tiberius Sempronius Gracchus and Caius Sempronius Gracchus, the Gracchi, tribunes of the plebs, had a real political program which was not reduced to the monthly distribution of a bushel of wheat at a reduced price to poor citizens. They tried to organize a profound change in society, notably through an agrarian reform (with a law limiting land ownership and providing for the redistribution of land to the poorest, with the foundation of 12 colonies of 3,000 men chosen among the poorest). In 123 BC, Tiberius Gracchus not only established a new principle by instituting the regularity of distributions, he also gave the people (as legislators) the authority in this matter instead of the Senate and the magistrates. Caius Gracchus then built many granaries. This wheat, which henceforth belonged to the people, came either from the tithe or from purchases made by the State. This law was not only intended, like many other Roman laws, to testify, but will be applied. Pages would not suffice to give an account of all the attempts of the richest to free

---

101. Peter GARNSEY, "Les raisons de la politique : approvisionnement alimentaire et consensus politique dans l'Antiquité" *in* Jean-Louis Flandrin and Massimo MONTANARI (eds.), *Histoire de l'alimentation, op. cit*, p. 245.

A political history of food. From the Pateolithic to our days

themselves from collective obligation by organizing their own banquets and redistributions, and this from the end of the 1st century B.C. to the beginning of the 1st century A.D. This conflict over the conception of a good society lasted three centuries. The Empire continued the republican adventure on this point by formalizing the cereal allocation and even gradually extending it to other products, while maintaining the principle of the state monopoly. The institution of the annone was reorganized on several occasions, notably under Augustus: 200,000 Roman citizens residing in Rome benefited from grain distributions, distributions that were sufficiently regular and abundant to allow them to live normally, and even to resell a surplus.

The Romans did not invent this system *ex nihilo*, but from multiple experiences. Athens had faced the terrible famine of 329 BC thanks to wheat distributions. The island of Samos had even set up a permanent system financed by the rich taxpayers. We could also cite other examples, in Egypt, and even in Mesopotamia. What is new with the Roman system is its scope, its ideology and, above all, the fact that it no longer concerns periods of food crisis or abundance, as Greece had done, but becomes systematic. Before the establishment of this annunciation system, the Senate already distributed cereals episodically from the first centuries of Roman history. Then, from the 2nd century BC, it was the town councillors who collected the wheat and organized sales at moderate prices in case of supply difficulties. The stroke of genius of Caius Gracchus resulted from a lucid examination of the situation in Rome. It takes note of the transformations appeared in the economic conditions of the market of Rome, henceforth supplied by the provincial regions, it also takes note of the considerable urban development of Rome[102]. Caius Gracchus therefore established the revolutionary principle that it was the government's right to ensure the city's supplies: "For the first time in Rome, the care of supplies appeared to be a constant public responsibility that the government of the Republic had to ensure [...] The frugal law of Caius Gracchus replaced the practice of extraordinary distributions with the commitment to ensure regular distributions to all Roman citizens. It was only after Caius Gracchus that measures were taken to fix a precise number of beneficiaries and thus to limit, within the body of citizens, the number of entitled persons"[103]. I will recall that the distributions are not free then, but less expensive. The objective is above all to avoid the usual

---

102. Henriette Pavis d'Escurac, *La préfecture de l'annone, service impérial d'Auguste à Constantin*, "Bibliothèque des Écoles françaises d'Athènes et de Rome", Publications de l'École française de Rome, 1978.
103. *Id. at ibid.*

wastage due to disordered mass arrivals, which are therefore unable to be stored. The system of free distribution, imagined by Caius Gracchus, is particularly well organized: only a part of the adult male citizens, domiciled in Rome, are entitled to it. The State drew up a list of entitled persons and kept it within strict limits. Cato in 62 BC and Claudius in 58 BC granted the right to wheat to almost all the plebs. Caesar, in 46 BC, reduced the number of beneficiaries from 320,000 to 150,000[104]. These distributions were never called into question, however, and they gradually included other foodstuffs such as oil, salt and pork. Thus, in 367 AD, 317,333 people benefited from pork distributions. These distributions were the object of conflicts to suppress or increase them: Claudius was thus taken to task by the crowd which bombarded him with bread croutons. Septimius Severus left, at his death, in the granaries housing the State's wheat, reserves equivalent to seven years of free distributions, proof that the system worked well[105]. These free distributions will never suppress the evergetism, the private liberalities, because its finality differs. In 28 B.C., Octavian had a quadruple ration of wheat distributed; in 23 B.C., Augustus financed, with his own money, 12 distributions of wheat to the plebs.

Setting the rates

The edict of the maximum, issued by the emperor Diocletian in 301, is the third type of food policy. It set the prices of the main foodstuffs on sale in the markets. It generalized ancient practices. During the French Revolution, the Conventionnels remembered this with the law on the maximum (1793).

The legend of Apicius

Apicius is a bi-legendary cook whose name serves as much to idealize as to demonize the Roman table. It does not matter that Apicius actually lived and that he was the author of the famous *De re coquinaria*, the only great recipe book of Roman antiquity that has come down to us[106]. Some people

---

104. *Id., ibid.*

105. Catherine Virlouvet, "La consommation de céréales dans la Rome du Haut-Empire [Les difficultés d'une approche quantitative]" in *Histoire & Mesure*, vol. 10, n° 3-4, 1995, thematic issue: *Consumption*, p. 261-275.

106. Bruno Laurioux, "Cuisiner à l'antique : Apicius au Moyen Âge" in *Médiévales*, vol. 13, n° 26, 1994, thematic number *Savoirs d'anciens*, p. 17-38 ; Bruno Laurioux, "Athénée, Apicius et Platina. Gourmands et gourmets de l'Antiquité sous le regard des humanistes romains du XVᵉ siècle" in *Pratiques et discours alimentaires en Méditerranée de l'Antiquité à la Renaissance*. Actes du 18ᵉ colloque de la Villa Kérylos à Beaulieu-sur-Mer, les 4, 5 & 6 octobre 2007, "Cahiers de la Villa Kérylos", vol. 19, n° 1, Paris, Académie des Inscriptions et Belles Lettres, 2008, p. 389-407 ; Jacques André, *Apicius. L'art culinaire. De re coquinaria*, Paris, C. Klincksieck, 1965.

praise Apicius because he was able to dust off the Roman table thanks to his borrowings from Greek tradition. The Greek model that Apicius seems to defend is in fact that of a Romanized Greece, but Romanized by an Empire already decadent (subjected to the good pleasures of the rich). The name of Apicius is still attached today to some food feats (or misdeeds), such as the chartering of a ship to fetch shrimps reputed to be better in Libya, but, disappointed by their size, the crew returned empty-handed. Pliny also mentions the stews of cockerel's crests torn from the living animal, mixed with goose feet, as part of this "great Roman cuisine". Many, like Seneca, will not cease to denounce "all the monstrosities of a luxury which, disgusted with the whole piece, chooses certain parts of the animal, forsaking all the rest, such as the dishes of tongues of pink flamingos". For Apicius' detractors, what is at issue is not the waste of food (in the economic sense), but a loss of the sense of the table. Many people make Apicius responsible for the Roman decadence, and therefore for the loss of its culinary tradition. In the 1st century AD, the poet Martial wrote a very critical funeral oration: "You had already, Apicius, sacrificed twice 30 million sesterces to your greed, you still had a good ten million left. Not being able to make you with a situation which represented for you hunger and thirst, you swallowed - supreme beverage - a cup of poison. Never Apicius, you showed yourself more greedy." The emperor Tiberius, intending to do a political pedagogy, is served (and let it be known), during the great ceremonies, the remains of the previous day or "simply" a half-boar, declaring that it has the same qualities as a whole boar.

Julian the Apostate

The figure of Julian is more surprising in a work devoted to the political history of food because he was an emperor and not a cook, but also because he is especially (badly) known for having abjured his Christian faith. Julian the Apostate proposes a new articulation between frugality and abundance, by advocating and practicing private frugality and public abundance. Julian takes up an old tradition that the Empire had forgotten. The perfect aristocrat is the one who knows to sacrifice for the common good. I believe that it is also on this ground that one must seek to understand Julian's sacrificial zeal rather than to denounce his hypothetical madness. What is certain is that Julian's soldiers will be obese from eating meat. Our chance is that Julian not only sacrificed a lot, he also wrote a lot about the meaning of sacrifice itself. He considers sacrifice useless for the immaterial gods, but indispensable for the gods of the sublunary region who are in charge of protecting men in their nation. The Jewish god is thus the material god in charge of this nation. The bloody sacrifice is indispensable from the political point of view, according to Julian, because it makes it possible to build a nation through the distribution of the sacrificed meat.

What do the Romans eat?

The Roman diet is structured around two main moments: the midday meal called the *prandium* and the evening meal called the *convivium*[107]. For the Romans, real eating meant eating cold, hard food and *fruges*, but in the evening they indulged in meals where meat, hot food and soft food occupied a central place. There is no contradiction, however, since these two meals do not have the same function and do not address the same organs. The meal based on meat, hot and soft dishes, is addressed to the *gula*, which cannot be assimilated to mere gluttony, because it is an organ located between the throat and the esophagus. While the *prandium* aims at nourishing the body, which implies that it relies on *fruges*, on cold dishes and on dishes that harden, the *cena* does not aim at nourishing the body but at purging it, which supposes that it manages to soften it beforehand.

The prandium

The Roman ideal of life, both from the individual and collective point of view, is action, so the meal of the active Roman can only be the *prandium*. This meal is valued because it is frugal, vegetarian, cold and ideally made of leftovers. This is why the Roman is a vegetable eater par excellence. The soldier is a bread eater because bread is a symbol of citizenship. We can thus try to establish a parallel between the Greek banquet, symbol of citizenship, and the Roman bread, symbol of the "mobilizable peasant", thus of citizenship. We find the tension between the symbolism of the gesture and the symbolism of the food. This bread, political symbol, becomes, with the Christianization, a religious symbol. But what is an action worthy of being cited in the eyes of the Romans? The

---

107. Florence Dupont (*in* "Grammaire de l'alimentation et des repas romains", art. cit.) takes up the classic opposition of the *cena* and the *prandium* and cites the tension between *cena* and *convivium*: "The Romans knew two opposite types of meals, the *cena* and the *prandium*. The first brings together men who always lie down (if there are women, they are traditionally seated) in a covered place - house, portico or garden topped with a *velum*; a well-defined social group - family, clientele, friends of the same age, professional or priestly college, neighbors - shares the pleasures of the table on the occasion of a feast. The number of guests is limited to about ten, but the number of dining rooms can be increased. If the bankers can be limited to the inhabitants of a farm - a peasant, his wife, his sons, his brothers, his grandsons, a few farmhands - the *cena* remains a feast, despite its limited luxury; it is never part of everyday life. When it takes on important dimensions, the *cena* can be called *convivium*."

philosophers answer: the professions of soldier, peasant and politician, in short everything that keeps one away from home, everything that forces one to *prandium*.

A cereal eater made of mush

The Roman is not initially a meat eater but a cereal eater. The porridge was for a long time the emblem of the Roman table (originally barley porridge) because it was the emblem of frugality and civilization (working the land).

Three ages can be distinguished: that of porridges, unleavened cakes and that of bread. This change is essential on the culinary and symbolic level, even if the private and public life will remain punctuated by cereal rituals. The mythical king Numa Pompilius, in founding the religious ritual of Rome, would indeed have given a central place to cereal offerings. The vestals, guardians of the temple where the hearth of the *Urbs* burned, prepared the *mola salsa*, a sacred composition made of roasted and salted flour. The demarcation of properties is also done (symbolically) with offerings of porridges and cakes (specific recipes). The young bride, guardian of the home, receives a flour cake. Varro, a Roman writer and scholar, who was interested in agriculture, defended the association of porridge with the very idea of civilization because "as far as food is concerned, nothing is older than porridge", so eating porridge, like the Romans, is to be part of the very long term. This traditional porridge, made of cereals (barley, wheat, wheat), is seasoned with herbs, olive oil, goat cheese, honey, eggs. It is sometimes accompanied by meat, but more often still, by fish. This feature does not disappear with the adoption of bread, from the 2nd century BC, because it is always accompanied by vegetables (cabbage, leeks, cucumbers...).

The adoption of bread

The good society is at the origin of the passage from porridge to unleavened cakes and then to bread. Bread takes with it an essential dimension since it becomes the symbol of commensality, as the famous scene where Caesar punishes a slave for having served non-identical breads attests. To serve different pieces of bread is to commit a social fault, it is to disrespect the commensality, thus transgressing the very meaning of the meal. This does not mean that there is only one type of bread, quite the contrary. Bakers prepare dozens of breads expressing different meanings. These breads differ according to their flours, their shapes, their tastes, their colors, their smells, etc. The first message is of course social. Not everyone can afford a white bread, made with flour. The servants eat bread made with flour mixed with bran. However, one must take into account the messages associated with the shapes, colors and spices. The *pistor* ("baker") masters these codes perfectly, for example concerning the presence of honey, anise, cumin, etc. I will not go back over the difficulty of the baker's work, which has been pointed out by so many authors. I will insist on the fact that the work of cereals (a product that is nevertheless valued) is the work of slaves or women, as if the one in charge of feeding (because cereals are the very symbol of food) had to be dominated.

Aristocratic Rome will debate endlessly about this passage from cereal porridges to bread-making, made possible by the abandonment of spelt in favor of naked wheat. Isn't the characteristic of the Roman to be a porridge eater? Some philosophers and agronomists, such as Varron, refuse for themselves and the society this passage to bread, symbol of Hellenization (envied or decried), therefore mark of an identity loss, of softness. This change had an effect on the food balance because, to the detriment of cereals considered less noble and lucrative than wine, the Romans reinforced the place of the vine, especially around the cities. The emperor Domitian forbade, in 92, (without apparent success) the planting of vines in and around Rome, to defend the vegetable gardens and fields.

Canned vegetable eaters

The Romans were supposed to eat cereal porridges and bread, but their consumption of vegetables and legumes was considerable. The ideal of life for every citizen is to have a vegetable garden, because eating vegetables and legumes is a reminder of his peasant origins. The Romans eat more or less the same vegetables as we do, but they use them in a different way since they mainly consume preserved food. The techniques of conservation are varied, but all have the consequence of modifying the organoleptic characteristics of the foodstuffs without this bothering the Romans, who prefer modified products. Vegetables were preserved in brine, in vinegar, in absinthe mixed with water, but also dried, crushed, grilled, etc. The Romans ate beans, lentils, which were also the soldier's food because they were supposed to give strength, salads, leeks, garlic and onions, parsnips, carrots, cabbage, asparagus, cucumbers, artichokes, etc. I give special importance to lettuce (lettuce of course, but not only) because if the Romans are salad eaters, it is because, for them, it symbolizes the grass, therefore the vegetable world. Eating grass has regained, for the Romans, a legitimacy lost by the Greeks. Salads are usually eaten at the beginning of the meal (with the eggs). They are eaten by hand, simply dipped in a

A political history of food. From the Pateolithic to our days

bowl of sauce. The Romans also made great use of legumes. These foods are the support of food symbolism: beans are the food of manual work, because the Romans, who like to play with etymology (often erroneously), explain that the beans, *fabae* come from *faber* which means "made with art", "ingenious" and by extension "worker", "craftsman"[108]...

From olives to olive oil

Olives, preserved by brining, were served as a complement to bread (access to different varieties of olives depended on social status), but the Romans used, like all Mediterranean tables, olive oil as the main source of fat. This oil has a deeply distorted taste due to its storage conditions. The sealing of the earthenware jars is done with wax or gums. The oil, the coarsest, intended for lighting, was also used to feed the poor. Diocletian's edict distinguishes three types of oil: first-pressed green oil, the best, but totally inaccessible to the common man; second-pressed oil costs half as much as green oil but is reserved for the well-to-do; ordinary oil costs a quarter of the value of green oil but remains too expensive for many. There are therefore by-products, second or third press oils. While some people pride themselves on recognizing the best oils by their purity, many flavour them with herbs to make them edible.

Spices and condiments

The Romans did not only eat to live, as shown by their great use of condiments, a sign of the search for taste, and therefore pleasure. Besides garlic, the condiment of the poor, the Roman table was flavored with celery, coriander, bay leaves, lovage, mint, mustard, cumin, myrrh, onion, oregano, parsley, savory, thyme, fennel and, of course, the famous *garum*, the emblem of Roman cuisine. This product actually dates back to the last centuries of Roman history.

Garum is a semi-aqueous solution, composed of three layers of fish intestines macerated with dry herbs. This product has a very strong taste and is used to season dishes. Real *garum* factories offer very different products. Connoisseurs know how to distinguish between the different recipes and talk about them with gusto. The most valuable is the Cartagena garum made with mackerel intestines. Its recipe is based on the principle of mixing, dear to the Greeks, and the principle of successive layers, so dear

---

108. Mireille Corbier also notes this approximate etymology, but how revealing: "Some dishes - and especially vegetables, such as beans or chard - are only poor or "worker" foods (a play on words justified by the combination of *faba*, "bean" and *faber*, "worker" (in *Histoire de l'alimentation, op. cit.* p. 215).

---

to the Romans. Anticipating developments, I think that the symbolism is different since the mixture refers to the great invariants of the political world, while the principle of superimposed layers is a sign of abundance, of generosity. The Roman aromatic bouquet is very diversified but more than a subtle balance of flavors, the guests like to find dominant tones. Some people explain this taste by the mainly vegetal character of their diet, but comparative history shows that nothing is systematic in this field: sometimes, people whose diet is largely vegetal use very few condiments, and vice versa. The search for taste is not unanimously shared by all, nor especially the taste (very Roman) for the confusion of flavors often under the dominance of one of them... The use of *garum* is such that it competes with salt, knowing that the *garum* is itself concocted by strongly salting entrails. However, *garum* will never have a real political status, which is why it does not appear in the (free) food distributions, while salt will be there alongside bread, wine and oil.

Plutarch describes salt as an indispensable complement "without which nothing is edible", "because as colors need light, flavors need salt to excite the sensation, otherwise their contact is heavy to the taste and disgusting". Salt is therefore both the main preservative (vegetables, meat, fish) and the emblem of the search for taste. The enriched Romans also made great use of exotic spices, such as pepper and ginger. This search for an excess of taste through seasoning is not unanimous. Thus, the comic poet and philosopher Plautus protests strongly: "I do not season a dinner like other cooks who serve you a whole meadow to season their dishes; who take the guests for oxen and present them with herbs that they accommodate with other herbs. They put coriander, fennel, garlic, parsley; they add sorrel, cabbage, chard and chard; they dilute a whole pound of silphium juice; they pile mustard, an awful drug, which cannot be pounded without making the waiters' eyes water."

The right question is not to appreciate (or not) the seasonings used by the Romans, but to note their importance, a sign, on the one hand, of the search for taste and pleasure, and, on the other hand, of their will to denaturalize the dishes. In other words, even if we could grow the same varieties from seeds found in the excavations, even if we cooked them in the same way, the preparations would no longer speak to us mentally. Nothing seemed to be better than a product from agriculture (and not from gathering), as long as it was transformed to the point of not recognizing it anymore. Spices and condiments, considered a public resource, were massively stocked by the authorities. Thus, Caesar destocked several hundred tons of silphium to finance the civil war.

The status of the pastry shop

Pastry-making gradually lost its initial religious character, even if it was still a question of making cakes as similar as possible to animals: for example, many birds were made with wheat paste. The desacralization of pastry making made the happiness of the small itinerant merchants and the profession of pastry maker (*dulciarius*) moved away from the temple. The ancient substitutes offered as sacrifices became delicacies, but the main ingredients remained the same, such as, of course, honey. The roborative character of this pastry is often evoked, but without sufficiently questioning the meaning of these alternating layers of semolina and cheese in a pastry crust. The analysis of this type of cake (*placenta*) however helps to understand the meaning of the compositions. This *placenta* was initially made in a religious setting, either at home or purchased from a specialized pastry chef, the *placentarius*. This cake, necessarily large, is intended to be cut into squares. This pastry, made with leafy dough, is a symbol of wealth and fertility. The word *placenta*, which became the generic name for all cakes, was gradually replaced by that of *dolcia* (idea of sweetness). Cato gives a recipe for *placenta* in his *De agricultura*: it is mainly flour and sheep's cheese in layers. This layered cuisine (placenta/fish and meat dishes/garum) is a promise of fertility and fertility.

Honey is the last product that we must mention, underlining its ambiguous status, at the same time product offered in sacrifice and, as such, basic ingredient of pastry, but also product of common use. Honey is found (almost) everywhere: in drinks, as food, as a preservation process... The edict of Diocletian distinguishes three types of honey and sanctions the numerous adulterations, like the addition of water or starch. The Romans used a lot of honey in drinks: honeyed wine (*mulsum*), honeyed beer, honeyed water, without forgetting the mead (honeyed water exposed to the sun to ferment). To question the place of honey is also to question the status of sweetness. It has been said that it would be the counterpart of a table with burning flavors, notably during the Empire, with an extravagant use of pepper. We can also think that honey refers to the fascination of the Romans for beehives, as a model of society, with hard-working and frugal bees.

Boiled, roasted, simmered

Many authors justify the Romans' preference for boiled food by its more economical nature, while also pointing out the considerable waste that the "great Roman kitchen" caused. This choice of boiled food probably has other justifications: the first one is the one given by Varro who, in establishing a chronology of the successive cooking methods, notes that humanity passed from the age of the grill, to that of the roast, and, finally, to the boiled food, thus doing away with the simmer. The Romans generally respected this principle of civilization, even if they debated it much less than the Greeks and if they did not hesitate to boil the meat before roasting it, a process that has become classic, which however constitutes a transgression of chronological sequences. Let us remember, with Marcel Detienne, that the superiority of broth over roast meat is not primarily culinary but cultural. However, the Romans also appreciated simmered cooking (slow cooking with a sauce), as shown by the abundance of lids and other dish covers and casseroles for stews. The pieces of meat that are simmered are usually first roasted in the oven. Lévi-Strauss, after having adopted several versions of the culinary triangular model (the raw, the cooked as a cultural transformation of the raw, the rotten as a natural transformation of the raw) with three methods of preparation (roasting/boiling/smoking) corresponding to the three poles of the culinary triangle, will enlarge it with a third axis, that of oil, to form a roasted/boiled, smoked, fried tetrahedron. Lévi-Strauss will be more and more interested in mixed cooking and in more complex cooking methods. The Christian apologist Arnobe wrote that grilled meat is half cooked. Eating boiled food is therefore for a Roman more civilized and cultured. The other reason is that boiled food is perfectly suited to the culinary strategies that underpin the kitchens of metamorphosis or subterfuge. Boiled meat allows for much more complex compositions, it gives the cook the possibility of having the whole animal at his disposal and therefore, for example, to be able to stuff it more easily or to hide other dishes in it. A final, more trivial reason is put forward insofar as the choice of boiling would be the obligatory consequence of salting, boiling salted pork quarters is undeniably the simplest way to use them. Florence Dupont writes (*in* "Grammaire de l'alimentation et des repas romains", art. cit.): "Lévi-Strauss's culinary triangle, applied to Roman foodstuffs, shows that edible animals are distributed along an axis ranging from the most raw to the most rotten, from the hardest to the softest, from lard to oysters. The oyster, soft, wet and cold, is already so corrupted that many men eat it hot (roasted) and peppered, even if it means seriously damaging their liver and stomach. Bacon, the fatty meat of the pig hardened by desiccation (salting, drying, smoking), is the only animal flesh that can be preserved and eaten boiled."

A political history of food. From the Pateolithic to our days

The political status of vegetables

The Romans are therefore eaters of cereals, vegetables and fruits, but not by necessity, not in the same way and for the same reasons as we do. To eat cereals, vegetables and fruits is to be civilized. The Romans, who loved these products, never ceased to expand the range of plants available, thanks to conquests, trade and agronomy. Roman agronomists were all the more important because every Roman, and especially every aristocrat, wanted to be an amateur agronomist for whom it was appropriate to have a garden and farmland and to cultivate them oneself. Jacques André has clearly seen this political-philosophical perception of vegetable products, a sign not only of civilization but also of property[109]. The Romans argued endlessly about the characteristics of products, especially the new ones that they had imported from their colonies. The same product, such as cabbage for example, can be adulated for different reasons. Felius (Caius Laelius) praises it because he is a Pythagorean and a vegetarian. Cato the Elder, the most important agronomist of Roman antiquity, also praised it because he saw it as a symbol of frugality. He even proposed dozens of recipes while conceding his preference for cabbage eaten almost plain. He makes the loss of frugality a cause of decadence, therefore of softness.

Always more meat!

The Roman table was initially less meaty than the Egyptian and Greek tables, because if the consumption of meat was never taken for granted in ancient civilizations, it was even less taken for granted in the Roman civilization. Meat has an ambiguous status: it is both a danger in an agricultural society and the sign of social, economic, but also political success. This is already why a large part of the population is forbidden to eat meat, because its consumption is considered derogatory to its social status and needs. This is the case of slaves, the poor and, in general, of rural people. It is also the case for pregnant women and young children. Meat may be all the more reserved for the elites as less and less meat is sacrificed than in Greece and this meat is redistributed to the senators only or sold for the benefit of the public treasury, thus not offered to the people. As for the meat from private sacrifices, it belongs to those who offer it.

The Romans classified animals, but in a different way than we do. They distinguished animals according to where they lived, in the water, on land or in the air. The livestock is the usual one (cows, oxen, sheep, goats, etc.), but with a very marked preference for very robust animals. No doubt the

---

109. Jacques ANDRÉ, *L'Alimentation et la cuisine à Rome, op. cit.*

desire not to distinguish between butchery and hunting meat explains, at least in part, this preference for large animals. This confusion between breeding and hunting led in parallel to the raising of game in enclosures (*Leporaria*, a term coming from *lepus*, "hare"), in particular wild boars, roe deer, stags, hares, and to the construction of aviaries for thrushes, turtle doves, pigeons, ortolans, quails, partridges... These animals, raised in a semi-wild manner, were fed differently according to the tastes sought: thus a wild boar can be fed exclusively with flours or acorns, according to the gustatory intentions of the owner.

Meat in Republican Rome

The meat, even consumed by the good society, is of poor quality because it is mainly cull animals. Literary testimonies abound, which establish that the Romans were not meat lovers. Petronius writes that no meat has a pleasant taste in itself. It would simply be the art of the cook who, by denaturing it, would make it acceptable. Meat is generally eaten very well cooked and cooked in sauce. This cutting into pieces does not have the same political status as in Greece: it is simply a matter of making edible what otherwise would not be. Much has been written about the appeal of stuffing and offal used in stuffing, without sufficiently noting that this is already a way of euphemizing meat. One should not imagine that the Romans were vegetarians, for if they ate little butcher's meat, they devoured pork and poultry.

Pork meat

Pork is almost not a meat for the Romans, or at least not a meat like the others. It is already a food in itself. It can therefore be consumed widely since it is naturally "cooked" and "hard". Pliny adds a culinary argument: no animal provides more food for gourmandise: its meat has about 50 flavors, while that of others gives only one. I am only partially convinced by this thesis because it seems to justify *a posteriori a* choice already made. The pig is indeed the only animal raised exclusively for the butchery. Its exceptionality is more profound than its organoleptic characteristics. The most sought-after cuts are the vulva and the sow's teat. They can be offered as gifts or twice at the same banquet. The encyclopedist Macrobius makes it the very prototype of the luxurious meal. This predilection for (feminine) stockings has a sexual connotation. The Romans also consumed bull's testicles but without giving them the same importance.

The Roman henhouse

The Roman henhouse is very diversified: chickens, wood pigeons, ducks, doves, thrushes, geese, chicks, guinea fowl, peacocks, flamingos, woodcocks, partridges, pheasants, etc. This enumeration voluntarily mixes domestic and wild poultry, because the Romans, in this field as in others, chose to mix the genres. The wild poultry that was captured was parked and very often fattened. Geese, but also pigeons, pheasants... were fattened with the best, like figs or flour mixtures. The Romans reacted to the laws that forbade the consumption of hens (in favor of eggs) by learning to castrate roosters to make capons. The consumption of eggs is considerable in the whole society. We have seen that eggs (from ducks, peacocks and hens) are most often eaten as an appetizer (during the moment called *gustatio*), their shells having to be broken immediately after consumption to prevent an evil spirit from using them to cast a spell.

Meat in Imperial Rome

Imperial Rome was much more carnivorous than republican Rome, even if the Church, triumphant since the conversion of Constantine in the 4th century, looked with caution on any consumption of meat, potentially diabolical since it was the result of sacrifices to false gods, and therefore to demons. This change in diet concerns only a few of the popular masses. Firstly, for financial reasons: the plebs had less and less means to buy meat because of the weakening of the middle classes; secondly, because this more meaty diet gave rise to social tensions, because of the monopolization of land for the benefit of livestock.

The transition to a more meaty diet is not only justified by a practice of social distinction, but by the concern to develop values more in line with the new ideological imperatives, which are those of imperial Rome, i.e. its warrior spirit, and therefore carnivorous. Hunting is thus valued but as a preparation for war. It has an educational value because it trains courage and boldness but it also has a religious value because it interferes with funerary themes. The Romans copied the Hellenic hunts and created an important venry. The roe deer, until then privileged, gave way, under the Empire, to the wild boar, the latter presenting physiological and symbolic characteristics more exploitable within the framework of the spectacularization of the table. A sumptuary law from the beginning of the 1st century B.C. had already tried to reduce the consumption of wild boar during large feasts, but obviously without success.

The fish

Unlike butcher's meat, which is largely excluded from the popular table, fish is particularly present thanks to the fish markets organized independently of the other markets, but also in the form of *hallec* (or *allec*, residues of fish flesh from the manufacture of *garum*) and *garum*.

Cheese lovers

Cheese occupies an important place in the Roman table. Civilization began for the Romans with cheese because it was based on human work (and incidentally provided reserves). On the other hand, drinking milk remains, even more than eating meat, a barbaric behavior, unworthy of a civilized Roman.

What do the Romans drink?

It is said that Rome was a civilization of wine, that is saying too much or not enough. The Romans drink wine and know how to drink it, but not in the way of the Greeks. The Romans distinguished four types of wine. The *calda*, wine in the current sense of the term, always consumed diluted with water and, in principle, hot water; the *posca*, which is a spiked wine, but not yet at the stage of vinegar, a drink initially intended for soldiers but which will become that of the workers; the "piquette", made with vinegar diluted to the tenth, is the drink of the plebs, the *lora*, made by passing water over the marc after pressing, initially reserved for slaves during the three months following the harvest, will be bought by the common people, particularly because of its low cost. The average consumption of wine (all categories combined) is estimated at 1 hectoliter per person per year, knowing that wine is strictly forbidden to women under penalty of death, because it is accused of being responsible for giving birth to monsters. The Romans drank a lot of wine, but not in the way of the Greeks because they did not make it the basis of the *convivium*, nor of the Egyptians because it was not a drink reserved only for the aristocracy.

Wine accompanied every moment of the day, thanks in particular to the taverns (*tabernae* and *popinae*). Wine was an integral part of the diet, beyond its caloric intake: it was used to "wet" the bread consumed during breakfast (*jentaculum*), it was often part of the *pulmentarium*, to which everyone was entitled, including slaves. Cato concedes them, for example, three quarters of a liter of wine per day. For a long time, the plebs demanded that wine be part of the free distributions. The emperor Augustus, questioned by the crowd, refused to take charge of the wine to face the shortage. Suetonius gave him the following answer:

A political history of food. From the Pateolithic to our days

"My son-in-law Agrippa, by building several aqueducts, provided sufficiently for no one to be thirsty" (Suetonius, *Aug.* , 42, 1). Wine was finally included in the free distributions, but only from the 2nd century AD. I am not sure that the water/wine mixture had the same status in ancient Rome as in Greece, even if the Romans gave it (at least) the same importance. Thus Caesar judged the Gauls to be "barbarians" because they drank their wine pure, and one could be punished for not cutting one's wine. The status of the Roman mixture refers to the control of drunkenness and especially to that of luxury.

The ceremonial of wine is complex for practical and cultural reasons. Wine is naturally thick, so it must be filtered through sieves. It is also necessarily cut with water (if possible hot but sometimes cold), this water is itself often "prepared" to be purified. It is usually boiled and then, sometimes, cooled in a snow bath thanks to products sold by ice merchants. Martial reminds us (*Epigrams*, XIV, 117) that we should not "drink snow, but water that the snow has frozen, it is an invention of our ingenious thirst". Wine is mostly drunk outside of the meal, with the exception of honeyed and flavored wine consumed with hors d'oeuvres. The consumption of wine at the end of the meal is the most important and occurs regularly at the time of the *comissatio* "a feast with music and dance followed by a walk in procession to bring back one of the guests and to start again the feast", which can go until the "orgy", another meaning of the word *comissatio*. A slave holds the role devolved, at the time of the Greek *symposion*, to the symposiarque. The Romans used special kettles to keep the water hot throughout a meal, thanks to a compartment with embers in the center of the container.

The conservation of wine in jars coated with pitch or resin modifies the taste of the liquid... and not to its advantage. Moreover, many Roman wines were smoked because they were kept above the kitchens, and the cooking fumes pierced the porous walls of the terracotta amphorae. In addition, the Romans did not shy away from certain curious mixtures, such as wine with sea water. More classic are the flavored wines which they make a great use (honeyed wine, wine with spices, wine of violets, wines of roses, etc.). In the classification of wines, the Romans opposed young wines to old wines, but a wine is said to be old as soon as it exceeds one year. However, one drinks vintages that are several decades old. The ancient vinification is more efficient than those of the following centuries thanks to the application of a coating of boiling pitch which sterilizes the containers/amphorae and to the use of corks or terracotta lids which allow gas exchanges. In conclusion, it should be noted that the Romans did not recognize the value of wine as being comparable to that of the Greek table and drank at least as much mead and beer as wine, which was used massively in cooking, for the preparation of sauces.

The convivium

The term *convivium* insists on the objective of a friendly conviviality[110]. The Roman *convivium* is neither the Egyptian worldly meeting nor the Greek banquet. However, it obeys rules that are just as restrictive[111]. Let us recall that the *convivium* is an "anti-prandium" because it is addressed to different organs. We shall see, however, that the *cena* has progressively moved from a friendly meeting to a new device where everyone competes for wealth, to the point of calling into question the notions of gift and counter-gift.

The organization of the convivium under the Republic

The *cena* has three main moments. The *gustatio* allows the serving of appetizers, most often eggs, salad, vegetables, fish in brine, more rarely shellfish, all washed down with a honeyed wine (*mulsum*): "My steward has brought me laxative mallows and the varied riches of my garden, the flattened lettuce and the leek to be sliced, without forgetting the flattering mint and the arugula that brings love. Minutely cut eggs will crown anchovies on a bed of street food, and there will be sow's teats spiced up with tuna brine" (Martial, X, 48). Everyone will have already understood that the principle of the *gustatio* is to serve only cold dishes. The second moment is that of the *primae mensae* (or "first service") with meats, roasted or boiled fish, always accompanied by vegetables: "A kid saved from the teeth of a ferocious wolf, grilled chops, broad beans and young green cabbage. To this will be added a chicken and a ham that has already survived three meals" (Martial, X, 48). The third moment is that of the *secondae mensae* (or "second service") during which one offers fruits, olives, lupine seeds and other salted dishes, sometimes cakes, wine, which can certainly accompany all the meal but which frames especially

---

110. Konrad Vössing, "Les banquets dans le monde romain : alimentation et communication" in *Dialogues d'histoire ancienne,* Supplément n° 7, 2012, p. 117-131, numéro thématique : *L'histoire de l'alimentation dans l'Antiquité. Bilan historiographique* - Journée de printemps de la SOPHAU, 21 mai 2011.
111. André Tchernia, "Le *convivium* romain et la distinction sociale" in *Pratiques et discours alimentaires en Méditerranée de l'Antiquité à la Renaissance.* Actes du 18e colloque de la Villa Kérylos à Beaulieu-sur-Mer, les 4, 5 & 6 octobre 2007, "Cahiers de la Villa Kérylos", vol. 19, n°1, Paris, Académie des Inscriptions et Belles Lettres, 2008, p. 147-156.

the entry and the after-meal: "When you will not be hungry any more, I will serve you ripe fruits, a bottle of Nomentum freed from its dregs and which reached twice three years under the Consulate of Frontinus (98 apr.C.)" (Martial, X, 48).

While the Greeks had to talk about serious things and therefore to be dressed in a serious way, the Romans were going to abandon the toga (clothing reserved for business and public life) to wear a light and elegant tunic (*cenatoria*), or even amusing disguises. Several practices aim besides to exclude the serious discussions, particularly the obliged use of clothing different from those used to lead business or to make politics, the presence of the women with equality with the men, the good taste which consists in excluding the remarks concerning the business or the politics, the practice which consists in enlivening the totality of the feast by making play wind instruments by slaves. This body of slaves, specialists in banquets, can be compared to that of the Greek "parasites", but without the political dimension which was attached to them.

One goes to the meal at the exit of the thermal baths, that is to say at the end of the eighth hour in winter, of the ninth in summer. It is the schedule adopted by Pliny the Younger (*Correspondence*, III, 1, 8-9) and by Martial, who gives an appointment to his friend Iulius Ceralis, at the eighth hour to take him to dinner at his place, after the bath (Martial, *Ep.* X, 52). One removes one's shoes before lying down, one also rinses one's hands. The beds (*lectus*) are placed in a "U" shape. The classic arrangement is three table beds with three places each (*triclinia*). It is possible to add multiples of three. This limitation of the number of guests does not answer the same objectives as within the framework of the Greek banquets: one remembers that the Greek banquet founds the citizenship on the friendship, it is thus possible to speak about it about policies of the friendship put at the service of the citizenship and the city. The guests must choose each other as a pledge of friendship. The feast is a *convivium*, its purpose does not exceed the private framework. The Roman table, because of the parvenus, made conviviality a luxury. The plebs, except perhaps the average plebs (under the Republic), no longer had the material conditions to receive guests (no sufficiently large spaces, no table beds, no servants, no expensive food). How do we know, on the other hand, that the conviviality of the taverns did not satisfy the desires of the plebs? What do we know about the conviviality in the *popinae*? Undoubtedly the plebeians found some pleasure there if one believes Juvenal, whose description of one of them enjoying the aroma of "a sow's vulva in a warm tavern" (*Satires*, XI, 79-81) was mentioned above.

The Romans (even more than the Egyptians and Greeks) placed considerable importance on the rules of precedence. The order of precedence on the beds was always from right to left, with the last place on the bottom (left) bed reserved for the most modest guest. With two exceptions, however, the place of honor is the third place in the middle bed and the host occupies the first place in the left bed, thus just opposite the guest of honor. The Roman *convivium* thus only apparently follows the figure of the fraternal circle. One eats necessarily leaning on the left elbow - which allows one to block the left part of the body (the feminine part) - and with the fingers, but in principle using only two fingers of the hand and dirtying only the first phalanx, it is customary to throw on the ground the remains of the meal to feed the powers of the earth and the souls of the dead. The sweeping is done (contrary to the Greek banquet) only after the departure of the guests.

This ritual will evolve with the adoption of the personal table bed but without upsetting the rituals. The maître d'hôtel, who for a long time was to remain an "altar master", since the profane and the religious were intermingled, ensured that the procedures were respected. The Roman table (the piece of furniture) could be round or square, it is in principle a piece of furniture with three curved legs in the shape of animal paws, the table is always covered with a rich fabric, the dishes and some food are stored there. This table occupies the central place devolved in the Greek banquet to the crater, sign of a shift from drink to food and, through them, from the mouth to the *gula*.

The figure of Lucullus

Lucius Licinus Lucullus (c. 115-c. 57 B.C.) is praised in all the gourmet stories. This statesman and Roman general hated by his troops is however representative of all the drifts of the Roman table, friend of Cicero and Sylla, leader of the conservative current opposed to the Gracchi. These men have for adversaries the *populares* who militate for the suppression of the debts of the poor peasants, the sharing of the grounds, the distributions of foodstuffs. One will keep simply of him the maxim "Lucullus dines at Lucullus" which means to make a sumptuous meal at its residence, without having guests, thus in violation of all the usual rules of the Roman commensality. Lucullus is the "anti-convivium" par excellence.

The end of the Republic is the golden age of great feasts (1st century BC)[112]. The Romans replaced the discourse on frugality and simplicity with another on abundance and luxury. The table gains in prowess what it loses in sharing. Its symbolism was transformed. The symbols are no longer primarily philosophical in nature, but serve to express power, and therefore remain political. They say the richness, the opulence, therefore the power, an economic power. The Roman *convivium* does not serve any more to say the friendly conviviality but to express relations of clientelism and ostentatious rivalry. It escapes the logic of gift and counter-gift because it is simply no longer possible to give equally, the richest not accepting to limit or restrict themselves. Under the Empire, the number of table beds and the number of guests increased, because the practice of friendly conviviality gave way to ostentatious practices. The number of dishes and services was multiplied and, in so doing, the duration of the *cena was* extended. We have a clear testimony of the decline of the Roman feast in the fact that women who used to participate in it only in a shifted way, by remaining seated on chairs, access the table bed, and thus the discussions. I don't think we can say that they imposed their presence, because they are admitted only because the *cena* loses its political dimension and because many customs forbid to talk about serious things. The participation of women is not the prelude to orgies but first the symptom of a privatization, then of an ostentatious strategy. One sufficiently insisted on the debauchery of luxury which relates to the dining room, the decoration, the crockery, the beds of table, the table, the dishes, the linen of table (which concerned initially the bed itself), the slaves (which must be beautiful, young, effeminate, dressed of luxurious clothing) to remain about it with the essential. During the 1st century the bed with one place (*stibadium*) replaces that with three places. One spoke about a search for comfort but it would be better to mention the loss of the significance of the bed of table. The abandonment of the *triclinium* ("bed with three places") is the mark of the abandonment of the Greek model. By abandonment, one should not understand the result of a reflection, but the abandonment of a use that no longer speaks. Pliny the Younger draws a picture of the debauches of luxury, to which this substitution of the bed with one place to the bed with three places gives rise: "The white marble *stibadium* is shaded by a trellis, supported by small columns, also of marble; from the

---

112. Konrad Vössing, "Les banquets dans le monde romain : alimentation et communication", art. cit.

table bed, as if the weight of the one who has just taken his place there made it gush, pipes pour water that falls on a hollowed slab and that is then held by a finely worked marble basin, which, thanks to an invisible mechanism, remains full without overflowing. The tray of appetizers and the heavy dishes are placed on the edge, the light dishes float here and there on displays in the shape of boats and birds" (Pliny the Younger, V, 6, 36-37). Each bed can be the object of a long and expensive work in cabinet making and goldsmithing. Some tables are worth the price of a farm. There is a growing distinction between tableware (intended to be used) and ceremonial tableware (which rests on the display stand). It is also customary to reduce the cuts in the kitchen in order to play with the kitchen of metamorphoses (and possibly deceptions) and to make animals presented whole, live birds, in front of the eyes of the guests, and, in order to enjoy the spectacle of cuts always more extraordinary. This function of cutter will later give birth to that of cutting squire. One always builds more *triclinium* (here *triclinium* (plur. *triclinii*) means "dining room") of summer in the open air, one installs them most often beside a fountain, but certain dining rooms are installed in caves (to play with mythology), the places are magnificently decorated with frescos, still lives, mosaics on the ground, etc. The motives, generally food, are so many invitations to enjoy, first by the sight, the dishes which are proposed as one enjoys the landscapes. We must not read these scenes (frescoes or mosaics) as distractions, because the Romans still believed in the omnipotence of images. Paul Veyne is right to say that this imagery means two things: "This is what life was like for them" and "so should we live because life is short". We find there the feeling that one must be aware of one's mortal character to be fully happy; but while the Egyptians and Greeks used morbid figurations, the Romans prefer to exhibit the beautiful life. Shows are given with mainly allegorical re-enactments which may refer to the guest of honor or to the food that will be served: hunting scenes are reproduced for game, fishing scenes for fish. These representations can mobilize many extras.

This luxury cuisine is designed to go against tradition. It is a way for the rich to secede by reversing the codes. Since the Roman kitchen is a thrifty kitchen, the kitchen of luxury of luxury must be a kitchen of waste. Mireille Corbier describes this opposition between the "great kitchen", a kitchen of waste, and a popular kitchen that recovers everything[113]. It was at this time that the Romans introduced the napkin, but it was not a piece of cloth used to wipe one's hands, because the use of the finger bowl

---

113. Mireille CORBIER, "La fève et la murène : hiérarchies sociales et nourritures à Rome", art. cit.

　　　　A political history of food. From the Pateolithic to our days

presented regularly by the servants was systematic, but a piece of cloth used to carry away the remains of the meal. This practice testifies to the survival of the tradition of offering gifts to the guests (from the food to the slaves who provided the service) and it is also a way of reintroducing evergetism, officially framed by the Roman laws. The parasites (this time in the modern sense) are now lacking in measure. Thus the poet Martial harshly denounces their abuses: "Everything that is served to you, you swallow from right to left: sow's teats, pork chops, rooster served by two, half a chicken and a whole wolf, fillet of moray eel and chicken leg, pigeon sprinkled with its juices, all of this is swallowed up in your soaked briefcase and then you give it to your young slave to take it home. As for us, we stay at the table without having anything more to do. If you are shameless, give us back our dinner; I did not invite you here tomorrow" (*Eph.*, II, 37).

Petronius, in the *Satiricon*, shows Trimalcion proposing, during his banquet, that a table be set for each guest as a sign of profanation of what was always the rule of sharing. However, it is not known if the questioning of commensality went that far, or if this example is the product of Petronius' cruel imagination towards the parvenus. The symbolic presence of a single table does not mean that all the guests are received with equal treatment. To be well served, everything depends in fact on the place granted on the beds and the instructions given to the slaves. It was customary to only take the pieces that were placed in front of you. The distribution of the dishes (from the best to the worst pieces) follows that of the places. The practice of taking one's own slave to help with one's personal service corrects, at the margin, this fundamental asymmetry.

Haute cuisine and contempt for cooks

The richness of the kitchenware of the rich houses is known, it concerns all the utensils necessary for the various types of cooking: the frying pans and sauté pans for frying and sautéing, the oven dishes for roasting, the pots for boiling, without forgetting all the necessary for grinding (mortar, filters), decorating (molds), cutting and seizing...

The more the cooking methods diversify (grilling, braising, sautéing, roasting, simmering, boiling), the more the know-how of the *coquus* ("cooks", plur. *coquii*) increases, the richer the kitchen becomes, the less the people in charge of preparing these sublime meals are considered! First indication of this change, when the kitchen migrates from the center of the house (where the same hearth was used to make offerings to the deities and the ancestors and to prepare the meals) to unhealthy outbuildings, not ventilated, not equipped with a smoke evacuation system. The second indication of this change is the creation of the profession of *coquus* in the service of the powerful, who were certainly in charge of preparing a ceremonial kitchen but who were decried. Thus Cicero (*De Officiis*, book I) condemns all the professions of mouth without exception. "All craftsmen devote themselves to a vile trade, the workshop cannot comprise anything well born and the least acceptable are the trades which are with the service of the pleasures (*quae ministrae sunt voluptatum*): fishmongers, butchers, cooks, pastry cooks, fishermen [...] "It is the Greek philosopher Athenaeus, hired by the Roman emperors, who will try to rehabilitate the kitchen and cooks... Athenaeus recalls that the foundation of the kitchen is found in Epicurus and Democritus, in short, the cook is as much the one who roasts the meat of the sacrifices, as the one who makes renounce to the raw meat, in short, it is a civilizer.

There is thus a Roman paradox: no civilization before Rome has carried so far the culinary arts but none has so despised the cooks. Why this detestation of the *coquus*? Why so few cookbooks? Why make it a slave or woman's job? Jack Goody helps us understand this paradox[114]. The "great cuisine" cannot go without class contempt (which some great chefs will escape). The Romans like to etymologically associate *coquus* and *cuculus*. The cook (*coquus)* evokes the *cuculus* ("cuckoo") in the sense of imbecile, lazy but also gallant. Cuckoos don't take care of their offspring, so they don't need to live in a couple like other birds and therefore they have a reputation of infidelity, passivity, in short of falsifiers. The *coquus-cuculus* is thus readily compared to the *adulterio* in that it is false and deceitful... Decadence (which is the great Roman fear well before the barbarian invasions) is always considered as an import of the softness attributed to the defeated and of which would testify their food practice, hence the fear in front of the "invasion" of the Greek, Syrian, Egyptian cooks and pastry cooks... i.e. Eastern. The formation of schools of Roman cooks does not please more. Thus Columella protests (and he is not the only one) against this innovation: "We have schools of rhetors, geometers, musicians; I have seen some where the most vile professions were taught, such as the art of preparing food, of making it more delicious, of ordering a sumptuous meal [...]" Seneca evokes the stoves of the dissipators (*sic*) which attract the youth while the schools of philosophy are empty. The indictment can be summed up in one word: the refusal of sluggishness, that is to say of the dumbing down of bodies and minds caused by cooking. According to

---

114. Jack GOODY, *Kitchens, Cooking and Classes, op. cit.*

  A political history of food. From the Pateolithic to our days

Pliny, the *coquus is* by definition a "vile profession", its art would be practiced mainly by slaves specialized in the art of swallowing their master's fortune. Martial draws the portrait of these mistreated cooks: "Who, tell me, has been inhuman enough, who has had so little consideration for you to make you, Theopompe, a cook? Can it be that one dares to disfigure this face by the soot of a smoky stove, that one soils this hair with grease from the fireplace? Where can one find more worthy than you to hold the drinking cups and the crystals? What hand, in preparing the falerne, will give it more flavor? If such an end awaits the servants gifted with divine beauty, let Jupiter hurry to employ Ganymede as cook." Everything (or almost) is said: not a civilization that gave so much importance to the table and so little to cooks...

It was necessary that this small world of the kitchen fell well low so that the Greek grammarian Athenaeus of Naucratis felt obliged to intervene: "From the cook to the poet, no difference: the art for the one as for the other is born of their spirit. He gives pride of place to Greek cooks, citing Mithaikos and his treatise on Sicilian meat, Chrisippus of Tyana and his treatise on baking, Diphilos of Siphnos and his diet for those in good health and for the sick, etc. He also praises the natural products... in the Greek way. Critics underestimate his famous work *The Deipnosophists* (or *The Banquet of Wise Men*) which he wrote at the request of Emperor Marcus Aurelius. Fifteen books make up this treatise, too quickly qualified as a simple compilation, whereas it helps to understand the mutation between the imaginary of the Greek table and the Roman table, whereas it shows where the rupture goes without being able to say it. Petronius' *Satiricon* continues this criticism by recounting a banquet at the home of a rich parvenu, Trimalcion, a freed slave[115]. While Greek banquets are programs to be accomplished which belong to a utopian principle, the *Satiricon* exposes what happened to a decadent society. Trimalcion embodies, as Simon Byl writes, the absolute non-citizenship, since Trimalcion is the example of the man deprived of philosophy and politics. This criticism is the one of the money which is exchanged against all.

<hr>

115. Émilie GÉRARD "Le *Satiricon* de Pétrone : la caricature picaresque" in *Vita Latina*, n° 157, 2000, p. 39-47 ; Robert BEDON, "Pétrone, *Satiricon*, XXX : le *dispensator* Cinnamus" in *Bulletin de l'Association Guillaume Budé*, n° 2, June 1996, p. 151-166.

Sixth service : The Gallic table

Prehistoric Gaul experienced a renewal of its population between the Mesolithic and Neolithic periods, with a significant immigration of short-skulled (brachycephalic) and brown-haired men from the East. There is no ethnic continuity between the hunter-gatherers that we left in the chapter devoted to the prehistoric table and these first farmers of the Bronze and Iron Ages. There is no continuity either in their conception of food and their ways of eating. The situation is even more complex since the first Greek colonies date from the first Iron Age, as does the massive immigration of the Celts. Each migrant people brings its own culinary traditions and table manners.

The second Iron Age, that of the conquest by the Galli, hence the name of Gaul, marks the beginning of the systematic exploitation of the land for agriculture. However, while they perfectly mastered the techniques of agriculture and animal husbandry, the Gauls still remained largely hunters and gatherers, thus provoking the incomprehension of other peoples.

This was the time of the first real cities, divided among about sixty peoples, each with its own territory, its own fortified place and its own chiefdom. These fortified cities were linked by an important road network, which later allowed Julius Caesar to cross Gaul easily.

We all have in mind a series of epinal images such as those of the great Gallic feasts that we owe to the Asterix album series. The album *Asterix at the Olympic Games* contains some truth... The Greek athletes had to make do with an olive because the most important thing was to share, and it didn't matter what was shared, the Romans took care of their diet and ensured that dietary rules were respected, while the Gauls had a feast. Confronting this imagery with historical knowledge is of little interest because the purpose of these images is not to accurately reflect reality. The Gallic tables are, with the image of the various tribes, necessarily plural, but of this diversity will be born, paradoxically, a certain unit. Two words characterize the Gallic banquets: clientelism and waste. Of what to offend Greeks and Romans who are also frightened of the habit, that they despise, that have the Gauls to consume their pure wine, without cutting it of water.

The great Gallic banquets

Greek and Roman travellers expressed their astonishment at the table manners of the Gauls, whose rules seemed very strange to them. The philosopher Posidonios of Apamea (135-51 B.C.) reports that Prince Luern, Celtic king of the Arvernes, whose reign was in the middle of the 1st century B.C., "sometimes enclosed a space of 12 square stadia with vats filled with expensive drinks and such quantities of victuals that, for several days, everyone could freely enter the enclosure and enjoy the food that was prepared there and served to all comers without interruption. This account is far from being isolated. The historian Phylarch, quoting Athenaeus, reports that "a very rich Celt made a public promise to treat all the Celts for a year, and he kept his promise in the following way: in the places of the country the most favorable from the point of view of the ways of communication, he established stations along the principal ways; surrounded by palisades of reeds and wicker, each site could contain four hundred men and even more, the installation was envisaged for the crowds which were to flood from the cities and surrounding villages. There were large cauldrons which, in his plan, he had taken care to have forged during the previous year by craftsmen called from other cities. A great number of oxen, pigs, sheep and many other animals were slaughtered every day. Tuns of wine were prepared, as well as large quantities of flour of hulled barley" (Athenaeus, *The Deipnisophists*, 34, 150)[116].

One can return reason of these great banquets only by taking time to understand the political and religious operation of Gauls.

An aristocratic society

Independent Gaul was made up of about sixty peoples who were largely autonomous from one another, each with its own senate, its own

---

116. Matthieu Poux. "Votive spaces - festive spaces. Banquets and libation rites in the context of sanctuaries and enclosures" in *Revue archéologique de Picardie*, vol. 1, n° 1, *Les enclos celtiques* - Actes de la table ronde de Ribemont-sur-Ancre (Somme), 2000, p. 217-231, *loc. cit.* p. 218.

    A political history of food. From the Pateolithic to our days

administration, its civic assembly, its magistrates and its clergy. Each tribe was divided into clans, and the latter grouped together several families. Each territory is thus occupied by a people and forms a separate state, certainly member of a confederation but the weakness of the link is such as the unit of Gaul is unceasingly called into question by rivalries and conflicts. The Gauls experimented with various political regimes, ranging from democracy to elective kingships, via aristocratic regimes in which the chiefs were elected by the nobles and the druids alone.

Each year, a meeting of the various states designates the "patron people", responsible for organizing future meetings, thus banquets, to resolve certain legal disputes and, eventually, to create a common army to face militarily an invader. The legal call to fight cannot be ignored and, in case of refusal, the recalcitrant is punished by the loss of nose, ears or eyes. The last one to arrive at the place of assembly, in case of mobilization, is systematically put to death. These declarations of war and mobilizations are accompanied by agape.

Gallic clientelism
The great Gallic banquets which astonish so much the foreigners are to be put in connection with this political operation and in particular the clientelism which remains the principal characteristic of this society founded on the honor. The Gauls are often the customers of rich "bosses" who, in exchange for their political support, must ensure them a constant protection. Urbanization, already well underway, seems to have upset the traditional conditions of clientelism, since while rural clients remain dependent on a family, which means that this clientelism is hereditary, urban clients are only committed to one person, which means that their children find their total freedom unless they conclude a new pact. Some rich "patrons" maintain clienteles of several thousands of individuals who, in times of peace, constitute their procession and accompany them during various events, in particular on the occasion of the great banquets, and who, in the event of armed conflict, are obliged to support them militarily.

Relationships of clientelism also existed between small and large Gallic states, since a small state could put itself under the protection of a larger one in exchange for vassalage and the payment of regular tribute. Individuals as well as states thus competed in generosity to increase their credit, which required the respect of the word and a generosity in food. Even the vergobrets, supreme magistrates appointed for one year, who exercised absolute power since they had the right of life and death over their constituents, did not escape this obligation of food political evergetism.

Many Gauls are thus "customers" of powerful people but also members of professional (craft, cultural) or religious brotherhoods. This structuring, in the form of complex concentric circles, gives place to great banquets which are the occasion to compete in two fields: initially in generosity, which, with the art of the war, is constitutive of the honor; then, in eloquence, since all is regulated at the time of oratorical jousts. These oratorical duels are largely the specificity of the Gallic banquets. The winner is designated by clamors and by the noise of the clashed weapons. The loads are entrusted at all the levels of the society (of the *domus* with the *civitas*) to those which regale the others and speak best...

Supervision by chiefs

The Gallic society includes three great social classes: that of the aristocrats, great landowners or men at arms (horsemen), that of the free men, and that, finally, of the clergy which counts itself three bodies: the druids, who intercede with the divine and natural world, say the right, make justice and are masters of the philosophical and physiological teaching; the ovates (or vates), in other words diviners in charge of the exercise of the worship and the celebration of the sacrifices, which also practise the auguries; the bards, poets and singers, charged to maintain the memory of the genealogies, to transmit the national traditions, to constitute and preserve the accounts of the warlike exploits, to write and to sing the sacred hymns accompanied by a music also sacred (since the harp is the divine instrument par excellence).

The population is thus strongly supervised by these various chieftaincies. I will insist on the existence of the hereditary equestrian class, descended from the ancient hunters, and which is largely at the origin of the civilization of the *oppida*, these fortified towns characteristic of the Gallic Iron Age at the time of the passage from the primitive villages (from 50 to 200 inhabitants) to the agglomerations. These *oppida* are the cradle of a Gallic way of life, and therefore of eating. The Gallic city is an enclosed city, a city too small to integrate all the urban population, a city bearing the name of its people, contrary to the Roman (and Gallo-Roman) cities which will always be open cities. Also, in spite of a rather late urbanization, the Gauls count at least 150 *oppida* which exhibit, since the second Iron Age, their enclosures, their towers, their bastions, symbols of power on the surrounding territories, but also their chapels, their meeting places, their important statuary. There are chief *oppida* which dominate other *oppida* (many chief oppida will change their name in the first and second centuries, such as Lutetia, which will become Paris).

     A political history of food. From the Pateolithic to our days

The religion of the Gauls

The druids, considered to be the descendants of the ancient theocratic leaders, enjoyed considerable power since they were high priests, magicians, soothsayers, magistrates and, sometimes, great electors. They were exempt from taxes and escaped general mobilization in case of war. They have the power to excommunicate, that is to say to forbid sacrifice. This social death is often accompanied by physical death, because there are no penal sanctions against anyone who has injured or even killed an excommunicated Gaul. The druids are in charge of the education of the young aristocrats: this learning is done by reciting by heart a considerable number of verses and by learning to observe nature, since it is it which is supposed to reveal the future.

The Gallic religion is polytheistic, just like the Egyptian, Greek or Roman religions, but its gods are, since the 1st century BC, of an anthropomorphic nature. The multiplicity of local cults does not prevent, moreover, the existence of a celestial hierarchy with a few great gods, including Taranis, god of the Sky and of the Storm. This divine world, with its female deities, remains very close to nature, with its sacred woods and mountains, with its trees that walk, its stones that turn, etc. One could think that with such naturalistic cults, which create an interdependence of all the living beings, plants included, the religion and the Gallic society would have remained frozen in out-of-date conceptions, but the Gauls developed at the same time a conception of the immortality of the soul which places them in this register well in advance of the other religions. This dogma is unrelated to any idea of punishment or reward. I will not enter the debate to know if the philosophical-religious doctrines of the druids were close to those of Pythagoras, but I will note that in religion as in politics, the Gauls are quite different in the landscape.

The Gallic evergetism

We can now find our Gauls banqueting. Historians note that the enclosures are generally a few tens, at most a few hundreds of meters, thus very far from the dimensions underlined by Phylarch and Posidonios (12 square stadiums equivalent to 800 meters of side). One benches in smaller committee, even if sometimes certain much larger enclosures constitute a kind of repetition of the great religious sanctuaries. These enclosures are generally implanted on the communication routes, which testifies to the will to allow meetings (thus alliances) between neighboring communities, or between State-patrons and State-clients...

The organization of the enclosures

The archaeologist Matthieu Poux proposes an enlightening analysis of these banquets[117]. Why indeed make enclosures to organize festivities since, after all, these events could just as well take place on open ground, suitable to favor this opening of the festival "to all comers"? According to Matthieu Poux, this is a deliberate and skilful staging. A staging of the community since the enclosure is a way to make a circle. Every enclosure represents a *tenemos* in the etymological sense of the term (from the Greek *temnein*, "to cut") since "the first goal of this type of structure was undoubtedly to mark a strict distinction between the daily and festive spheres, but also between the profane and sacred world"; "The enclosure marks a border beyond which the whole of the consumed or sacrificed goods belongs primarily to the divinity or the inviting power [...Toasts, libations, sacrifices [...] deliberations, games and ritual fights have a meaning that goes far beyond mere entertainment."

This staging of the break between the community and the rest of the world does not, however, go without creating a division within the community itself. The guests are indeed arranged in a series of concentric circles around the host, from the richest and most powerful to the poorest and most dependent. These privileges granted to the notables within the banquet are noted by the witnesses of the time but also attested by the work of researchers. Matthieu Poux speaks of an enclosure within the enclosure that could accommodate about thirty people. The enclosures were designed for one-time use and were therefore not used for long, despite the heavy investment in time and materials required (the need to level the ground, erect the palisades and dig the ditches). These quadrangular enclosures are oriented on the cardinal points. Matthieu Poux adds that the staging also concerns food and drink since their grouping in the form of heaps, at the bottom of the ditches, or along the enclosure of the sanctuaries, is part of a ceremonial framework: "These treatments are the expression of a very particular relationship to the act of eating or drinking, leaving the physiological domain for that of ritual. Thus, deposits of amphorae voluntarily broken and incinerated, to the exclusion of any other category of ceramic. On the other hand, there does not seem to have been any atypical butchery cuts, even if the consumption methods differ according to the species: for pork, it is mainly the heads, ribs, shoulders and hams, with the exception of the feet; for sheep, it is more the ribs, shoulders and

---

117. Matthieu Poux, "Espaces votifs - espaces festifs. Banquets and libation rites in the context of sanctuaries and enclosures", art. cit.

A political history of food. From the Pateolithic to our days

legs, but neither the heads nor the feet... The consumption of beverages is also very ritualized, especially that of wine, since this libation, which is necessarily collective, always takes place in the center of the peribola. The quantities of amphorae represent a volume of several hectoliters.

The obligation to waste

Matthieu Poux draws attention to the importance of reliefs of all kinds. The power of a chef is measured by the amount of food and drink he can offer, but also and above all by the amount of leftovers and waste. I insist: we do not only throw away what has not been consumed, we voluntarily throw away food and beverages not intended for consumption! Patrice Méniel also insists on the importance of sacrifices during the Second Iron Age and even at the beginning of the Roman period: a significant part of the animals killed are not consumed nor intended to be[118] : consumption implies indeed a disarticulation and a boning contrary to the direct burial in which the bones are intact. These sacrificed animals come overwhelmingly from domestic livestock (very few hares, foxes, fish): pigs, sheep, goats, dogs, are cut up for butchery, while oxen and horses are not or hardly ever consumed. Poultry is almost absent from sanctuaries and banquets, although it is part of the ordinary diet.

Such a system of clientelism, with the waste that it supposes, is only possible because Gaul is then an exceptionally rich territory. It was ahead of other countries in terms of agriculture, as evidenced by the ease of supply for Julius Caesar's armies. Some specialists, such as Michel Py and Stéphane Verger, maintain that it was precisely this system of clientelism that served as the driving force behind the economic development of Gaul[119] , because it required learning to mobilize considerable resources in order to meet expectations.

From banquets to political functions

The Gallic banquets are not only places of evergetism and waste, they also fill a quite particular political function. We will see that if it is indeed a question of making politics - i.e. to (re)define relations of force

---

118. Patrice MÉNIEL, *Les sacrifices d'animaux chez les Gaulois*, Paris, "Les Hespérides", Éditions Errance, 1992.
119. Michel PY, *Culture, économie et société protohistoriques dans la région nîmoise*, 2 vols, Paris-Rome, École française de Rome, 1990; Stéphane VERGER, *Rites et espaces en pays celte et méditerranéen. Étude comparée à partir du sanctuaire d'Acy-Romance (Ardennes, France)*, Rome, "Collection de l'École française de Rome - 276", École française de Rome, 2000.

---

and alliances, even to continue debates -, but under another form or by speaking about another thing, it is however strictly prohibited to speak about politics in a direct way. One will thus make politics through jousts and oratorical or physical duels. Athenaeus writes in *The Deipnosophists* that "the Celts, sometimes, during the meal, fought in single combat. Indeed, being excited and equipped with their weapons, they first engage in an imaginary combat and end up coming to blows with each other and sometimes even with wounds; and sometimes, irritated by the latter, if (their relatives) who are delighted (with the scene) do not stop them, they go so far as to take their own lives. We find in this description the essential role of the customers of the chiefs. These duels, verbal or physical, which oppose the chefs or sometimes their clients, but in their name, are not only a great opportunity for entertainment but they contribute to constantly redefine the power relationships and alliances. Eating together is therefore inseparable from this work of political division. As Stéphane Verger analyzes: "Gallic society as described by Posidonius or as it appears in the *Commentaries* is characterized by a constant redefinition of the relative ranks of the great figures who are at its head: no one is safe from an irremediable setback in an assembly, from a challenge, from a murder by deception, which call into question his place in the complex game of honor and prestige. It is this image that gives the Gallic banquet such as it is presented by Posidonios, according to Athénée (*Deipnosophistes* IV, 152b-c). On the one hand, the guests are placed there according to a very precise order of precedence, according to their inherited or acquired qualities: "When they dine in great enough number, they sit down in circle, the most important in the middle, like a chief of chorus, who prevails on the others by his warlike skill, his birth or his wealth. The host sits next to him, then on each side the others according to their rank." But on the other hand, this precise order is unstable and liable to renegotiation at any time: "In the past, when a hindquarters was served, the most important one took the leg of lamb; if anyone objected, [the rivals] would rise and fight a duel to the death"[120].

If everything ends with banquets and fights in the style of Asterix, we should not be misled by the nature of the words exchanged. One might think that these are all the more the occasion for great debates since the prior political meetings are strictly framed. One said much, taking again in that the contemptuous judgement of the Greeks, that the Gauls were the

---

120. Stéphane VERGER, "Société, politique et religion en Gaule avant la Conquête", *Pallas*, n° 80, 2009, thematic issue: *Rome et l'Occident, IIe siècle av. J.-C. au IIe siècle apr. J.-C.*, p. 61-82.

    A political history of food. From the Pateolithic to our days

champions of the eloquence at the time of the popular assemblies, a codified eloquence made of metaphors and resting on a figurative language. It is especially necessary to insist on the fact that the Gauls have the obligation to listen in absolute silence to each speaker and that the recalcitrant ones are strongly called back to order by specialized magistrates, because they must testify noisily their agreement or disagreement only at the end of the speech. But the historians also recall that it is interdict to speak about the public affairs apart from the regular and controlled popular assemblies, so much so that the travelers are interdict to evoke the situations of the other Gallic States before having obtained the authorization on behalf of the magistrates. In the same way, at the time of the annual meeting which is held in the territory of the Carnutes, the delegates of the various States swear to preserve the absolute secrecy on the deliberations which will take place, under penalty of death.

Funeral banquets

The Gauls, like many other peoples, developed their aptitude to banquet on the occasion of the funeral banquets of the chiefs and the humble. However, one can, by crossing the analyses, suggest that these great Gallic feasts do not result so much, as with the other peoples, from the cult of the ancestors, but directly from the very early belief in the immortality of the soul, already briefly evoked (cf. *supra*, § "The religion of the Gauls"). The philologist Erwin Rohde (1845-1898) already maintained that this belief could not be the extension of the cult of the souls of the ancestors because "the immortality of the soul necessarily supposes its divine nature, and such a nature inevitably induces a form of equality between men and gods"[121]. The archaeologist Jean-Louis Brunaux adds that this belief could only have developed in philosophical sects living on the bangs of society, but since the expansion of Druidism in the second and first centuries BC, the Druids have been organized into brotherhoods, some even thinking of Pythagorean connotations[122]. The Gallic funeral banquets thus have a very particular statute taking into account the "faces of death and the dead in Celtic Gaul" (Jean-Louis Brunaux). Julius Caesar speaks, in his *Bellum Gallicum* (the Gallic *War*), of magnificent and sumptuous funerals with regard to the degree of civilization that he recognizes in the Gauls. The

---

121. Erwin Rohde, *Psyche, le culte de l'âme chez les Grecs et leur croyance en l'immortalité*, Paris, Payot, 1928.
122. Jean-Louis Brunaux, *Les religions gauloises. Rituels celtiques de la Gaule indépendante*, Paris, Éditions Errance, 1996.

Gauls despise death all the more because they believe in their immortality. Aristotle made of these Gallic warriors, leaving naked with the combat and weak protected by their weapons, the example even of unreasonable beings: "Among those who go beyond measure, there is the one who fears nothing, this one has no particular name [...] It would be a madman or an insensitive one, the one who would fear neither the earthquake nor the raging waves, as the Celts do, so they say" (*Ethics to Nicomachus*, III, 7, 7). Researchers have established the importance of suicide within the Gallic civilization. The Gauls displayed a certain contempt for human remains; during battles, the corpses of enemies, and even those of the Gauls, were not buried. The skulls and long bones were transformed into trophies or everyday objects. Another paradox is that many dog bones are found in the burials, although the dog was an important animal among the Gauls. Jan de Vries even made it one of the five sacred animals of the Celtic religion[123]. The dog is also linked to the cults of healing water and agricultural abundance. The dog is described as the spirit of wheat by F. Jenkins[124]. The dog is killed in certain regions of eastern Gaul.

An original food situation

The Gauls were reputed to like to "eat well" and drink excessively. Meals were usually eaten sitting at tables, on benches, with cakes, cheese, cold cuts, grilled beef but especially with a lot of pork and sheep. They drank mead and mead. They mastered many preservation techniques and stored in granaries, silos, pits, sacks, baskets, crates, barrels and vases. These *dolia* contain from 40 to 120 liters of liquid or grain. The silos do not exceed 1 meter in height to reduce the risk of fermentation. Cereals, acorns and vegetables were isolated from the ground by a bed of straw. The Gauls knew how to ensure efficient drainage and create ventilation shafts. The stocks represent at least one year's food. This storage is generally collective and brings together several families at the same time. The kitchens are equipped with ovens, often of very small dimensions. The Gauls used a lot of basketry, earthenware and ceramic containers, they had bottles, bowls, cups, vases, pots, both for cooking, preparation, presentation and consumption. The presence of numerous cheese bowls attests to the manufacture of cheese.

---

123. Jan DE Vries, *La religion des Celtes*, Paris, Payot, 1963.
124. F. JENKINS, "The Role of the Dog in Romano-Gaulish Religion", Brussels, *Latomus*, 1957, pp. 60-76.

     A political history of food. From the Pateolithic to our days

Gauls still gatherers and hunters

The Gauls of the Middle Neolithic (between 3500 B.C. and 2500 B.C.) maintained lifestyles that combined agriculture, livestock breeding and survivals of older lifestyles (sometimes intensive gathering, hunting, fishing). Gathering continues largely despite the number of plants cultivated since the second millennium BC, especially acorns and hazelnuts. Acorns are very rich in tannin, so their bitterness must be removed. To do this, after the skin has been removed, the acorns are boiled and then roasted on plates covered with clay or in contact with hot stones, then they are ground, mixed with cereal flour to make cakes or kinds of bread.

Many fish and shellfish (clams, scallops, mussels, periwinkles, sea urchins, crabs, etc.) were caught at sea and in rivers. The Gauls also remained hunters because of the importance of forests: small game represents up to a third of the remains in the ossuaries. Hunting large game is certainly an essential activity of the Gallic aristocracy (at the time of independence and then under Rome), but Arrien notes, in his treatise on cinegetics, that it does not live from hunting and simply seeks pleasure and, I would add, a military education there.

The Romans rely on the rich

The social inequalities and consequently the differences in food increase as the exploitation of large agricultural domains makes the breeding secondary, not only because the breeding is more easily communal (with the practice of the communal pastures), but because Rome takes support on these large owners and rewards them[125]. It is already of them of which speaks the emperor Claude when he declares about 47: "Already the manners, the arts, the alliances confuse them with us: that they also bring us their gold and their richnesses rather than being alone to have them!" The solution will be to make them, in 212, full Roman citizens. Consequence: the notables of the cities start to imitate the Roman way of life and go to their country *villae* to hunt, but even the notables of the countryside adopt the Roman way of life, not hesitating to make destroy their old house to live in the Roman way. It is the beginning of the dispersed habitat, contrary to the grouped Gallic habitat. These notables also adopted the chimney instead of the fireplace which smoked the room.

---

125. André LOYEN, "Résistants et collaborateurs en Gaule à l'époque des Grandes Invasions" in *Bulletin de l'Association Guillaume Budé*, n° 4, *Lettres d'humanité*, vol. 22, 1963, p. 437-450.

On the agricultural side

The Gauls are reputed to be, at the time of independence and then of the conquest, excellent farmers. They had a real superiority. Superiority in tools because they were masters in the art of working metals and knew how to make working instruments (knives, sickles, pruning hooks, scythes, hoes, harrows, ploughshares, etc.). Superiority of cultivation techniques because they used soil fertilization, rotation and crop associations; they were also the inventors of ploughs and harvesters. Gaul was therefore self-sufficient in grain and even exported, even if its economy remained mainly subsistence for cultural reasons. Agriculture was based on wheat and barley (then millet and oats) and it was only gradually (and belatedly) that the Gauls cultivated legumes such as peas, broad beans, beans, lentils and oil plants such as hemp, flax, poppies and camelina. Vegetable plants are quite similar to ours: onions, cabbages, turnips, parsnips, garlic, carrots, lettuce, nettles and various herbs. These plants were eaten in salads, soups or added to popular porridges. The Gauls consumed a lot of wild fruits and berries (sloes, apples, cherries, raspberries, strawberries, plums, grapes, elderberries, currants, hazelnuts, acorns). Bread was reserved for members of the aristocracy.

On the breeding side

The Gauls were not only excellent farmers but also breeders. Animal husbandry will always be as important as agriculture, which is already an anomaly by the standards of the Greeks and especially the Romans. From the Bronze Age onwards, animals were no longer used only for their meat but for transport, riding, milking and their by-products. Beef is both a draught animal and a butcher's meat; cow's milk is massively used to make cheese and butter; dogs could be consumed as a substitute for pigs, with the same cuts; horses are not (or no longer) consumed nor used in agriculture, since they are used for war and prestige ceremonies. Livestock farming concerned beef, pork and ovicaprines (sheep and goats). However, the Gauls raised far fewer goats than sheep. Apart from banquets, poultry is prized as much for its eggs as for its meat. The Gauls, who had a strong attraction for salt, used it for salting (meat preserved in large earthenware salt rooms) and for charcuterie of which they were the best specialists according to the Romans. Varron proclaims that the Gauls make the "fattest and best of all charcuterie". The Gallic animals were selected until they became very small, therefore docile, better suited to family consumption. Rome will bring its cattle, its butcheries and its way of consuming meat[126].

What do the Gauls drink?

Beer is the traditional drink, but it is not true that making beer is easier than making wine. Beer, unlike wine, can never ferment spontaneously. The basis of fermentation is a malt of germinated, roasted and powdered barley grains. The Gauls preferred barley beer (which has a lot of starch) and sometimes wheat beer. They made beers flavored with honey in particular. The *kourmi* is a beer brewed with barley, the cervesia is made with wheat (or spelt), the *korma* is a wheat beer with honey added. The Gauls brewed a wide variety of beers and used the foam as a beauty product for women's faces. The manufacture of beer became almost industrial with a real division of labor: most of the work is done in the countryside (cleaning, soaking, germination, kilning, preparation of malt), then the beer is finished in the immediate vicinity of cities[127]. The Gauls consumed wild fruit spirits such as sloe, which had sufficient sugar to allow fermentation of the juice.

The Gauls were not wine drinkers, although wild and even cultivated vines existed since the 6th century BC, probably at the initiative of the Greek colonists. They drink it only exceptionally and they drink it as one drinks beer or mead, not mixed with water. The Gauls, on the other hand, are attracted to flavored wines, flavored with rose, wormwood, pepper, honey, saffron-colored wines, etc. Ordinary wine is very pungent (we speak of *picatum vinum* or "stained wine") because of the treatment of amphorae with a layer of resin, and also because the Gauls did not shy away from adding this pitch (from cypress, pine, larch, mastic, terebinth) to the wine itself. They have a reputation for drinking a lot and not shying away from drunkenness.

---

126. Sébastien LEPETZ, "Effets de la romanisation sur l'élevage dans les établissements ruraux du nord de la Gaule : l'exemple de l'augmentation de la stature des animaux domestiques" in *Revue archéologique de Picardie*, n° 11, 1996, numéro thématique : *De la ferme indigène à la villa romaine. La romanisation des campagnes de la Gaule*, p. 317-324; Pierre Jaillette, "*Fert... pecuaria gallus*. Le bétail en Gaule romaine tardive. Inventory of literary data" in *Revue archéologique de Picardie*, vol. 1, No. 1, 2003, thematic issue: *Cultivators, breeders and artisans in the countryside of Roman Gaul*, p. 249-261.

127. Fanette LAUBENHEIMER, Pierre OUZOULIAS and Paul VAN OSSEL, "La bière en Gaule. Sa fabrication, les mots pour le dire, les vestiges archéologiques : première approche" in *Revue archéologique de Picardie*, vol. 1, n°1, 2003, thematic number: *Cultivators, breeders and craftsmen in the campaigns of Roman Gaul*, p. 47-63.

The destruction of the Druidic clergy

The defeat of Alesia in 52 B.C. is remembered for the surrender of Vercingetorix. It is forgotten that this was the largest battle of antiquity with 300,000 combatants involved. It is also forgotten that this defeat is due to the betrayal of a part of the Gallic chiefs and their people of which the Aedui and the Arvernes: approximately 100 000 Gallic soldiers did not take part in the combat[128]. It has been said that Gallic civilization disappeared in a few decades, because of its divisions and the congenital weakness of the Druidic system with its oral tradition, since, as soon as it was banned by Rome, it could no longer provide the backbone of society. It is true that the Romans wanted the Gallic clergy to disappear because it was the main obstacle to the policy of assimilation necessary to the *pax romana*. The resistances are however numerous in spite of the collaboration of the elites, as testifies the assassination of the notable carnute Tasgétios, placed at the head of Gaul by Caesar, and the persistence of the Gallic naturalist cults[129].

The Romanization of Gaul

The Gallo-Roman encounter took place in two stages: from 120 BC, the Romanization of southern Gaul, then, from 50 BC, the rapid Romanization of the three Gauls. The situation is thus very different according to the Gauls: Gaul narbonnaise (in the south of France) is very Romanized at the time of the conquest, but it is also subjected to the Greek influences because the Roman colonization was preceded by five centuries of Greek colonies.

Romanization accelerated under Augustus. Lyon became the administrative capital of the Three Gauls. Augustus created the federal council of the Gauls which met every August 1st on the Croix-Rousse hill. The delegates of the 60 cities took part to present their wishes and grievances to Rome. The imperial power takes largely support on the local notables. The Romanization of Gaul was financed by the theft of the treasures of Egypt. Claudius continued the policy of Augustus, especially since he was born in Lyon, in 10 B.C. He came to power in 41 A.D. and exercised his *imperium* for thirteen years.

The Romanization of Gaul, during the 1st century AD, marked the birth of a new Gallo-Roman civilization due not to a change in population (the "occupying army" numbered 100,000 soldiers), but to

---

128. Joël Le Gall, Le siège d'Alésia... en 1985 [Conférence prononcée à Paris, le 31 janvier 1985], in *Bulletin de l'Association Guillaume Budé*, n° 1, mars 1986, p. 8-21.
129. Paul Marie Duval, *Travaux sur la Gaule (1946-1986)*, Paris-Rome, Publications de l'École française de Rome, n° 116, 1989, chapter: "Autour de César, 2, La déformation historique dans les commentaires, d'après Michel Rambaud", p. 139-161.

A political history of food. From the Pateolithic to our days

the acculturation of the Gallic nobility, who were largely collaborators. Benefiting from the pacification of the conflicts between the Gallic cities, from the development of the trade and the cities with the Roman way, i.e. not fortified, from the construction of imposing monuments like the theaters, the amphitheatres, the hippodromes, the thermal baths, bridges and aqueducts, opportunities to make a career in the service of the colonizer and then of the Roman Empire, after the latter had granted Roman citizenship to the Gauls, the Gallic aristocrats became the propagandists of the Roman way of life. They not only adopted Latin but also agriculture with the creation of large estates (*villae*), the retreat of the forest, the development of the moors, the rise of the vine, and, in Languedoc, of the olive and fig tree, the transformation of the livestock in favor of large Roman animals. They even adopted table practices (notably the table bed and wine). Romanization led to a split between the new food of the elites and the people of the countryside. Instead of wheat and barley porridge and boiled or roasted meats, the good society began to consume large round loaves of bread, symbol of wealth, seasoned meats, more cheese and seafood. The prefect of the Gauls, Ausone, was a great lover of oysters.

Ausone, architect of the Romanization

The Roman administration will come to replace the Gallic political system and the Gallic civilization thanks to the collaboration of the majority of the elites and the support of certain Gallic people already largely Romanized. Decimus Magnus Ausonius known as Ausone (309-394) is the symbol of the rise of the Gallic notables, a rise conceived like a strategy of class. His maternal grandfather, Arborius, was one of Constantine's teachers, his father was a physician and prefect, his son was appointed proconsul of Africa, prefect of Italy, and then prefect of the Prefectory of Gaul - his entire family monopolized the highest positions in the Western Empire. Ausone, a professor at the University of Bordeaux, a successful poet, tutor to the young prince Gratian in 364, became, in 378, when the latter acceded to the throne, prefect of the Gauls. Among a score of works, he wrote the *Book of Eglogues*, a veritable doctrine of a good life according to Gallic culture, and gave a large place to food[130].

---

130. Robert Étienne, "Ausone et la forêt" in *Annales du Midi : revue archéologique, historique et philologique de la France méridionale*, vol. 90, n°138-139, 1978, numéro thématique : *Hommage à Philippe Wolff*, p. 251-255 ; Charles-Marie Ternes, "La sagesse grecque dans l'œuvre d'Ausone" in *Comptes rendus des séances de l'Académie des Inscriptions et Belles-Lettres*, 130ᵉ année, n° 1, 1986, p. 147-161.

The consequences of Romanization on meat consumption

The Romans not only brought with them urban butcheries but also the primacy of beef, which was considered a work companion. The Gallo-Romans at the head of large Roman-style farms needed a new work force, which was to modify the meat diet. This period is the one of conflicts of use between traditional Gauls, more fond of goats, and Gallo-Romans defenders of oxen. Goats and sheep are opposed by their function and their diet: the ox needs green fodder, from the meadows in the summer, and supplementary fodder in winter. It is therefore necessary to reserve good land for it. Sheep, on the other hand, are content to graze on fallow land, they feed on stubble after the harvest and accept straw, which large cattle do not appreciate. The goat is even less difficult, but rare (one goat for 20 sheep). Sébastien Lepetz and Véronique Matterne have studied the transformation of livestock and food between the end of Gallic independence and the beginning of the Gallo-Roman period[131]. It is known that in Gaul the domestication of animal species, from the Neolithic period onwards, resulted in a reduction in the size of animals: the stature of oxen, horses, sheep and pigs continued to decrease. But the Gallo-Roman period saw the appearance of much larger animals: Roman cattle are about 20% larger than the Gallic species. According to the researchers, this evolution was not based on native strains, but on the importation of much stronger breeds. This increase also concerns the size of goats and pigs. A herd with small animals corresponds to a deliberate choice, that of a family slaughter, with its own cutting techniques. We know that other regions, such as Brittany (the name of England at the time), resisted the importation of herds according to these Roman standards. One can be content to put forward the teaching of Latin agronomists, such as Varon, Cato and Columella, and their choice of larger and stronger animals, but this would be to miss the purely dietary implications of these choices. The importation of Roman animals imposes, in fact, to eat in the Roman way: the Gauls pass from their types of slaughter, cutting and cooking, to other ways of doing things. The meat was systematically offered in small quarters, as it was consumed in the form of stew, without any preference for pieces. This meat was sold at a single price (depending on the type of animal). In 30 A.D., the edict of the maximum fixes the price for each species, but does not establish differences in price between the various pieces of meat. Martine Leguilloux

---

131. Sébastien LEPETZ and Véronique MATTERNE, "Élevage et agriculture dans le nord de la Gaule durant l'époque gallo-romaine : une confrontation des données archéologiques et carpologiques" in *Revue archéologique de Picardie*, vol. 1, n° 1, 2003, thematic issue : *Cultivators, breeders and craftsmen in the countryside of Roman Gaul*, p. 23-35.

A political history of food. From the Pateolithic to our days

has analyzed this link between urbanization and the creation of butcher shops, the type of cut and cooking in the form of stews, insisting on the fact that as this Roman model was imposed, many Gallic domestic and wild species were no longer consumed[132]. For example, in the region of Marseilles, seven types of animals are now eaten. Small ruminants, sheep and goats, became the majority, while pigs and cattle became much rarer, and small livestock (poultry and rabbits) as well as wild fauna (deer and wild boars) almost disappeared. The slaughter of new breeds is done later (adult animals), because the herds have above all the objective to produce raw materials (wool, leather) and not meat for slaughter. The Gauls began to eat the animals that had been culled from the wool industry. Cattle are consumed as adults after reform of the carting work. The only exception is the pig, raised only for meat. Equines slaughtered after culling are in principle not consumed.

The increase in the size of the animals responds above all to the needs of wool, leather, work (traction), at the base of the new agricultural and craft productions. The increase in the size of the sheep meets the needs in fabric of the notables. The ox is used in the cereal and food productions. As Sébastien Lepetz has shown, the precepts of Roman breeding are turned exclusively towards the production of draught animals and ploughing[133]. Columelle believed that sheep should be given first place because their wool protected them from the violence of the cold, hence the improvement in their quality. This explains the weak presence of the goat, although its meat is good, its milk is excellent, and it has a great capacity to adapt to difficult environments. I am therefore not convinced by the thesis that the Roman breeds were adopted because of the Gallic demographic increase, even if the "big" animals are indeed more economical, since an animal of 1,000 kilos consumes less than two of 500 kilos, requires less peasant work, generates less losses and waste during slaughter, etc. The challenge is above all to supply the new, enriched urban classes!

The Romanization of the Gallo-Roman table is a wonderful illustration of the impact of political choices in terms of agriculture, and therefore of food. In Roman times, domestic mammals provided the majority of the

---

132. Martine Leguilloux, "À propos de la charcuterie en Gaule romaine : un exemple à Aix-en-Provence (ZAC Sextius-Mirabeau)" in *Gallia*, vol. 54, n° 1, 1997, p. 239-259 ; *id.* Note on the cutting of butchery in Roman Provence" in *Revue archéologique de Narbonnaise*, vol. 24, n° 1, 1991, p. 279-288.

133. Sébastien Lepetz, "Les restes osseux animaux du sanctuaire gallo-romain de la forêt d'Halatte (commune d'Ognon, Oise). Vestiges sacrificiels et reliefs de repas ?" in *Revue archéologique de Picardie*, vol. 18, n° 1, 2000, thematic number : *The Gallo-Roman temple of the Halatte forest (Oise)*, p. 197-200.

meat consumed, while wild animals only represented 3%. In urban sites, pork reached 50%, while in smaller settlements, sheep were the primary source, and in rural areas, beef (cull animals).

The consequences of Romanization on plant consumption

Romanization also modified the varieties of food plants. If in the north of Gaul one remains with the culture of the starch tree, in the south, the wheat with naked grains, of the wheat type, supplant the dressed wheat (of the spelt and starch tree type). The processing of dressed grains is longer and more complex if they are to be consumed as bread instead of porridge. Cereals must be threshed several times to obtain clean grain. "The substitution of wheat for starch [...] from the beginning of the Roman period shows that these crop choices do not depend on dietary habits"[134]. The cities became grain reserves for bread-making cereals. We also witnessed the development of legumes, including in storage structures. The cultivation of rye appears. In short, cereals still dominate, but there is the beginning of a transformation in consumption patterns.

In the same way that the maintenance of the clandestine naturalist faith explains why the establishment of Christianity proved to be much later in Gaul than in other regions of the Empire - which will oblige the evangelizers to carry out a ferocious fight, until the 6th century, whereas other regions, This forced the evangelists to wage a fierce struggle until the 4th century, when other regions, such as Ireland, which played a role in the evangelization of Gaul, were already completely Christianized. The Romanization of food customs, which only concerned "good society", was never strong enough to put down the ancient Gallic grammar of the table. This one will arise again as soon as the Roman Empire collapses. We will then see a new marriage between Gallic, Gallo-Roman and barbarian traditions.

---

134. Sébastien Lepetz and Véronique Matterne, "Élevage et agriculture dans le nord de la Gaule durant l'époque gallo-romaine : une confrontation des données archéologiques et carpologiques", art. cit.

Seventh service: The Merovingian table

This chapter could have been entitled "the barbarian table" as this qualifier fits this period, which runs from the 5th to the 7th century, that is to say from the end of the Western Roman Empire to the change of dynasty and thus to Charlemagne[135]. This period is often identified with a phase of regression in the architectural, economic, agricultural, cultural and political fields. This vision of things is now denounced for what it is: a bias forged in particular by the Carolingians to justify their coup d'état. Notwithstanding the wars, the raids, the voluntary destruction of harvests and materials, this period is rather a time of abundance and diversification of supplies in the field of food[136].

The Merovingians liked to eat, they even ate a lot, but differently than the Gallo-Romans and the Franks, the new masters of the country. These barbarian elites were beer drinkers and big meat eaters, especially of large domestic and, if possible, wild quadrupeds. They ate seated in front of a table (a board on trestles), not like Gallo-Roman citizens, but like women and slaves. They liked to eat in large company, unlike the Romans; they also shared their meals with their wives and children; in short, they ate, in the eyes of the Gallo-Roman aristocracy and the first Christians, but for different reasons, like Barbarians and pagans. Among the Merovingians, we know that the organization of banquets constitutes, with hunting, a major political ritual since the king being itinerant, it is the occasion for him to gather the aristocracy from which he draws his power. The Merovingians will have to invent a new culture of table, acceptable by themselves, the

---

135. Alain DIERKENS and Liliane PLOUVIER, *Festins mérovingiens*, Brussels, Le Livre Timperman, 2008.

136. Bernadette CABOURET, "D'Apicius à la table des rois 'barbares'" in *Dialogues d'histoire ancienne,* Supplément n° 7, 2012, p. 159-172, numéro thématique : *L'histoire de l'alimentation dans l'Antiquité. Bilan historiographique* - Journée de printemps de la SOPHAU, 21 mai 2011.

Gallo-Roman aristocracy and the Church, in the territory of the current France which counts then approximately 10 million inhabitants.

During these three centuries, there were two major overlapping phases. The first phase is that of a wider return to gathering and hunting as a complement to cultivation and breeding, which allows the "populi" (I call them the "little people", as opposed to the powerful) to have access to a sufficient and diversified diet. The second phase is that of a compromise between the new and the old masters, which results, through new table practices, in sending the populi to the side of barbarism and the powerful to the side of civilization. The "barbarians", they are not any more those who eat meat and drink milk, but those who are uncultivated and live of the *incultum* (forest, marshes and moors)[137]. We will see agitating some characters like Ausone (of which we already spoke), Sidonius Apollinaire, Anthime (or Antime), Vinidarius, all convinced of the need for reforming the table to give the Merovingians a political base. Many of those who wrote about food were either prominent politicians or close to kings and emperors. During these two centuries, the Frankish table will develop an ideology whose markers will remain those of the French (almost) until today.

No initial dualization of the table

I would like to emphasize the lasting absence of dualisation of the table due to the numerical, but also ideological, importance of the peasant-warriors. This class, known as the "king's freemen", composed of small and medium-sized landowners, members of the royal army, retained a very important political weight until the beginning of the Carolingian era, which saw its collapse, the major causes of which were the development of large-scale property, the gradual mutation of the freemen into subjugators and the formation of a military caste from which the peasants were excluded. Moreover, everything will be done to prevent the populi from exercising sylvo-pastoral activities. The powerful gradually monopolize the forests and massively deforest, appropriate the big game and will end up sending the populi back to the products of the earth (cereals, legumes). The food will evolve and become more vegetable, even if we continue to eat meat as long as the hunting of small game remains legal.

---

137. Fabrice GUIZARD-DUCHAMP, "Les espaces du sauvage dans le monde franc : réalités et représentations" in *Actes des congrès de la Société des historiens médiévistes de l'enseignement supérieur public*, vol. 37, n° 1, 2006, p. 117-129, thematic issue: *Construction of space in the Middle Ages: practices and representations.*

A political history of food. From the Pateolithic to our days

The Merovingian political context

One cannot understand the mutations of the table during these centuries without taking into account the political context resulting from the great migrations and the collapse of the Roman Empire generating a new alliance between old and new masters, but also between royalty and Christianity.

This Merovingian dynasty, which was to modify the Gallo-Roman conception of the table, owes its name to Merovius, the mythical father and grandfather of Childeric and Clovis, both kings of the Franks. Clovis is the real founder of the dynasty, because he came to power at the moment when the Western Roman Empire disappeared and because of his military victories, in 486, against the "Roman" Syagrius whose "kingdom" extended from the Somme to the Loire, then in 507, at Vouillé, in Poitou, against the Visigoth king Alaric II, whom he killed at the very beginning of the battle. This quick death was interpreted by his troops, who were very religious, as a "judgment of God" and the Visigoths stopped fighting. The army of Auvergne, come to support the Visigoths, is laminated and the son of Sidonia Apollinaire, who led it, dies during the fights.

In the meantime, Clovis, as a good political strategist, had himself baptized as a Nicene Christian in 496, in Reims, by Bishop Remi, who was to be his eminence grise. He was not the first barbarian king to convert, as legend has it, but the last, since all the other Germanic kings and peoples became Christians, but they chose the other side, that of the Arian Christians. Clovis and the Franks were the only ones to have preserved the old German religion and to maintain the cult of Odon, but better, in the eyes of Rome, to be pagans than heretics, like the Visigoths and Burgundians who inhabited Gaul. It is true that the conversion of Clovis facilitated the Frankish conquest among the bishops in search of military and political support after the collapse of the Roman Empire, but the mass of the Salian Franks remained faithful to their gods and their table.

It was the Council of Orleans, in 511, which sealed the alliance between Clovis, the Gallo-Roman elites and the Church. Clovis recognized the privileges of the powerful, that is, the existence of an unequal society with laws that differentiated between the "free" and the "non-free" and the "semi-free", and, among the "free", the *optimates* ("best") or *nobiles* ("noble") and the "mediocre", according to their proximity to the king, but also according to the size of their landed properties. Clovis recognized the rights of the Nicene Church against the Arian Church. By making this choice, he adopted Christianity in its imperial version, which conferred on him and his descendants a new sacredness in exchange for his mission to defend the Church and ensure order in the kingdom. Faced with the failure of politics, the bishops took over many temporal tasks, such as supplies, irrigation, fortifications, etc. The sons of Clovis continued this policy of good understanding with a Church that obtained in return immunity (i.e., the prohibition of judges from seizing a case involving the Church), as well as the exclusive right to preach. The conversion to Christianity was not really completed until the 7th century.

Towards the political unity of Gaul

Thanks to Clovis and his successors, the Franks achieved political unity in Gaul. They relied on a particularly powerful army (especially with its elite corps: the antrustions), on the Church, whose importance and weight increased, and on the heritage of the Roman Empire, numerous lands but also some large palaces, rural or urban, such as those of Braine, Berny-Rivière and Brennacum, located in the Aisne, but above all Attigny, a royal residence purchased by Clovis in which a draft of "national" administration develops the acts of government. These palaces were also places of pomp and ceremony where councils could be held. For two and a half centuries, the institution of councils was in fact confiscated by the Merovingians, who used it as one of the main tools of royalty to exercise their authority, while state structures remained embryonic[138].

In these palaces are received all the important people in this country in the making and foreign embassies that one wishes to impress with banquets. The agricultural land attached to the palaces provided the bulk of the subsistence. Indeed, Gaul was almost non-existent at the time of the battle of the Franks. With the exception of the central Massif, which still claimed to be part of the Empire, the Burgundians, Visigoths and other peoples shared the spoils. The Visigoths crossed the Alps in 412, coming first as guests and soldiers of the Empire in exchange for land in southwestern Gaul. They initially traded the sword for the plow, but took up arms again. The Franks were given the mission of protecting the province of Belgium. To these constant clashes between barbarian peoples to seize more land, each with the support and legitimacy of its own church, is added the fact that a significant part of the population has literally seceded, especially in the South, on the model of the movement

---

138. See Odette Pontal, *Histoire des conciles mérovingiens*, Paris, CNRS, Éditions du Cerf, Institut de Recherche et d'Histoire des Textes, 1989.

A political history of food. From the Pateolithic to our days

of Bagaudes[139] which threatens the power of the nobles by demanding more equality. These vagabonds formed armed bands of several thousand people, their leader, a doctor by the name of Eudoxius, took refuge with the Huns[140].

The Salian Franks, a chosen people

The Franks wanted to be a different people from the others because they were chosen by God. They aspired to benefit from a different kingship but also from a different culture in which hunting and eating took pride of place. The Frankish state differed not only from the Empire in the narrowness of its territory but also in its conception of power and therefore its practice of politics. The Gallo-Roman system, based on the cult of law, was replaced by the Germanic system, where kingship was based solely on the "good pleasure" of the king. The Salian Franks recognized the pre-eminence of a royal family whose men wore long, flowing blonde hair, which was forbidden to others. The loss of this hair also deprives the princely state[141] : Queen Clotilde, widow of Clovis, preferred to see two of her three grandsons strangled, on the orders of their uncles, rather than see them live with their hair cut off and therefore without the possibility of accessing the throne one day. François Gaulme sees in the attachment to this hair a solar myth, as in the ritual of burial on a chariot (or on a chariot wheel). The famous oxcart is the symbol of the solar expression of royalty. Germanic historians have developed the concept of the "ethno-genetic" model, which places kingship at the center of the process of formation of peoples. The people only exist by aggregating around it. The Merovingian

---

139. "The 'Bagaude' was, in the first half of the 5th century, a striking fact and an episode among others of the decline of the Roman Empire. The social movement, with indiscernible beginnings, perceptible especially towards 415-418, affected mainly the countries of the Gallic west. It is generally considered by modern historians as a recurrent succession of rural troubles, a series of peasant uprisings exasperated by the exactions of the 'powerful', the great landowners and the imperial tax authorities" (H. MARTIN, "Réflexions sur les Bagaudes", *Annales de Normandie*, vol. 49, n° 1, 1999, p. 78-79).

140. We know little about this doctor: Bruno POTTIER ("Can we speak of popular revolts in late antiquity?" [Bagaudes and social history of Gaul of the 4th and 5th centuries], *Mélanges de l'École française de Rome - Antiquité*, 123-2,| 2011, p. 433-465) writes: "The physician Eudoxius may have become the leader of a dissident community of the Bagaudes, whatever its nature, going as far as separating from the Empire and rallying Attila." See also Jacques ANNEQUIN and Juan Carlos SÁNCHEZ LÉON, "Les sources de l'histoire des Bagaudes" in *Dialogues d'histoire ancienne*, vol. 23, n°2, 1997, p. 175-176 ; André LOYEN, "Résistants et collaborateurs en Gaule à l'époque des Grandes Invasions" in *Bulletin de l'Association Guillaume Budé, Lettres d'humanité* n° 22, December 1963, p. 437-450.

141. Jean HOYOUX, "*Reges criniti*. Chevelures, tonsures et scalps chez les Mérovingiens" in *Revue belge de philologie et d'histoire*, vol. 26, n° 3, 1948, p. 479-508.

---

king is thus obliged to make a great circuit after his election. He travels the country in a carriage harnessed to oxen driven by a herdsman. It is in this carriage that he leaves the palace for everything that is important, such as going to the "plaid", the annual public assembly of his people, as well as meeting other kings, and going to large banquets. Régine Le Jan explains that this oxcart refers to very ancient fertility rites: the peoples of the North worshipped Nerthus, representing the mother goddess who, each year, left her island in a cart pulled by heifers[142]. The oxcart is therefore inseparable from the clientelism that the Merovingians developed by distributing land to the nobles, but especially to the Church. The Franks took over from the Germans another ritual for the elevation of kings with the enthronement, which made the elevation on the shield (another solar symbol) disappear in the 6th century. The expression "lazy kings", which was later used to designate the Merovingians, was coined by Eginhard (or Einhard), Charlemagne's biographer, to justify the illegitimate seizure of power by the Carolingians. These kings were caricatured as having thought only of eating and drinking. This moral disqualification is accompanied by a physical decline since they are represented as "monsters", explaining that hair runs all along their spine, like pigs (*sic*).

Less picturesque is the prologue to the Salic law, the foundation of the Frankish legal system, which maintains that God is at the origin of the race of the Franks. The king of the Franks would therefore be closer to God, which is why he is addressed as "Lord". From the 2nd century onwards, the whole of Gaul became identified with the Frankish kingdom: political and religious relations were henceforth established on a national level. This period is that of the transition from warrior kingship to territorial kingship, since these kings had to learn to exercise their authority over different peoples, imitating the Roman imperial model. The fragility of this system is the mode of succession with the sharing of the territories between the king's sons. This dynasty therefore experienced two major phases of decline: the weakening of central power following the division of the kingdom between the four sons of Clotaire I in 613, who, like his father Clovis, had managed to save national unity while preserving the authority of the various local kings; and after 613, the decline of royalty with the revolt of the nobles. Indeed, the Merovingian system took over the territorial organization into counties that existed in the Roman Empire. This constitutive weakness of the Merovingian

---

142. Régine Le Jan, "La sacralité de la royauté mérovingienne", *Annales. Histoire, Sciences Sociales,* 58ᵉ année, n° 6, 2003, p. 1217-1241.

A political history of food. From the Pateolithic to our days

dynasty forced it to constantly compromise between several civilizations or several cultures, as evidenced in particular by the compromises made with regard to food.

The beginning of the Christianization

The Church played a central role under the Merovingian dynasty by choosing to ally itself with the only non-Christian people, the Salian Franks, in order to better fight against what was left of Gallic paganism, but above all against the Arianist Visigoths and Burgundians[143]. This Nicene Church will put its fight against paganism in the background to devote itself to its total war against Arianism, another Christian current, then dominant in Gaul, based on the thought of Arius (256-336). The Arian Church defends the thesis according to which the son is not of the same substance as the father, it thus testifies of God but is not itself God. It supports the primacy of the general council over the pope and respect for the decisions of the councils. It joins, on the other hand, many religious forces considered orthodox by advocating an integral asceticism and an absolute rigorism, which leads it to reprove the sexual act, even in marriage, and to advocate a food frugality very far from the Gallo-Roman and barbarian practices. The Visigoth kings were very pious and allowed themselves to be led by their own bishops. The military victories of Clovis sounded the death knell of Gallic Arianism. The bishop of Poitiers will thus be able to restore the unity of the Gallic episcopal body. But as soon as Arianism was defeated, the fight against indigenous paganism resumed. The Church destroys or hijacks the chapels and pagan temples, hunts down the domestic lараries, the Gallo-Roman works of art are systematically broken, buried in pits, thrown into wells, rivers, etc. It resumed the fight against the consumption of meat from sacrifices. Once paganism had been defeated, the Nicene Church continued to destroy paganism by hijacking its places and objects of worship, for example by making altars out of holy water fonts, or even by using sarcophagi to deposit its saints in. This victorious Gallic Church, made up of small local communities grouped around their bishop, includes in its ranks many members of the

---

143. Martin HEINZELMANN, "L'aristocratie et les évêchés entre Loire et Rhin, jusqu'à la fin du VIIe siècle" in *Revue d'histoire de l'Église de France*, vol. 62. n° 168, 1976, p. 75-90, numéro thématique : *La chritianisation des pays entre Loire et Rhin (IVe-VIIe siècle)* ; Stéphane GIOANNI, "Moines et évêques en Gaule aux Ve et VIe siècles : la controverse entre Augustin et les moines provençaux" in *Médiévales*, vol. 19, n° 38, 2000, p. 149-161, thematic issue: *L'invention de l'histoire.*

educated elite and many former Gallo-Roman prefects. The "good society" turned to it, which seemed to be the only heir to the Empire[144].

Nicene Christianity thus emerged victorious in the 4th century, but only in the cities, and still in an ambiguous way because the adult catechumens (coming from paganism) delayed as much as possible the reception of the sacrament which had the virtue of erasing all the sins committed before. The *rustici* are considered as pagans attached to their pagan cults. The Merovingians therefore continued the Christianization of Gaul, but while it had begun with Greeks and Orientals (the Rhone Valley), in the 5th century they supported the efforts of Saint Martin to evangelize the countryside. Bishop Gregory of Tours tells us that the bishops of Embrun and Gap "spent most of their nights feasting and drinking". This particularly rigid rule of Saint Columban was based on a system of compulsory denunciation and punishments, including food deprivation. It was gradually abandoned in the following century for the rule of Saint Benedict. The Church endeavored to Christianize the frairies and particularly monitored their banquets and funeral feasts, which were considered abominable. In this area, they called for an end to the concessions made during evangelization. Too many death feasts were the occasion of rites considered pagan. The bishops proclaim it: the time for compromise is now over.

An agreement between the Church and the aristocracy at the expense of the people

At the beginning of the 4th century, Christianity appeared in the middle and lower urban classes, while the peasant masses and the aristocracy remained pagan. When Christianity triumphed, these social strata that had carried it were in retreat, mainly due to de-urbanization. The Church chose to escape the collapse of the superstructures of the Lower Empire by disassociating itself from the urban classes that had ensured its success until then. The aristocracy replaces these middle classes at the cost of numerous deformations/distortions, notably in terms of "good conduct". With this erosion of the middle classes from the 5th to the 7th century, the gap widened between the uneducated mass and a cultivated elite belonging to the Church. The barbarian chiefs, bishops and abbots of barbarian origin adopted the "Christian" way of life, a condition for their social ascension, but by adapting it. The regression of the secular culture was soon paid for by a contempt for the people. One sees besides

---

144. Luce PIETRI, "La Gaule chrétienne au IVᵉ siècle" in *Vita Latina*, vol. 172, n° 1, 2005, p. 60-71.

                    A political history of food. From the Pateolithic to our days

developing social disorders of great extent. Edward Thompson explains that the Bagaudes are not an ordinary banditry but a revolt of the Celtic peasants against the Romanized elite and the State. They represent a more egalitarian trend within this period. In the Gaul of the early Middle Ages, there was a change in the boundaries between the civilized and the Barbarians. The Barbarian becomes the people. This alliance between old and new masters with the support of the Church and on the back of the people is expressed in particular by a new food ideology.

Resistance fighters against "collabos" but all frugal

With the great migrations that tore its territory apart, Gaul experienced a conflict between resistance fighters and collaborators, similar to the one that had opposed Dumnorix and Vercingetorix to the Druid Diviciacos, a friend of Caesar.

Many Gallo-Romans were convinced that the end of the world was near and that Gaul was paying for its sins. This is the case of Salvian (400-470), a great scholar, converted to asceticism with his wife (chastity in marriage, donation of his goods to the Church and to the poor, retreat in a place favourable to asceticism). He defends the Visigothic Christians of Toulouse, but also the Bagaudes, and denounces the interior fornication that are the spectacles. He explains, in *The Government of God*, that the fall of the Roman Empire corresponds to a universal plan of God to punish the moral decadence and to reward the moral purity of the Barbarians, more civilized than the Romans. He was convinced that the Visigoths of Toulouse were part of God's plan and that they would come under the Catholic faith once their mission was accomplished. He advocated a frugal diet, which he believed was in accordance with God's will, but also the need for repentance to make up for the faults of the Gallo-Romans. To the question: "Why, if God really takes care of this world, are the good people more miserable than the bad? Why do the Barbarians, who are godless or heretics, triumph over the Christian empire?" Salvian replies, "You complain about your misfortunes, but you only get what you deserve. From whatever side you look, you see only cowardice, greed, debauchery [...], on the social level, they are nothing but brigands' morals: the poor are stripped, the widows groan, the orphans are oppressed. The Roman is a wolf to the Roman [...] In adversity, in the midst of wars and battles, one thinks only of the spectacles of the circus or the amphitheater, which are only an interior fornication, an apostasy of the faith. One sees everywhere only impurity, orgies and debauchery". Salvian sees himself as an enemy of Hellenism. He explains that the king of the Vandals, Genseric, had suppressed pederasty and prostitution in Africa and forced the Roman to be faithful to his wife. He rallies to the Germanic forces in the name of moral recovery. Better, he says, to live free under the appearance of slavery than to be a slave under the appearance of freedom. The Church and the monasteries will thus collaborate, at first, mainly with the Barbarians. This is the case of Avitus (395-456), an Arverne nobleman who joined Theodoric II. The king of the Visigoths had him appointed Western Roman emperor (455-456). Avitus is, moreover, the father-in-law of Sidonius Apollinaris (of which we will speak again). He also denounced the excesses of the flesh and called for food deprivation.

On the side of the resistance, Majorian (420-461), recreates an army and pushes back the Visigoths and the Burgundians. The Gallo-Roman aristocracy rallied to him. The bishop of Tours, Perpetuus, attributes his success to religious intercession. Majorian, military and legislator, introduced more justice and humanity and denounced the depravities of the nobles. He wanted to reduce the weight of the Church by forbidding women to bequeath their goods to it at the expense of their children and by proscribing the confinement of young girls in convents. He died in an attack in 461. The old Gaul will not recover from it. The North in particular seceded and took support on a new force: the Franks.

These resisters and "collaborators", beyond all that divides them, finally share the same ascetic vision of existence, the same condemnation of the pleasures of the flesh and of *gula*, in short, they have a dynasty ahead of them since this message will be taken up more under the Carolingians than under the Merovingians, due to the weight of the Church.

The Franks save (temporarily) the greed

Liliane Plouvier rightly writes that for the Merovingian period we have "a rather extensive culinary corpus, all the more astonishing because, during the following centuries, gastronomic literature will enter into hibernation, at least in Christian Europe. It was not until the 16th century, or even the 13th century, that new manuscripts were created with unpublished recipes.[145] The essential point is perhaps elsewhere: in the capacity of Merovingian society to acquire a political identity in which the good eater is first and foremost a big eater, and even an eater of meat, especially raw bacon. Sidonius Apollinaris, despite his death in 486, was soon taken over

---

145. Liliane PLOUVIER, "L'alimentation carnée au haut Moyen Âge d'après le *De observatione ciborum* d'Anthime et les *Excerpta* de Vinidarius" in *Revue belge de philologie et d'histoire*, vol. 80, n° 4, 2002, numéro thématique : *Histoire médiévale, moderne et contemporaine* p. 1357-1369.

A political history of food. From the Pateolithic to our days

by the Franks, along with Vinidarius and Anthime, to build a new conception of the table capable of taking its place in their political ideology.

Sidoine Apollinaire or the defense of voracity

Sidonius Apollinaris, politician and poet, was a child of Gallic notables since his father and grandfather were prefects of the Prefecture of Gaul[146]. He benefits at first from the support of his father-in-law Avitus, one time Roman emperor of Occident, with whom he frequents the court of the Visigoth kings of Toulouse, then puts himself at the service of Majorien, the murderer of his father-in-law, by becoming his panegyrist. After the fall of Majorian, he returned to Gaul and offered his pen to the new emperor Anthemius (467-472), whose panegyrist he also became. Fleeing Rome, threatened by famine since the Vandals cut off the supply of African wheat, he withdrew again to Gaul. He was soon appointed Nicene bishop of Clermont in 470 and distinguished himself by leading a fierce military resistance against Visigoth troops for three years with his brother-in-law Ecdicius, a Gallo-Roman senator. In 475, Clermont was finally betrayed by Rome which preferred to exchange Auvergne for the departure of the Visigoths from Arles and Marseille. He was imprisoned for two years, then released after having praised the new masters. He died in 486, otherwise he would have ended up rallying Clovis, his son's murderer.

Sidoine Apollinaire is a troubled but endearing character because he knows that much is at stake in the table practices of the powerful people he meets. He understands that the banquets are the principal structure allowing the "good society" to continue to reign in this troubled period. The table thus constitutes, in his eyes, a tool of expression of the identity of the elites. He exhibits a series of portraits of "good" and "bad" eaters in order to help the aristocracy to constitute itself by distinguishing itself from the populi. The researcher Emmanuelle Raga develops a fruitful analysis of these portraits by showing that they displace the border between "good" and "bad" eaters, because it does not pass any more between Gallo-Romans and Barbarians but between cultivated people and uncultivated[147]. A social frontier replaces the ethnic frontier. This criterion also covers the distinction between cultivated and uncultivated land. The Gallo-Romanized Barbarian as well as the Gallo-Romanized Barbarian constitute the prototype of the

---

146. Françoise Prévot, "Sidoine Apollinaire et l'Auvergne" in *Revue d'histoire de l'Église de France*, vol. 79, n° 203, 1993, p. 243-259.
147. Emmanuelle Raga, "Bon mangeur, mauvais mangeur. Pratiques alimentaires et critique sociale dans l'œuvre de Sidoine Apollinaire et de ses contemporains" in *Revue belge de philologie et d'histoire*, vol. 87, n° 2, 2009, p. 165-196.

"good" eater against that of the "bad" popular eater. Sidonius Apollinaris will have to propose adjustments to the table of the powerful to make it conform to the new imperatives. He revisits, in a new way, the opposition between frugality and abundance but where, for example, Julian opposed private frugality and public abundance, he proposes to marry the alternation between exceptional sumptuous banquets and sober ordinary meals, with the new imperative of fasting linked to Christianization. Emmanuelle Raga notes the eminent place that Sidoine Apollinaire also grants to the compensation of the "frivolity of the art of banqueting" by noble practices like readings or religious conversations, or at least serious ones. The poet makes his own the thesis of Symmachus, theorist of the traditional Roman identity, who maintains that the aristocrat makes himself guilty if he leaves his *virtus* unfruitful because "it is not enough to possess this precise gift", it is still necessary to take part in the race to the public functions, to recommend his friends, to maintain the *amicitia*, to develop his own literary talent and to encourage that of the others, in short, the aristocrat must live his life of aristocrat... He must therefore also bank, but with the necessary compensations. Emmanuelle Raga believes that what is at stake behind this discourse is the defense and promotion of a true class solidarity among the powerful. I agree much less when she writes that this position would not be motivated by hostility towards the "lower" classes, since they would in no way constitute any kind of danger for the elite. However, this contempt is displayed in numerous texts, including those of Sidonius Apollinaris, who describes these popular circles as "onion-eaters"; this was also the period when the Church was advancing new theses that were rather hostile to the populi, and finally, it was the period when the Bagaudes threatened the power of the rich. I think therefore that even if Sidonius Apollinaris still lacks the words to say it (they will come later, notably with the theory of social tripartition), his love of the aristocracy is proportional to his contempt for the populi. It is necessary that aristocracy and people are two antagonistic poles to be able to justify the common agape of the old and new masters. How, otherwise, could a Gallo-Roman nobleman feel closer to a barbarian chief than to a Gallo-Roman peasant or to a barbarian peasant? Apollinaire is thus the champion of convivialism on the back of the populi. The only way, according to him, to save the power of the aristocracy converted to Christianity is to allow him to take part in the banquets of class. Raga notes that the condemnation of the luxurious banquets and the valorization of the fasting by the Christian religion are in contradiction with the aristocratic ideal, except to practise the fasting between the banquets and to compensate the terrestrial foods by spiritual

A political history of food. From the Pateolithic to our days

foods (recitation or reading of texts). Raga notes that Sidonius Apollinaris insists on the participation in the banquets and not on the marriage, nor even on the accumulation of wealth, sign that the "participation in the class banquet would be the most aristocratic activity for the senatorial elite". When Sidonius Apollinaris evokes the banquets organized by Theodoric II, in 455, with prohibition to speak, except to say really serious things..., what he says of the heretical Visigoths is perfectly appropriate to Clovis and Rome! Sidonius Apollinaris brings a classy answer to Christianization by evoking the senator Vectius, big consumer of meaty foods but who compensates by the simultaneous absorption of spiritual foods: "In the meantime, it is the assiduous reading of the Holy Books that allows him, during meals, to absorb spiritual food more often; he frequently reads and rereads the psalms, he sings them even more frequently, and by this new way of living, he realizes the perfect type of the monk, not under the hood but under the mantle of the great Lord [...]" Sidonius Apollinaire thus puts forward two ways of reconciling the contradictory constraints of the aristocratic and religious worlds that will leave a lasting mark on French history. For its part, the Church will have to make other compromises by authorizing, for example, its bishops to take part in class banquets, real places of power, even if they have to go so far as to abstain from eating meat on lean days.

The cult of meat according to Anthime

The new elites can therefore be "good" eaters by participating in class banquets but can they continue to devour meat[148]? Several great authors of the time will try to answer positively. Anthymus is a Greek doctor (end of the 5th and beginning of the 6th century), banished from Byzantium under Zeno, in 478, for having conspired against the Goth Theodoric Strabon. He took refuge in Italy with the king of the Goths, Theodore the Great, who sent him as an ambassador to Thierry I, king of the Franks and son of Clovis (who reigned from 511 to 534). He wrote him a culinary treatise: *De observatione ciborum*. It doesn't matter what his intentions were because this work will take on a significance in history that he could not possibly have foreseen. According to Liliane Plouvier, Anthime inaugurated a new discipline, that of medical cooking, which would reach its peak in the late

---

148. Martine LEGUILLOUX, "Alimentation et élevage à Marseille au Vᵉ siècle après J.-C. d'après les études de faunes" in *Méditerranée*, vol. 82, n° 3, 1985, p. 85-92, numéro thématique : *Les origines de Marseille. Environnement et archéologie* ; Gaëtan CONGÈS, Martine LEGUILLOUX and Françoise BRIEN-POITEVIN, "Un dépotoir de l'Antiquité tardive dans le quartier de l'Esplanade à Arles" in *Revue archéologique de Narbonnaise*, vol. 24, n° 1, 1991, p. 201-234.

Middle Ages. He would be the creator of snow eggs, puffed quenelles and pike mousseline. Many of his inventions were forgotten until they were rediscovered. The main thing seems to me to be the fact that Anthime writes a "carnivorous book", but he does it in a diplomatic way, starting with bread and concluding with grapes (and therefore, potentially, with wine). I think that, beyond its culinary or medical merits, Anthime's work is first and foremost a political book: it both romanizes and barbarizes the Merovingian table to make it shareable by new and old masters under the aegis of the Church. In speaking of a book of compromise acceptable to Barbarians, Carl Deroux is right, but this book was also to be acceptable to Gallo-Romans and the Church[149]. This work includes, besides its preface, 91 chapters. Bread is certainly given as the central food, a politically correct position, but the book does have seven chapters on pork. Carl Deroux notes that Anthime inserted a chapter on three drinks (cervoise, honey wine and mead, absinthe wine) between those on bacon and pork kidneys. He explains this strange classification by the fact that a Greek could not but bring closer the barbaric use of the raw bacon and these drinks of which two at least (cervoise and wormwood wine) are typical of the Gallic or Frankish customs. Anthime chooses, in the Roman style, not to differentiate between animals for slaughter and game and to present them in an anarchic way: cow, sheep, lamb, wild boar, deer, fawn, roe deer, pork, suckling pig, beef, salted meat of cow and beef, hare, bacon, pork kidneys, stomach of beef and sheep, vulva of sow, sow's teat, double fat, pig's liver, etc. It rehabilitates the cow, but only of reform, and subjects it to a triple cooking: it must be blanched, steamed and finally browned. The aim is not to soften the flesh but to "harden" it. Anthime devotes several chapters to poultry, distinguishing between domesticated birds and those fattened in captivity, and mentions two preparations: chicken quenelles and a kind of draft of snow eggs. He then discusses fish and mollusks, followed by vegetables (mallows, chard, leeks, cabbage, lettuce, celery, etc.) and legumes. He continues his letter with dairy products and concludes with fruits (quince, apple, pear, plum, peach, cherry, etc.). Anthime shows once again his diplomacy by showing that if the Franks drink sour milk, they also drink wine, a way of saying that the opposition between milk drinkers - who would be on the side of barbarism - and wine drinkers - therefore on the side of culture - does not hold. However, he considers

---

149. Carl DEROUX, "Anthime, un médecin gourmet du début des temps mérovingiens" in *Revue belge de philologie et d'histoire*, vol. 80, n° 4, 2002, numéro thématique : *Histoire médiévale, moderne et contemporaine*, p. 1107-1124 ; Liliane PLOUVIER, "L'alimentation carnée au haut Moyen Âge d'après le *De observatione ciborum* d'Anthime et les *Excerpta* de Vinidarius, art. cit.

                    A political history of food. From the Pateolithic to our days

milk as a delicacy (*melchia*) and advises against raw milk, unless it has just come out of the udder and is still warm.

Carl Deroux adds that Anthime's letter testifies to the use in cooking of beverages such as wine, oxymel and *posca*, condiments such as salt, brine, vinegar, *garum*, *hydrogarum* (*garum* with water), spices such as pepper, costus root, ginger, cloves, etc. Anthime makes a negative judgment of *garum*, which was still widely used in Merovingian times and was indispensable to any refined cuisine. Carl Deroux justifies Anthime by the fact that *garum* can make one think of decay, which cannot fit in with his conception of digestion (opposed to another analyzing it as putrefaction and not as cooking). For Anthime, therefore, there would be a dietary ban on eating rotten food. Faithful to the teachings of the Ancients, he recommends boiling but ends up admitting roasting over a low heat because of the preferences of the new masters. He insisted on the importance of cooking, convinced that digestion (and therefore health) begins in the kitchen. Carl Deroux notes that "the idea is not new, but Anthime's radicalization of the principle that digestion begins in the kitchen leads him to give the latter a place to which other physicians have not accustomed us. For example, he devotes a great deal of time to the cooking of eggs: he asks that they be cooked in cold water over a low heat, stirring carefully with a spatula, for fear that the egg will be overcooked on the outside and undercooked on the inside. Anthime does, however, make three transgressions that he knows to be major, but essential to the success of the enterprise: he argues that lard can be substituted for olive oil in the manner of the Franks, that lard can be eaten raw (although he prefers to substitute boiled lard), and that mead and mead are noble drinks. The physician-diplomat thus provides the ideological framework needed by the elites to increase their consumption of meat: meat is a means of acquiring strength, it is the food of the powerful. The Merovingian banquet is the occasion to eat a lot of meat.

The cult of pork according to Vinidarius

Another work, from this period, extends this rehabilitation of meat. It testifies that a Merovingian banquet is first of all the sharing of a pig. The *Excerpta* (*Extracts*), attributed to Vinidarius, constitute the last part of the book of Apicius (beginning of [life]), but the language and the style are different. Little is known about him except that he was an Ostrogoth of noble birth. His book contains 31 recipes, but they are mostly about meat in sauce and fish in sauce. Of the 17 meat recipes, 7 are exclusively for pork and the other 10 are divided between lamb, kid, chicken, turtle doves, partridge and hare. The *Excerpta* also devotes 13 recipes to fish (scorpion fish, albacore tuna, surmulet, moray eel, sole, lobster). Liliane Plouvier speaks of "culinary modernity": Vinidarius indeed takes from Apicius what is best, such as emulsified sauces of the mousseline type and his recipe for mayonnaise, he proposes new sauces, notably a custard, and would even be the inventor of the tartar sauce. Without openly criticizing *garum*, he introduces verjuice, a very acidic immature grape juice, in its place. However, I would like to emphasize the importance of pork-based dishes: suckling pig with coriander, suckling pig with wine sauce, suckling pig marinated, pork in sauce, pork with thyme, grilled pork, etc. This centrality of the pig in the Merovingian table cannot be explained only by the presence of large oak forests. The pig is the emblem of the forest, which is no longer the symbol of barbarism. It even became the unit of measurement for trade instead of grain. This period is the one of the return of the legends about the regeneration of the Great Pig. Massimo Montanari notes that "the legends of these peoples attribute to the perpetual regeneration of the Great Pig the same magical and propitiatory role as the fertility rites of the Mediterranean peoples to the Great Mother Earth"[150]. This cult of the pig, especially the wild one, refers to a new reading of the opposition nature/culture which supposes a wild part and a domesticated part. This dehumanized wild part is the empire of a vital, sacred and superhuman energy, the one that only the hunter can acquire through his activity, the one that also allows us to establish an analogy between the king and the wild animal and that tells us that neither the animal nor the king are subordinate to anyone but God.

What do the Merovingians eat?

The new dominant culture is more sylvo-pastoral than agrarian. Thanks to this, the Merovingian table will benefit from a real enrichment and widening of the range of vegetable and meat products. It was not until the end of the Middle Ages that a period of carnivorous food was to be found. The forest regained its rights and the landscapes were marked by enclosures because a "barbaric" law stipulated that any open field was a common good. It was not until the 13th century that a vast movement of "de-enclosure" took place with the rise of village communities. This period

---

150. Massimo MONTANARI, "Romans, Barbarians, Christians: at the dawn of European food culture", in Jean-Louis Flandrin and Massimo MONTANARI (eds), *Histoire de l'alimentation, op. cit.* p. 279-282, *loc. cit.* p. 281.

     A political history of food. From the Pateolithic to our days

was one of great diversity of production because not only Gaul, but each "country" lived in a quasi autarkic regime.

The cereal/meat/milk and butter/beef quadrilateral

The Merovingian table seems to adopt the wheat/olive oil/wine triangle, but this is actually an apparent concession to the Church. These ingredients are integrated into the Christian culture where they are the symbol of the sacrifice that took place once and for all with the crucifixion. They are therefore the justification for the refusal of bloody sacrifices: it is no longer necessary to sacrifice, especially since the sacrifices were offered to demons. The Merovingians abandoned the Gallo-Roman triangle (bread/oil/wine) for the quadrilateral of meat/cereals/milk and butter/vegetables. Enough has already been said about the primacy of the animal over the vegetable, and in particular about the importance of butcher's meat and game. However, they eat mostly pork, the other meat animals are rather intended for other functions such as traction or by-products. Raw lard, and no longer vulva or teat, is the Merovingian dish par excellence. One could speak of a transgression of the principle of superiority of cooked over raw, but this is to forget that pork is considered as already cooked.

The consumption of charcuterie remains important among the nobility. The Merovingians did not differentiate sausages according to their animal origin but according to their forms (sausages, sausages, saveloys) and their spices. Specifically, they liked very spicy sausages but also rillettes, pork heads, salted or smoked shoulders, etc. Their meat is often salted or smoked, probably for conservation reasons. This meat is eaten in porridge with cereals, vegetables or legumes. The nobles eat meat that is roasted or grilled. It was customary to roast the pieces far from the fire (a compromise with boiled meat?). Specialists note that the butchers mastered the cutting techniques since there are few splinters and the joints are intact.

The Merovingians also had an abundant farmyard, they continued to fatten geese but also consumed hens, roosters, peacocks and pheasants. The Merovingians were lovers of game, especially large game. The nobles consumed the products of noble hunting, i.e. deer (considered the king of the forests), roe deer, wild boar, heron, pheasant, etc. The populi were content with small game: hares with snares, birds with nets or glue. Freshwater and sea fish were very much consumed, especially on the lean days that the Church was beginning to impose: fish was mostly eaten salted and dried. Herring is very appreciated.

The Merovingians consumed a lot of curdled milk and cheese, especially goat and sheep, because cows were used for other purposes. Another major change: butter and lard largely replaced oil, whose use did not disappear for all that because olive oil was still used but otherwise in the South and walnut oil in the North.

As far as cereals are concerned, the powerful turn to rich wheat and white bread, while the peasants still choose to "eat a lot" and in a more secure way, rather than "eat well" according to the criteria of the rich. They prefer poor but better yielding wheat, such as rye, spelt, buckwheat, oats and, in the South, barley and millet. The wealthy Merovingians systematically added linseed, aniseed, caraway and poppy seeds to their bread. White bread was reserved for the very rich, meteil bread (wheat and rye) was the ordinary bread of good society and barley bread was consumed by the same circles on fasting days. Within the working classes, this period is characterized by a decrease in the consumption of pancakes without the bread becoming generalized. This dualization was all the more marked after the 6th century when King Dagobert made milling a feudal right in 630, i.e. he made it compulsory to grind one's grain at the common mill (which was under the banner of the local lord), with payment of a fee in kind; in the cities, as in Paris, the millers paid a tithe to the bishopric. These fiscal choices are one of the reasons why soup and porridge (of millet and chestnuts, for example) were maintained for a very long time, because they did not require the use of mills and communal ovens. The people therefore preferred cereal porridges, meat broth and curdled milk.

The Merovingians were excellent gardeners, especially since no taxes were levied on vegetable gardens. Vegetables and legumes are therefore numerous: turnips, broad beans, turnips, broad beans, chickpeas, pumpkins, turnips, cabbages, leeks, carrots, parsnips, salads, etc. The nobles had an orchard offering apples, pears, cherries, plums, figs, walnuts, almonds, grapes, etc., while the populi were satisfied with wild berries. Merovingian cuisine likes to mix spices and uses many aromatic and edible herbs. Sauces are bound with honey. Honey is also used a lot in the stuffings that accompany meats. The Merovingians, who planted a lot of vines, consumed the same drinks as the Gallo-Romans, they liked wine a lot, especially flavored wines and adopted the absinthe wine, brought by the Barbarians. They also drink a lot of "cervoise". Cervoise was made with pitch (a variety of wheat) and sometimes oats. Barley was only later introduced as a cereal and for drinking. Beer was (re)made with hops. The authors of the time often considered that the Great Invasions had reinforced the penchant for alcohol and drunkenness at all levels of society. From the end of the 6th century to the 9th century, all the councils stigmatize the consumption of wine.

Popular food dominated by the incultum

The popular diet partly escaped the shock of the great migrations thanks to the importance of the *incultum* which compensated for the massive destructions. The Gallo-Romans and then the Merovingians opposed the world of crops (land conquered from nature) to that of *incultum* (forest, moors and marshes). Fabrice Guizard-Duchamp has written a study on the wilderness of the Franks[151]. This wild universe has certainly been anthropized for a long time, which explains that nature is a cultural and political reality with its rights of use. The wild is more than the *incultum* and the *incultum* is more than the forest. The wild has not the same status according to the social or religious circles. For the populi, the *incultum is* what provides products of the wild, game, small and large, acorns, hazelnuts, berries, fruits of brambles, edible and aromatic plants and herbs, mushrooms, fish, etc. These products of the gathering, the harvesting of the wild and the harvesting of the wild, are the products of the forest. These products of gathering, hunting and poaching are then vital. For the Church, the wilderness is first of all the place of demons and paganism. Christians preferred the vertical axis that joined earth and heaven and distinguished between reptiles, other animals, humans and then angels. The savage is rehabilitated if it becomes the equivalent of the desert and allows the encounter with God. For the powerful, the wild is the territory of the "noble hunt" whose codification will be done progressively, to end in the 9th century around the figure of the king hunter and with the prohibition made to the people to practice hunting. The sylvo-pastoral activities will thus be progressively marginalized because of their competition with the new needs of the powerful, as shown, for example, by the creation of forest reserves in the 6th century for their sole use. The king no longer reserved for himself the killing of certain wild animals in order to appropriate their magical power, as was still the case in the 6th century, he had to become the absolute master of the forest in order to appropriate its sacred power. The royal forests multiplied and the nobles followed suit.

Towards the change of dynasty and table

The weakening of Merovingian power can be explained by the personality of certain kings, but above all by the regression of secular culture in the face of the strengthening of the power of the Church, especially

---

151. Fabrice GUIZARD-DUCHAMP, *Les terres du sauvage dans le monde franc (IVᵉ-IXᵉ siècle)*, Rennes, Presses universitaires de Rennes, 2009.

the bishops, by the material and mental disorganization caused by the rise in power of the Muslims, with the blockade of the Mediterranean, with the displacement of the geopolitical center of gravity to the North and East, to the Germanic countries, with the weakening of cities such as Marseilles, and by an economy that was less and less sylvo-pastoral. All of these factors contributed to the rise in power of the "mayors of the palace", who were at first simple stewards, responsible in particular for supplies, and then central figures in the Frankish state. The history of the change of dynasty and the passage from the Merovingian to the Carolingian table is first and foremost that of a family, the Pippinids, great aristocrats of Germanic origin, who assumed the functions of mayor of the palace of the Merovingian kings. Pepin of Landen (Pepin the Elder) was an extremely wealthy nobleman, mayor of the palace of Austrasia, ally of Arnoul, bishop of Metz. His son Pepin II of Herstal (680-714) fulfilled the same functions, but with a concentration of town halls. The son of Pepin of Herstal, Charles (714-741) - later nicknamed Martel - was the "principal minister", the "sole butler" of Thierry III. He received the title of duke and prince of the Franks and benefited from the support of the missionaries. He developed a policy of clientelism among the nobles by massively distributing the king's lands but also those of the Church... This rise in power of the mayors of the palace is in fact the translation of a rebalancing of power between the king and the great aristocratic families. After the death of Thierry III, in 737, Charles forgot to return the power. In 741, Charles Martel made the mistake of dividing the kingdom between his two sons, Carloman and Pepin (the Short), and Charles' territorial conquests were soon called into question to the point that his heirs saw fit, in 743, to put the last descendant of Clovis, a certain Childéric III, back on the throne. Around 746-747, Carloman became a monk, and Pepin the Short was strengthened in his position, even if the legitimist (Promerovingian) faction violently opposed him. He then seeks and obtains an alliance with the papacy and the ecclesiastical party whose animator is the priest Fulrad (chaplain of the mayor of the palace). Pepin the Short relegated the Merovingian king to a convent and seized the crown, thus legitimizing the de facto power exercised by his family for three quarters of a century. He obtained the support of Rome thanks to Fulrad and sent a delegation to Pope Zachariah to ask him what should be done with kings who were royal only in title. The pope's programmed answer was clear: those who actually exercised power should be raised to the throne. The nobles ratified the decision and Pepin was elected king according to the custom, that is to say raised on the bulwark, during an assembly at the Field of March in 751. However,

 A political history of food. From the Pateolithic to our days

he was anointed by Archbishop Boniface and consecrated by the Gallic bishops according to the Pope's command. This usurpation of the power causes however some popular disorders. The pope soon asks in return the support of Pepin during the attempt of invasion of the Eternal City by the Lombards. He even takes refuge in 753 in the Frankish kingdom. Pepin the Short, respecting the old protocol of Constantine, is his squire on part of the journey to demonstrate his dependence on the pope. He took the opportunity to be crowned a second time, giving his power another legitimate basis than the election by the nobles of the kingdom. He had his two sons crowned at the same time. Medieval kingship, both priestly and secular, was born in these brand new ceremonies[152]. Everything is thus ready to invent a new table.

---

152. For the historical aspect of this paragraph, see [Collectif], *Histoire de France pour tous les Français*, tome 1 : *Des origines jusqu'à 1774*, Paris, Hachette, 1950, chap. IV by Édouard PERROY, "L'empire carolingien", p. 61-63.

Eighth service: The Carolingian table

Of course, the change of dynasty does not cause a brutal rupture in the diet of the nobility, and even less in that of the people, because in this field it often takes hundreds of years, sometimes even thousands, to change practices. We will present more archetypes corresponding to the Carolingian project. Two periods must be distinguished: that which goes (almost) to the end of Charlemagne's long reign (771-814) and which is characterized by the attempt to invent food policies; that which is confirmed with Charlemagne's son, Louis the Pious, and continues with his grandson, Charles the Bald, and which is characterized by the victory of the most intransigent rigorist religious trends. This period, known as the "Carolingian renaissance", saw the abandonment of Charlemagne's plan to be a great nurturing king and was reflected in the great weakness of the state. The public power withdraws to give way to charity and the inescapability of God's plan, which simply calls for more prayers and discipline through the penitentials[153]. This hatred of the flesh, of matter, and therefore not only of gluttony but also of the belly, which already existed under Charlemagne in a contained way, will be deployed with the last Carolingians.

The two periods mentioned above - Charlemagne's reign itself and the "Carolingian renaissance" - mark the transition from an imperial theocracy to an episcopal theocracy, each of which imposed its own table. This Carolingian period was a great moment for the Church, but a bad moment for the table, especially for the people. This observation is all the more stinging since the outcome could have been different if certain religious dogmas had not undermined Charlemagne's claims to reinvent food policies.

---

153. Cyrille VOGEL, "La discipline pénitentielle en Gaule des origines au IXᵉ siècle : le dossier hagiographique (suite et fin)" in *Revue des sciences religieuses*, tome 30, fasc. 2, 1956, p. 157-186.

One cannot understand the Christianization of the Carolingian table without mentioning the functioning of the imperial theocracy. In the end, this period was much more concerned with relics than with questions of provisioning and food. The alleged abuses of the *gula* were denounced with increasing fervor, but the clerics and nobles multiplied the abuses arising from the cult of relics. Alcuin of Tours, Charlemagne's main adviser, echoed this.

The Carolingian table in the age of imperial theocracy

The Christianization of the table would not have been possible without the choice of the Church to make an alliance with the nobles against the little people, in particular the one of the cities which had however made its own success. The Church never ceased to assert its power by placing itself at the service of the Carolingians and by using this new dynasty. It first took advantage of the weakness that marked the beginnings of the Carolingians in the face of Merovingian legitimists, furious and always at work, to make itself indispensable, especially in 754, when Pope Stephen IV, who had come to Gaul to renew Pepin's coronation and at the same time crown his sons, satisfied Pepin's wish by forbidding the faithful to choose a king outside of their descendants. This priestly monarchy lasted for two centuries, during which the Church ensured the legitimacy of the Carolingian kings by approving their coronation and by consecrating their sons and future monarchs during their father's lifetime. In return - it was necessary to pay for the support of the papacy and to deliver it from the Lombards, who were threatening Rome - Pepin led two campaigns (754 and 756) in Italy to ward off the Lombard danger. This exchange of goodwill meant that at the death of Pepin, in 768, Charles, nicknamed the Great, of whom we have made Charlemagne, and Carloman II, crowned in 754 at the side of their father, each had their kingdom. The hostility between the brothers only ended with the death of Carloman II, in 771, allowing Charlemagne to seize his throne and thus save the unity of the kingdom. His long reign of forty-three years could begin.

A new covenant with the Church

Charlemagne, knowing that his power could be doubly challenged by the last Merovingians and the descendants of his brother Carloman, chose once again to make an alliance with the Church by becoming first and foremost the chosen one of God (and of Rome) before the nobles. Charlemagne wanted to realize the great design of St. Augustine and to build politically an order inspired by the earthly Jerusalem. Charlemagne was undoubtedly sincerely Christian, he attended mass every morning, he participated in other services if possible, he wore a reliquary around his neck that was supposed to contain the hair of the Virgin (even though the emblem of his political power was the belt that he wore, like all those who held public office at the time, and whose trim, as far as he was concerned, was a true work of art). Charlemagne hesitates, for a time, between being the guardian of bodies, a new nurturing king, and that of souls, a principle that prevails because, in his words, life is short and the moment of death uncertain. He claims to have been appointed to lead the Christian people to their salvation. This notion of "Christian people" was essential because it meant that he had to rely on necessarily "national" traditions, especially in the area of food, while always presenting them as conforming to the religious precepts of the Church. As a result, he clericalized the Frankish state, gave his conquests a slight air of religious wars, and constantly mixed the affairs of the empire and those of the Church in his legal texts. The Carolingian penal law of 785 was particularly severe, providing for death sentences for paganism, for the cremation of the dead, for the worship of woods and trees, springs and fountains, for the looting of churches or for the non-observance of the Lenten fast.

Charlemagne was made emperor by Pope Leo III on December 25, 800, in the Lateran basilica. But if Pepin owed his coronation entirely to Rome, the pope made Charlemagne the emperor that he already was in fact... Charlemagne would therefore have had sufficient power to emancipate himself from the Church, but Rome's chance lay in Charlemagne's geopolitical project, which was the Christian restoration of the old Roman Empire. This Carolingian civilization was a civilization of the Bible and politics itself remained dependent on sacred teachings. Great readers of the Bible, especially the Old Testament, the Carolingians sought to reform society entirely according to its prescriptions, including, of course, in terms of food.

A state in the hands of the religious
The Carolingians, in their concern for forced Christianization, profoundly modified the functioning of the Frankish state by calling into question the mechanisms inherited from the Merovingians. While the Merovingians surrounded themselves with numerous laymen, the Carolingians only brought clerics into the palace, thus ensuring the pre-eminence of the Church over society for several centuries. While the local functions (dukes and counts) and palatine functions were separated,

Pepin the Short chose to bring them together, as soon as he became king, which Charlemagne confirmed, in order to better impose his views. Charlemagne, after a trip to Italy, abandoned the last Merovingian methods of government by making the court no longer a place of prestige and great banquets, but a real decision-making body and control of the execution of decisions. Charlemagne had a large ceremonial hall (*Aula Regia*) built on the 20 hectares of the palace of Aachen, which could accommodate up to a thousand people for plaids (*placita)* or banquets. This imperial theocracy did not, however, lapse into absolutism, for Charlemagne knew he needed the aristocracy. He consulted the nobles regularly: every year he convened the plea, which, taking the name of "general council", brought together counts, bishops, abbots, vassals, and the faithful, a whole beautiful world that the texts describe as *populus*, making this minority the Frankish people instead of the millions of former peasant-warriors. Charlemagne also defended the bishops, including against the archbishops, because they were indispensable to him during the pleas and because he needed the servants of God for the affairs of the century. Only they were capable of disciplining the little people. However, Charlemagne was aware of the fragility of his system, which is why he extended the oath of fidelity to the king, which had been put into effect by Pepin, to all free men aged 12. Only monks who observed the rule of St. Benedict were exempt. Charlemagne had about 500 counts and 800 bishops at his disposal to Christianize Francia occidentalis (or West Francia), to whom he added his *missi dominici* (the "master's overseers") who always went in pairs (one cleric and one layman) to control the nobles. Indeed, through the history of his own family Charlemagne knew only too well the weight of betrayals, which is why, although he knew how to surround himself with the great intellectuals of the time (Clement of Ireland (750-818), Peter of Pisa (744-799), Theodulf of Orleans (750-821), Alcuin of Tours (733-804), Charlemagne directed this elite with the concern of giving an answer to Juvenal's question, *Quis custodiet ipsos custodes?* ("Who watches over the watchers?"), and named himself *episcopus episcorum* ("the bishop of bishops"). He also refused the appointment of a Patriarch of the Frankish Church. He explains, in the capitulary *of Villis* (812), "that one should not make mayors of men who are too powerful, but rather of people of mediocre importance. They are faithful." The end of Charlemagne's reign, however, was marked by a rise in the power of the clergy and by the creation of a great many private churches, set up by rich landowners who hired priests. These private churches, under the orders of the powerful people who owned them, became the network of parishes responsible for

A political history of food. From the Pateolithic to our days

supervising the rural population. Charlemagne, while sometimes criticizing the growing temporal power of the Church and asking the bishops to take care of souls, generalized, with the capitulary of Herstal in 779, the principle of tithing, always to compensate for the spoliations of Charles Martel from which the powerful had benefited and which the little ones would therefore pay.

A Christian army

Charlemagne, as a good king of the Franks, was first and foremost a warlord: he led the Frankish army, which was several thousand strong and had become officially Christian, which meant that soldiers were obliged to wear the cross, attend church services and were forbidden to eat meat during certain periods. Because of the prohibition of looting in Christian lands, each soldier was obliged to bring three months of "marching supplies" which, in principle, he had to show at each mobilization. However, this system did not work well, so Charlemagne, while maintaining the ban on looting, generalized paid requisitions. Live animals therefore accompanied the movement of troops. In 811, Charlemagne led a campaign against drunkenness. The drunken soldier was excommunicated and condemned to drink only water until he was convinced of his unworthiness. Charlemagne also forbade asking another soldier for wine.

The Christianization of the table

This little Christian France, which took on the mission of evangelizing populations that were still considered pagan, particularly in terms of food, invented numerous legends to justify, first of all in its own eyes, the coercive power that it had. These legends are based on a centralist and hierarchical conception of the conversion of Gaul, which will very quickly become the matrix of a centralism in many other fields. This legend is that of Saint Denis, evangelizer of Paris in the 1st century, whose companions are said to have founded the bishoprics themselves. This legend is that of the baptism of Clovis, which would have marked the entry of France into God's plan, with the myth developed by Eginhard, Charlemagne's official memorialist, of a dove that would have brought the holy chrism, the holy ampulla, from heaven, thus guaranteeing the bishops of Rheims the exclusivity of the power of coronation and making the Frankish king different from the other monarchs[154].

---

154. This holy bulb was destroyed on October 8, 1793, during the French Revolution, see Gustave LAURENT, "Le Conventionnel Rühl à Reims. La destruction de la sainte-ampoule" *Annales historiques de la Révolution française*, 3ᵉ année, n° 14, mars-avril 1926, p. 136-167.

Eighth service: The Carolingian table

West Francia, which thus became the other Promised Land, the one in which the Christian faith would be purer and deeper, then adopted a series of symbolic signs such as the lilies of the Virgin. This exceptional kingdom of lilies must eat in a different way from other peoples, of course, but eat in a Christian way[155]. This "French" exceptionality, the eldest daughter of the Church, was to be paid for at the price of a repression of its customs, particularly its food customs. The people of West Francia had to abandon the carnivorous diet and the "cervoise" of which they were so proud and adopt a new food triangle based on bread, wine and "companage" (*companagium*), that is to say, the complements to bread, most often vegetables and various condiments. This conversion was paid for not only by restrictions linked to the alternation of fatty days and lean days forbidding the eating of meat, eggs, animal fats and dairy products, but also by the prohibition of drinking wine, between 100 and 200 days a year, depending on the time and the region. These restrictions concern of course Lent, the 40 days preceding Easter, the fasts of the four times, the Wednesday, Friday and Saturday of the week marking the beginning of each of the four seasons, the "vigils" (*vigilia*), i.e. the eves of religious feasts, then innumerable with the patron saints of the villages and professions, but also all Fridays, day of abstinence and not of fasting, since only meat is prohibited. Until the 7th century, during periods of fasting, no food was allowed before the only meal of the day, which was normally held after sunset. The periods of food crisis lead to defying the prohibitions (consumption of food reputed to be foul and even cannibalism)...

The repression of popular eating habits

The Church will have a lot of difficulties to impose its new diet just as the Carolingian Empire will have difficulties to impose its agricultural reform. This people, who used to eat four times a day, will have to learn to be satisfied with only one meal; this people, who used to eat diversified, because of the vegetable gardens but also because of the importance of gathering, will have to get used to a more monotonous diet because of the supremacy of bread. It is repeated that the bread having replaced gradually the meat of wild animals, the cereal growing would have progressed to the detriment of the forests and the moors, but also of the largely drained swamps. Certainly, but it is not to see that with the "small hunting",

---

155. The flowers without pistil are considered as feminine, the three petals represent the triple virginity: the ring which joins them evokes the closed garden. The lily is without stem because conceived without human intervention (*in* Colette BEAUNE, *Naissance de la nation France*, Paris, Gallimard, 1985).

   A political history of food. From the Pateolithic to our days

the people of the countryside ensured more its autonomy than with the cereals, while sharing a meaty food with the powerful ones, even if it was different (small and big hunting); it is not to see either that the cereals necessary to the manufacture of the bread are fragile and that it is enough of a bad harvest to miss food; it is also not to see that this Carolingian agricultural revolution benefits first of all the powerful because it allows the development of breeding and wheat, this noble cereal which the poor did not want because of its weak output and which they cultivated only to feed the rich and the taxman... This agricultural revolution, which began just before the 10th century and ended in the 13th, would eventually result in a decline in production - despite the increase in productivity - the end of free peasants and the rise of serfdom, and the differentiation of the table, which would be legitimized by the Church and the medical profession... Let us not believe that this revolution was made without resistance. Not only did the peasants continue to defend the old ways, but they also resisted certain changes in technology, such as the switch from the cereal sickle (with teeth) to the scythe, because the latter, which was so much more productive, was first and foremost a cause of waste, since the brutal impact on the stalks caused many grains to be lost.

The new penitentials
The Church and the Carolingian power had the means to impose the Christianization of the table, which first benefited the richest. They played on coercion and fear. Jacques Le Goff has drawn attention to these veritable institutions of propaganda that were the monasteries, the chancelleries, the preachers, the orators or the heralds. I would like to insist on the central role of penitential discipline in the field of the repression of alimentary mores. This period is indeed the one of the setting up of the system of confessions based on interrogations, led by priests, allowing to sanction anodyne behaviors judged deviant. This new penitential practice, invented in Great Britain and Ireland in the 5th century, initially in a monastic context, spread to West Francia through the intermediary of Irish monks with the support of the nobles. The role of the priest consisted in applying a priced penance, which required, on the one hand, obtaining a confession, thus a more explicit confession, and, on the other hand, a list of offences that needed to be punished. The people were thus closely monitored in all areas that the authorities considered important, such as the prohibition of pagan cults or the obligation to observe the lean days and the Lenten fast. The Church kept the haunting of the consumption of meats consecrated to other deities because, from its point

of view, the pagan meal structures the pagan religion. The capitulary *De partibus saxoniae* (785) condemned the pagan custom of eating sacrificial meat and instituted the death penalty against those who refused the quadragesimal fast and ate meat "in defiance of Christianity" (*pro despectu christianitatis*). In West Francia, additional fasts were often pronounced, meat consumption was forbidden for varying periods of time, but which could last for several years, and corporal punishment and fines were also used. Finally, the Church advocated the "expiatory pilgrimage", born in Ireland, and introduced it on the continent in the 12th century at the same time as the system of paid penance... However, the flagellant penitents took over from the pilgrim penitents at the beginning of the 13th century, because the Church considered pilgrimages to be dangerous because of the physical promiscuity they imposed. The Church established a simple principle: for public sin, public penance; for hidden sin, hidden penance. The same fault is thus likely to be sanctioned differently according to the notoriety of the facts.

The penitentials thus draw a new border between the pure and the impure. They almost always mention dietary prohibitions and set out sanctions in case of transgression. The historian Pierre Bonnassie lists seven types of prohibitions concerning foodstuffs considered inedible, abominable and filthy between the 6th and the 9th century[156]. These prohibitions relate to meat products. Vegetables are considered pure in accordance with the vegetarian ideal of the Church. These prohibitions concern the flesh of animals qualified as impure by their very nature (dog, cat, rat), eating their meat is in principle worth 40 days of penance, the flesh of animals immolated to pagan divinities, the flesh of animals soiled by sexual contact with man (they must be slaughtered and their meat given to the dogs), the flesh of animals that have eaten human flesh or drunk human blood (pigs, chickens), food soiled by any contact with an animal already partially devoured by animals, undercooked food (three days of penance for the one who consumes it without knowing it, seven days in the other case), flesh of carrion (any animal not killed by man is indeed considered as filthy). These religious prohibitions of the Carolingian period therefore mostly ignore those of the Bible. They also resorted to fictions: salting (soaking in brine) purified the meat from its original defects and from the stains that might have tainted it. The two main taboos remain of

---

156. Pierre BONNASSIE, "Consumption of foul food and cannibalism of survival in the West of the High Middle Ages" in *Annales. Economies, Sociétés, Civilisations*, 44ᵉ année, n° 5, 1989. p. 1035-1056.

                        A political history of food. From the Pateolithic to our days

course blood and semen. The great challenge remains the elimination of sacrificial cults and hippophagic practices.

A period of food miracles

This period of repression of popular eating habits is also the period in which stories of miracles... in food are multiplied. God uses food as an instrument of communication. This profusion of legends can be linked to the debates of the time on the real presence of Christ in the Eucharist. Stories of miracles in which recluses fed themselves with a host for years were repeated all the way to the top of the Church. Peter the Venerable tells in *De miraculis* that a simple but pious man, locked up for a year in a mine after a landslide, was found alive thanks to a miraculous loaf of bread found each day when his wife lit a candle for him. The scenes of the multiplication of the loaves or the transformation of water into wine constitute, says Massimo Montanari, one of the "normal" forms of divine intervention in everyday life, most often realized through pious characters.

Chivalrous banquets and hermit meals

This period of Christianization, marked by the repression of the popular table, sees at the same time flourishing a whole series of valorizing representations on the knightly banquets and on the food of the hermits. Chrétien de Troyes established the link between chivalry and Christian sociability. We owe to Anita Guerreau-Jalabert a tasty description of the table of the Grail through the analysis of a series of accounts which seem to oppose knightly banquets and meals of the hermits[157]. These two types of meals are certainly opposed to each other, but they are opposed, in my opinion, first of all to the popular meal; it alone sends the popular "bad eaters" back to the side of barbarism, without any hope of being saved. The eremitic triangle is composed of bread, water and vegetables, whereas the chivalric banquet is based on bread, meat and wine. The bread is thus the only food common to both triangles, but as Guerreau-Jalabert notes, it is not the same bread, since the chivalric bread is a pure product whereas the eremitic bread is an extremely coarse product, black and rough, made not of wheat, but of barley and oats, and which must be obligatorily consumed in the form of porridge, thus soaked with water. It can be seen that the hermits eat badly and their diet sends them back to the stage of gathering, but they are nevertheless saved, to the point of being confused with all the

---

157. Anita GUERREAU-JALABERT, "Aliments symboliques et symbolique de la table dans les romans arthuriens (XIIᵉ-XIIIᵉ siècles)" in *Annales. Économies, Sociétés, Civilisations*, 47ᵉ année, n° 3, 1992, p. 561-594.

---

religious, insofar as their diet translates not the idea of barbarism but that of poverty and abstinence, characteristic of their state. The knightly diet is certainly marked by its carnivorous dimension, but as salt and wine are necessarily present in their agape, these elements Christianize their table as faith civilizes the forest.

Eating "Franc-Christian" in the time of Charlemagne

This period is that of a transition between, on the one hand, the tables of Antiquity and the Merovingian period, and, on the other hand, those of the clerical-feudal model. The people continued to eat a lot, except in times of famine and shortage, but they ate less and less diversified and less and less "noble". Once again, the system sought to exclude the humble from the forest, the moors and the marshes, that is, from "small-scale hunting", fishing and extensive gathering. They often have a vegetable garden, both in the cities and in the countryside, which supplies them with green vegetables (and sometimes legumes), but already bread replaces meat, and this bread, which was given as the complement of everything else, becomes the central element. This degradation is, however, limited by a representation of society that does not yet distinguish those who work from those who fight and those who pray, but those who work from the secular clergy and the regular clergy. This classification, with a border that passes inside the world of the clergy, sends all the rest of society to the same (bad) side and reduces the capacity to think of a dualisation of the table on the basis of the social state alone.

On the side of the powerful
Charlemagne is the very picture of a true Frankish king: an excellent horseman, a great hunter, a good (i.e. fat) eater. He usually ate only one meal a day in the middle of the afternoon, a sign that he was already succumbing to the clerical model that was being imposed. He is usually served five dishes, one of which must be of great venison (prestige and warlike and sexual strength are required). This meat is of course roasted on a spit, as it should be for a king. Paradoxically, the chroniclers only know of one fault: he did not drink much. He preferred, like all his time, very acidic white wines. Charlemagne, even if he preferred the company of a few intimates, knew that the organization of large banquets was essential not only to his office, but also to the organization of power itself. Its table is conceived like an important moment of its diplomacy. The banquets at his court are naturally carnivorous banquets, except lean days and

A political history of food. From the Pateolithic to our days

fasts which he respects and makes respect scrupulously, more especially as the deprivation of meat is a current sanction for the nobles who have demerited, in particular on the battle fields. The etiquette foresees that the emperor's guests occupy a place at table determined according to their merits. The use of the so-called "French service" allowed for asymmetrical relationships to be marked, since the guests had at hand, depending on their place, dishes of different quality and quantity. Banqueting together can therefore mean drinking different drinks and eating different dishes. Each banquet obeys a particularly rigorous protocol in the layout of the room, the preparation of the dishes and the organization of the service. (We will evoke the whole of these elements in the next chapter.) I insist simply here on the clericalization of the Carolingian banquets since, because of the already evoked thesis of the compensations to the *gula*, the meals are in principle silent, with reading of sacred texts of great religious works (in particular extracts of *The City of God* of saint Augustin), of dynastic biolegends and listening to music and sacred songs. We find one of the great specificities of haute cuisine, the presence of a numerous, qualified and always male staff: the maîtres queux, roasters and other confectioners who officiate in the kitchen, the panetier in charge of the preparation of the tablecloths, the slicers and the nave of the powerful[158] , the squire in charge of cutting up the food in the dining room and reserving the best pieces for the most important people (such as the heads and necks of the birds), the cupbearer in charge of serving the wines, mixing water and wine at the guests' discretion, but also of using the "unicorn horn" (in fact, extracted from the tusk of a narwhal) supposed to detect poisons.

The Christianization of the table was therefore not an obstacle to large banquets, even under Louis the Pious or Charles the Bald, who were quite bigoted. One of the former students of the Palatine Academy, Ermold le Noir, recalls the feast organized at the court of Louis the Pious for the baptism of King Harold: "Meanwhile, the resources of the imperial household were being prepared, various dishes and wines of all kinds. Peter, head of the bread makers, and Gunzo, head of the cooks, are actively setting the tables. They put white woolen napkins on the tables and arrange the food in dishes as clear as marble. One takes care of the bread, the other of the meats, and one sees golden vases placed in front of each dish. Another officer, Otho, directs and stimulates the cupbearers, preparing pure and thick wines [...] The Danes admire the feast, the emperor's furniture, his officers."

---

158. The "nave of the powerful" refers to the nave of the table, which is a small ornamental receptacle designed to contain the objects used by the master of the house: knife, spoons, salt and spices.

On the people's side

Under the Carolingians, the popular table began to lose certain attributes of the Merovingian table. For a long time, it remained relatively meaty, but beef began to dethrone pork, while in the South, sheep and lamb kept their place[159]. The products of gathering and the vegetable garden remained essential, but cereal production made considerable progress. We could say, by forcing the line, that we pass from meat to bread. A new bread-wine-companage triangle (everything that goes with bread) will soon replace the Merovingian cereal-carnassier triangle, with butter, milk and beer. While it was still explained that bread was used to accompany everything else, it is this everything else that will now accompany the bread which has become central. Bread is always associated with wine because it is consumed with it: indeed, pieces of bread are soaked in wine in the morning. Bread is also consumed in soup in the evening, since a vegetable broth, exceptionally meat broth, is poured on a slice. This term of bread must be understood in a generic way, because if it designates, for the good society, the bread in the current sense, it commonly designates for the humble people pancakes or porridges. One makes, but not for long, one's bread at home, when the powerful do not yet impose the banality of mills and ovens (which belong to the lord and for the use of which the peasant pays a royalty), but one chooses to consume barley, rye, spelt, millet, buckwheat, starch, even oats, and to cultivate wheat only to supply the powerful: the owners of landed estates require it in their royalty. The supplements to the bread come from vegetable gardens or from gathering and exceptionally from breeding, hunting and fishing. Fresh vegetables are the same as in previous periods, but with a clear preference for cabbage and onions, followed by leeks, turnips, spinach, parsnips, etc. Pulses are very popular, especially beans, lentils, chickpeas, vetches and chard. We still eat wild vegetables such as dandelion, watercress, asparagus, edible and aromatic herbs (thyme, sage, laurel), we pick mushrooms but also snails and various mollusks, we eat wild fruits and berries and especially dried fruits such as acorns, nuts and hazelnuts. Meat consumption has begun to decrease and, with the exception of pork, it is cull animals (sheep, goats, cattle). The slaughter of the pig allows to eat fresh meat at the beginning of the winter and to consume the rest in the form of cured meat. The poor do not eat poultry, it is monopolized by the rich. The popular table remains nourishing with rations of 4,000 to 6,000 calories per day, which

---

159. Frédérique AUDOIN-ROUZEAU, *Ossements animaux du Moyen Âge au monastère de La Charité-sur-Loire*, Paris, Publications de la Sorbonne, 1986.

                    A political history of food. From the Pateolithic to our days

is three times the current standard, but the proportion of bread in these calories is constantly increasing. One will soon eat 1 or 2 pounds of bread per day, and much more of the false millet bread than of the wheat bread. The popular table becomes more monotonous and especially precarious because the wheat harvests are always uncertain.

We are thus seeing a strengthening of the dualisation of the table between poor and rich, as the middle social strata disappear. This phenomenon concerns the cities as well as the countryside. The banquets of brotherhoods could have allowed, even occasionally, to bring together the two diets, but the Church will use its power to control and restrict them. Water remained the main drink consumed. It was also used to make soups and other porridges. Good water" should have no taste, no smell, no color. However, it was not appreciated because it was considered to be the drink of children, women, the poorest, slaves... Drinking water was also a sign of punishment: a Carolingian capitulary condemned soldiers to drink only water if they had shown cowardice in battle, and a Colomban penitential condemned them to water and bread in the event of a serious offence. These sanctions could last for several years.

The banquets of brotherhood (between the populi and the powerful)
In principle, all professional activities were supervised in the Carolingian era by a guild: the trade (masters, journeymen, apprentices) thus received its statutes from a municipal or royal authority. These guilds were coupled with a brotherhood that grouped only the masters and provided both religious services and mutual aid between their members, without the intervention of the bishops. This period could have been marked by the banquets of brotherhood, the *potatio*, annual banquet held at the time of the festival of the saint patron of the profession, and the university banquets, held for the obtaining of the diplomas (of which already the baccalaureate), if the Church had not chosen to condemn them, just as it had already before condemned the mortuary meals judged propitious to the pagan rituals. This time, the Church put forward as a pretext the defense of public order because the Christian framework of spiritual kinship would be used, in these banquets, in such a way as to challenge the very foundation of Christian society, that is to say its hierarchical character and the will of God from which one cannot escape. Charlemagne had moreover prohibited, in 779, like the Church, the oaths taken between members because one can take oath only to the authorities. The system will try to get hold of the guilds after the 11th century.

These banquets of brotherhood, organized at least once a year, are obligatory for their members who cannot abstain from taking part in them to the point that even in the event of major impediment of one of them a delegation carries the meal to his residence. One cannot better say that it is indeed a question of sharing the table to share a feeling of brotherhood which does not need the Church to maintain itself. The banquet of brotherhood allows a redistribution to oneself (to others oneself), they affirm thus their eminently egalitarian character, the more so as all kinds of food were served there, even those traditionally reserved to the powerful ones.

Franc-Christian drinking: French wine versus English beer

The Carolingian era will bring a new rule to the grammar of the French table with the praise of the French wine against the bad English beer. The Carolingian empire owes (almost) everything to England and to Alcuin[160]. Alcuin instructs the clergy through a clear writing of the homilies, the Gregorian sacramentary, etc. Religion is not so much a matter of inner adherence as of outer practice and conformity to the law (biblical religion, legal religion). The objective was to create the same people regardless of the country: the *populus christianus*. Charlemagne is the *christianitas*, the society of believers united under the same leader in the common will to realize the kingdom of God on earth.

Alcuin Albinus Flaccus (Alcuin of Tours), an Anglo-Saxon monk (circa 735-804), often presented as the preceptor of the West, Charlemagne's main advisor, founder and director of the Palace School of Aachen in charge of training the children of the kingdom's nobles destined for high office, will be our main guide, because of his particularly polemical stance on intoxicating beverages[161].

At the time of these debates, Alcuin was the head of the abbey of Saint-Martin de Tours, which Charlemagne had entrusted to him in 796, a classic procedure at the time for granting an income to the great intellectuals/ideologists of the regime (Fridegise succeeded him in 804 and became chancellor to Louis the Pious). Our Anglo-Saxon monk took

---

160. Jean Chélini, "Alcuin, Charlemagne et Saint-Martin de Tours" in *Revue d'histoire de l'Église de France*, vol. 47. n° 144, 1961, p. 19-50 ; Samuel Loewenfeld, "Une lettre inédite d'Alcuin" in *Bibliothèque de l'École des Chartes*, vol. 42, 1881, p. 8-11 ; René Martin, "*Vinum dulce, gloriosum... le thème du vin dans la poésie latine médiévale*" in *Bulletin de l'Association Guillaume Budé, Lettres d'humanité*, n° 49, December 1990, p. 356-370.
161. Alban Gautier, "Alcuin, la bière et le vin : comportements alimentaires et choix identitaires dans la correspondance d'Alcuin", in *Annales de Bretagne et des Pays de l'Ouest*, tome 111, 2004, p. 431-441.

part in the debate between the archdeacon Pierre de Blois and Robert de Beaufeu. The latter considered that beer was the source of the liberal and generous character of the English, which was contested by Pierre de Blois, who judged that all the evils that characterized the English were due to it. Alcuin, after having recalled that abstinence is certainly preferable, chooses the French "wine drinkers" against the English "beer drinkers", the choice of Christian France against pagan England. Alcuin multiplies his letters against the drunkenness of the English and their bad habits at the table: drunkenness, and particularly theirs, is like the mouth of hell; *gula*, and particularly theirs, is the door to all vices. For Alcuin, the English are close to the pagans by their table manners, their behavior, their clothes, their hairiness, their poetry, etc. Alcuin pushes the English out of Christianity because they resemble pagans. The English and pagans share a number of practices. The English and pagans are drunkards, beer drinkers, unlike the Franks and Romans who would be temperate wine drinkers. The English were also horse meat eaters, a sign of paganism. Alban Gauthier adds that Alcuin uses Gildas to explain that not to behave like a good Christian is to do worse than the pagans. Alcuin is himself a wine drinker, and he bases this choice on biblical texts (Book of Chronicles, Song of Songs, Proverbs and the story of the wedding at Cana). Wine, he says, is justified by the Bible because it is the liquid of the Eucharist, unlike beer, a native liquid that councils and island synods must constantly proscribe for the celebration of the Mass. Indeed, beer had become a pagan drink since the middle of the 6th century. Alcuin is not afraid of the association of feast and wine, his poems testify, for example, the description of the court of Charlemagne where wine flows in abundance. It is therefore normal to drink, moreover no monastic rule prohibits the consumption of wine in the West. Beer is non-Roman, non-Christian, non-legitimate, therefore vernacular, pagan and popular. Alcuin finally denounces a triple confusion: between Christians and pagans, between clerics and laymen, between the only legitimate learned culture and the illegitimate vernacular culture. I follow Alban Gauthier less when he considers that Alcuin's agenda is the definition of a religious and not a national identity. It is true that this question will be stronger in the 12th century at the time of the Norman conquest, but it mobilizes previously fixed schemas. Alcuin thus made wine an element of the national cement that was then in the making. During the second Carolingian period, we will see the construction of the national identity leaning this time on the hatred of the Germanic table.

What is drunkenness?

Charlemagne, Louis the Pious and then Charles the Bald will take numerous capitularies to fight against the drunkenness of the soldiers and the people. Gregory of Tours reserves long letters to the question of alcoholism. It is difficult to know what is reality and what is an ideological need to find simple ways to oppose "good" and "bad" Christians. The consumption of alcohol is indeed important in monasteries. Benedict of Aniane foresees 3 liters of wine per day for the canonesses or 2 liters of wine and 2 liters of beer. He also establishes an equivalence between water and beer and therefore allows people to drink freely. Saint Thomas Aquinas certainly condemns drunkenness in his *Summa Theologica* (13th century) but remains very tolerant: he multiplies the cases where drunkenness does not constitute a sin, because the drinker did not know that the drink was so strong, or because he was unaware of his own weakness towards wine. Saint Thomas Aquinas even adds that he who abstains to the point of harming his health commits a fault... Pierre Abélard (1079-1142) follows this tradition by reminding us that "according to whether the wine drawn from its fruit is taken with or without measure, it makes known to man the good or the evil."

The failure of Charlemagne's food policies

The Carolingian kings were the main landowners of Francia, due to the former properties of the Roman Empire passed first to the Merovingians, then to their own dynasty, and due to military conquests and purchases of estates by the palace.

The rules imposed on their own domains influenced the diet of many, especially since the properties of the Church, second landowner, and those of the nobles, received from the Merovingians and Charles Martel, followed the same standards. Charlemagne tried to impose a new conception of food through his capitularies and other legal rules, in which agriculture took precedence over hunting and breeding and cultivated cereals over gathering (herbs and berries). Charlemagne first used the old Merovingian mechanisms. In 744, he fixed the prices of wheat and various breads "in times of abundance as well as dearth". Oats were the reference grain, barley was worth twice as much as oats, rye three times as much, and wheat four times as much. For one denarius, one could have 12 loaves of wheat, 15 loaves of rye, 20 loaves of barley or 25 loaves of oats. The State bought cereals which it stored in the tax granaries and sold them at twice the normal price in times of crisis. Faced with the famine of 779, Charlemagne ordered the nobles to give alms. He also developed a policy to revive the vegetable gardens. Everything that was produced there was thus exempt from taxation. The capitulary *De villis*, which deals with economy and agriculture, makes it compulsory to cultivate dry beans and chickpeas to ensure the gap between two cereal harvests. All cereals, edible herbs, fruits, etc. are registered administratively. There are more than 200 species of pears in the palace properties. Some other texts can be cited, such as the capitulary against famine, adopted in 805, which includes both effective precautionary measures such as the prohibition of exporting foodstuffs, and acts of devotion such as the obligation to implore the mercy of God. A capitulary of 806 laid down the principle that every great man must feed his poor, but more than an obligation placed on the prelates and counts, it was a question of restricting begging and above all of forbidding the manants to go begging outside their county. Charlemagne also forbade the trampling of grapes and imposed clean working, making the use of iron-rimmed barrels compulsory, etc.

Charlemagne can therefore be credited with a real renewal of agriculture. He introduced three major innovations that would have an impact on the content of food during this period: the three-year crop rotation, the marning of the soil (the addition of marl, i.e. a mixture of limestone and clay to improve the soil, an old practice that had been abandoned since the end of Antiquity), and the use of the collar with a frame for horses to replace the ox. The Roman emperor Theodosius had forbidden the pulling of a horse weighing more than 500 kilos for fear that it would strangle itself, due to the well-known fragility of its neck... These Carolingian policies gave, at first, important results, as shown by the rather rapid shift from popular consumption of meat to bread. These changes were not without conflicts of use due to the clearing of land, the control of the nobles over the forests, marshes, etc. The *missi dominici* report the new tensions around the questioning of the rights of gleaning, affouage and glandage. Shortly after 800, the Carolingian system abandoned the project of returning to the model of the nurturing king, even before that of the hunting king developed. Historians note a complete abandonment of food risk management policies as early as 806, not because the Frankish state no longer had the capacity to intervene due to the collapse of its structures, but because of the apogee of obscurantist religious currents. This "failure of Charlemagne", to use François Louis Ganshof's formula, is the consequence of a certain "Christianization" made of contempt for matter, of the damnation of humans, prelude to the passage from an imperial theocracy to an episcopal theocracy.

A new clerical-feudal model will be set up, with as new decision-makers not the emperor and the palace any more, but the archbishops, the bishops, the abbots, the princes, the counts, in short, a whole new class, in particular seigneurial, which finds its own interest to interpret the situations of famine differently. The food crisis is thus not any more the consequence of natural events and the negligence of the temporal power, but a divine sanction. Pierre Toubert notes that there is no difference in behavior between secular and ecclesiastical lords, nor between towns and countryside. The only response to the risk of food shortages was now to be found in the ideological field of almsgiving, which was now a simple duty of *caritas* and no longer a duty of the State.

The conception of the table in the age of the episcopal theocracy

This second period of the Carolingian dynasty was one of regression in many areas, particularly in the area of ordinary food. The model, initially conceived for monastic life alone, was to inspire the discourse and measures taken against the whole of society, since the monasteries, models of religious perfection, were also considered to be the political foundation of the state. This drift explains the "failure of Charlemagne", who, after the death of Alcuin, let his son Louis (the Pious), then under the influence of the monk Benedict of Aniane, give an obscurantist character to all his policies. This transition from Alcuin to Benedict of Aniane marks a rise in power of a rigorist and ascetic theology (which does not only concern the monks) but is translated by the abandonment of policies aiming at guaranteeing an adequate popular food supply.

The interventionist policies of the empire were replaced by almsgiving by Louis the Pious and then his son, Louis the Bald, who went so far as to forbid priests to sell church property for charity, and to explain that malnutrition and famine were part of God's plan from which men could not escape unless they reformed spiritually. New movements such as the "Peace of God" movement, which emphasizes the confession of the faults of the powerful in relation to the divine order, rather than measures of food production, storage and distribution at maximum price, will soon be put to use. This new course is all the more easily imposed as currents advocating contempt for the body and matter, and therefore necessarily for food, are reinforced. This period is the one in which a new conception of the capital sins is deployed, making *gula* (gluttony) one of the seven capital sins that many consider to be, along with the story of Adam and Eve's apple, the very foundation of original sin.

A political history of food. From the Pateolithic to our days

The monasteries given as models

We would be wrong to take the later deviations in the field of the table for the reality of the time: monastic life, given as the most perfect, is made up of restrictions notably on the food level. Monasteries are not, contrary to what they will become, places where one eats better than in the rest of society and especially among the people. To be a monk is to obey a strict rule, and the regulations, and even more so the customs in force, are particularly severe with regard to the table. The restrictions concern the quantities, the qualities and the times of the meals, beyond the periods of fasting. The rule of St. Benedict, which became generalized under the influence of the Carolingians, forbade all consumption of meat, except for the sick; some monasteries even forbade vegetables prepared with fat. Monks were generally allowed only two frugal meals. The morning snack (usually bread and wine) is often forbidden. White bread was reserved for the sick and the monks were content with a coarse bread made of wheat, barley, oats, millet and vetch. They were forbidden pepper and cumin, which were widely consumed at the time. They eat eggs but very little fish, although it is allowed, and even less poultry. The Church would question the status of poultry at length. Their consumption was totally forbidden by the Council of Aix-la-Chapelle in 816 before another one, the following year, authorized it for eight days a year. The *pulli volatilia were* indeed a luxury food since they were much more expensive than butcher's meat. On the other hand, there is no problem for the Church to recognize without question that the tail of the beaver, because it is (almost) always in water, is equivalent to a fish.

The time is no longer so much about dietary miracles as about stories of vines voluntarily rendered sterile by the sprinkling of holy water by more pious monks than others, and about divine punishments for clerics who do not respect the fast. Thus, "during a meal at the home of the bishop Prix de Clermont, three guests, who abstained from eating meat, were laughed at by all the other guests. The room collapses and only the three abstainers or *paetitentes* are safe and sound...[162]" The monastic model is certainly given as specific since the Carolingians consider that society is composed of three different states, that of the monks, that of the other clerics (priests, bishops, etc.) and that of the laity (without differentiating between peasants and fighters, because of the figure of the peasant-warrior, inherited from the Merovingians). This monastic diet was progressively

---

162. Cyrille VOGEL, "La discipline pénitentielle en Gaule des origines au IXᵉ siècle : le dossier hagiographique" in *Revue des Sciences Religieuses*, vol. 30, n°1, 1956, p. 1-26.

given as an example not only to the clerics, but also to the laity, notables and commoners. The condemnation of the matter is not indeed valid only for the monks and each one, clerics or laymen, must be inspired by them to restrict themselves. This dialectic between religious specificity and the model it constitutes is not sufficiently taken into account. It is however it which explains that the table of the powerful, and in particular (we will see it) that of the Great of Spain - Spain is then the dominant power -, becomes so frugal and that the rich eat only twice a day, contrary to the people who continue to take four daily meals.

The sin of gluttony

The Christianization of the Frankish civilization will result in a multiplication of prohibitions. Certain restrictions initially intended for monks were to extend beyond the monasteries. The introduction of the deadly sins, their new classification and their interpretation will have a great influence on the conception of the popular table but also on that of the elites[163]. The Church once again made something new out of something old. The Assyrians and Babylonians had already imagined that human vices were the work of seven great animal demons. Clement of Alexandria made the sow the sign of gluttony, long before the Church. This link between the list of vices and a bestiary is logical, because animals are linked to the earth, to the flesh, in short to matter, so they represent everything that prevents the soul from rising. The idea of a sin of gluttony was born within the eremitical communities established in the Egyptian desert. Around 365, the monk Evagrius the Pontic lists eight vices by which the devil would manage to seize monks. Gluttony is the first of these temptations, lust the second. Thus we already find at work the couple *gula/luxuria* which will mark so much the Christian world until our days. Another monk, John Cassian, took up this list of the eight vices around 420 and transmitted it to the monasteries of the West. In his *System of vices*, he always gives the first place to gluttony, because it would be the oldest vice from which all the others derive. He speaks about *gastrimargia*, madness of the belly. This carnal vice is not accidental because it is explained by the very physicality of man. The monastic rule must therefore restrain the *gula* by limiting the number of food intakes, by defining the schedules, by specifying quantities and qualities of rations.

The repression of dietary practices has certainly existed since the Merovingian period and the introduction of the alternation of fat days

---

163. Florent QUELLIER, *Gourmandise, histoire d'un péché capital*, Paris, Armand Colin, 2010.

          A political history of food. From the Pateolithic to our days

and lean days, but it will especially increase during the second Carolingian period by taking support from a list proposed in 604 by Pope Gregory. It should be noted that in his mind this new list corresponded to the dangers linked to the cenobitic life of the West and not to the lifestyles of the faithful as a whole. He took up the seven vices and added pride. It was only with the new system of penitential tariffs and the adoption of confession (well before the principle of its annual obligation promulgated by the Council of 1215), which was based on precise questioning, that the Church asked priests to use this list, putting the *gula* in fifth place. The Church no longer spoke of vices but of sins, because what counted from then on was the act and it did not matter what the bad thoughts were. Anticipating the times to come, we can say that the *gula*, which in Roman times meant an organ and a pleasure, will remain one of the seven deadly sins. In the 13th century, Thomas Aquinas, in his *Summa Theologica*, defined gluttony as the sum of excess and refinement. In the 15th century, each capital sin had its own emblematic animal: the sin of gluttony became the pig, which not only could not stop eating, but grunted as it gobbled up its food before rolling in its own manure, similar to the gluttons who ate and drank excessively and without refinement. The question of the pig, an impure animal (*porcus diabolicus*) alongside the horse (declared inedible by Pope Gregory III (731-741) and whose meat was once again consumed after an 1866 order by the Paris Police Prefect) and the dog (much consumed in Germany), was settled with its rehabilitation, during the epidemic known as "mal des ardents" (the disease of the burning), with the transfer of the relics of St. Anthony from Constantinople to La Motte-Saint-Didier. The animals are always depicted in motion because they are heading, like the Ghouls, towards hell. The solution imagined was therefore to draw inspiration from monastic life - in which eating was totally regulated - to regulate the eating habits of the common people. I believe that we are mistaken in thinking that, from the point of view of the Church, the sin of gluttony only concerns, or even mainly, the rich and the powerful; because behind the incantatory denunciations, a conception of the table according to social rank is already being put in place which justifies these excesses. The sin of gluttony will soon no longer be eating too much but desiring too much.

Cassian distinguished three forms of gluttony that were common in the monasteries: anticipating the time of the meal, filling one's belly, and seeking out the finest or most carefully prepared foods.

Gregory the Great (pope in 590) adds the fact of eating excessively with regard to one's needs, and, above all, the fact of absorbing food under the spur of a desire that is much too ardent. He thus associates five vices with gluttony: silly joy, obscenity, loss of purity, excessive talkativeness and weakening of the senses. He denounces particularly the obscene songs and blasphemous remarks. Thus we see the idea that it is desire that really constitutes the vice of the *gula*, and not the excess of food in itself. The nobleman can eat a lot and even eat a lot of meat, without this constituting a sin, since he does so because of the obligations linked to his state, thus in accordance with God's plan; whereas a poor man can eat much less, but still be a sinner if he eats above his rank, that is to say if he envies the table of the powerful.

Thomas de Chobham maintains that one cannot impose on the powerful and the rich a diet that is too hard and that it is even preferable to organize alternative penances, in the form of alms and prayers. Gerson adds that a king who eats a lot, especially meat, does not commit a sin, but commits a sin by feeding his servants and the poor too much.

The Church fears the association of gluttony, loquacity and lust on the part of the powerful more than the excesses of the table. The sin of the language (*sic*) is indeed unjustifiable, even within the framework of its unequal conception of the society. Gilles de Rome attacks the speeches held in the banquets of the princes and proposes instead to read texts, according to the monastic use. He accepts however a compromise and suggests to read, instead of the religious texts, the customs of the kingdom, the gestures of the great elders and the manuals of instruction of the princes. What was progressively important was not so much the quantity of food consumed by the powerful, nor even its cost, but rather good table manners. Vincent de Beauvois was commissioned to write a manual of instructions for the children of Saint Louis.

The sin of gluttony is therefore variable and, for the poor, it is the fact of desiring above one's state, frequenting taverns and succumbing to drunkenness. Drunkenness is indeed worse than gluttony, for if gluttony is the idolatry of the belly, drunkenness is the worship of the devil: "Drunken people are the devil's worshippers and priests, who pray in his oratory or temple, that is, in the tavern; they worship him, sanctify him and sing."

Louis the Pious and Benedict of Aniane: the generalization of the hatred of the belly

The death of Alcuin of Tours, in 804, was to produce a real break in the Carolingian ideological system by allowing the more mystical currents to come to power and impose a much greater respect for religious prescriptions. The only surviving child of Charlemagne was Louis (778-840),

A political history of food. From the Pateolithic to our days

king of Aquitaine, who was brought up in the south of France, where the superstitious faction of the Church, steadfastly opposed by Alcuin, was strongest. Louis' preceptor was Benedict of Aniane (750-821), a leading figure in this rigorous faction; a Germanic aristocrat, a reformer of monasticism, a good connoisseur of the table and especially of wine, since he was the cupbearer of Berthe au grand pied, he founded a monastery in 774-775 on his property in Aniane, where he wanted to live according to Eastern traditions (dietary asceticism, begging, mortifications, sleep deprivation, etc.). His project did not meet with great success, so he soon adopted the rule of Saint Benedict, which was more flexible. His monastery spread rapidly and he became close to Louis the Pious again. In 813, when Charlemagne handed over his crown, Louis moved to Aachen and brought Benedict of Aniane to his court. They chased away Alcuin's former relatives and wished to integrate the monasteries even more into the heart of state institutions. Louis entrusted him with their reform in order to make them essential instruments of his power. Benedict of Aniane imposed the rule of St. Benedict on everyone and created the positions of *missi monastici* (modeled on the former *missi dominici* of Charlemagne) to ensure the strict application of his decisions. In 817, he and Louis the Pious convened a general chapter of all the monasteries and made several decisions: schools were henceforth reserved for future monks only, manual work was almost completely eliminated in order to renounce the world and separate from the profane world, the obligation to work for the conversion of pagans, the creation of prisons in the monasteries, an increase in the number of services and prayers, etc. He created a central monastic school in Inden (a monastery near Aachen) and each monastery in the empire was obliged to send two monks to train there. This period will reinforce the existing rigorist, if not obscurantist, tendencies. Some monasteries forbid washing because if the person is devoured by vermin, it is a punishment from God. It has been said that Benedict of Aniane prepared the work of Cluny, but this is to forget that he also prepared the abandonment of the little people to their sad fate and to hunger.

The condemnation of the belly

This period can be better understood by consulting the work entitled *The Contempt of the World (De contemptu mundi)* by Cardinal Lotario de Segni, the future Pope Innocent III, which he wrote between 1190 and 1198. This text is not only an ascetic treatise as there were so many of them, because it testifies to a will to put down all that is related to the body and matter. *The contempt of the world* no longer condemns only the excesses, but, in our field, the act of eating itself. Mankind did not have a native need to eat, then it ate only to satisfy its natural needs, then it succumbed to the sin of gluttony. This treatise takes up the thesis of one of the Fathers of the Church, Saint Ambrose, who maintains that the invention of food (on the sixth day of Creation) marks the passage from a world that grows to a world that is consumed, in short, a regression in Creation. This fall would have been limited, however, by the prohibition to eat the fruits of one of the trees of Creation. The first sin was therefore gluttony, but the evil was present through the existence of the belly alone. Ambrose writes: "And no sooner was food introduced than the end of the world began" even though it was "gluttony [that] drove out of the earthly paradise the man who reigned there." Certainly, Augustine would rectify this thesis by maintaining that what is primary is not gluttony, but the feeling of self-sufficiency, pride, disobedience, the idea that one can do without God. Carolingian society, however, remains marked by Ambrose's thesis, hence the repulsive representations of the *gula* given by the Church, hence his condemnation of excessive eating, hence his fight against drunkenness understood as a more particularly diabolical form of the *gula,* hence his disgust at everything that is matter, food and drink, and his conviction that humanity will one day no longer need to feed itself. Alcuin, who was far from being the most rigorous, expressed the mood of the times: "What you ate and drank yesterday is excrement today [...] This is what our pleasures are: excrement and decay. He quotes St. Paul: *Non est regnum Dei esca et potus* to remind us of the unimportance of food and drink for salvation, a sign of the irreconcilable nature of the belly, and not only of the *gula*, with the kingdom of God.

Louis the hunter

Louis is as much a hunter king as a pious king. The only thing he refuses is to be a foster king. He will gradually restrict the rights of the little ones on the forests and increase his own hunting grounds and those of the nobles around him. Eginhard, who worked for his glory after having worked for that of his father, reminds us that the practice of hunting is a cultural trait of the Franks..., by which he means the nobles and not the peasant-warriors. These royal hunts will not cease to develop until Louis VI with a capture of the game whose food goal is not the principal objective. This hunting of large animals was no longer a warrior training and became a simple court ritual bringing together the king and the nobles. Louis the Pious organized feasts in the middle of the forest without ever forgetting the pomp. He sits with his guests on golden armchairs while the other

A political history of food. From the Pateolithic to our days

hunters lie on the grass: "Soon the servants bring the roasted flesh of the animals killed in the hunt: a varied venison covers the table of the emperor. Hunger falls; they bring the cups to their lips, and in turn thirst is driven away by the sweet drink: the generous wine rejoices these bold hearts, and all return to the court with gusto."

Charles the Bald and Hincmar of Reims: the end of food policies

When Louis the Pious died in June 840, a period of turmoil related to the division of the empire between his sons, Lothar, Louis of Bavaria and Charles of Aquitaine began. After the treaty of Verdun (843) Charles, in addition to Aquitaine, saw his kingdom of Francia occidentalis (Western Francia) increase by the western part of Burgundy and Neustria, up to the mouth of the Scheldt.

Charles had his head shaved as a sign of submission to God, choosing the Church against the Frankish tradition that required a king to have long hair..., and became Charles the Bald. While he lives in a world of religious symbols, the Church keeps repeating that life is fleeting and death eternal, and he respects the dietary rules, he organizes great festivities for royal birthdays.

Charles the Bald took as his eminence grise Hincmar of Rheims (806-882), archbishop of Rheims (845-882), who was to develop a new political theology, the first consequence of which was to abandon the poor to their fate. Hincmar distinguishes between the *pauperes*, the *ignobiles*, just assured of their economic and legal existence, the mediocre, who live on little, then the well-to-do and the *nobiles*, and finally, the *proceres primores* and the sublimes. This vision of society is a way of allowing the State to withdraw from the last food policies still in place, while the Church, itself under the influence of Hincmar, strongly reduces its alms to the poorest. Everyone fulfills God's plan by staying in his place without changing the order of things. Man can only suffer his fate in order to better prepare his future life. God is given as the only master of the economy, to intervene would be to thwart his will. The enemy is not wealth or social inequality, but the hoarding that leads (the poor) to want to steal other people's goods. Envy is more sinful than wealth because it is contrary to God's desire. Hincmar intends to separate the clerics from the laity in order to build a counter-society: he forbids them to participate in collective banquets and intends to make them lose the taste for good food, drink and pleasures. He sacralized the goods of the Church, making the priests simple usufructuaries, without the possibility of hiring them to finance good works of charity.

After the death in 877 of Charles the Bald (elevated to the rank of emperor by the pope in 875) and the interlude of Carloman (877-884), Charles the Fat, son of Louis the German, temporarily restored the unity of the Carolingian empire (884-887/888). But incapable, cowardly, deceitful and brutal, Charles the Fat was deposed in 887 by his own Germanic subjects in favor of a bastard of one of his brothers, Arnoul, followed in 888 by the nobles of West Francia who went to look for a king outside the Carolingian dynasty. The unanimity is made to push back Arnoul, Germanic king pretending to the throne. However, the nobles of West Francia were divided over their choice: three candidates were vying for power. The Frankish Church tried to impose Guy of Spoleto, who came from Italy, but failed. An anecdote reported by Liutprand of Cremona, in the *Antapodosis*, is worth quoting, because it testifies to the arguments chosen to refuse Guy of Spoleto[164]. While the bishop of Metz was preparing to receive him to crown him king of the Franks and had great honors and a large banquet prepared for him, he learned of the frugality of Guy of Spoleto and therefore preferred him to Eudes, count of Paris, a fierce adversary of the Normans and a good eater, i.e., a lover of meat: "He is not worthy of reigning over us, the one who is content with a vile meal of a few cents. This frugal diet is called *contra naturam francorum*. Guy, hearing of Eudes' appointment, returned to Italy and became pope. The bishop Foulque crowns, however, January 28, 893, the anniversary of the death of Charlemagne, Charles the Simple, but the latter, to oppose Eudes he considers a usurper of the title, although he had sworn loyalty in 888, allies himself with the Normans, which provokes the fury of Foulque: "The God you irritate will lose you quickly." The only certainty of the nobles of West Francia is that, if they do not want a king bad eater, that is to say kneaded of Greco-Roman culture and not Frankish, they do not want either a Germanic king, fat but bad eater. Liutprand of Cremona praises the virtues of the *Rex francorum* by opposing him to the *Rex graecorum*, great lover of leeks and onions and drinker of water, displaying a sobriety and an excessive humility to be worthy of exercising the power...

---

164. Massimo MONTANARI, "Valeurs, symboles, messages alimentaires durant le haut Moyen Âge" in *Médiévales*, n° 5, 1983, p. 57-66, numéro thématique : *Nourritures*, sous la direction d'Odile REDON.

Germans, fat but bad eaters

The hatred of the beer-drinking Englishman never gave an inch during this long period, but it is now combined with a hatred of the German[165]. This was the period of the emergence of a lasting aversion between the French and German peoples, even if its solidified expression would not see the light of day until the 11th century. A new vocabulary was already appearing, which opposed Francie and Saxonia, the *populus francorum* and the *populus saxonorum*. We are not yet at the point where the king of the Franks, Louis VI the Fat, is said to have said to an envoy of the emperor Henry V: "Tpwrut [*sic*] Aleman", but the ground is prepared. This aversion has of course a linguistic basis, as witnessed by the violence between young people from the 9th century onwards. However, it is adorned, on both sides, with a culinary dimension. Certainly, the Germans ate a lot (like the Franks) but badly (according to the Franks). They ate barley, sauerkraut and buttermilk (the liquid left over after the milk was beaten to make butter). They consumed, supreme monstrosity, milk soup. The Germans reproached the Gauls for being too greedy and therefore sinful. These indictments miss the point: there are indeed two cultural areas, two different ways of eating. While the "French" banquet distinguishes between soups (food cooked in a sauce), then rôts and, finally, entremets; the "German" banquets oppose cold dishes (salads, boiled meats and fish, roasted, smoked and pâtés) to hot dishes and conclude with cold and hot sweet dishes. The organization of the banquets is also surprising for both Germans and French. On the German side, no one is allowed to serve himself, since the service is provided by servants and each guest has access to the same dishes, the dishes follow each other and are not all brought at the same time.

The Carolingian table of the second period laid the foundations for a poor table for the poor and a rich table for the rich. The aristocracy adopted other table manners, still luxurious but in the new respect of compensatory rituals. The food of the people was regulated by new capitularies and the Church was happy to receive the mission to supervise sexual and table manners. Thus, rules often invented to discipline the monks were imposed on the whole society at the cost of some compromises. The great innovative idea is however that the stomachs of the poor are not those of the rich. This thesis is defended in the name of science, faith and order.

---

165. Stephen MENNELL, *Français et Anglais à table du Moyen Âge à nos jours*, trans. Thierry Detienne, Paris, Flammarion, 1987.

We leave the Carolingian table for the clerical-feudal table at a time when the Church is no longer content to issue a ban against the hare, considered lewd, hermaphroditic and homosexual[166], but also begins to write treatises on popular food. The first of these was written by Peter of Spain, the future Pope John XXI, under the title *Thesaurus pauperum* (*Treasure of the poor*). The future pope explains that coarse meats, rye bread, etc., are better suited to the bellies of the working classes. It will be retorted that the medical theses went in this direction, maintaining that the work being not natural, since divine sanction, it produced a strong heat and burned the bad food. However, Massimo Montanari points out that Peter IV of Aragon, in his *Ordinacions*, indicates that wine that has gone sour, moldy bread, rotten fruit, rancid cheese... are perfectly suitable for ritual alms given to the poor.

166. Jean-Louis FLANDRIN, "L'alimentation et la religion pendant le haut Moyen Âge" *in* [Collectif], *Festins mérovingiens*, Bruxelles, Le Livre Timperman, 2008; Bruno LAURIOUX, "Le lièvre lubrique et la bête sanglante. Réflexions sur quelques interdits alimentaires durant le haut Moyen Âge", *Anthropozoologica*, 1988, p. 128-129.

NINTH SERVICE: THE CLERICAL-FEUDAL TABLE

We are beginning to enter a more familiar field, since works on the table in the Middle Ages and the Renaissance are numerous and well documented, with the exception of popular uses of the table. Jean-Louis Flandrin and Bruno Laurioux have written extensively on this history, but with little interest in its social, regional, cultural, culinary and even technical dimensions. The table in the Middle Ages served as much to create the divisions of society as to represent and stage them.

We are not only in the domain of images and staging but in that of a performative discourse. The powerful, especially clerics and doctors, create society by explaining how poor and rich should eat. The works of historians, in particular those of Bruno Laurioux, constitute a mine of factual information for those who want to take seriously what is at stake through the various rules of the feudal table[167]. He will therefore be our guide and we refer the reader to his works for further information. However, historians too often present the popular tables from the point of view of the powerful (which is what the available sources tend to do), but the poor are not "rich" people who lack only money, nor are they "nobles" without honor.

---

167. This work is based on the following works, even if I remain solely responsible for the analysis: Bruno LAURIOUX, Le *Moyen Âge à table*, Paris, Adam Biro, 1989; *id. Manger au Moyen Âge. Pratiques et discours alimentaires en Europe aux XIV* et XV* siècles*, Paris, "Littératures", Hachette, 2002 ; *id. Une histoire culinaire du Moyen Âge*, Paris, H. Champion, 2005; *id. Écrits et images de la gastronomie médiévale*, Paris, "Conférences Léopold Delisle", Éditions de la Bibliothèque nationale de France, 2011 ; Catherine LANOË, Bruno LAURIOUX et Mathieu DA VINHA (dir), *Cultures de cour, Cultures du corps, XIV*-XVIII* siècle*, Paris, Presses de l'université Paris-Sorbonne, 2011 ; Jean-Louis FLANDRIN and Carole LAMBERT *Fêtes gourmandes au Moyen Âge*, Paris, Imprimerie nationale, 1998; Éric BIRLOUEZ, *À la table des seigneurs, des moines et des paysans du Moyen Âge*, Rennes, "Histoire", Éditions Ouest-France, 2011; *id.* Nelly LABÈRE, *Être à table au Moyen Âge*, Madrid, Casa de Velázquez, 2011; *Banquets et manières de table au Moyen Âge*, [Actes du 21e colloque du CUERMA], Aix-en-Provence, CUERMA, université de Provence, 1996.

The humble make choices that are not only "choices of the necessary", for example by refusing wheat for themselves, because they know from experience that excessive cerealization is not good in terms of security for the little people. The table of the humble corresponds to another wealth, to other ways of eating and drinking. This table is however that of a social apartheid - I use this anachronistic term deliberately - justified by religious and medical considerations.

A dualisation of the table

The clerical-feudal table is based on the famous theory of the chain of being (which leads the nobles to prefer to eat birds and to leave the bulbs and the roots to those who are becoming serfs), but this thesis crosses another theory, But this theory intersects with another theory, that of the three orders, stated by Pope Zechariah and taken up by the bishop of Rheims, Adalberon, in a text expressing the profound meaning of the unexpected rallying of the Church to Hugh Capet, thus betraying its Ottonian allies, who wished to rebuild, from Germania, the empire of Charlemagne. Once again, the Church and the powerful allied themselves to defend their power and they did so by defining ways of eating. It was no longer enough to be a "good eater" to respect the calendar of lean days and meat days (*sic*), one still had to eat lean or fat, vegetables or meat, according to the "social" status defined by the Church. The populi, who had already lost the right to eat meat according to their own customs, would have to accept eating differently from those other Christians who were the powerful (clerics and lords) because of the choice of maximum cerealization and the control of the nobles over the forests.

We shall see that this new theory, elaborated from the 9th century onwards, which no longer opposes the laity to secular clerics, on the one hand, and to regular clerics, on the other, but which henceforth distinguishes between "those who pray", "those who fight" and "those who work", undoubtedly responds to lofty theological considerations, but also to the well-thought-out interests of the powerful! We usually like to insist on everything that distinguishes the tables of the warriors, the clerics and the workers, but behind these secondary differences, we notice that if the food situation of "those who pray" and "those who fight" improves, the majority of "those who work" undergoes a food regression, in spite of the ingenuity that "those who work" put in order to feed themselves and find pleasure in it.

We can therefore speak of a real dualisation of the table corresponding to the end of the last "free peasants", to the development of serfdom, to the weakening of the position of the old manual professions, to the appropriation of the land - in particular of the forests, moors, marshes, promoted as hunting grounds by a small minority, and finally to the concentration of habitats and settlements.

This evolution, which is summarized in the concept of *incastellamento* ("entrenchment"), led to the marginalization of the once important silvo-pastoral activities. This period, which marks a decline in common lands and common goods, such as mills or village ovens, continues, on the other hand, the policy of "great works" in terms of deforestation, draining of marshes, irrigation, but also the mutation of agricultural techniques, not all of which are beneficial to the greatest number, as the adoption of the scythe instead of the sickle, as also the fact, within the framework of the cerealization, of privileging the wheat, or, in that of the breeding, of facilitating the rise of the big ovine herds thanks to the transhumance to the contempt of the former uses.

The appalling record of successive periods of hunger and famine is all the more unacceptable when society already has the resources to make food choices that benefit the greatest number.

A programmed evolution
I understand that the Church will draw on existing ideologies to justify extending the realm of religious constraints beyond the straitjacket of lean days and other restrictions and prohibitions. We have seen how the sin of gluttony came to be used to denounce the aspirations of the beggars to eat better (above their state) rather than the wastefulness of the nobles in a context of poverty. I also understand that the political system started to change well before the election of Hugues Capet, in 987, that is to say before the nobles (the feudalists), who were already in power, finally imposed one of their own as king, with the explicit support of the Church. This was because feudalism really came into being with the capitulary of Meerssen in 847, which obliged each free man to choose "freely" a "senior" in accordance with the inegalitarian vision defended in particular by the Church: "We want each free man in our kingdom to receive as lord the one he chooses himself, either ourselves or one of our followers. Then, because the designation of Capet is only possible because since 888 the royalty is again elective in Francia occidentalis, sign of its decline.

The theory of the three orders

We always eat according to the representations of society that are ours. We cannot change the table without changing our cosmology. We have seen this with Egypt, Greece and Rome. We cannot understand how the clerical-feudal system managed to modify the diet of 20 million "French" without detailing its vision of the world, its conception of order and therefore of power[168]. We will follow this story "strangely" starting from the choice of Hugues Capet against Charles of Lorraine, a choice largely imposed by Archbishop Adalberon of Rheims, however a member of the Ottonian "party", favourable to the project of the German to reconstitute the empire of Charlemagne, but which the Church judged too "independent". This troubled period was marked by speeches in favor of restoring order in a society that had lost all sense of "natural" and divine hierarchy. Thus, the Carolingians were put on trial in the same way as the Merovingians themselves. To justify this "return to normality", the theory of the orders of Pope Zechariah was used, that is to say, a conception of society distributed in classes (which were not social classes at all) and each of which had a well-defined status in God's plan, which, moreover, legislation and dietary customs never ceased to specify.

This theory of the three orders succeeded the Carolingian division between monks, secular clergy and laity, elaborated at a time when every "free man" was a warrior. The new representation distinguishes between the *bellatores* ("those who fight"), the *oratores* ("those who ensure communication with God") and the *laboratores* ("those who work"). I would like to emphasize that from the Church's point of view it is not a question of making a sociological analysis, opposing, for example, free men and slaves or poor and rich. Among the *laboratores,* one finds slaves, serfs, craftsmen, rich bourgeois and extremely wealthy bankers. This classification is more ontological, one might even say "essentialist", since it is a matter of prescribing to each person a series of behaviors in conformity with God's plan. The consequence of this plan of God is first of all to isolate the clerics even more from the rest of society and to allow *in fine* an alliance (of class) between *bellatores* and *oratores*, largely coming from the same social circles and especially to imagine a "King-Priest" whereas he was until then only the representative of the peasant-warriors in the old representation. It is difficult to see today to what extent this representation of power went against the conceptions shared by many at the time. The Church had to

---

168. Auguste DUMAS, "L'Église de Reims au temps des luttes entre carolingiens et robertiens (888-1027)", in *Revue d'histoire de l'Église de France*, vol. 30, n° 117, 1944, p. 5-38.

fight ideologically to impose it, even among the *bellatores*. We have with the famous poem of Adalberon to King Robert an essential testimony on this ideological fight and on its consequences in terms of alliances. We will see that if Adalberon starts by speaking about war theology, he ends up speaking about cooking.

Adalberon, the three orders and food

Adalberon of Laon wrote his poem to King Robert in 1025, introducing into the conception of royal power the Christian theory of social order, the pivot of which is his vision of kingship[169]. This poem is sometimes presented as the most complete expression in the West of the new Christian conception of royal power. This poem is constructed in three stages: in the first movement, Adalberon shows that the king possesses all the attributes of youth (*juventus*), he is handsome, he is strong, he has great moral energy. A new law, that of the Cluniacs, promoters of the peace movement, has however turned the world upside down, since the monks have turned into *milites* and have built a carnival army incapable of resisting the Saracens. Royalty has thus failed in its function of guiding the youth. The second part of the poem is a call to rely on wisdom (*sapienta*) of which the king also possesses the attributes. He must use it to rebuild his kingship in the image of the heavenly Jerusalem. The knowledge of the divine law allows him to keep the clerics away from the world of the serfs. In the same way, the human law prescribes him to separate the condition of the nobles from that of the serfs. The interplay of these two laws leads to a tripartite division *oratores/bellatores/laboratores*, but in which the *oratores* and the *bellatores* have in common to distinguish themselves from the serfs. In the third part, Adalberon paints portraits: the serf is sent back to the plough; the clerics, protected from all defilement, no longer split the earth or stand behind the backs of oxen. They are neither butchers, nor innkeepers, nor pig farmers, nor shepherds. They do not sift wheat, nor do they cook. All these jobs that concern agriculture and food are given as impure and therefore reserved exclusively for serfs. The act of cooking is devalued and represented by a greasy pot. The table is impure because of its relationship with the animal world. To the impure food, prepared by the serf and the cook, is opposed the sacred food, the Eucharist, prepared

---

169. Claude Carozzi, "Les fondements de la tripartition sociale chez Adalbéron de Laon" in *Annales. Economies, Sociétés, Civilisations.* 33ᵉ année, n° 4, 1978, p. 683-702 ; Ferdinand Lot, "Une charte fausse d'Adalbéron, archevêque de Reims" in *Bibliothèque de l'École des chartes*, vol. 52, 1891, p. 31-45.

by the clerics. Claude Carozzi notes that in Adalberon there is a greater tolerance towards the vegetable world. The cleric can frequent the vine, the tree, the gardens.

To each his own table!

It is of course no coincidence that Adalberon, in the text that justifies the rallying of the Church to Hugh Capet, ends up talking about cooking. Indeed, this is the shortest way to illustrate the implications of the new worldview and its unequal order. This system of social tripartition will combine with the theory of the chain of being to define a new food grammar.

The new theory of the chain of being
The Church takes up and develops in its own way the old idea that the universe is ordered vertically from God to inanimate objects (minerals). The hierarchy of beings thus depends on their living environment. The divine creation is composed of four elements: fire, air, water and earth. These four elements are supposed to be arranged in concentric circles with water surrounding earth, air surrounding water and fire surrounding air. This theory allows us to understand the hierarchy of foods and therefore their distribution. The celestial food hierarchy thus descends from birds to fish and then from mammals to plants. The earth is the element furthest from the Creator: what comes from it is at the bottom of the celestial hierarchy, and therefore also of the food hierarchy. Bruno Laurioux explains that this great chain of being justifies the contempt of the powerful for vegetables. However, this category is itself subdivided: at the bottom are the bulbs (garlic, onion, leek, shallot), just above are the "roots" whose underground part is consumed (turnips, rabe, parsnips, carrots), then the vegetables whose leaves start from the root (lettuce, spinach) and, at the top, those whose leaves start from the stem (cabbage, peas).

The classification of mammals is also complex: game is of course superior to butcher's meat, but there are subtle gradations, so beef, initially depreciated, is however more noble if it is an ox rather than a cow. Distinctions are also made between fish by considering those that fly as more noble. Birds occupy a higher level but differentiating between those that fly the highest, those that never fly very high (chickens) and those that struggle to fly away (ducks and geese). The fourth element, fire, interferes with the cooking methods: the Middle Ages reverse the hierarchy by valuing direct cooking (by fire), semi-direct cooking (with the roast), and then indirect cooking (boiled).

                A political history of food. From the Pateolithic to our days

Thus the working classes, progressively forbidden to eat meat and even fish, had to make do with the worst kinds of vegetables and especially bad bread. We shall see that they never stopped cheating, notably through gathering and poaching. The powerful kept a mainly meaty diet, preferring waterfowl and poultry. They also ate pork, a symbol of the separation of Christians from Jews and Muslims, but as it was a (too) popular meat, they began to differentiate between raw and salted bacon. The powerful ate vegetables (the most noble ones) but almost always as an accompaniment to a dish. On lean days, they eat a lot of fish, a symbol of Christ (in ancient Greek, the word fish ichtus, (ἰχθύς, *ikhthús*), is composed of the first letters of the terms composing the formula "Jesus Christ son of God savior").

A medical discourse favorable to the powerful

Doctors consider that diseases are explained by disturbances between the four humors that run through the body: blood, bile, melancholy and phlegm. Their respective proportions define the personality of each person: sanguine, bile, choleric and phlegmatic. A sanguine individual must eat poultry because these birds borrow heat and humidity from the air, their environment of origin, and blood is a hot and humid mood.

What did we eat?

Historians of taste, notably Jean-Louis Flandrin and Bruno Laurioux, have questioned the idea of a "culinary international" that would have homogenized the table between the 13th and 15th centuries. There are national preferences that even work on certain common elements such as the attraction for a colorful table. For example, the French prefer "graines de paradis" to pepper and verjuice to vinegar. Laurioux notes that English cookbooks, even when written in French, are undeniably English, with, for example, a great use of beer in cooking, largely sweet dishes and a great use of color against the eat-white that characterizes French "good taste.

A very colorful table

The grammar of the table in the Middle Ages insists on the importance of the color of food, the techniques used to color it are abundantly explained, but without sufficiently saying that, among all these colors, "eating-white" is a national preference, whereas, for example, the English, but also the Germans, eat more colorfully. Eating-white undoubtedly refers to the domain of emblems such as the fleur-de-lis, which only the eldest daughter of the Church, i.e. France, can boast of. White is a symbol of purity but also of peace. It is therefore found in food and toppings. This white food is obtained both by dyes and by the choice of white substances such as white fish, poultry meat, rice, crushed almonds deposited in several layers, sugar (which is the only major use). Green sauce is also very common, but it never manages to dethrone the white food. It is sometimes explained that this debauchery of colors is a way to ward off collective anguish: these centuries are indeed centuries of great fear, skilfully maintained by the Church, but it should not be forgotten that theology then considers colors as an essential instrument to rise to the "light of God". To stay in the food domain, if white expresses purity, green evokes fertility, black power, yellow wisdom, gold and silver luxury and pomp, etc.. The white color is given by bread crumbs or almonds, the green is obtained with spinach juice, leek green, sorrel, parsley or sage, the yellow with saffron or egg yolk, the red with sunflower or orca-nette root, the black is given notably with burnt bread, other plants color blue, purple, etc. We would be surprised to see the color of some dishes: game, symbol of power, is colored in black while other meats are in pink/red. These different colors are also mixed with jellies, which are used extensively because they are appreciated for their brilliant colors.

A very acid and spicy table
Medieval cuisine is characterized by the search for an extremely acidic and spicy taste. This is possible because of the use of thick wine sauces, thanks to a binding with breadcrumbs or egg yolk and the importance of stuffed preparations. Not only meat and fish are spiced, but also soups, desserts and fruits, such as pears in syrup with cinnamon[170]. The taste goes rather to low fat sauces, contrary to the legends, but very colorful. The acidic taste is given by the use of verjuice (juice extracted from green grapes or sometimes from wild apples), vinegar, and sometimes currant juice. This attraction explains the preference for naturally more acidic white wines. The strong flavor is given by spices: specialists list more than 200 of them, some of them surprising like the secretions produced by the sex glands of the beaver. The most consumed spices are more ordinary, such as cloves, pepper, cinnamon, nutmeg, ginger, saffron, anise, etc. The French use maniguette much more than other peoples, not because they particularly like its taste, but because it is the only country where the fruits of this plant have been called "seeds of paradise". These seeds are the spice of the aristocracy, while pepper is neglected because it is far too popular.

---

170. Bruno LAURIOUX, "De l'usage des épices dans l'alimentation médiévale" in *Médiévales*, vol. 2, n° 5, 1983, thematic issue: *Nourritures*, under the direction of Odile REDON, p. 15-31.

This table particularly likes to mix spices, especially cinnamon and ginger. The study of the recipes shows a contempt for cumin. The preferred taste, and therefore dominant, is sweet and sour.

Specialists have questioned the reasons for this attraction to a spicy table. They all reject the thesis that this choice is explained by the need to camouflage the taste of decaying meat, an argument that reflects our ideological *preconceptions* about the past. Some believe that it is the part of dream associated with exoticism and marvellous stories that makes cinnamon, for example, a spice coming from the nest of the Phoenix, a legendary bird that became a symbol of the resurrection of Christ... Others explain this preference by the chain of being, since spices coming from hot and arid regions are associated with the element "fire", supposed to be the noblest of creation.

I would like to return to the controversy between Maxime Robinson and Bruno Laurioux. The specialist of the Arab world sees in the great use of spices an importation of the Arab taste, while the historian of the table inscribes the medieval cuisine, not so exceptional in his eyes, in the simple prolongation of ancient traditions. This attraction for oriental spices seems to me to be explained by the thesis then shared that the East is the region in which Eden existed. Eating spicy food is therefore an act of faith, even before being a gustatory preference, or rather, one likes to eat spicy food because it brings one closer to the imagined food of the earthly paradise. The only nation where the Arabization of the table is indisputable is England, which has a very pronounced taste for sugar while this ingredient remains largely shunned on the whole continent. France did not really discover sugar until the 15th century and used it differently: sapa, a must reduced by half, which had great sweetening properties, was used in wine sauces.

We know from the work of ceramologists such as Danièle Alexandre-Bidon that the Middle Ages were sensitive to the flavors added by the containers[171]. The taste of smoke or the taste of burning were hated to the point of changing (breaking) the pots that had taken on these odors. The taste of oak is sought after for soups, fish, butter, fruit, honey, vinegar. The taste of clay is sought after because it has the same origin as the human body from clay.

A deceptive table
The clerical-feudal table preserves the taste for unnatural products, i.e. transformed. The praise of naturalness did not appear until the 16th

---

171. Danièle Alexandre-Bidon, *Une archéologie du goût. Céramique et consommation (Moyen Âge - Temps modernes)*, Paris, "Espaces médiévaux", Picard, 2005.

century[172]. A good table should not allow for the immediate identification of the product, whether it is vegetables or legumes, fruit, and of course meat or fish. Cooks play with colors and spices, with cooking methods and with a whole art that consists in giving a deceptive appearance to products, in the spirit of the cuisine of metamorphoses dear to the ancient Romans. The great attraction of pâtés and pies is explained by the possibility of hiding food in them and giving them shapes that follow those of an animal, for example.

How the powerful eat

While the popular table became progressively poorer during the Middle Ages, that of the powerful became considerably richer. The main principle was not only to eat more and better than the little people, but also to eat more and better than one's peers. The table is thus a language of power within the good society, although it is different among those who only have a significant patrimony and among those who maintain vassalage ties. The nobility represented about 1% of the population, the clergy 1% and the *laboratores* (mainly peasants) 98%.

The Housekeeper of Paris

We have a precise knowledge of the eating habits of "good society" thanks to a series of works, including *Le Ménagier de Paris* written around 1390 by an elderly bourgeois passing on to his young wife practical and moral advice about the table[173]. The author recommends to his wife to exclude food that is too expensive, such as certain birds, because they are above their rank. A meal in "good society" must certainly offer poultry, but there is a whole gradation between those of the "little rich" (chicks, chickens, capons, roosters, hens, geldings, ducks, (chicks, chickens, capons, roosters, hens, geldings, ducks, pigeons, geese), those of the "average rich" (woodcock, plovers, quail, larks, thrushes, magpies) and those of the "great rich" or even the lords (swans, herons, peacocks, cranes, storks, cormorants, bitterns, etc.).). The table of the rich must also exclude fruits that are too popular, such as blackberries, chestnuts, pine nuts, rosehips, wild

---

172. Philippe Meyzie, *L'alimentation en Europe à l'époque moderne*, Paris, "Collection U", Armand Colin, 2010 ; Alain Drouard, *Les Français et la table : alimentation, cuisine, gastronomie du Moyen Âge à nos jours*, Paris, Ellipses, 2005.

173. Le Ménagier de Paris, *traité de morale et d'économie domestique, composé vers 1393 par un Parisien pour l'éducation de sa femme*, Jérôme Pichon (éd), Bibliothèque de l'École des chartes, vol. 9, n° 1, 1848, p. 353-354.

---

strawberries, mountain ash, alders, but offers sloes, currants, raspberries, walnuts and hazelnuts, and all cultivated fruits, such as apples, pears, cherries, plums, quinces... and in the South, olives, almonds, peaches, apricots, figs, grapes, etc. The author of the *Ménagier* adds that "to eat once a day is a life of an angel and twice a human life; but to eat three or four times a day or more, is a life of a beast and not a human creature". The possessors, respectful of their status, i.e. of the divine order, know how to restrict themselves, a sign of their relative idleness (because they do not need to eat like those who work), but also of their respect for good customs. They abstain from breakfast, have dinner in the late morning and supper in the middle of the afternoon. Those who do not respect this rule and those who cleverly cheat it are denounced. These transgressions, coming from the merchant circles, eventually reached the court: Charles V (king of France from 1364 to 1380), who got up around noon and had his first meal at 5 p.m., stayed at the table for three hours, then ate again heavily from midnight until 6 a.m. These table manners were the laughing stock of foreign courts: in Spain, for example, those Frenchmen who ate three or four times a day and did not hesitate to make themselves vomit between meals in order to continue eating were denounced. The great Catalan moralist Francesc Eiximenis even wrote: "Cursed be the land whose princes eat in the morning like children [...] It should be enough for everyone to eat twice a day."

Guillaume Tirel known as Taillevent
Guillaume Tirel (1310-1395), known as Taillevent, is the author of the famous book *Le Viandier*, a testimony of the dietary habits of the nobles[174]. He began as a master chef to King Charles V in 1373, and in 1388 became the first equerry to Charles VI. Taillevent intended to distance himself from the famous treatise of Apicius which remained the absolute reference.

---

174. *Le Viandier de Guillaume Tirel, dit Taillevent, enfant de cuisine de la reine Jehanne d'Évreux, queu du roi Philippe de Valois et duc de Normandie, dauphin de Viennois, premier queu et sergent d'armes de Charles V, maistre des garnisons de cuisine de Charles VI [1326-1395] ; published on the manuscript of the National Library, with the variants of the manuscripts of the Mazarine Library and the Archives de la Manche, preceded d'an introduction and accompanied by notes*, by Baron Jérôme Pichon,..... and Georges VICAIRE. *Attached are original pieces relating to Taillevent, reproductions of his seals and tomb, the reprint of the oldest known edition of his book, a new edition of the oldest treatise on cooking written in French and a table of contents.* In Paris, sold by Techener, 1892. In-8°, LXVIII-480 pages. (Plus an additional leaf, which contains the text of a letter from Philippe de Valois, dated November 1330.); Bruno LAURIOUX, *Le règne de Taillevent. Livres et pratiques culinaires de la fin du Moyen Âge*, Paris, Publications de la Sorbonne, 1997; *id.* Between knowledge and practices: the cookbook at the end of the Middle Ages" in *Médiévales*, vol. 7, n° 14, 1988, p. 59-71, thematic issue: *La culture sur le marché.*

The cuisine he proposed was rich, abundant and spicy, in accordance with the customs of the time, but above all free of Gallo-Roman canons.

The aristocratic diet

The French aristocratic diet inherited the obligation to "eat a lot" but added the prohibition of eating more than a member of a higher rank than oneself. A wife or child may also not eat or drink more than her husband or father. Different quantities of meat were provided according to the status of the guests: a prince received 2 pounds of meat, dukes and grand knights 1 pound, simple knights 1 half-pound, squires, chaplains and clerks a quarter-pound, servants an eighth, etc. (Banquet offered to Humbert II, dauphin of Viennese, 14th century.)

The nobles, apart from banquets, ate in their private apartments as a sign of power and left the common room called "tinel" to the servants. They also liked to have lunch on the grass, especially during the great hunts.

The meals of the nobles are structured around three moments (soups, roasts and entremets) which take on different dimensions and meanings depending on their private or public nature. Many other services are added. I insist first of all on the fact that if the "meats" are not necessarily "flesh", but all that allows to live, that the soups are not more soups, but dishes prepared in a pot, that the rôts are not necessarily roasted and that the entremets will become more spectacles than additional dishes, served between the dishes.

The French service, a political device

The so-called "French service" consists of sequencing the meal by bringing several different dishes, sometimes dozens, to the table. All these dishes are placed and removed at the same time, which implies a large staff. The principle is that each person can only eat the dishes that have been placed in front of them. This method of service requires a rigorous table plan, because, of course, the dishes are not placed indifferently on the table, but according to the status of each guest and his nobility[175]. This mode of service removes any idea of sharing dishes, which means that one can banquet together while having totally dissimilar meals. Everyone is not given the same dishes or the same quantities of food: the most important person is offered a heron, for example, while those just below his rank are served a bittern, while the others receive a plover. The rule, as we have

---

175. Jean-Louis FLANDRIN, *L'ordre des mets*, Paris, Odile Jacob, 2002.

     A political history of food. From the Pateolithic to our days

seen, is that the portions of meat are halved each time one moves down a rank. This principle does not apply to fruits and vegetables.

A meal with the nobles

Not sharing a meal (even when eating in separate rooms) is always seen as a social failure, so it is customary to invite each other on a regular basis. One cannot refuse an invitation, nor can one refrain from returning it for too long. The invitation to come to the table is usually made at the sound of the horn, and each one washes his hands: they are held over a basin and the servants pour water from a ewer and present a towel to wipe themselves. This ritual of hand washing is repeated at the end of the meal. The table is seated according to the table plan. Women often eat in a separate room and if not, except for their marriage, they are relegated to the bottom of the tables. Four characters play an essential role: the kitchen squire, who is the real organizer of the meal, a sort of maître d'hôtel and steward; the panetier, who is responsible for the tablecloths, the preparation of the slicers and the salt; the slicing squire, who is necessarily a nobleman, in charge of making the cuts for the main guests and serving them the best pieces, such as the heads and necks of the birds; the cupbearer, responsible for the service of the wines and who, at the table of the princes, carries out, with the sommelier, the usual operations, with the "horn of unicorn" (piece of narwhal's tusk) to make sure that the wine is not poisoned.

The first course is made up of seasonal fruits accompanied by scalded cakes, i.e. cakes made from bread dough and cooked in boiling water, salted dishes such as pâtés or sausages, all accompanied by sweet wines such as grenache, malvoisie, muscat, hypocras (white wine flavored with herbs and spices, such as cinnamon, ginger and pepper, and usually consumed hot). Fruits, which are cold and moist foods, are eaten at the beginning of the meal in order to be cooked in the stomach, except for pears, medlars and quinces, which are served at the end of the meal, most often cooked in wine.

The second service is devoted to soups, that is to say, food cooked in pots, such as meat, game, poultry, always served with vegetables. With the soups we find the principle of simmering characteristic of the ancient tables. Specialists remind us that among the soups, there was a distinction between brouets (meat cooked in a broth) and "crétonnés" (a piece of bacon cooked to take a shrivelled form).

The third service is that of the rôts. It is necessary to distinguish between the so-called "meat days" when meat cooked on a spit is served, and, if possible, at the table of the nobles, (water) game, large birds or poultry... and the lean days devoted to sea or freshwater fish, served boiled, on a spit or cooked in the oven. Meat is served in confusion when different kinds of meat are mixed together on a large plate.

The fourth service is the one of the desserts, extraordinary achievements and/or shows in the room (we will talk about it more in detail).

The fifth service is the dessert service, which consists of sweet fruit preparations, compotes, custards, pies, creams, doughnuts, etc. We also offer some fresh fruits such as pears or quinces in wine, as well as cheeses and dried fruits. The last moment is called "issue": hypocras is served, this time made with red wine (white wine opens the digestive tract while red wine is said to close it), accompanied by waffles, beggars, etc. Different wines are offered throughout the meal without any idea of food/wine pairing (unlike in Germany at the same time). Wines with honey, wines with cloves, cooked wines are appreciated. The recitation of graces concludes the meal. The tables are removed to free up space for dancing (except on Fridays). The amphitryon can invite in his private apartments a part of the guests for the boute-hors (or boutehors) dedicated to the sharing of a spicy red wine accompanied by room spices, such as fennel, anise, ginger, fruits (such as quince, walnuts and hazelnuts), jams, sugared almonds...

The French art of the great banquet

The staff in charge of the king's kitchen service numbered between 50 and 100 people, depending on the period and especially on the events. The highest position was that of kitchen squire, a position reserved for an aristocrat. Then there were the maîtres queux, the queux, the échansons and the sommeliers, specialized servants in the dining room and in the kitchen. A distinction was made between the "cuisine de bouche", which was intended for the preparation of dishes for the king, and the "cuisine du commun", which was intended for the other guests.

Eat beautifully

However, the French art of banqueting goes far beyond the service of dishes called "à la française". Already initiated by the first kitchen squires such as Taillevent, it was largely codified in the 15th century at the court of Philip the Good, Duke of Burgundy, by another kitchen squire, Olivier de La Marche. Philippe le Bon needed, as part of his strategy of conquering royal power, to invite and impress the country's leading electors. As one can hardly do better in terms of conception and refinement of the dishes, without risking to succumb to the sin of *gula*, one plays on everything that surrounds the meal: the decoration of the room, stretched with canopies and tapestries representing allegories, the clothes of the people in charge of the service, the organization of extraordinary shows, walks with visit of the orchard, games (of marbles, bowls, dice, chess, cards) or hunting parties or even tournaments in the banquet hall.

This evolution is logical in a society which rests largely on the art of the representation. Jacques Le Goff speaks of exhibitionist propaganda to transform men into *subditi* ("subjects"). This society is a society of monstration with its exhibitions, its tortures in the pillory or on platforms, its entrances of cities, in short, all the spectacles of propaganda of which the banquets of the nobles are largely part. To eat well, it is thus initially to eat beautiful, since all that is beautiful is supposed to be good.

Olivier de La Marche, the great codifier

This French art of banqueting was taken up by many foreign princes, including the kings of Spain, then the main political power. This art was codified by Olivier de La Marche, then kitchen squire to Philip the Good, then butler and captain of the guards to Charles the Bold, Duke of Burgundy[176]. It was he who had the mission of organizing the two greatest feasts of the 15th century: the one held in 1454 and known as the "Banquet of the Pheasant's Vow", whose objective is to convince the nobles to launch a new crusade (a heron is released in the banquet hall with a hawk to kill it); and the one held in 1468 for the marriage of Charles the Bold with Margaret of York, with seven different dining rooms each presided over by a close relative of the prince assisted by a butler. Charles the Bold ate alone in a room next to the chapel, while his wife ate with the other women, in the company of dukes chosen from among the oldest. Olivier de La Marche is the author in 1473 of *L'état de la maison* in which he describes the art of banqueting.

A staging of inequalities

This setting in scene of the power plays on other processes: the existence of several dining rooms; the existence of several tables in the same room; the possibility for the main character to eat alone at a table in an isolated room, or, in the same room while the other guests are spread over several tables; the presence for each table of a "top end" and a "bottom end" allowing to mark gradations; the exceptional right to an individual

176. *Mémoires d'Olivier de La Marche, maître d'hôtel et capitaine des gardes de Charles le Téméraire*, published for the Société de l'Histoire de France by H. BEAUNE and J. D'ARBAUMONT, Paris, Librairie Renouard, 4 vols, 1883-1888.

portion instead of the ration for two; the right to "service-covered" (the dish arrives covered in front of the guest), which makes it possible to eat hot, whereas one usually eats lukewarm given the distance of the kitchen from the dining room to avoid any propagation of fire; the right to occupy a throne, an armchair, a chair, or even an individual bench, rather than sharing, according to custom, a collective bench; the presence of a canopy (tapestry) behind one's seat; the right to a cutter under one's bread slicer; a personal cup and not for two, etc.

Many other procedures allow to stage the relations of power by reserving certain objects or moments of prestige. Thus the table reserved for the main guests is not only central but rests on a platform. A guest usually eats on a trench (a large slice of bread, often round, cut from several days' stale bread bought especially for this purpose) on which meat, vegetables and sauces are placed, and which is abandoned, at the end of the meal, to be given to the dogs of the house or to the poor. It is customary for this slicer to be placed for the nobles on a carving board, which may be composed of three other slicers placed in a triangle, or which may consist of a wooden, earthen, pewter, or silver plate, with precious stones. Guests are usually given one trencher for two but one bowl each. The goblet is shared and the knife is personal. The handles of the cutlery are harmonized with the liturgical calendar: for Lent, ebony handles, for Easter, ivory handles, for Pentecost, the two materials are mixed.

Contrary to a rumor, forks (with two or three prongs) already existed, but a legend maintained by the Church says that a Byzantine princess of the 10th century, Theodora Doukas, wife of Domenico Selvo, doge of Venice (1071-1084), suddenly died after using one, a clear and indisputable sign of divine punishment for the use of this tool... Historians insist on the presence of the nave, a monumental object reserved for great people. Bruno Laurioux specifies that this object in the shape of a ship can reach a weight of 81 kilos and a height of 90 centimeters, it is made of gold, vermeil, gilded silver and decorated with enamel or precious stones. The nave contains the cutlery, the saltcellar and the napkin of the nobles and allows them to put there, for the alms of the poor, all the pieces that they do not wish to eat and that they choose not to give to the dogs of the room. I would also like to mention the sideboards and other dressers that allow the most expensive and rare dishes, different from the ones used for the service, to be exposed to the guests.

The absence of a permanent dining room and of a table on legs, far from being a handicap, introduces a beneficial flexibility to these settings. The tables are simply set up in the most appropriate place, according to

A political history of food. From the Pateolithic to our days

the season, the number, but also the quality of the various guests. Trays are placed on trestles for this purpose. These makeshift tables have no value as such, especially since they are necessarily covered by large tablecloths. The latter, made of linen or hemp, are necessarily white and their quality testifies to the wealth of the host. Three tablecloths are often superimposed to refer to the Trinity and they must go down to the ground. The tablecloths are usually supplemented with a long strip of cloth on the guests' side, which serves as a napkin. The paved floor of the rooms is, for the big feasts, covered with jonchées (herbs and rushes) and strewn with odorous flowers.

The entremets: culinary feats with spectacular staging

One does not understand the principle of medieval feasts if one does not detail the entremets. This moment of "entre-les-mets" comes just after the rôts and is based either on exceptional dishes, or on staging of extravagant dishes, or on staging in which these dishes have disappeared to keep only the extravagant and exceptional character. In the Middle Ages, sight and sound were more important than touch and taste.

Originally, we can distinguish three types of entremets: those which remain in place during all the duration of the banquet, for example the wine fountains; those presented in the form of tables in connection with the topic of the banquet; those laid out on the tables and which are changed with each service according to its contents. However, the generalization of the entremets makes that the banquets are not necessarily any more moments devoted to drink and eat, but to look. Balconies were built so that spectators, who were not guests, could participate in the banquet while watching the entremets. The dining room is also organized in such a way as to allow everyone to enjoy the desserts, which is why the table is arranged in a "U" shape and the guests sit on one side only. One would miss the point if one imagined that these were only pleasant and amusing distractions. Entremets serve to express the power and authority of the host or of those whom we wish to honor, and they also allow us to convey political messages more effectively. The desserts are not only propagandistic but also didactic/pedagogic. We will have a fair idea of the tone of these entremets by recalling that Philip Augustus (1165-1223, king from 1180 to 1223), the seventh Capetian king, and his advisor, the theologian Pierre Le Chantre, refused for a long time to hire jugglers and comedians, and finally accepted them only on the condition that these jugglers, and then the trouvères, would sing, each in their own way, the deeds of princes and nobles of the kingdom as well as the lives of the saints, for the edification of the public. Gace Brulé, the most popular singer and poet, was one of the beneficiaries of the rents drawn from the king's estates and hosted some of the great feasts. Let us also remember the aversion of the French monarchy to blasphemous swearing, unlike the English kings: the guilty party was fined if he was rich, or plunged into water fully clothed if he was poor. This aversion to swearing is related to that of the *gula*: the mouth being the main source of evil. As for the clothes, those of the men of the 14th century mould the sex and the women have deep necklines. This period is the one where one kisses *beak to beak*.

For a long time, only the main guests were entitled to a dessert, first a simple dish such as colored porridges, eggs, vegetable purées, then a more refined dish such as a poultry stew or offal, or even a real culinary feat when the dish consisted of a swan (or a goose) covered with its skin and feathers. *The Viandier* details this fashionable preparation: the bird is first stripped of its skin and then cooked, it is then covered with its plumage, its beak and legs are gilded with fine gold, a clever device made of threads and wooden rods gives the impression that the bird is about to fly away. In 1420, Amiczo Chiquart had conceived, for Amédée VIII of Savoy, a castle whose four towers were used as support for four emblematic dishes; in the center of the construction a double fountain made spout wine and rose water.

The entremets are obviously signs of wealth and power, which is why the Council of Reims forbade them in 1304 (temporarily) to clerics. These entremets then became grandiose settings intended to glorify the main guests and to amaze the other guests. We speak of entremets "de peintrerie" to designate these shows using automatisms, or actors, musicians, singers, jugglers, acrobats, fire-eaters, trouvères, troubadours, animal showmen, etc. Bruno Laurioux insists on the dimension of political propaganda: it is no longer a question of coming to share a meal, besides many do not eat, but a grandiose spectacle which will necessarily make memory. This practice of the entremets explains the considerable lengthening of the duration of the banquets, thus that organized for the marriage of Charles the Bold lasts nine whole days. The most grandiose entremets are first the work of the court of Burgundy and Olivier de La Marche. Thus, during the famous Banquet of the Pheasant Vow, La Marche designed 80 entremets showing the duties of the nobles and justifying the crusade. Italy will be in the 18th century the country of the most beautiful sugar desserts in the form of sculptures.

From the nurturing prince to the predatory prince

Some people justify the excesses of the powerful by the fact that they could not consume everything and so they allowed a redistribution to the poorest (we know that the trench knife ended up as alms). Saint Louis is often quoted as welcoming 13 poor people at his table, as well as the creation of the position of general officer in charge of collecting the leftovers. However, this period was more one of reverse redistribution, taking from ordinary people to give to the powerful. I will not repeat here the trial of feudal taxation and the exemptions from which the nobles and the Church benefited. I would like to evoke these "obligatory food gifts" from which the lords and priests benefit, in an ordinary way, and, in a more exceptional way, the visiting princes. Much has been written about the importance of the rituals of welcoming sovereigns since the imperial *Adventus at the* end of Antiquity, and it has been said that they served to symbolically express the ideals of the community and to break the monotony of daily life, thanks to the great feasts. All this is true, but the cost of these "royal entries" represents up to 10% of the annual tax revenues that were thus spent in gifts, especially food, to the aristocracy. This phenomenon, which developed with the urban renaissance of the 12th century, continued, in different forms, until the 18th century. I would also like to emphasize that the processions that went to meet the king were initially only secular, without any religious presence, but that the Church, succeeding in imposing its presence alongside the provosts of the merchants, the aldermen and other officers of the town halls, then in the lead, changed the nature of these rituals. Originally, demonstrations of defense of local liberties, with the staging of the drawbridge allowing access to the city, first closed, then opened after the king's answers to questions posed by city representatives, the processions - just like the shows, performances and banquets - will lose their secular character to display loyalty to the king of France.

Some insufficient sumptuary laws
After the 13th century, France had new sumptuary laws limiting excessive luxury, but they never had the same impact as in Antiquity or as they had in Germany and Italy. France was more willing to accept wasteful spending at wedding banquets, funerals or among friends. Bruno Laurioux, however, cites the decision of the municipal authorities of Limoges to prohibit "large and excessive expenses made for the diapers and for the women's changing rooms". I would like to believe that no misogyny tainted this particular measure (one month after birth, women, until then

considered impure, were once again allowed to enter churches and to cook) because, at the same time, there was great tolerance towards monks who, through the custom - which was being rediscovered - of making pious donations to monastery foundations, were allowed to provide masses for the dead in exchange for (very) improved meals[177].

The renewal of food policies

The period that goes from the second Carolingian phase to the middle of the clerical-feudal system is marked by the quasi-disparagement of food policies, with the end of the great tradition of state intervention in this field. The time is to accept the human submission to the divine punishment (*peccatis nostris exigentibus*)[178]. The policies of storing and distributing food surpluses were therefore replaced by prayers, confessions, processions, but also by the observation of exceptional celestial pheno-mena (such as comets, eclipses, meteors) that were supposed to announce, through unfavorable astral conjunctions, the consequences of a foreseeable judgment of God. As processions, alms and repentances were insufficient to ensure the feeding of the people, policies in various domains gradually reappeared, starting in the 12th century, but especially in the 13th, 14th and 15th centuries. The number of capitularies on foodstuffs most likely to be spoiled (such as fish), tampered with (such as meat and sausages) or the most sensitive (such as bread, wine and various alcoholic beverages) increased. The pollution of water (springs and wells) was particularly monitored, but first of all because of the great fear of poisoning (of reli-gious inspiration). The codification of trades is also a way to ensure the quality of food products. In 1248, Louis IX (Saint Louis) formalized the profession of cook by creating the corporation of roasters, in charge of cooking poultry, game, roasts and roasts. This profession is the ancestor of the "maîtres queux". It is also compulsory to devote up to a third of the surface area to legumes, which are likely to ensure a bridge between two cereal crops with a deficit. The maximum price of various cereals was fixed in times of crisis. Public or private wells were multiplied, cisterns

---

177. Caroline Bynum, *Jeûnes et festins sacrés, les femmes et la nourriture dans la spiritualité médiévale*, trans. by C. Forestier-Pergnier and E. Utudjian Saint-André, Paris, Cerf, 1994.
178. Pierre Toubert, "Disettes, famines and control of food risk in the Mediterranean world in the Middle Ages" in *Pratiques et discours alimentaires en Méditerranée de l'Antiquité à la Renaissance*. Actes du 18ᵉ colloque de la Villa Kérylos à Beaulieu-sur-Mer, les 4, 5 & 6 octobre 2007, "Cahiers de la Villa Kérylos", vol. 19, n° 1, Paris, Académie des Inscriptions et Belles Lettres, 2008, p. 451-468 ; Thierry Lesieur, "Modèle clunisien de la justice divine et mode de la rationalité" in *Cahiers de civilisation médiévale*. 46ᵉ année, n° 181, janvier-mars 2003, p. 3-21.

     A political history of food. From the Pateolithic to our days

were created to collect water by infiltration or drainage, and numerous fountains were created, even if Parisians had, for example, only 1 to 2 liters of water per day. Cities, such as Provins in 1273, created systems of water distribution to homes, in exchange for a fee, with pipes created and managed by the municipalities.

On the side of the monasteries

While this long Middle Ages saw the degradation of the popular table, this period also saw an improvement in the diet of the secular clergy, but also of the regular clergy who were subject to the vows of poverty, obedience and chastity[179]. The principle of the collective meal was maintained, and being excluded from the common table was a very serious sanction pronounced against a monk. The Carthusian order is an exception, because by merging the constraints of monasteries and those of eremitism, it obliges the monks to take their meals alone. The religious refectory is the ancestor of institutions like schools. The rule of silence is imposed in the refectory which obliges to speak with the hands, while one reads sacred texts. A sign language was thus developed for the monks.

This lightening of the constraints comes from far, since the adoption of the rule of Saint Benedict, much more flexible than the others, allows the abbot to multiply the dispensations, once the principle of non-consumption of meat has been solemnly reaffirmed. This improvement of the monastic table can be explained by the social origin of the monks, who often came from "good society", so they ate wheat bread (like the rich and powerful) and not bread substitutes like the poor; then, because while formally respecting the restrictions, they developed a refinement in the preparations, even if it is, in principle, always strictly forbidden for a monk to specialize in the function of cook. Bernard de Clairvaux thus protested against the "dozens of ways of preparing eggs" in force at Cluny, the flagship monastery of Christianity, and Pierre Abélard wondered about the meaning of eating more expensive fish than meat on lean days. Meat, at first served only to the sick, was now consumed by the "weakened" monks, but outside the refectory, it was then admitted during meals to celebrate feasts or great events. Banning meat already implies an agreement on what is called meat. As early as the Carolingian period, it is maintained that Saint Benedict only forbade the meat of quadrupeds and therefore

---

179. Aline Rousselle-Estève, "Saint Benoît d'Aniane et Cassien. Study on the *Concordia Regularum*" in *Annales du Midi : revue archéologique, historique et philologique de la France méridionale*, vol. 75, n° 62, 1963, p. 145-160.

authorized the meat of fowl and other birds... It is also considered that sea and river birds, such as beaver tails, can be assimilated to fish... Offal that is not meat can be eaten in pâtés or pies. The time of the single meal was also brought forward to mid-day from October to Easter and during periods of fasting, which made it possible to add a snack in the evening (the word snack comes from the name of the short lectures given by the monk Jean Cassien in the 5th century). The system of supplementary rations was also invented to celebrate events, local saints or to respond to requests for masses financed by donations. The "pittances" were additional rations served for two monks while the "general" rations were served individually. They include eggs, cheese and fish...

The peace banquets

The Church, at the end of the 10th century, launched two great movements to regain control of society after its own errors. First of all, the movement of the peace of God, assemblies of clerics and nobles in which the *bellatores* confided their sins committed against peace understood as the cohesion of Christianity[180]. These assemblies aimed at reconciling God and his people in order to avoid punishments such as famines. Then, the other movement, which is that of the truce of God forbidding fighting during the period of Lent and on Sundays. At the crossroads of these two movements, the famous "peace banquets" developed. God's will was supposed to preside over the peace relations, either because the peace obtained was a miracle, since the oppositions were considered to be strong, or because God directly intervened with natural elements to force the belligerents. Extraordinary meteorological phenomena were at the root of the success of peace nego-tiations with the English or between French princes. The devil sometimes intervened to prevent peace: he caused a flood or the death of the negotiator.

What do the people eat?

The situation differs according to the regions, the times and the economic conditions, but there are common characteristics that are constantly mocked by the powerful while imposing them and justifying them ideologically. More than anything else, we must avoid the trap of miserabilism, because what characterizes this period is not so much lack as a succession of periods of relative abundance followed by periods of famine

---

180. Dominique Barthélemy, "La paix de Dieu dans son contexte (989-1041)" in *Cahiers de civilisation médiévale*. 40ᵉ année, n° 157, January-March 1997, p. 3-35.

and starvation. We must not underestimate the ingenuity of the working class, based on the art of muddling through and plundering.

People eat on average four times a day, but the dishes are always more similar. We find again the triangle bread/wine/companion (complements of bread), but it works differently[181].

To eat is to eat bread

Everything is done to lead the people to eat mainly bread, to the point of identifying food with bread. But at the same time, bread making was made more and more expensive and difficult by granting the lords the monopoly of the mills (for the flour) and the ovens (for the baking). The situation in the cities was often different, if only for safety reasons: it was usually forbidden to make bread at home. Its manufacture is divided between several trades: the blazers who trade in wheat or grain, the millers who produce the flour, the bakers who knead the dough and the bakers who bake the bread. Charlemagne had already issued a capitulary requiring that each baker's post be effectively occupied. The public authorities were therefore watching over the grain (dare we say it!): thus in Paris, bakers were subject to the authority of the Grand panetier de France, a royal officer in charge of applying the 1305 statute. Among the obligations: the obligation to bake bread every day, even on Sundays, a day that is a mandatory holiday for other trades. The specificity of the baker's trade is also marked by the prohibition to make cakes and pastries.

To eat is thus to eat bread, and that will remain it during centuries, but to eat bread is to maintain the bond of feudal subordination. This period invented a way of putting the people in check through their way of eating. The people forced to eat bread eat bad bread and false bread (oat bread).

Wine to drink or eat

The use made by the people of wine is not in conformity with the official canons of the powerful: the already thick wine is eaten more than drunk, since it is used to soften and make edible a bad bread. This popular use of wine also provides an essential part of the calories. The production represents a consumption of 1 to 2 liters per day and per inhabitant, without taking into account the consumption of women and children. Can we speak of a failure of the Church, but also of the monarchy, in their declared will to reduce alcoholism? I must admit that I have some

---

181. Louis STOUFF, *Ravitaillement et alimentation en Provence aux XIVe et XVe siècles*, Paris-La Haye, Mouton et Cie, 1970.

doubts about the effect of the measures taken against alcoholism because they consist more in maintaining a sinful people than in amending them. It should be noted that the official wine rations for sailors, especially those of the king, are 3 liters per day and that Benedict of Aniane, however rigorous, generously granted 3 liters of wine per day, or 2 liters of wine and 2 liters of beer, to the canonesses.

However, the State was able to show its efficiency during this long period to regulate the consumption of other drinks. The Salic law already condemned those who uprooted apple and pear trees, at the risk of reducing the consumption of cider. The increase of its production in the Middle Ages is due to a voluntarism which will take the form of the importation of new varieties of apple trees, more productive, from the South-West and Spain. However, cider will only replace cervoise for political reasons, due to the desire to preserve cereals for bread only. I would like to take this opportunity to remind you that there are different categories of cervoise, from those with a low alcohol content to strong and very strong cervoise, but also cervoise with honey, marjoram, bay leaf, mint, sage, etc. Saint-Louis took several measures prohibiting the brewing of cervoise. The first treaty on cider, *De Vino et Pomaceo*, was published in 1588 by Julien de Paulmier[182]. Different ciders exist such as pommé, apple cider, and perry, pear cider. Beer was just beginning to be drunk again (by adding hops to barley and wheat). John without Earth will found the order of the Hop, sign of official recognition of the beer, only in the 14th century, that is to say well after the conflict between Franks and Anglo-Saxons does not concern any more the choice of the wine against the beer.

Bread complements... without meat

The "complements of bread" were poorer and poorer, with less and less meat, never poultry, almost no small game, and only the smallest cuts of cattle (cull cows) and pork. Meat remains aristocratic, sometimes for different reasons: this is the case with game, a symbol of power, and therefore reserved for the nobility, and poultry (domestic or wild), considered not very nutritious, and therefore suitable for the stomachs of idle nobles. Many people only ate fresh meat at the beginning of the winter, when the pig was killed, and were satisfied with salted meat for the rest of the year. The small people of the South enjoy a greater consumption of sheep and goats. Fish from the sea and from the river reached the

---

182. See the edition proposed by the National Library of France on the site http://gallica.bnf. fr/ark:/12148/bpt6k378700n : *Traité du vin et du cidre* par Julien de Paulmier, *Docteur en la faculté de Médecine à Paris, à Caen chez Pierre Le Chandelier, 1589.*

                                   A political history of food. From the Pateolithic to our days

tables of the poorest people but remained expensive. The people of the cities ate sea fish, especially herring, called the "bled [wheat] of the sea", which was very abundant, inexpensive, and could be preserved for a long time by being smoked or salted. Bruno Laurioux notes that from the 14th century onwards, a new preservation technique, called "caquage", made it possible to consume herring for a year: emptied of its viscera, it was packed in barrels alternating with layers of salt. Other fish such as cod, salmon, hake, trout, pike, carp, mackerel, anchovy, and even whale, which was very common on the coast, were consumed. The eel is the most appreciated fish. Fish has an ambiguous status because it is, at the same time, the "meat" of lean days and penitence but also that of the festivals, except for cod and herring. Fish is fried or prepared in rumps, pies, pâtés, macerated in wine or vinegar, often accompanied by sauces based on fruit juice and spices or sour sauce. Milk is discarded, except in the Northwest, because it is tainted by the idea that it is a "poor man's food", not only economically, but because it evokes the childish condition. The era also remains dependent on the thesis of Aldebrandin, who maintains that the nature of milk is close to that of blood: it acquires its white color only in the udder and transmits the characteristics of the animal or the mother, which is why it is forbidden to feed a Christian baby with Saracen milk. Milk is therefore consumed by the only small people in various forms: fresh, curdled, whey, clear milk, drained, hot, honeyed cow's milk, milk soup with croutons, etc. The consumption of butter remained limited, until the end of the 15th century, because it was forbidden for religious reasons for a third of the year. Salted butter (always) was reserved for the sick. The opposition of a France of butter and a France of oil will only come much later. The Flemings were mocked as "butter eaters" because they added it to their beer and wine. The rich used (olive) oil and the more humble did not consume any or fell back on walnut, flax, hemp seed, camelina oil, etc. The main fats remain lard and bacon, except for Lent when only bad oils remain. The consumption of cheese concerns now the whole society because it is considered that it serves to make the meat go down in the stomach. One eats fresh, fatty, dry, grated, crushed, chopped cheese, in pies, in flans, in stuffings, gratinated with herbs and spices, etc. The "good society" abandoned cow's cheese in favor of goat's and sheep's cheese. Cheese, like bread, was marked with the sign of the cross incised on its crust. Eggs, which are very cheap, are massively consumed, cooked, braised, fried, soft, poached, in stews, scrambled, in omelettes, in flans, cakes, pies.

Popular taverns

Not only do the "people of little" do whatever it takes to get enough food, but they also seek pleasure in sharing good things[183]. The great peasant meals that punctuated the events of life attest to this interest. The small people of the cities eat more meat than those of the countryside, including for wedding meals sometimes composed only of bread, milk, eggs and cheese. The cities and towns offered many catering services for roasted meat, pies, pork pies (stuffed with pork, quail, larks, woodcock, salmon, eels, etc.) and waffles, which were bought for immediate consumption in taverns serving only drinks. Meat and fish pies, which were very popular at the time, were purchased from pastry stores or from the "forgetful", who were very numerous street vendors. Many of these taverns are the result, especially in the rural world, of the old collective ovens in which the women cooked bread and brewed beer. These ovens were first conceded in exchange for their maintenance to real professionals who gradually transformed them into drinking establishments, more rarely into restaurants. In the 14th century, Paris had 500 taverns but also inns. Wine, beer and cider were served. The tavern trade was one of the few in the 13th century without a guild, allowing anyone to set up and operate. In 1268, the city of Paris regulated the status of the cervoisiers and therefore the quality of the products. In *Le Livre des métiers,* Étienne Boileau reproduces the recipe for the ordinary cervoise, made of water, barley, meteil (a mixture of wheat and rye) and "dragées" (a mixture of vetches, lentils and oats). The guild of pork butchers, organized in 1476, had a monopoly on the sale of sausages, pâtés and boudinaille.

The popular tables do not suffer from chronic insufficiency, since historians recall that the "normal" caloric rations reach the triple of ours, but of precariousness, even of extreme fragility, because of the too big place granted to the bread, and with the contempt (of the table) of the humble ones from which they dissociate themselves by making fun of the aulx and salted bacon eaters.

Faced with famines and shortages

This long period was marked by famines and shortages regular enough to reduce the French population from 20 to 10 million. I am not unaware of the climatic conditions of these periods, but their consequences are all the more terrible because the agricultural choices imposed by the powerful/owners weakened the food supply of the greatest number. The

---

183. Jean VERDON, *Boire au Moyen Âge*, Paris, "Pour l'histoire", Perrin, 2002.

ravages of the Black Death of 1348-1351 can be explained by the chronic undernourishment that resulted from these policies.

Pierre Toubert, studying the consequences of the famines and the plague, shows that in certain valleys of the South-West, orphaned and female fires represent 40 to 50 % of the houses, and that the inactive population (the elderly, the very sick and infirm, and children under 10 years of age) reaches 30 %[184]. The feudal power reacted by increasing the taxation on active households, while the village communities developed the principle of solidarity. In the 14th century, food assistance schemes multiplied, first in rural areas, and then on the initiative of the population itself. Pierre Toubert notes that the post-plague period will have its downtrodden and its upstarts, since a few rich people, peasants or not, were able to take advantage of the depopulation of the countryside to enlarge their domain. Social inequalities, far from decreasing, will finally experience a new boom.

What assessment should be made?

The polemic has never ceased between those who consider that an improvement occurred between the Merovingian and feudal eras and those who, on the contrary, speak of regression. Medieval bread certainly replaced Merovingian meat, but this bread was made of cereals, which made the food supply more fragile, since a bad harvest was enough for the poorest to lack food. Cerealization also led to conflicts over the allocation of the best land, either to produce the cereals of the poor (millet, millet, oats) or the wheat of the rich. Similar conflicts exist with regard to intensive livestock farming, especially sheep, which, in defiance of ancient customs, competes with them and is heavily invested by urban capital in search of large and rapid profits. This is why village communities are bringing numerous legal actions against these new "pastoral entrepreneurs" who, by generalizing the transhumance system, are changing the popular relationship between cultivated and uncultivated land. Two other political events, already mentioned, contributed to the deterioration of the food supply of ordinary people, even during TIMES of crisis: the ban on domestic mills, which made it impossible to make flour at home and made it too expensive to use the so-called "banal" mills, which the lords had secured for themselves in exchange for payment of a fee (often in kind), and the ban on baking bread anywhere but in the lord's oven, which was

---

184. Pierre TOUBERT, "Perception et gestion des crises dans l'Occident médiéval" in *Comptes rendus des séances de l'Académie des Inscriptions et Belles-Lettres*, 153ᵉ année, n° 4, 2009, p. 1497-1513.

also too expensive. The other event that contributed to the degradation of the common people's diet was the strengthening of the claims of the powerful on the products of the forest, the moors, the marshes, the rivers and the reduction of the communal lands.

The people will learn to develop alternative foods such as wild plants, like "bread of scarcity" made with hazel catkins, immature ears, fern roots, and sometimes even with earth like clay mixed with bran. One also turns to "foul" foods (dogs or rats). Some chroniclers mention the consumption of human flesh, an accusation that always has the "merit" of making the victims of the famine the culprits. Thus, around 1032, the Burgundian monk Raoul Glaber evokes in these terms the famine that struck in the year 1000: "When the wild animals and birds had been eaten, the men began, under the influence of a devouring hunger, to collect for eating all sorts of carrion and things horrible to say. Some resorted to the roots of the forests and the herbs of the rivers to escape death. A raging hunger made men devour human flesh..." It is a pity that the Church did not speak of the multiplication of loaves and food miracles, but called for more processions and repentances!

Renaissance cuisine

Before leaving the Middle Ages, we will evoke one of the most established legends for centuries, according to which the revival of the French table is due to Italy, and in particular to the role played by Catherine de Médicis who came from Italy to France with her own Italian cooks. It all started in Italy with the famous Platina, librarian at the Vatican...

The Platinum Affair and its Honest Voluptuousness

In the 15th century, humanists set out to rediscover Latin works from antiquity. They did so most often at the request of the Church, which is how they rediscovered the treatise of Apicius, *De re coquinaria*, a text, it will be remembered, promoted under the Carolingians by Raban Maur, known as Abbot Fulda, who had studied under Alcuin, and who communicated it to Abbot Loup de Ferrières, a pupil of Raban's and a close associate of Charles II the Bald[185]. The treaty of Apicius, so unchristian, soon fell into oblivion and might never have reappeared without Enoch d'Ascali, who was on a mission at the request of Pope Nicholas V, in the reserves of the library of the monastery of Fulda. The work did not seduce

---

185. Jacques ANDRÉ, *Apicius. The culinary art. De re coquinaria, op. cit.*

the pope and it was necessary to rediscover it a few years later by Giulio Pomponio Leto, the grand master of the Roman Academy, so that it could finally become famous... This rediscovery took place, however, in 1468, in the context of the plot against the pope of which the members of the Roman Academy were accused and which led them to prison where they were tortured. They were accused of eating meat during Lent, under the pretext of wanting to live like Romans (togas, pagan cults, etc.). It was in this troubled context that a sulphurous character appeared, Bartolomeo Sacchi, known as "il Platina" or "Platina", the author of the most important treatise on cooking in the 15th century, which revolutionized the Italian table[186]. Platina, born in 1421 in Piadena near Cremona and died in Rome in 1481, was a former soldier who became an "abreviator" for Pope Pius II, but when the Curia abolished this function, he openly threatened to denounce this act of despotism. He found himself locked up in a strict Vatican prison for four months. Cardinal Francis of Gonzaga obtained his freedom and he became a member of the Roman Academy, founded by Giulio Pomponio Leto, just when the latter was accused of being a group of irreligious libertines, plotting against the Church. Platinum was again arrested, tortured and locked up in the Castel Sant'Angelo. He was released in 1469, cleared and hired, in 1475, as a librarian at the Vatican. He published and soon dedicated to the cardinal of Saint-Clement in Rome (1476) his famous *Opusculum de Obsonnis, Ac Honesta Voluptate et Valetudine* (*Honest pleasure and good health*), better known as *Honest voluptuousness*. This cookery book will be reprinted often during three centuries but often under different titles. However, Platine understood the limits of his freedom of expression, which is why he weighed his epicureanism with theses acceptable to the Church. He thus maintains that if the main concern that must guide the cook is to distribute joy, health and well-being, it is nevertheless appropriate that each one eats according to his own rank. Let the humble people beware of coveting and eating the dishes that make the rich happy. Platinum is in fact the author who made it possible to Italianize the European table by replacing spices, for example, with lemon or orange juice, by revaluing vegetables without hesitating to quote 15 different kinds of salads. He recommends eating outside in the summer, in the spring, placing flowers on the table, in the winter, burning fragrant herbs, serving meals on clean white tablecloths, using plenty of clean dishes; He advocates starting the meal with raw food, such as fruit

---

186. Bruno LAURIOUX, "Le prince des cuisiniers et le cuisinier des princes : nouveaux documents sur maestro Martino", *Médiévales*, n° 49, 2005, p. 141-154.

and salad, simply seasoned with oil and vinegar, he rehabilitates cheese at the end of the meal to close the stomach, he indicates that any meal must be accompanied by wine for pleasure and salvation, etc.

The legend of Catherine de Medici

The case seems to be heard: Catherine de Medici would have arrived in France with her own cooks, she would have "Italianized the French cuisine". She would be at the origin of the great French royal cuisine that would become the jewel of Europe. Historians have long since debunked this fable, which seems to have originated with Montaigne. Montaigne made a negative judgment which only became positive thanks to a collaborator of Diderot for his *Encyclopedia*. The French cuisine of the Renaissance remains a medieval cuisine, still very spicy, with sauces that are still thick because they are still bound with breadcrumbs, but certainly less acidic. The only important transformation concerns sugar, which is much more used, so much so that Jean Bruyerin-Champier, François I's physician, makes a sharp criticism in his *De re cibaria*, published in 1560, in which he tries to promote a life and a food called "more natural". The Great French Cuisine will only be born in the 16th century in the respect of the "French" traditions. This culinary legend is a political legend born twice: first in the context of the Wars of Religion, then in order to take support from Italy to better distance itself from the Spain of Charles V, a dominant power in decline. France needed to invent a prestigious elsewhere, a beacon country, utopian, to make its own traditions live and evolve.

The table appears less regionalized at the beginning than at the end of the Middle Ages because, Laurioux tells us, of the rise in power of local specificities. I understand that all feudal regimes lead to the splitting up of territory, but I think that this renewal of diversity can be explained first of all by the choices made in the face of the dramatic consequences of the double food and demographic crisis that characterizes this period. On the one hand, we see a clear decline in ploughed land, a return to natural grasslands, an advance of forests and moors, and, on the other hand, more small game, a rediscovery of nature's free resources (gathering and collecting snails). We do not share the same resources with 10 million less French people, we eat differently, with other foods. The 16th century is therefore effectively a reversal with a more carnivorous table. Fernand Braudel even speaks of a new carnivorous Europe[187] at the end of the

---

187. Fernand BRAUDEL, *Civilisation matérielle, Économie et Capitalisme, XVᵉ-XVIIIᵉ siècle*, tome 1 : *Les Structures du quotidien, in* chap. 3 "Le superflu et l'ordinaire : nourritures et boissons", § "L'Europe des carnivores", Paris, Armand Colin, 1979, p. 159-170.

Middle Ages, but which will never question the position of bread. Bruno Laurioux estimates the average consumption of meat by French people at 200 grams per day, while that of bread is 1 kilogram.

This improvement of the popular table seems also to be explained by a crisis of regime, with shaken feudal institutions and a beginning of "dechristianization" which is perhaps only the possibility to make less pretence. This power, which the powerful lost, was temporarily returned (before the victory of the absolute monarchy) to the village communities, which recovered at least partially the means of organizing themselves and resisting the plundering of the rich, but it also benefited the poor, who were thus able to return to modes of eating that were more beneficial to them than the largely cereal-based diet that had been imposed on them for so long. However, the primacy of bread will never be questioned (before the end of the 20th century). Eating remains eating bread and it doesn't matter, as we will see later, what it is made of.

Tenth service:
The table of the absolute monarchy

Louis XIV's regulations for table service inspired many foreign monarchies before being decried by the Revolution and taken up again with zeal by the Emperor Napoleon. However, the absolute state was not created in a day. It is the result of a long process of two centuries, from François I to Louis XIV, then Louis XVI. Norbert Elias has shown that the Versailles system was also inspired by the court of Henry III. However, we will see that the time of Louis XIV introduced a break in the table practices of high society for political reasons and not for agricultural or culinary reasons. The table of the absolute monarchy is largely due, on the one hand, to its ability to build itself independently from foreign tables and, on the other hand, to the Trojan myth of the origins of the nobility, which justifies that it eats differently from the people. We shall see that this separatism of the elites led the little people to have to make do with a diet that was not only often insufficient, but unhealthy, all the more so since the authorities chose to abandon the mechanisms for regulating the grain and bread markets in the name of the omnipotence of the market, thus causing shortages and provoking riots.

Should we skimp on the table?

This table which wants to be more "natural" but claims to defend a new "good taste", based on the cult of reason, on the search for moderation in all things, on geometry and symmetry, and no longer on obscurantist excesses, cannot be understood outside the context of the religious wars which bled France, outside the ideas of the Renaissance and humanism, outside the weakening of feudalism and nobility to the benefit of the king. This table is that of the passage from a warlike nobility to an administrative monarchy symbolized by the punishment of the city of Marseille, in 1660,

---

with the siege of the city, the elimination of the nobility from the Council of the city to the benefit of the new rich that are the merchants. This table is also the one of the disappearance of the moral conception of the economy in favor of the new mercantilist doctrines. We thus see capitalism gaining ground. We have with *The Famous Company of the Lésine, or Alesne. That is to say, the Manière d'espargner, acquérir & conserver,* a marvelous collection of texts, dated 1604, which constitutes a true manual for the perfect small capitalist and rentier. This text reviews all the aspects of the table with a single objective: to save, to save everything, fish, meat, salads, knives, toothpicks, etc. The verb "to skimp" will even become common usage. The Compagnie de la Contre-Lésine, or the Marmite Grasse, responded by opposing the code of saving with that of spending, dealing with gastronomy, wine, clothing, hunting, etc.

Rather than following the slow evolution of food from the clerical-feudal period to its apogee under Louis XIV, Louis XV and Louis XVI, we will go to the heart of the matter to show that it is indeed for political reasons that the table is transformed, although it does so from its own traditions and not from a legendary import of Italian cuisine via the entourage of Catherine de Medici (1519-1589), wife of Henry II and Queen of France between 1547 and 1589. The France of this period will have its Gallican table, independent of those of other nations and the Church, and its "absolute" table in the image of its State.

Gallican religion, Gallican table

The kings of France, although "eldest sons of the Church", did not cease, from Philip the Fair (1285-1314) to Louis XIV (1643-1715), to ensure that the State had its autonomy vis-à-vis Rome thanks to the promotion of a Gallican Church displaying its particularities, including food.

This Gallican table was built in the face of two counter-models: the English, symbol of a diabolical table, and the Spanish, emblem of all excesses and submission to the authority of the pope.

This table "à la française" will mobilize a certain number of characteristics that it will borrow from the Renaissance and then from the humanism of the Enlightenment to better distinguish itself from the religious model.

The English and Spanish counter-models

Devout Spain appears as a counter-model, especially in terms of food. We have seen that, under Charles V, the Spaniards made fun of French eating habits - let us remember the words of the great Catalan moralist

Eiximenis: "Cursed be the land whose princes eat in the morning like children [...], it must be enough for each one to eat twice a day" -, but it is now the Spanish habits that are ridiculed at the French court. It did not matter that this counter-model was being constructed at the same time as Spain was adopting Burgundian-inspired table rituals, for its image remained associated with the pious Charles V (1519-1556), great-grandson of Charles the Bold. However, as Jeanne Allard has shown, the tables of Charles V, Isabella of Castile, and Ferdinand of Aragon were marked by the greatest austerity, since the king, the image of God on earth, could have no contact other than etiquette: thus, he could only share his table (and even then only exceptionally) with cardinals. The ritual thus deprives him of "all conviviality"[188].

This austerity is more of etiquette than of content, because Charles V and Philip II suffer from gout, linked to a great consumption of fish, meats, and, for Philip, pastries. To break with the customs of the Great Spanish, it is to break with the supremacy of Spain, it is to dissociate itself from its political model and to take position vis-a-vis the Inquisition. It doesn't matter that this counter-model is constituted in the Golden Age (1530-1640), that is to say precisely at the moment when the power of Spain declines. Eating differently from the Spaniards became a political and even religious obligation.

England appears as the incarnation of evil because of the excommunication of its king Henry VIII, in 1534, after his marriage with Anne Boleyn, despite the refusal of the pope to ratify his divorce with Catherine of Aragon (in order not to displease Charles V, whose niece she was), and, of course, because of the triumph of Anglicanism, which consisted of reducing the pope to his function as bishop of Rome, but, above all, because of the beheading in 1649 of Charles I. Eating differently from the English became, from then on, a religious as well as a political obligation.

An autonomous monarchy, an autonomous table

The table of the absolute monarchy is above all that of a State that frees itself from the tutelage of the Church and intends to make food a political and economic matter before being religious. We must therefore make a detour through this history to better understand the foundations of the new grammar of the table that developed under the absolute monarchy. Indeed, it was necessary to get rid of the excesses of the Christian table,

---

188. Jean-Louis FLANDRIN and Jane COBBI (dirs), *Tables d'hier, tables d'ailleurs*, Paris, Odile Jacob, 1999.

symbols of submission to Rome, while continuing to claim to be Christian and to fight the Jews and the representatives of the "so-called reformed religion" (RPR) who rejected the individual practice of fasting[189]. They invented, in a way, the "fasting gourmand", just to say that we are indeed Christians, but Gallican Christians, good and great eaters to better venerate God. The boundaries, as one can imagine, are not easy to draw. The champions of Gallicanism are divided between those who call, with the encyclopedists, to throw away the old recipes... even if it means ending up on the positions of the RPR and those who intend to save the essentials of dogma. Thus, the Jesuit Father Guillaume-François Berthier, guard of the Royal Library, in charge of the education of the young Louis XVI, resolute opponent of Voltaire and Rousseau, is opposed to the innovations that lead to espouse the theses of the "so-called reformed religion": "It is not reasonable to make a general law of abstinence and fasting, that true fasting is to give the body, only what is necessary to maintain it in health [...] All these proposals [...] the faculty of theology condemned them all for its greatest joy" (in *History of the Gallican Church dedicated to our lords of the clergy*, by Fr. Jacques Longueval).

A short history of Gallicanism

We underestimate too much the violence of the confrontations of the time to be able to understand how the table was such an important stake, more in France than in other countries. This history will know two acme, under Philip the Fair in the 13th century, then under Louis XIV in the 17th century. These two kings modified the rituals (especially of the table) to better express their Gallicanism.

In 1296, King Philip the Fair opposed Pope Boniface VIII by wanting to tax the clergy. In 1302, the pope released the king's subjects from obedience and prepared his excommunication. Philip the Fair then convened a council of French bishops to condemn the Pope, as well as assemblies of nobles and burghers (inventing the matrix of the future Estates General). He even sent a troop to try to arrest the pope in Italy in order to have him judged by a general council. Unlike some emperors, Philip the Fair did not wish to compete with the Pope, but rather to reaffirm the autonomy of the

---

189. Protestants practiced little food fasting, both to distance themselves from Roman Catholic excesses and because they rejected self-justification practices. "My whole life is penance", Luther wrote, thus closing the door on any practice of penance. This debate about Protestant fasting is still relevant today, as evidenced by the recent statement from the Protestant news agency Protest info: "No fasting rather than bad fasting." (protestinfo.ch/201404046866/6866-the-young-at-protestants-better-sabstain-than-do-a-penitence.html site).

          A political history of food. From the Pateolithic to our days

state in the face of Rome, because, as Marsilio of Padua, a famous Italian heterodox political theorist opposed to any earthly power of the Church, argued, the power of the king (of France or elsewhere) came from the people, not the Pope. The first consequence of this conflict was, in 1307, the suppression of the Templar order, symbol of the earthly (financial) power of the Church: Rome had to take care of its own business! The second is the great Western schism (1378-1417) with the appointment of a pope in Avignon. Christianity was then ruled by two popes, with two networks of bishops, priests and tithes. The palace of the Popes of Avignon will be the laboratory of a Christian high cuisine. Certainly, the Council of Constance, convened by Emperor Sigismund in 1411-1418, reunited the Church, which was no less weakened because it had to mourn the loss of its project for a great Christian empire. It was unable to mobilize for a new crusade and was obliged to sign concordats with the States, whose autonomy was in fact recognized.

A few centuries later, Louis XIV, in conflict with Pope Innocent XI (Pope from 1676 to 1689) on the question of the preponderance of national councils over papal authority, remembered this episode: he had Bishop Jacques-Bénigne Bossuet draft the *Four Articles* (1682), which he had adopted by an extraordinary assembly of the clergy of the kingdom of France. We know the famous reply of the pope to the French ambassador who presented the text to him: "If the councils are superior to the popes who derive their power from God, the states general should have the leisure to formulate the same claim against the king. This formula, certainly premonitory, is then an attempt to extract a new historical compromise between the Church of Rome and the powerful (as under Clovis, Charles Martel, Charlemagne...). It led, moreover, to Louis XIV withdrawing the *Four Articles* in 1693 but without ever questioning Gallican principles, the king having even informed Pope Innocent XII (Pope from 1691 to 1700) that if he did not accept the philosophy of the *Four Articles*, he promised him "the consequences of a pontificate worse than that of Innocent XI. This contested papacy could only be weakened despite the desire of these various currents to maintain pressure on the little people, notably through the respect of prescriptions concerning ordinary life.

Perhaps we should date from this period the beginning of "declericalization" and even of "dechristianization", movements that will become even more visible in the 18th century, not only with authors such as Voltaire, Helvétius or Diderot, but with the decline in religious vocations and, above all, with the progressive decrease in church attendance. When one knows that the number of "non paschalizers" (those who do not make their Easter) is estimated in many regions, like the South-West, to be more than half of the population on the eve of the Revolution, that among the "paschalizers" not all follow the dietary prescriptions of the Church, one understands that another conception had to/could have developed. Good taste" for a Christian table implies respecting the calendar of fat and lean days, fasts, food penances, the principle of almsgiving, etc. Good taste", outside of this context, implies the conception of other rules that are not simply codes of politeness.

The question of (good) taste

The question of (good) taste was at work in the 16th and 17th centuries, which were plagued by existential doubts: it was indeed necessary to compensate for the retreat of simple, not to say simplistic, religious reference points with new rules of civility. We thus witness a profusion of treaties of good manners, which do not all have the reputation of the one that Erasmus of Rotterdam published in 1530, at the age of 73, known under the title *Manuel de savoir-vivre à l'usage des enfants*, otherwise called *La Civilité puérile*[190]. This treaty, written for the young prince Henri of Burgundy, devotes a long chapter to the table manners, the good manners of eating and drinking. It has been mistakenly thought that it is simply a treatise on good manners for those who wish to succeed in the nobility, because the author recommends, for example, to put both hands on the table, never to join them, never to put them on food or on one's chest, to place one's glass and knife on the right side of the plate, one's bread and napkin on the left side of the plate, and to grasp meat with only three fingers of the right hand, etc. The author, a regular canon of Saint-Antoine, author of numerous libels including the famous *Manuel du soldat chrétien*, of the *Éloge de la folie* or of *L'Institution du prince chrétien* (written for the young Charles of Habsburg, the future Charles Quint), was then the friend of the greatest intellectuals of his time, for example of Thomas Moore whose execution he experienced as a personal tragedy, and he kept up an assiduous correspondence with many princes. It is worth asking why such a central figure took the time to write a treatise on civility. The answer lies in his great project of reforming Christian civilization in order to build a Europe based on tolerance and peace. His great intuition concerns the importance of the ordinary, the everyday, and therefore also the table, in the construction of a humanizing civility. The same spirit guided a few

---

190. Yveline Fumat, "La civilité peut-elle s'enseigner ?" in *Revue française de pédagogie*, vol. 132, n° 1, 2000, thematic issue: *Evaluation, pedagogical follow-up and portfolio*, p. 101-113.

 A political history of food. From the Pateolithic to our days

years later the Protestant Claude Hours de Calviac, banished from France by Henry II because of his convictions, who, inspired by Erasmus, wrote his own treatise on puerile civility[191] , this time trying to defuse conflicts between peoples linked to etiquette (in a concern for interculturality): "The Germans chew with their mouths closed and find it ugly to do otherwise. The French, on the other hand, half-open their mouths and find the Germans' procedure unsavory. The Italians proceed very softly, and the French more roundly, so that they find the Italian procedure too delicate and precious."

The aim of Erasmus, like that of Calviac, was to move the frontier between peoples and to establish it between the human and animal worlds, by proscribing everything that brought man closer to the beast, such as licking one's bowl, "letting off water and wind" at the table, making incongruous noises, etc. We are therefore very far from earlier treatises, such as the famous Italian work of the end of the 13th century, *Fifty courtesies of the table* (*De quinquaginta curialitatibus ad mensam*), written by Bonvesin della Riva, a member of the penitential order of the Umiliati, advocating a life of silence and frugal and austere obedience... The ideal of life is no longer the model of the monastery. For the new school, on the contrary, talking too much and not talking at the table are two sides of the same sin, the same social fault. One could quote, of course, Rabelais (without falling into the trap of believing that he was defending through his characters a way of life that he disapproved of). Rabelais (1483 or 1494-1553), a great admirer of Erasmus, is not indeed Rabelaisian or gargantuan, but, close to the Protestants whose indignation against certain abuses of the Church he shares, he makes eating a real mode of knowledge[192].

We could also quote Montaigne (1533-1592) who had the sentence of Saint Paul written on the walls of his library: "Do not be wiser than you need to be, but be soberly wise." The philosopher, who intends to

---

191. http://www.bvh.univ-tours.fr/Consult/index.asp?numfiche=591

192. Gérard Haddad's book *Manger le livre* provides exceptional material. It shows, for example, that among Jewish children, learning to write is linked to the notion of food. Thus, the little Jewish boy traces letters on a tablet which will be covered with honey and which the child will lick. Thus writing is eaten... The book is eaten. Among Christians, the host is the body of Christ. Among the marabouts, a person is cured by having him swallow the name of God on a parchment dissolved in water. In China, the ideogram of writing is that of a stylus placed on the mouth. To eat is thus to incorporate a history, values. Haddad then links Claude Lévi-Strauss in the light of this hypothesis: fire is the mediator between the raw and the cooked, but also between the sun that burns everything and the rotten that devours. The fire corresponds to the culture, one deduces from it that the fire is already the book thus the word which corresponds to the paternal function. Haddad is also interested in the figure of Dionysus and associates the term libation with *liber*, "the book".

---

harmonize the body and the mind by means of the soul, knows that this harmonization is difficult, even at the table. The body (senses) and the mind (reason) being imprecise instruments, "it would be essential to the full functioning of our taste sensations to increase the impact of the soul, our third tool, on the balance of body and mind"[193]. The researcher concludes that the logic of Montaigne's table is that of the trial (as in philosophy): it is a question of proceeding by trial and error, by experimentation. We are very far from the definitive prescriptions of the Church intended to discipline the soul by the body. José Alexandrino de Souza Filho, professor of literature, recalls that when Montaigne received Henri de Navarre, the future Henri IV, the latter did without the service of his servants, including his cupbearer. He became a philosopher by tasting and eating, like Montaigne, with his hand.

The choice of "moderation"

This choice of (good) taste is already defended by claiming moderation in all things. The enemy here is no longer the barbarian but the sectarian. This bias can only be understood in the light of the intransigence of the Church in previous centuries. Claude-Gilbert Dubois has clearly seen in what this discourse aims well beyond the table: "Dietary restriction is part of the whole penitential and flagellatory apparatus which consists in overcoming the beast to spread its angelic wings and to hypertrophy, by concrete measures, guilt to take horror of the sin linked to the human condition which we know, however, is incurable.

The clerical-feudal table led, in fact, to the martyrdom of its nature because of a real death drive that nourished a dolorous posture: this was the era of the flagellants (who were forbidden to participate in public life) and of the massacre of the Jews, who were accused of spreading diseases by poisoning wells and fountains. Moderating not only the excesses of the table, but also those of the religious prescriptions, is therefore to display a compassionate attitude. This position is of course opposed not only to that of the ultras but also to that of the Jansenists who develop a pessimistic vision of salvation in which everything derives from the curse of Adam. This moderation is, of course, very relative in the light of Louis XIV's wars of aggression or his religious policy against the Jansenists and Port-Royal and against the "so-called reformed religion", of which the revocation of the Edict of Nantes was the high point, forcing more than 200,000

---

193. Wim Bots, "Montaigne, du boire et du manger", in *Le Boire et le manger au XVIe siècle*, Actes du 11e colloque du Puy-en-Velay, 9-11 septembre 2003, Publications de l'université de Saint-Étienne, 2004.

Protestants into exile. This middle way morality, applied to table manners, will already pass by the rehabilitation of the material, thus of the nature.

Eating "natural"

The condemnation of matter, and therefore of the body, and therefore of food, led to the demonization of both the act of eating and certain foods. The foods of the poor (roots and vegetables) were naturally less Christian than those of the rich, according to the "chain of elements". The (good) taste will therefore rehabilitate nature, and thus the natural, by re-legitimizing what was devalued. The (good) taste will be to eat less processed, therefore less spicy, less mixed, to prefer milder flavors, and, even, to eat vegetables and to multiply the lunches on the grass. Already, at the end of the 17th century, the famous cook Robert criticized spices and excessive mixing. Nicolas de Bonnefons published in 1655 *Les délices de la campagne*, a true hymn to Mother Nature. The color palette also favors natural colors (with green vegetables, red meat, bread as white as possible, etc.). We start to mix less sweet and salty and we move the sweet towards the end of the meal, we diversify the cooking methods according to the pieces of meat in order to preserve the flavors (some pieces are braised, others are baked or fried), we use more fat to coat without masking the taste (thanks to the generalization of the use of butter which passes from the religious status of fatty food to that of lean food), We adopt the red copper pot which preserves the organoleptic characteristics of the products much better than the old black bottom pot, we reject very acidic preparations (such as meats simmered in a base composed of vinegar, leek, celery, fennel), we preserve less vegetables and fruits in vinegar, but more in salt or sugar, we witness the decline of the acidic white wine in favor of red wine and even gray and clear wines, with a dress considered until then as indecisive, etc. This rehabilitation of naturalness in the kitchen, and therefore of nature, is to be compared with the thinking of the physiocrats, but also with that of Jean-Jacques Rousseau. Nature is good. Social life is bad. Medicine will follow by replacing the practice of bloodletting by the idea of a healthy diet. In 1759, Duhamel du Monceau explained that most diseases were due to the use of salted meats... and therefore to their denaturation.

Eating "rationally"

This period is that of a systematic rationalization of supplies, of recipes with books that begin to resemble ours, of work in the kitchen, of service, of entertainment, of table manners... The legend of Catherine de Medici perhaps contributes to repress another revolution, which will mark the table well beyond the Renaissance. What is new is not the imaginary importation of Italian cuisine into France, but the affirmation of rational thought. The search for symmetry is the great characteristic of this period, because a good table is above all a beautiful geometric table. I think that this symmetry does not have primarily an aesthetic function but corresponds to a new intelligence of the table which rests on the marriage of the dishes and the words, in short, on reason.

The search for symmetry

The main question in the 16th, 17th and 18th centuries concerned the arrangement of dishes on the table. The table plan was first of all a plan of the dishes, which reconciles harmony and symmetry in the respect of the requirements of the court and its strict ceremonial. Nicolas de Bonnefons, the king's valet de chambre, author of the famous book *Le Jardinier français*, shed light on the placement of dishes: "Let there be strong and weak ones on one side, and on the other, at equal distance, as far as possible, mixing his service so well that it seems that there are no double dishes, because of the distance between them, and the change of side" (Nicolas de Bonnefons, *Les délices de la campagne*, 1655). The symmetry of the arrangement of the dishes is therefore essential but complex to achieve, especially since the table must never be left empty: the dishes removed are immediately replaced, so each service has an equal number. This symmetrical composition is necessarily done around a spectacular "middle dish", itself surrounded by other dishes. The "main course", made of golden vermeil, will gradually replace this "middle course". Each service lasts between a quarter of an hour and half an hour.

The choice of aesthetics

The analysis of Claude-Gilbert Dubois leads to the side of the aesthetic. He insists on the fact that "aesthetics is founded on mathematical bases: those of ratio and proportionality. Wouldn't there be a kind of golden ratio to govern the beauty of the table, as there is to determine the forms pleasant to the eye. A menu is established as a work of architecture intended for everyday life, not too high, not too massive, not too narrow, not too humble. The appropriate term is seyant, which is associated with pleasant, in short, it is the union of the useful and the pleasant. Battista Platina, in his work on *Honest Pleasure*, says that *every table is divided into three tables*: this means that every menu consists of three main courses or has three services; first of all light dishes (salads, sweet confits, eggs, fruits).

A political history of food. From the Pateolithic to our days

This is what we call, with a word that also has an architectural meaning, an *entrance*. Then comes the body of the house, *the second table* according to Platina, including *soup* (pot-au-feu), based on meat and vegetables, or fish and roasts. Finally, what we call *dessert* (it is the serving or the exit, to use the architectural metaphor) which consists of cheese and dried fruit. Claude-Gilbert Dubois adds: "This ternary division corresponds to one of the most universal categories in the division of three-dimensional space, time (past, present, future), logic (major, minor, conclusion) and dialectics, and constitutes the basis of pyramidal compositions or porticos with three arches, of which the central one is the main one, and which can be found in the Roman triumphal arch as well as in Gothic facades"[194]. He adds that the five-course meals are only a variant of the ternary rhythm, we find, as in architecture, the same continuity with an ornamental supplement. Everything would thus be a matter of measure around the three elementary substances: bread, wine, flesh.

The choice of secularization

I would like to insist on the dimension of secularization that underlies the quest for symmetry. Symmetry is the praise of reason, calculation, propor-tion, in short, of geometry, contrary to the choice of excess and bigoted unreason. One remembers the famous maxim supposedly inscribed at the entrance of the Academy of Philosophy founded by Plato: "Let no one enter here who is not a geometer", and which is a call to develop one's capacity for abstraction, to go beyond the stage of sensations that keep us in the order of the empirical world and prevent us from rising to the truth. I believe that if the French table of the Enlightenment, in its monarchic and then republican versions, makes pastry the jewel of the "science of mouth", it is because pastry is considered a branch of architecture, itself a daughter of geometry, and therefore of reason. This quest for symmetry is a new language that should be adopted in addition to, or in compensation for, or instead of, religious discourse. The era is one of criticism of dietary habits which, in the name of faith, lead the rich to eat on lean days with more expensive food than on fatty days, to bring in foodstuffs (such as fish) that are rare and therefore expensive, from ever further away. Erasmus was not mistaken, who, in his *Praise of Folly*, relativized the role attributed to fasting and abstinence in relation to charity. Michel Jeanneret allows us to continue this analysis by

---

194. Claude-Gilbert Dubois "À table au xviᵉ siècle : les mets et les mots de la table" in *Le boire et le manger au xviᵉ siècle*. Proceedings of the XIth colloquium of Puy-en-Velay, 9-11 September 2003, Publications of the University of Saint-Etienne, 2004, p. 11-29.

insisting on the marriage of food and words[195]. He reminds us first of all that "the common etymology of flavor and knowledge promises pleasures of the body and mind [...] Table talk gives the eater ownership and awareness of his pleasure". This speech is codified since it is necessary to avoid two excesses: *garrulitas*, the chatter that monopolizes the attention and *taciturnitas*, the laconism that throws a cold. Michel Jeanneret then notes that there are, in banquets, precious guests that he calls the "gourmands grammairiens", adding that "the symposia scene is for literature a precious ally: it gives back to ideas their verbal substance, it restores them to the world of flavor and play". I feel like daring a double parallel with the Greek parasites and with the Latin of cooking. Michel Jeanneret finally notes that, at the time, Germany and Italy were ahead of France. He speaks of "arch-banquet" for these organizations that allow creativity, verbal performance, puns to the point of coarseness and scatology. He defines this banquet as a feast of the language. He opposes him the *cena trimalchionis*, that is to say the famous banquet, certainly, but served to uncultured people. The symmetrical banquet would be thus an apprenticeship of the conciliation of the freedoms of the "barbarian" and the knowledge of living of the "civilized".

Absolute monarchy, absolute table

Two major phenomena characterize Versailles: the absence of religious subjects in the decor and the disappearance of public ceremonies. The only religious subjects are found in the chapel, while everywhere else the architects and decorators draw from mythology and pagan divinities to better stage the cult of Louis XIV. His official emblem is a shining sun, shining on the whole globe. The political intelligence of the Sun King and his advisors was to have organized the court life in such a way that everything happened at Versailles, in the presence of the courtiers only. Louis XIV only uprooted 2 to 3% of the aristocracy to transplant them to Versailles (less than 5,000 people out of more than 200,000 nobles), but the impact of the court on the "gens de biens" was considerable, allowing the creation of a *royal and bourgeois* cuisine, according to the title of a treaty.

The absolute monarchy "invents" the absolute table
The absolute monarchy, by choosing to centralize the whole life of the court at Versailles, no longer had to justify its own excesses, as attested by

---

195. Michel JEANNERET, *Des mets et des mots, banquets et propos de table à la Renaissance*, Paris, Corti, 1987.

its mad spending at the very moment when finances were bad, forcing an increase in taxes. I will illustrate the specificity of the table of Louis XIV by evoking the legend of the chicken in the pot of Henri IV, then the comedy-ballet written by Nicolas de La Chesnaye to denounce the banquets[196].

The story of the chicken in the pot of the "good king" Henri

The story of the chicken in the pot is only one element of the Henri IV legend still maintained today by the Henri IV Association. This anecdote is the conclusion of a conversation at the Jeu de Paume between Henri IV and the Duke of Savoy. The king of France certified that "there will be no ploughman in my kingdom who will not have a hen in his pot" every Sunday. Let us remember that a ploughman belongs to the rich elite of the peasantry. This legend of the "good king", which developed as early as 1590 to reinforce his historical legitimacy to the throne, integrates a corpus of anecdotes, including the "white plume" and the "chicken in the pot", in a work published shortly after his death (*Histoire du Roy Henry le Grand* d'Hardouin de Beaumont de Péréfixe, 1662)[197]. The legend plays with the idea of a return to the good and nurturing king and substitutes the image of the "Christian king" with that of a "French monarch who was both gallant and famous for his good words. In 1722, Voltaire published *La Henriade* in honor of the good King Henry and religious tolerance. The portrait he paints is that of a philosopher king, a free thinker, a philanthropist, a true precursor of the Enlightenment. The people can identify with their king all the more because he is presented with all the characteristics of a country gentleman (his familiarity, his common sense, his proverbial appetite, etc.). This praise of Henri IV also serves to magnify Sully, Minister of Finance, emblem of rural France[198].

The Banquet Condemnation

The specificity of the table under Louis XIV can be better perceived by rereading *La Condamnation de Banquet*, a text written in the 16th century by the kitchen squire Nicolas de La Chesnaye[199], special adviser in this field to Louis XI and then to Louis XII. This play in two acts is a come-

---

196. Barbara KETCHAM-WHEATON, *L'Office et la Bouche*, Paris, Calmann-Lévy, 1994; Roland JOUSSELIN, *Au couvert du Roi, XVIIe-XVIIIe siècles*, Paris, Éditions Christian, 1998.
197. René GANDILHON, "Henri IV et le vin", in *Bibliothèque de l'École des chartes*, vol. 145, n° 2, 1987, p. 383-406.
198. *The Legend of Henri IV*. Acts collected by Pierre TUCOO-CHALA and Paul MIRONNEAU, Pau, Association Henri IV, J & D Editions, 1995.
199. Nicolas DE LA CHESNAYE, *La Condamnation de Banquet*, critical edition by Joëlle KOOPMANS and Paul VERHUYCK, Geneva, "Textes littéraires français", Droz, 1991.

dy-ballet intended to be danced. In the first act, three merry men, Dîner, Souper and Banquet, offer, each, a meal to young ladies, Gourmandise, Friandise and Accoutumance, accompanied by Bonne-Compagnie, Passe-Temps, Je-bois-à-vous and Je-plaige-d'autant. The hosts have asked a group of helpers named after diseases that afflict heavy eaters (Colic, Apoplexy, Gout, Paralysis, Epilepsy, etc.) to hit their guests at both meals. The guests run away except for four who die. The three companions are therefore prosecuted before a jury, under the presidency of lady Experience assisted by Sobriety, Bleeding, Clysteria, Diet, etc. Remède pronounces the sentence: Dîner and Souper are acquitted because they are considered indispensable to life, on condition that there is always a six-hour interval between them, Banquet, condemned to death, is hanged.

A table worthy of the Sun King

For Louis XIV, the abandonment of the traditional state rituals of his predecessors had of course a political purpose: it was above all a matter of nourishing a social separatism based on the legend of the Trojan origins of the French nobility and on the desire to create a perfectly centralized state apparatus. This political project leads to the definition of a complete program in which every detail counts. The table plays its own score in this concert.

We will come back to the ordering of the table, the fixed schedules of the three daily meals, the determination of who is allowed to speak and when, etc. Let's just remember that 5,000 nobles could attend or participate in the king's meal! I will insist more on the political voluntarism that led the absolute monarchy to invent a "French-style" table, as it already had a "French-style" architecture with Charles and Claude Perrault, "French-style" gardens with the architect and landscape designer André Le Nôtre, French" music with Lully, "French" painting and sculpture with Charles Le Brun, "French" literature with Jean Chapelain, "French" madrigals and sonnets with Isaac de Benserade, balls, ballets and fireworks, "grand hunts"[200], etc.

The table received the same attention as the other domains, with the same intervention of special advisers and the King's secret council. Colbert

---

200. Alain GUERY, "Versailles : le phantasme de l'absolutisme (note critique)" in *Annales. Histoire, Sciences Sociales*, 56ᵉ année, n° 2, 2001, p. 507-517 ; Jean-Pierre Néraudau, "La mythologie à Versailles au temps de Louis XIV. Architecture, jardins et musique" in *Bulletin de l'Association Guillaume Budé*, n° 1, mars 1988, p. 72-85 ; Gérard SABATIER, "La gloire du roi. Iconographie de Louis XIV de 1661 à 1672" in *Histoire, économie et société*, 19e année, n° 4, 2000, thematic issue: *Louis XIV et la construction de l'État royal (1661-1672)*, under the direction of Olivier CHALINE and François-Joseph RUGGIU, p. 527-560.

          A political history of food. From the Pateolithic to our days

was at the center of this political system. The table, with its complex ritual intended to produce above all hierarchy, with its decorum, with the primacy of service over cuisine, constitutes an ideological program serving to express the unique character of power; just as the garden, with its groves, its labyrinths of greenery, populated with stone animals, statues, fountains, waterfalls, conceived as a parable of royal authority, with Apollo sitting at the center of the Great Basin, and designed to attract all the eyes of the nobles; just as the Hall of Mirrors, whose iconographic program was revised overnight by Charles Le Brun on the recommendations of the King's Secret Council... This state propaganda based on a state patronage is framed by numerous academies, the Academy of Painting and Sculpture founded in 1648, the Petite Académie, in 1663, in charge of the king's representation devices, including medals, equestrian statues, the Academy of Sciences in 1666, the Academy of France in Rome in 1666, the Academy of Architecture in 1675, the Royal Printing Office, the workshops of the Louvre, the manufacture of Gobelins, etc.

The Trojan myth of the origins of the nobility

One cannot understand the mutations of the table of the powerful (and not only of the court) if one does not question the great political myths which will end up characterizing the absolute monarchy. These legends are stories in which one truly believes and which therefore have a power of creation and ordering of reality. The powerful "French" are entitled to eat and drink in a different way than the other powerful Europeans, and also, naturally, than the little people, because they belong to a different blood. We must go back, with Colette Beaune, to the legend of the Trojan origins of the Franks, to the different versions that were given between the 7th century and the 17th, until we arrive at the thesis of a nobility of a race other than that of the people[201].

A first legend drawn from texts of the 7th and 8th centuries recognizes an exceptional value to the whole of the Frankish people: "Francion (or Priam the young or Anténor) and his companions leave Troy in flames to found the city of Sycambria on the Danube. At the request of the emperor Valentinian, they exterminate the Alains, refugees in the Palus Meotides, in exchange for ten years of exemption from tribute. Refusing to take back the payment, they withdrew to Germania and did not enter Gaul until the

---

201. Colette Beaune, "L'utilisation politique du mythe des origines troyennes en France à la fin du Moyen Âge" in *Lectures médiévales de Virgile*. Actes du colloque de Rome (25-28 octobre 1982). Rome, Publications de l'École française de Rome, n° 80, 1985, p. 331-355.

4th century with Marcomir and Pharamond. This legend is then used to justify the prestige of the nation and as an argument against the papacy; it also justifies the crusades to recover the Trojan soil; it explains, finally, the attachment of the Franks to another civilization with, for example, the culture of much and eating well... The political problem created by this legend is that this myth concerns only the Franks and not the Gauls, so it suggests that the "French" people is not homogeneous. The monk Rigord (1145-1209?), one of the main founders of French monarchical ideology, therefore proposes another version: he assumes that a part of the Trojan exiles would have emigrated to France, in the 9th century B.C., with the duke Ybor; they would have been joined, in the 4th century A.D., by Marcomir and Pharamond. The Gauls would have come from the first migration and the Franks from the second, but all have the same ethnic purity. Jean Lemaire (1473-1524), librarian of the house of Burgundy, then official historiographer of Louis XII (1462-1515), explains that the Gauls, descendants of Noah, left to found Troy, would have returned to the soil of the mother country. This legend was very useful at a time when the pope was opposed to the king whose legitimacy was contested by the English and when the French nobility was beaten on the battlefields.

According to Colette Beaune, this reinterpretation of the Trojan myth gave rise to the notion of a "French nation" by placing it in a history dating back to Troy and mobilizing great holy figures such as Denis, Clovis, Louis and Michel. However, this same myth ended up pitting the nobility, the bearers of Trojan blood, against the people. The nobles were thus exempted from taxes from the 14th century onwards because of their difference in blood. On May 29, 1418, a revolt opened the gates of Paris to the Burgundian bands allied with the English. The fall of the city was compared to that of Troy: the Parisian people, like those of Troy in the past, would have betrayed their king and their nobility, forcing the latter to flee, as those of Troy had done. The English are thus the deserved punishment for the sins of the people, for which they must repent. The divorce of the elites with the people is thus consummated.

This myth is also used to claim independence from the pope. The argument is defined during the conflict of king Philippe le Bel with the pope Boniface VIII: the original independence of the Trojan people justifies the current independence towards Rome. The Franci never submitted and the Galli, even when submitted, were always in rebellion. Colette Beaune also evokes the anti-English role of the Trojan myth: Anténor the Trojan traitor is the ancestor of the English who are only "a mixed race capable of all bad actions". The proof is in their practice of murder, their abundance

A political history of food. From the Pateolithic to our days

of bastards, their penchant for drink and their foul ways of eating. This Trojan myth also arouses all the "oriental" food curiosities since the site of Troy is imprecise, confused with those of other cities...

The reversal of sumptuary laws

The myth of the Trojan origin of the French nobility justified the reversal of the sumptuary laws. Indeed, the rise of a merchant bourgeoisie directly threatens the aristocratic monopoly on luxury. What would happen to society if the rich could eat or dress like the powerful? The kings will therefore try to preserve or recreate social/biological distances. These new sumptuary laws were no longer intended to reduce the waste of the richest, but to defend the nobles against the bourgeois. The differences must be able to be displayed in the choice of fabrics, in their color, in the use of metals and precious stones. From François I to Henri IV, 11 sumptuary edicts talk about restricting luxury under the pretext of directing capital to the state coffers in the service of "Nous and the public thing". The sumptuary ordinance of Philip the Bold, in 1279, deals with the affairs of the table, that of Philip the Fair, in 1294, also concerns the costume. Each class had its own law, which it could not violate without incurring heavy fines. The great peacemaker of the Wars of Religion and Chancellor of France, Michel de l'Hospital, before being chased away by the ultracatholic current, tried, with the laws of January 1563, to regulate the drinks and food served in the inns by imposing a standard menu and by requiring that each commune enforce the law. However, there were far fewer sumptuary laws in France than in Germany or Italy. Neithard Bulst's team identified more than 3,500 sumptuary ordinances in Germany, including texts regulating celebrations for weddings, baptisms and funerals[202]. The accounting records confirm that the fines were indeed enforced and that specialized personnel were in charge of control. The aim was to defend the social order by imposing a code of behavior that assigned everyone a place in the social hierarchy, including the marginalized, prostitutes, delinquents, and even adulterers, etc. Since the public authorities were unable to enforce these texts in the private home, it was made compulsory to organize these banquets publicly and specialized houses were created for this purpose. These *Hochzeitshaüser* ("wedding houses") were particularly numerous in the 15th and 16th centuries. An ordinance of Regensburg in 1661 even formally forbids the creation of paintings that do not respect the regu-

---

202. Neithard BULST, "Les ordonnances somptuaires en Allemagne : expression de l'ordre social urbain (XIVᵉ-XVIᵉ siècle)" in *Comptes rendus des séances de l'Académie des Inscriptions et Belles-Lettres*, 137ᵉ année, n°3, 1993, p. 771-784.

lations in terms of clothing, decoration, and the food present. Another ordinance (Göttingen, 1340) states that all those who receive alms from the city lose the right to wear colored shoes or to eat certain foods. We should not be misled by Voltaire's condemnation of the sumptuary laws, who explained in 1756 that all these laws (especially those written between 1572 and 1580) proved above all that the government did not always have great views and that it seemed easier to the ministers to proscribe industry than to encourage it (in *Essais sur les mœurs et l'esprit des nations, et sur les principaux faits de l'histoire, depuis Charlemagne jusqu'à Louis XIII*). What the philosopher condemns is the counterproductive character of these laws which, far from curbing excesses, arouse the desire of vain expenses. Montaigne criticizes, on the other hand, the splendor and the extravagances, that it is about the food field or the clothing (the fly). He qualifies as fetishism the choice of a too expensive crockery, because, in this case, the financial value exceeds the value of use at the point to make lose the utility. Montaigne, in his *Essays*, uses a fable to explain that objects that are too expensive corrupt morals: "This is what King Cotys did; he paid liberally for the beautiful and rich crockery that he had been presented with; but because it was singularly fragile, he broke it immediately himself, to avoid such an easy matter of wrath against his servants"[203].

Hunting reserves

The predatory character of the nobility is also apparent in its practices of large and small hunts. The tendencies, already outlined at the time of the Carolingians and of feudalism, are reinforced. The poor are systematically excluded from the forests and therefore from the consumption of (small) game. The monarchs were the first to set a bad example, like Louis XI who, in 1482, issued a decree prohibiting all hunting on his lands. The royal hunts even ended up encroaching on the necessities of agriculture, especially since the powerful no longer recognized hunting restrictions according to the agricultural calendar. Versailles, before becoming a 23,000 hectare estate under Louis XIV, was already the hunting grounds of Henry IV and then Louis XIII. Louis XIV hunted between 110 and 140 days a year; Louis XV, three times a week; according to Hippolyte Taine (in *Les Origines de la France contemporaine*, t. 1 et 2, *L'Ancien Régime*, 1875) Louis XVI, who hunted 200 times a year, shot 189,251 pieces and 1,274 deer between 1774 and 1787[204].

---

203. Montaigne, *Essais*, Livre III, chapitre X "De mesnager sa volonté", Paris, "Bibliothèque de la Pléiade", Gallimard, 1967, p. 992.
204. Grégory Quenet, *Versailles, une histoire naturelle*, Paris, "Sciences humaines", La Découverte, 2015.

A political history of food. From the Pateolithic to our days

A new way of staging meals

Kings eat differently from the people and other nobles in all societies, but this specificity can be marked in various' ways depending on the message one wishes to communicate. For example, does the king eat alone or with others, and are the guests only spectators or are they guests? It has been shown that until the reign of Louis XIV, the main objective of the regulations was to establish and enforce a distance between the king and his subjects, including the nobles[205]. It was not yet a question of organizing a court life as at Versailles, but of instituting the king. The main part of the ceremonial was therefore based, until Louis XIV, on the three orders of Henri III, promulgated in 1578, 1582 and 1585, which aimed to maintain a distance between the king and his subjects, forbidding him to be spoken to, to lean on his chair, or to stand too close. Barriers are installed to better isolate him. This distance imposed towards the king is then introduced towards his food. No one was allowed to approach his meat, blow on his wine, touch his bread, etc. The fear of poisoning exists, but the essential thing, in my opinion, is to "sacralize" the person of the king by sacralizing his food. His dishes are prepared by a different staff than the one who cooks for the queen or the dauphin, the table rituals, sometimes the dishes, differ. The king eats alone in the center of the room, with his back to the fireplace, seated in an armchair, he may invite people standing to sit on stools or folding chairs and grace them with a few pieces of his food.

The regulation of ceremonial is therefore not so much aimed at ensuring the representation of power as at producing an organization in which each gesture, each posture, designates the place, the status and the power to which each person can lay claim. This thesis of Norbert Elias[206] is confirmed by all the historical monographs. Edward Shils insists particularly on the relationship between the position of power and the space occupied[207] (which is more or less close to the center). This distribution of the guests indicates to each one the place which is his and the gestures to be accomplished.

Everything is significant in this ceremonial: the position in relation to the center of the room, the distance from the table and the king's seat, the

---

205. Claudine Haroche, "Position et disposition des convives dans la société de cour au xvii⁰ siècle. Éléments pour une réflexion sur le pouvoir politique dans l'espace de la table" in *Revue française de science politique*, 48e année, n° 3-4, 1998, p. 376-386.
206. Norbert Elias [1969], *La société de cour*, Paris, "Champs essais", Flammarion, 2008.
207. Edward Shils, *Center and Periphery: Essays in Macrosociology*, Chicago and London, University of Chicago Press, 1975.

right to occupy a seat or to remain standing, the type of seat on which one sits according to one's rank: stool, folding or armchair...

The generalization of a permanent court life will deeply modify this scenography because it imposes to define with whom to eat (or not). The table of the Sun King was no longer primarily used to establish the king, but rather the relationship of each person with him, hence the need to invent a service that would allow for a whole range of gradations. It is no longer enough to have a place when hundreds, sometimes thousands of people attend the meal; one must also know what place it is. This evolution occurs when a new object appears on the table: the plate. It is not only a modernized version of the old trencher and bowl (although it replaces both of these objects), but a new way of saying that the main thing is to determine who has the right to the banquet and to which part.

I would compare the substitution of the plate for the trencher to that of the padlock in the nave, the padlock certainly allows the napkin folded in four to be placed on top of the bread and cutlery, but it no longer has compartments for the relief. While the trench knife was still a reminder of the obligation to share with the poor, since it was distributed to them at the end of the meal (something that Saint Louis would ensure by enacting strict regulations), the plate simply becomes the sign of inclusion in one of the spheres that touch power. Claudine Haroche recalls that the word "plate" comes from the acceptance of a guest sitting at the table[208]. The plate, which initially signified a status, will gradually designate a utensil that allows each person to eat at the assigned place. The plate "thus gathers in it the origin and the function of table manners: the posture, the position, the arrangement, the technical instrument". Saint-Simon describes in detail the king's dinner, the small table setting, the rank of those who were allowed to take part in it, the precise moment at which they were to enter, the position assigned to them, the king's brother presenting the napkin, etc. He also recalls how Mlle d'Alessandro was able to serve the king at the dinner. He also recalls how Mlle d'Alençon, the niece of Louis XIII, wife of the Duke of Guise, was served by the latter, specifying the type of seat to which he was entitled and the place assigned to him.

The organization of the offices of the king's household

Christophe Blanquie will be our guide thanks to his study of the offices of the king's household[209]. The king's household consists of the domestic

---

208. *Id., ibid.*
209. Christophe BLANQUIE, "Dans la main du Grand maître [Les offices de la maison du roi, 1643-1720]" in *Histoire & Mesure*, vol. 13, n° 3-4, 1998, thematic issue : *Varia*, p. 243-288.

officers who serve the king and who are placed under the authority of the Grand Master of France, who is responsible for establishing the officers' quarters and for receiving the oath of those who do not take it directly from the king. This office of the Grand Master took over from that of the Dapicer, which succeeded that of the Mayor of the Palace. The Princes of Condé held the office of Grand Master of France from 1643 to the Revolution. The domestic officers could transmit their charges with the approval of the Grand Master. There were 52 charges: 9 for the maître d'hôtel au serdeau, 7 for the "petit commun", 33 for the "grand commun", 3 more specialized charges (bakers, purveyors and wine merchants), which represented a total of 350 officers (who therefore worked in shifts). There is, also, a charge concerning the "guard of the extraordinary crockery"...

Seven offices concern the king directly (paneterie, "échansonnerie bouche" and "cuisine bouche"), the commensals include the "paneterie commun", "échansons communs", "cuisine commun", as well as the fruiterie and the fourrière. The "petit commun" retained the service of the Grand Master and the chamberlain, the "grand commun" the service of all the officers. These offices could be transferred with the agreement of the Grand Master. As Christophe Blanquie mentions, "there are no small offices in the king's house": to hold an office, even a mediocre one, is to be an officer in the royal liturgy, of which every detail is specified. Thus, the 1681 regulation defines the manner of bringing the dishes to the king's table as a procession giving it its solemn character: "His Majesty's meat will be carried in this order : two of his guards will walk first, then the hall ushers, the hostel master with his staff, the gentleman servant panner, the general controller, the controller of the mouth, the controller clerk of office and others who will carry the meat, the kitchen squire and the dish guard, and behind them two other guards of His Majesty who will not let anyone approach the meat." The officers of the king's household retain their office, even when the king dies, unlike those related to the person of the queen or the princes. One can therefore consider that the notion of continuity of the state derives, paradoxically, from the affairs of the table. The principle is stated in an edict of Henry II in 1554: "The House of the King is not broken, nor does the King die. The officers of the House of the King are transferred to the successor of the predecessor. This irremovability of domestic officers thus anticipates, as Christophe Blanquie points out, the theory of the "two mystical bodies of the king", hence the transformation of domestic offices into offices of the Crown, hence the fact that the Grand Master of France succeeds the Grand Master of the King's household. The domestic office is thus at the heart of the monarchical construction, since the king's house is as much the condensed expression of the kingdom as a mirror of the king's power. These officers are an extension of the old custom of the king being served by nobles: "When he [the king] sits down, a prince of the blood brings him his napkin, failing that another prince, or in their absence an officer of the Crown."

The holder of a "small office", dependent on a head of office, received a "brevet de retenue" which meant that the king "retained and retains him in the state of office of...". As soon as the oath is taken, the officer takes his rank in the king's household and receives the wages attached to his office... This analysis by Christophe Blanquie can be completed by that of Norbert Elias in order to understand the drift of the ceremonial towards fetishistic gestures such as the one that wants the queen, naked as Eve, to wait for the ceremony of presenting her shirt to be completed, or this other one that sees the dishes pass between so many hands that they arrive cold.

Service before cooking

The importance given to protocol meant that the main focus was no longer on the food, and therefore on the cooking, but on the organization of the service at the table. The old back service was abandoned in favor of a front service which increased its importance. The servants were no longer required to stand aside because they participated in the pomp of power. This front service allows to magnify the distribution of the dishes and in particular the cuts of meat. This will be the great era of the sharp squires. The works multiply to describe this ritual. One is right to insist on the fact that this spectacular cutting of meat, most often done in the air with a knife and a two-pronged fork, was a male activity for a long time performed by a nobleman, then by the most qualified servant or the master of the house, but it should be added that this cutting allowed the pieces to be distributed in an even more discriminating manner. The difficult adoption of the fork within the court can also be explained by the defense of good taste: eating with the hands requires an important know-how which consists in dirtying only the first phalanges of three fingers of the right hand, without ever, for example, touching the pieces of one's table neighbors. The fork then appeared to be much too simple to use, too "democratic" one might say, as it did not allow the nobleman to differentiate himself from the gentleman and the latter from his servants. France therefore adopted the fork well after other countries and for medical reasons (fear of contamination by touch). A compromise will do for a long time: the pieces are seized with the fork in the collective dish, put in its individual plate, then eaten with the fingers. One keeps one's hat on one's head to eat in order to be able to greet each new service, one is thus obliged to keep one's coat, and therefore also one's sword... The staging of power becomes heavier to the detriment of a joyful sociability. The only exception, lunches on the grass but also the service of coffee, tea or chocolate.

Another way of marking inequalities was to differentiate the service of wines according to rank. The rules established under Henry III specify that the bottles should never be placed on the table, but arranged on dessert tables, with a gentleman standing behind the king. The wine was first tasted by the first physician, then by the sommelier and the cupbearer to check its taste. There are four kinds of wine for the table: vin de bouche (for the king's mouth), vin de table (for the other guests), vin de suite (for the valets), vin commun (for the servants). The wine is aged on beechwood shavings for a month after it is made.

The sweet honors

The royal splendor applies to the king's travels. We know quite well the customs thanks to the publication of works that recounted the conditions of the receptions, as soon as they were made. For example, one of the books details the conditions of the reception of the king in Metz, in 1744, with the construction of triumphal arches, with fountains from which wine flows, with the realization of porticoes and columns, with paintings of bacchantes, basins and water jets, fireworks, gifts, banquets, etc. Distributions of bread and meat are organized. The staging of power counts much more than the strict consumption of food. Thus, when Henry III visited Venice, the city organized extraordinary festivities in order to seduce him and obtain his support against Spain and the Church. This episode is revealing, because the debauchery of achievements has a spectacular function since the French king eats only dishes prepared by his own cook. Venice was therefore going to display "sweet honors"[210] , that is to say, constructions in wood, marble, but above all in sugar, intended to arouse wonder, to arouse astonishment (*sic*), thanks to allegories, myths that were all political allusions. These sculptures in sugar, but also in chocolate, will not cease to develop under the monarchy. For the success of these feasts, the powerful ensured the participation of the greatest artists, Leonardo da Vinci was, for a time, superintendent of the tables of Ludovico More, Titian at the service of the Este family.

---

210. Daniela AMBROSINI, "Les honneurs sucrés de Venise", in *Le boire et le manger au XVIe siècle. Actes du 11e colloque du Puy-en-Velay, 9-11 septembre 2003, Publications de l'université de Saint-Étienne, 2004, p. 267-284.*

The supply contracts

The nobles did not eat like the people, if only because they obtained their supplies differently. Pierre Couperie, in a 1964 issue of *Annales ESC*, describes the central institution of food supply contracts: "The mistrust felt towards their servants by the great lords of the 16th and 17th centuries has given rise to a fairly abundant series of documents (including) those of the "Marchés de pourvoierie", signed before a notary, by which a provider, who was at the same time a contractor and a domestic officer, undertook to provide a regular supply of certain foodstuffs at prices agreed in advance[211]. This system was very widespread: pastries, wine, bread and flour, oats [...], meat, roast meat, and fish: each of them gives a list of more than 200 items with corresponding prices. These contracts stipulate the obligation for the outfitter to follow the nobleman in his travels and to provide him with a certain number of commodities at a price fixed in advance. Pierre Couperie writes that this trade required great skill, a lot of dexterity, as well as considerable capital. However, this activity was particularly lucrative, and on the very day of the signing of the 1659 contract, the king's provider received 30,000 livres for his start-up costs... The delivery schedule was uniformly set to allow for unforeseen events: fish had to be delivered at 7 a.m. between October 1 and April 1, and at 5 a.m. the rest of the year. Meat, consumed in the evening, is delivered at 2 p.m. If the food was of defective quality, the provider received only a smaller sum; if the food was inedible, the officers bought other food at the provider's expense. This system of supply will have as a consequence to make known, even to create, local and regional specialities, such as the andouilles of Troyes, the cervelas of Bologna, the ham of the Basque Country and of Mainz, etc. France began to be recognized as the country of cheeses since the treaty of Gilles le Bouvier, herald of Charles VII, who published around 1450 the *Livre de la description des pays (Book of the description of the countries)* specifying, for each province visited, its landscapes and its natural and agricultural productions, in particular cheeses, which constitute so many natural treasures.

The art of sauces

For a long time, the new French cuisine has been defined as "Italian cuisine with the added art of sauces". We know that the thesis of the importation of Italian cuisine into France is only a legend, but the transformation

---

211. Pierre Couperie, "L'alimentation au xviie siècle : les marchés de pourvoierie" in *Annales. Économies, Sociétés, Civilisations*, 19e année, n° 3, 1964, p. 467-479.

 A political history of food. From the Pateolithic to our days

was indeed made by inventing a new art of sauces, by abandoning thick sauces based on bread crumbs or egg yolk and by considerably reducing the use of acidic flavors. Sauces began to gain importance as early as the 17th century, but especially in the 18th century. François Marin (1739) in his *Dons de Comus*[212] proposes about fifty recipes for sauces which he describes as the soul of French cuisine. In his *Suite des dons de Comus*, published in 1742, he details 95 new recipes. This new cuisine, which developed in the context of the philosophy of the Enlightenment, made great use of Champagne wine, which would remain the emblem of bourgeois cuisine in the 19th century. Voltaire said that champagne, described as "sparkling foam", was the living image of France.

Can we invent a royal and bourgeois cuisine?

We can often measure the progress made in a few years by comparing a few books: that of Master Chiquart, author of *Du fait de cuisine* composed for Amédée VIII of Savoy in 1420; that of Jean de Bockenheym (Johannes Bockenheim), author of the *Registrum coquine* (early 15th century) composed for Pope Martin V ; or the translation, at the request of Charles V, of the Franciscan Bartholomew the Englishman's *De proprietatibus rerum* (*On the properties of things*) dating from the 13th century; and the various books from the second half of the 17th century. It has been said that the medicalization of the table, the invention of a new dietetics, helped a lot to its evolution, to its rationalization. Conflicts between doctors and cooks are numerous, the first preaching moderation, the second striving to achieve sometimes unhealthy gastronomic feats. The health journal of Louis XIV, kept by his doctors, criticizes, for example, the abundance of dishes responsible for digestive disorders... I would like to insist on another cleavage: is it a question of creating a cuisine for the nobility or should it also be accessible to the "good bourgeois"?

François Pierre, known as "La Varenne", kitchen squire to the Marquis d'Uxelles, is the author of the book *Le Cuisinier françois*[213] (1651) which will be published in more than forty editions in half a century. He proposed a cuisine that broke with the usual frameworks by seeking to bring the table of the aristocracy closer to that of the wealthy bourgeoisie. Pierre de Lune, also a kitchen squire, but working for the Duke of Rohan, published *Le Cuisinier* and *Le Nouveau et Parfait Maistre d'hostel royal*[214] in 1656, which are in the same vein. Pierre de Lune innovates by daring, contrary to La

---

212. http://gallica.bnf.fr/ark:/12148/bpt6k1108709.
213. http://gallica.bnf.fr/ark:/12148/bpt6k114423k.
214. http://gallica.bnf.fr/ark:/12148/bpt6k1339465.

Varenne, to order his work according to the seasons and not according to the calendar of fat and lean days. The counter-attack was to come through a work entitled *L'Art de bien traiter*, signed with the three initials L.S.R. and published in 1674[215]. This book was a fierce attack on La Varenne, whom he accused of (class) treason by wanting to make the aristocrats eat wheat porridge and Jerusalem artichokes (*sic*); he even spoke of the "absurd and disgusting lessons that the Sieur de Varenne dared to give". However, the nobility cannot stop history. In 1691, François Massialot publishes a new work whose main interest lies in its falsely anodyne title, *Le Cuisinier roïal et bourgeois (The Royal and Bourgeois Cook)*, a fine way to put an end to the food privilege of the nobility.

On the people's side

The key word in terms of popular food is not only precariousness but a chronic insufficiency which, at the slightest climatic problem, causes food shortages. The fear of not having enough to eat is now part of the daily lot of the humble. The causes are multiple: deforestation, overgrazing, predominance of wheat. The powerful evoked human submission to divine punishment (*peccatis nostris exigentibus*), some rationalists envisaged exceptional celestial phenomena (such as comets, eclipses, meteors). It is necessary to wait for the Enlightenment to question the policies.

Numerous regional monographs describe the popular food, rural and urban, during this rather dark period. The popular table was characterized by its poor quality and extreme monotony: bad bread largely replaced meat. The people of the cities had more access to meat, but it was often unsuitable meat. For centuries, there is a self-consumption of waste according to the formula of Madeleine Ferrières[216] : we sell at the market the best (to be able to buy seeds and some tools), for example the successful salted meats, and we consume only those that have failed and that are the cause of many poisonings and deaths. The working classes do not eat the same bread as the bourgeoisie, nor the same bread as the servants of the bourgeoisie. The people ate bread that was often poorly baked in order to save wood... The basic cereals were rye flour with barley added. In case of shortage, oats are added. This soup is eaten three times a day, with more or less salt according to the amount of the gabelle and the abuse. It is sometimes supplemented with cabbage, turnips, lettuce, onions, carrots

---

215. http://gallica.bnf.fr/ark:/12148/bpt6k6565874p.
216. Madeleine Ferrières, *Histoire des peurs alimentaires. Du Moyen Âge à l'aube du XXᵉ siècle*, Paris, Éditions du Seuil, 2002, republished in pocket "Points Histoire", 2006.

     A political history of food. From the Pateolithic to our days

and celery. One also consumes soups made with pearl barley, which looks like rice. On other occasions, a piece of bacon is added. The consumption of pork has become very low. Except for a few exceptions, people no longer eat cold cuts because the pigs are too sickly and the expensive salt makes the cold cuts very peppery. Milk and cheese are in short supply because of the low number of livestock and the lack of pastures. In the countryside, the best wine to drink was water reddened with "petit vin", while the people in the cities drank 300 liters of wine per year per person. In the 17th and 18th centuries, the Church again attacked funeral meals, which were provided for in many wills and consisted of bread, meat and wine, because they were still accused of maintaining a pagan vision of death.

The cohabitation of several generations under the same roof became the rule and tended to replace the marriage contracts providing for the obligation to provide food to parents. This period, known as the period of the great confinement of the poor in hospices and prisons, saw the degradation of the food system in institutions: historians note a significant decrease in meat consumption, even though the ration of a soldier in the 16th century was still 212 grams (this decrease was therefore later for institutions than for the rest of the population), as well as an overconsumption of dried or ground, salted or cooked food, comparable to the practices of the rural or urban population. When it is not simply replaced by bread, the meat consumed by the people is often tainted... Two files therefore deserve a specific detour, that of the bread known as "à la Reine" and that of meat.

The case of the bread known as "à la Reine"

For political reasons, bread has become the main food of the French with almost a kilo and a half per day and per person. And it doesn't matter what it is made of (oats, for example)... Bread is therefore the symbol of food policies, but also of social inequalities. Marc Bloch writes: "Throughout the centuries, there has been no clearer criterion of class than this one." The Enlightenment did not question the supremacy of wheat, even though agricultural societies multiplied. Voltaire wrote in 1750 that "the nation began to reason about wheat"; Louis XV said he was very interested in the discoveries of Mathieu Tillet (member of the Academy of Sciences) about the wheat fungus. Bread, always bread.

It was in this context that the "Queen's bread" affair broke out in 1668. The body of bakers, neglected under the Merovingians and at the beginning of the Carolingians, had become a highly regulated profession, even more so than butchers. There are two distribution systems offering

---

three types of bread. In Paris, for example, there were public bakers and fairground bakers (from Gonesse and the surrounding area), who sold a popular bread twice a week, called "Gonesse bread". The public bakers offer three types of more expensive bread, white chapter bread, bis-white bread or bourgeois bread and bis-or brode bread. According to the regulations, the prices range from one to three. Bakers were allowed to make other types of bread (notably the so-called "Queen's bread" consumed by the wealthy classes). This bread is not made with traditional leavening (giving a poorly aerated bread, therefore heavy), but with brewer's yeast giving a much more swollen bread, therefore much lighter and tender. This leaven is essentially used to make rolls: if it is simply a salted roll, it is called "soft bread", if milk is added, it is called "Queen's bread" (in reference to Marie de Médicis). This affair of the bread known as "à la Reine" will mobilize public opinion for a long time because of the lawsuit brought by the public bakers to the cabaretiers, who buy the bread from the fairground bakers. The cabaretiers defend themselves by explaining that the bread of the stores, that is to say the bread of the public bakers, is made with beer yeast and that it is harmful. They based themselves on a decree of La Reynie of 1669, motivated by a vote of the faculty of medicine against the use of yeast, considered unhealthy. The public bakers defended themselves by explaining that in 1670 the Parliament had re-established the legality of using yeast for bread rolls.

Consumption of tainted meat

The absolute monarchy is often credited with the multiplication of food hygiene rules. These rules exist, certainly, but not for all! For example, the regulations concerning meat, a sensitive commodity.

There are, in fact, not two or three distribution channels, as is often heard, but four or even five. The first two circuits of butcheries are aimed at the "good" clientele: the "public butcheries", which sell beef, mutton and pork, and the "low butcheries", which offer meat from so-called inferior animals (such as the horse or the goat). A third circuit, that of the triperies, holds the monopoly of the low cuts for the people. The fourth circuit concerns the legal marketing of spoiled meat. This market is quite official and has its own regulations and is therefore controlled. Stores had to display a white flag, in particular to sell spoiled pork: "Pigs whose flesh is still only over-seeded with a few grains of spoilage can be sold [...] If the flesh is not yet corrupted, salt can correct the malignancy [...] the over-seeded pork flesh will be put in salt for forty days and then sold in a particular corner of the halls [indicated] by a post and a white flag" (Nicolas Delamare, *Traité de la police*, 1729, II). Meat recognized as totally unfit for human consumption was destined for the king's prisoners under Louis XI, or thrown into the Seine under Louis XIV, but sometimes distributed to the poor or in charitable establishments, as part of what we can consider a fifth non-commercial circuit. The slaughtering being obligatory *within the city walls*, traffic jams of animals clogged the streets, the meat had to be sold within forty-eight hours maximum, the display of the sex was compulsory, because male meat was considered better. In case of fraud, butchers are fined and sometimes corporal punishment.

The paradox of the frumentary revolts

The great period of Versailles is first of all that of the subsistence crises (1693-1694 and 1709-1710) because of a shortage of wheat, rye and barley. The only crisis of 1693-1694 caused 2 million deaths. It was the greatest catastrophe for centuries. It is explained, of course, by a drought, but also and above all, on the one hand, by the excessive specialization in the production of wheat to feed the rich and the cities, and, on the other hand, by the abandonment of the interventionist policies of the State[217]. The Church first organized processions to implore God's forgiveness, then, after the good harvest of 1694, the Archbishop of Paris ordered that all churches organize forty-hour prayers to "give thanks to God for this year's harvest, which abundantly repaired the sterility of the last two years..." The respite was short-lived with a new crisis in 1709-1710.

We owe Louise A. Tilly has a good understanding of the subsistence crises, but especially of the frugal revolts that marked the 17th and 18th centuries until the Revolution of 1789[218]. Louise A. Tilly explains that it is not in the simplistic economic formula "scarcity equals hunger equals riots" that one must seek the explanation of the frugal revolts since the 17th century, whereas scarcity disappeared more than a century before the last revolts, but in the non-interventionist attitude of the State and the pre-eminence given to wheat production, which the people disapproved of. The revolts did not take place where prices were highest, but where the needs of the metropolis, the army, and the large cities made supply a concern.

---

217. Cynthia BOUTON, "Les mouvements de subsistance et le problème de l'économie morale sous l'Ancien Régime et la Révolution française" in *Annales historiques de la Révolution française*, n° 319, 2000, p. 71-100.
218. Louise A. TILLY, "La révolte frumentaire, forme de conflit politique en France", *Annales. Économies, Sociétés, Civilisations*, 27e année, n° 3, May-June 1972, p. 731-757.

Before exposing the responsibility of new doctrines such as mercantilism, it is appropriate to quote Nicolas Delamare, first grain commissioner, then "great policeman" and author of the famous *Traité de la police* of 1719 (constantly republished until the Revolution), half of which was devoted to the food trade: "Public safety is never more exposed than in these times when bread is lacking or can only be obtained with difficulty…". Three types of riots can be distinguished: two classic ones, which date back to antiquity, and the other, a modern one, a consequence of the liberalization of the food markets, especially the grain market. The market riot, an urban version of the frumentary revolts, was directed against bakers whose selling prices were too high and bread too scarce; the hindrance, a rural form of the grain revolts, consisted in preventing the wagons and barges loaded with grain from leaving (at the beginning of the 17th century). The new form was popular taxation, which consisted in seizing grain or bread, selling it at the "right price" and paying the owner.

The great frumentary revolts did not occur at the height of food crises but when the government decided to abandon policies to protect the common people. The system of regulation of the grain market, first modified in the 17th century, was abandoned at the end of the 17th century. Previously, grain had to be sold on open markets and bakers and merchants could only buy after consumers had been able to buy. Thus, wheat, once offered for sale at a given price, had to remain on the market until it was completely sold. On the third day, it could be sold at a reduced price. No one was allowed to buy standing wheat or store it in granaries (except producers and consumers, but not speculators). It was compulsory to destock in case of a shortage. Thus, a sufficient quantity of cereals was kept permanently, either on sale or in stock. A similar system worked for bread, whose administered prices had to be posted. In the event of a shortage, the quantity of bread was reduced without affecting the selling price. Employees monitor compliance with the regulations.

This old system based on consumer protection was to be undermined by the rise of a new economic doctrine: mercantilism. This doctrine advocated the transfer of the management of the economy from the communes to the state. Attempts to impose it failed in the 16th century, but they succeeded in the following century, because mercantilism became the economic counterpart of the political centralism of Louis XIV. Paris ordered the setting of prices in a centralized manner, even for distant markets, just as Paris intended to impose the same law.

A political history of food. From the Pateolithic to our days

However, in 1709, the King's Council debated one last time the necessity of taxing prices, but the inquiry entrusted to Nicolas Delamare concluded that all the authorities were opposed to it. In contrast to taxation, the new dominant economic theory postulated that the "fair price" could only be that of the market (i.e., the meeting of supply and demand) and that regulations should be abolished. This conception of the economy was largely a Jansenist emanation with Pierre de Boisguilbert, as Gilbert Faccarello has shown[219]. Choiseul promulgated the edicts of 1763 and 1764 which established the free circulation of grain throughout the kingdom and opened up trade to all without the need for registration. These edicts were repealed in 1770, as were similar decisions by Turgot in 1774-1775, because of a combination of forces: poor harvests, popular opposition accompanied by riots, and parliamentary opposition[220]. Despite the repeal, the damage was done. The old regulations that fixed prices, prohibited, for example, the transfer of grain from one region to another, and required speculative merchants to register in order to trade in grain, were never restored.

Turgot (1727-1781) reveals the contradictions of the Enlightenment. He was close to the physiocrats, a friend of Diderot and the author of the article in *the Encyclopedia* on misery ("It is the sovereigns who make the miserable"). He wrote a thesis on the progress of the human spirit and was appointed by Louis XVI as Secretary of State for the Navy and later as Controller General of Finance. In the spring of 1775, he responded to the hunger riots and the looting of Parisian bakeries by having two alleged leaders, one 28 years old and the other 16, hanged in the Place de Grève. It is also him who will have the chestnut trees destroyed, in particular in Limousin, to substitute them the culture of the potato, in the name of the physiocratic theses[221].

The principle of tariff taxation would never again cease to be a popular demand. Edward P. Thompson offered a suggestive analysis of this period, showing how this new monarchical policy marked the end of the "moral

---

219. Gilbert Faccarello, *Aux origines de l'économie politique libérale : Pierre de Boisguilbert*, Paris, Éditions Anthropos, 1986. I would add, as I showed in *La face cachée du pape François* (Paris, Max Milo, 2016), the heavy responsibility of the Franciscans... One can read on this point the masterly study of Giacomo Todeschini, *Richesse franciscaine. De la pauvreté volontaire à la société de marché*, translated (ital.) by Nathalie Gailius and Roberto Nigro, Paris, "Verdier poche", Verdier, 2008.
220. Gilbert Faccarello, *Aux origines de l'économie politique libérale : Pierre de Boisguilbert, op. cit.*, p. 739.
221. Cf. the following chapter on the republican table where the theories of the physiocrats are discussed.

economy of the poor. The riots were thus a way of forcing the authorities to apply, or to apply themselves, the traditional measures: "The appearance of the frumentary revolts politicized the problem of subsistence and gave it a national dimension. They were inspired in the popular consciousness of a model of what should be in its eyes the economic functioning." The French Revolution is not so far away, with its laws on the maximum and its projects of great fraternal banquet.

Eleventh Service: The Republican Table

I would have liked to call this chapter the revolutionary table, but as the Thermidorian reaction, the Directory and the Consulate, which succeed the great revolutionary experiments, resemble strangely the last years of the absolute monarchy, I preferred to speak of the republican table because the Revolution, as soon as it tried to respond to the needs of the most humble, notably those of the quarter state[222] (which was never recognized), by taxing foodstuffs, it followed in the footsteps of the currents, notably the physiocrats, who wanted to free the market and put an end to popular eating habits.

We will discover, for example, that what is at stake in the destruction of chestnut trees, already well underway under Louis XVI by Turgot, and in the generalization of substitute foods, in a direction even worse than that

---

222. This term refers to the fourth-order list of grievances, that of the daily poor, the infirm, and the destitute, drafted at the time of the 1789 Estates General by Louis Pierre Dufourny de Villiers (1739-c. 1796), known as Dufourny. This revolutionary protested against the exclusion of the poorest from the writing of the cahiers de doléances. The Third Estate was only a fraction of the people, since one had to pay six pounds of taxes to be a member. In November 1789, Dufourny called for the foundation of "fraternal committees" bringing together workers and poor people on an equal basis. He will be president of the directoire of the department of Paris after August 10, 1792. Suspected of being linked to the Indulgents (Danton, Desmoulins, Fabre...), he will be arrested, Robespierre having strongly accused him on the 16th of germinal year II at the Jacobins. Released after the 9-Thermidor, he participated in the hunger riots in Germinal year III and was arrested again after Cambon accused him of having been involved in the massacres of September 1792. The amnesty of 4 brumaire year IV gave him back his freedom. It was to die shortly after. The expression "quarter state" (*vierde stand*) can be found in earlier texts in Dutch. The term "quarter state" became famous with the famous painting by Giuseppe Pellizza da Volpedo, completed in 1901 and titled *Il Quarto Stato*, after its author had discovered the term in the famous *Socialist History of the French Revolution* by Jean Jaurès. The book *Histoire de la langue française*, published in 1900, also explains that "among the compounds formed by an adjective and a noun, 'three dots' usually refers to the Freemasons and 'quarter state' to the proletariat".

---

which Turgot himself had dared to imagine, is the consequence of political choices that will make the French one of the most malnourished peoples! We will even have the luxury of a new famine and our livestock will be one of the sickest because of the blindness of scientists and politicians... A double postulate supports their policies: on the one hand, the idea that the poor have a good stomach and no taste, and that they can eat anything, and, on the other hand, the idea that it is good that they sweat blood and water to be able to eat to their hunger rather than counting, with chestnuts, on a miraculous "breadfruit tree."

We cannot, on the other hand, pronounce on what the revolutionary table would have been if the Revolution had not ended up devouring its children, Enragés, hébertists, Indulgents, robespierrists, then babouvistes, until the Directory which organized the victory of the bourgeoisie and capitalism.

This republican table is the child of the Enlightenment in all its best and worst aspects. On the positive side, we find the idea that the well-being of the people is the ultimate criterion for judging a society and that food must be good to think about, and therefore rational, thus allowing the Republic of the bellies to be married with that of the reason and the heart, and, on the negative side, we find economic liberalism applied to the grain market and the blissful faith in science that is supposed to feed 28 million French people.

When the Revolution meets the table

The revolutionary period also has the merit of reminding us that in France, if everything does not necessarily begin and end with a good meal, questions of food are never very far from the terrible hours. The collective memory, mixing real facts and biolegends, will never cease to maintain the link between food and revolutionary issues. One wanted to explain (too quickly) the Revolution by the bad harvests. One savors the image of the 7,000 women and 20,000 men of the National Guard going to Versailles in October 1789 to fetch Louis XVI, Marie-Antoinette and the Dauphin, a sign that they still believed that "the baker, the bakerywoman and the little butler" still corresponded to the figure of the good and nourishing king. It will never be forgotten that during the banquet of the bodyguards offered to the regiment of Flanders, called from Douai by the king to intimidate the Parisian popular movement, and held in the room of the Opera of the castle of Versailles on October 1, 1789, officers of the nobility withered the tricolour cockade, a gesture that triggered the insurrections of

October 5 and 6 for the respect of the "sacred sign of the French liberty", but especially because the rumor ran that to have bread, it was necessary to withdraw Louis XVI from the influence of the court and to bring him back to Paris.

According to the legendary account attributed to Camille Desmoulins and taken up by Alexandre Dumas in his *Grand dictionnaire de la cuisine* (1873), Louis XVI was arrested in Varennes because he took time to taste pig's feet in Sainte-Menehould. Lamartine will dwell on the description of the last banquet of the Girondins in the chapel of the Conciergerie: "The funeral supper was prepared in the large dungeon. Sophisticated dishes, rare wines, expensive flowers, numerous torches covered the oak table of the prisons. Luxury of the supreme farewell, prodigality of the dying who have nothing to spare for the next day... the meal was prolonged until the first twilight of the day. Vergniaud placed at the center of the table presided over it with the same calm dignity that he had kept the night of August 10, while presiding over the Convention.... Nothing indicated for a long time, in the faces and words, that this meal was the prelude to a torture" (Alphonse de Lamartine, *Histoire des Girondins*)[223]. The six months between the subsistence riots of February 1793, the days of March 9 and 10, the insurrections of May 31 and June 2, the sectional movement of August, and the days of September 4 and 5, are essential for understanding what was at stake around the question of subsistence, with the successive laws establishing the "first maximum" (May 4, 1793) and the "general maximum" (September 11, 1793). What was at stake, and this was the objective of these important laws, was to establish the link between the price of subsistence (and not only the necessities) and the level of wages, and to sketch out what could have become a true public food service thanks to the network of granaries of abundance throughout the territory, through the recognition of the right of each person to obtain what he or she needed to eat and to live[224].

Thus, during the most glorious but also the darkest hours of the Revolution, Robespierre, Danton, Saint-Just, Marat, Babeuf, will never stop talking about food! Not that they were gourmets (with the possible exception of Danton, who was undoubtedly more of a gourmand than a gourmet), but they knew that the fate of the Revolution depended on its

---

223. http://gallica.bnf.fr/ark:/12148/bpt6k10495068.
224. For a good and synthetic overview of this question of subsistances, see the art. For a good and synthetic overview of this question of subsistances, see the art. "Subsistances" by Claude Gindin in the *Dictionnaire historique de la Révolution française* published by the Presses universitaires de France in 1989 (see *below* the precise references for this book).

ability to feed some 650,000 Parisians and a revolutionary army of one million citizen-soldiers.

From the subsistence crisis to the Revolution

"They don't have bread? Let them eat brioche!" This famous phrase, falsely attributed to Marie Antoinette, is considered the justification for the Revolution and almost the signal for its outbreak. However, this formula runs from one country to another, since it appears, as early as the 16th century, in Germany and Latvia. Christine Shojaei Kawan and Véronique Campion-Vincent have established that it is used to describe three types of accusation: stupidity or ignorance when it involves women, outrageous cruelty when the protagonists are men, and the arrogance of the powerful in all cases[225]. This formula also testifies to the fixation of thought on the sole question of bread, a focus that is more the product of an ideological war than a simple observation about food.

I would like to return to the thesis developed by Guy Lemarchand: "The crisis of 1789 was not a thunderclap in a serene sky, it followed a rise in various tensions over several decades." Contrary to the legends cleverly maintained, the Revolution is not the consequence of a bad harvest but that of bad political choices carefully thought out. Guy Lemarchand, to whom we owe a brilliant analysis of subsistence troubles, shows that these troubles, which multiplied between the end of the 17th and the beginning of the 18th centuries, sanctioned, on the one hand, the edicts of 1763-1764 which liberalized the grain market, and, on the other hand, the unilateral seizure of communal lands by the hobereaux (closure of forests, draining of marshes, etc.)[226]. This policy was by no means accidental, since it corresponded, since the 17th century, within the framework of the Catholic Counter-Reformation, to the desire of the ruling classes to limit, or even prohibit, popular festivities, carnivals, balls and other gatherings deemed dangerous. [227]The historian agrees with the analysis of his colleagues Florence Gauthier and Guy Ikni, who write that in seeing the popular movement as a retrograde agitation, recent historians have allowed themselves to be impressed by the liberal authors of the 19th

---

225. Véronique CAMPION-VINCENT and Christine SHOJAEI KAWAN, "Marie-Antoinette and her famous saying. Two scenographies and two centuries of disorder, three levels of communication and three accusatory modes" in *Annales historiques de la Révolution française*, n° 327, 2002, p. 29-56.
226. Guy LEMARCHAND, "Troubles populaires au xviiie siècle et conscience de classe : une préface à la Révolution française" in *Annales historiques de la Révolution française*, n° 279, 1990, p. 32-48.
227. *Id., ibid.*, p. 40.

A political history of food. From the Pateolithic to our days

century, who themselves were heirs to the theses of the physiocrats: "The little people simply demanded the right to life within the framework of an optimistic vision of the possibilities given by the natural environment and an egalitarian conception of society. The people's expectations were therefore precise: to regulate the grain and bread trade in order to limit the negative effects of the development of the market economy. As Guy Lemarchand analyzes, three centuries of food riots forged a political consciousness: "The personnel of the food riots, like those of the anti-fiscal unrest, constituted a sans-culotterie before the letter of the law: artisans, small merchants, laborers, and winegrowers were numerous. In this way, throughout the three centuries of the Ancien Régime, a tradition of social struggle and, especially in the cities, of questioning the powers that be was forged, the first step towards a political consciousness that prepared the popular intervention during the Revolution. It prefigured the suspicious demand of the crowds from 1789 to 1794, of taxation and seizure of goods by the authorities. It will facilitate the formation of rural popular societies which, in turn, will extend popular economic and political action, as in Provence."

The ways of speaking about bread during the Revolution

The question of bread is consubstantial with the Revolution. The 1789 grievance books accuse the vine of usurping wheat land. The people learned to oppose politically the wine to the right to bread for all. This thesis is an old debate since, already under Louis XV, a decree of the Council of June 5, 1731 forbade "to make new plantations of vines in the extent of the Provinces and Generalities of the Kingdom and to restore, without the express permission of His Majesty, those which will have been two years without being cultivated, at the risk of each offender, of 3 000 livres of fine and under greater punishment if it falls to it; which permission will not be granted unless the land has been examined beforehand by the orders of the Intendant, to see if it is not more suitable for another crop than for being planted with vines. Although overturned in 1759, this ruling reserving the land for cereals marked the progression of capitalist property and the death of the figure of the nurturing king.

We already know that the equality of bread and food was imposed on the people in the cities, but especially in the countryside, to the detriment of another diet based on meat, other cereals, herbs, chestnuts. As the powerful often succeeded in imposing their point of view, the people, at first hostile to the "white bread of the rich", the cause of famine, ended up

---

demanding it and made the "right to bread" the emblem of their struggle. However, it is only from the point of view of the dominant that the dominated reduce their thoughts to their stomachs because, as Jacques Guilhaumou and Denise Maldidier's study on the political discursive confrontations around bread[228] proves, the way of speaking about bread divides society. The authors note that while the simple expression "Bread!" was the cry uttered by the people throughout the subsistence riots[229] that marked the Ancien Régime, something new was created around the events of October 5 and 6, 1789, since people demanded bread and something else: "Bread and to Versailles! "is the slogan of the women and national guards marching to bring the king back to Paris: "The food riot takes a new form; it is inscribed in the revolutionary political space. We see another manifestation of it in the general cry that erupted in front of the gates of the castle: "Bread and the end of business", where the demand for bread is associated with the denunciation of the hoarding ministers. The assassination of the baker François, who was hanged and beheaded in the Place de Grève on October 21, 1789, was certainly a pretext for the adoption of martial law, signed by Louis XVI, but its principle had been under debate since the days of October 5 and 6, because the powerful had clearly perceived the deep meaning of the revolt, as did Robespierre, who castigated this measure (it was "immolating freedom"). On the other hand, the Jacobins opposed the Enragés during the debate on the promulgation of a law on subsistence, each with their own slogan. Jacques Guilhaumou and Denise Maldidier write: "The confrontation was organized around two competing coordinations: "Bread and the Law" opposed "Bread and Freedom". A delegation was received on February 12, 1793: "We are told that a good law is impossible [...] No, a good law is not impossible; we have come to propose it to you". In March and September 1793, we witness the rise of a new slogan: "Bread and iron", which this time accompanies the birth of the Hebertist movement. The Jacobins of Marseilles translated the demand for a revolutionary army

228. Jacques GUILHAUMOU and Denise MALDIDIER, "Coordination et discours. 'Du pain et X' à l'époque de la Révolution française" in *Linx*, n° 10, 1984, numéro thématique : *Syntaxe & Discours*, p. 97-117.
229. *Id., ibid.,* p. 98: "From 1789 to 1795, a series of statements containing the sequence 'Bread and X' marked the high points of the revolutionary process. This structure of coordination seems to attest the emergence of new meanings in the field of revolutionary discourses. It is through coordination that the traditional cry of the people "Bread" is inscribed in the political space: "Bread and Versailles!" cry the women on October 5, 1789; "Bread and liberty" specify the Jacobins in the face of the revolutionary rise in 1793; "Bread and iron" claim the partisans of the Maximum (1793-1794); "Bread and the Constitution of 1793" proclaim the Parisian sans-culottes in front of the Thermidorian deputies in 1795.

    A political history of food. From the Pateolithic to our days

against the hoarders into this new slogan: "We must say, as in Marseilles: bread and iron to the sans-culottes and that will do. The deputy Favre adds: "It is necessary that the people of all the republic have also iron and bread and that they enjoy peace and happiness" (April 28). The partisans of the free circulation launched a counter-slogan through the voice of the deputy Philippeaux: "Bread and the Constitution, here is the petition of the free man, of the true republican... The Romans said *Panem et circenses*, bread and the games of the circus" (May 4). The slogan "Bread and iron" was taken up throughout this period by Jacques Roux, leader of the Enragés. It was inscribed as a motto on the banners of the popular societies of the South, gathered in congress in Marseille: "Bread and iron, that is the union, the ambition of the true revolutionaries". Marat wrote on February 21, 1793: "The duty of the faithful representatives of the people is not to push the people to despair by exaggerated alarms to force them to receive, at the same time, irons and bread. Their duty is not only to give bread to the people, like food to the vilest of animals. Despots also give bread to their subjects... We, the representatives of the nation, want to, and must, assure them of the liberty, peace, and abundance that are the fruit of just laws"[230].

Gracchus Babeuf and the administration of subsistence

The solutions for supplying bread to the 650,000 or so Parisians therefore varied according to whether they adhered to liberal or socialist theses on the economic level. This period was one of constant redistribution of political cards: thus Jean-Paul Marat, the editor of *L'Ami du peuple*, found himself overtaken on his left in February 1793 by the Enragés, the hébertists, and the friends of Babeuf, such as Fournier l'Américain, who engaged in a polemic against him. Marat feared that the agrarian law would lead to absolute equality and opposed the maximum contrary to his liberal economic convictions. This period was also one of extreme ideological confusion. Thus Camille Desmoulins denounces the danger that the counter-revolution will be made in red bonnets. In February 1793, Babeuf wrote a vitriolic pamphlet against Marat (who had had him released from prison in July 1790 after he had been imprisoned for his activism against indirect taxes). His text, *Législation des sans-culottes ou la parfaite égalité, réclamation des droits des 24 millions d'hommes sur le 25e million*, after having praised Robespierre's draft Declaration of Rights insofar as this Declaration recognizes the true rights of humans, calls for

---

230. *Id., ibid.,* pp. 105-106 and 108-110.

taking seriously its article 17 to claim from society "all that is necessary for its happy existence".

François-Noël Babeuf, who took the pseudonym of Gracchus Babeuf in 1794 in homage to the Gracques, initiators of an agrarian reform in ancient Rome, is famous for having led the "Conjuration of Equals" against the Directory, along with Buonarroti, Sylvain Maréchal, and Félix Le Peletier de Saint-Fargeau, in order to achieve "perfect equality" and "common happiness" by means of collectivization of the economy and a direct political democracy. Babeuf was arrested, the people tried to free him twice. He was sentenced to death in a context where the death penalty had just been voted for those who advocated the Constitution of 1793 and rebelled against the Directory. Babeuf tried to commit suicide when the verdict was announced, but was guillotined on May 27, 1797. He was certainly only a secondary actor of the Revolution, except in the field of food, since he was appointed secretary of the administration of subsistence under Garin, that is to say during the most critical period of the Revolution in terms of food, but also during the last attempts to do something really new with the so-called "maximum" laws. Babeuf, who took office in mid-May, just as the maximum law (the "first maximum") voted on May 4, 1793 by the Convention came into force, was therefore a particularly well placed witness to understand the balance of power. On September 27, 1792, the Paris Commune had already set a maximum selling price for certain products, but this measure proved insufficient. So on May 4, 1793, the Convention extended the law of maximum prices (on grain and flour), which was already in force in Paris, to the whole country, hoping that this harmonization would allow the city to be supplied. It established the taxation of grain prices by department according to the average price during the first months of the year, made it mandatory to declare the quantities of grain held by farmers and their marketing at the market, and entrusted the census of stocks and controls to the municipalities, which had an absolute right of requisition. This law, which also proved to be insufficient due to speculation by the wealthy peasantry and the depreciation of assignats, was literally imposed by the sans-culottes on the Convention, as it was contrary to the liberal ideas of the deputies. This law was more of a concession that many wanted to be temporary. It was, however, necessary to calm the people because the harvest of 1793 had been good and nothing explained this situation of shortage in the middle of abundance, if not this "wheat strike" led by the well-to-do peasantry who had seen their role grow on the grain market thanks to the abolition of feudal rights and tithes and the acquisition of the property of the clergy and emigrants. Babeuf will not cease, from his position at the administration of subsistances, to denounce the real sabotage of the law of May 4 by local administrations which prefer to live economically in autarky. He multiplied the letters of protest addressed to the districts and departments concerned and wrote reports for the Committee of Public Safety. But the Jacobin leaders themselves were still reluctant to enforce their own law, and it was not until the riots of September 4 and 5, 1793, that they ceased their procrastination and embarked on the policy of the general maximum.

The sectional movement of August 1793

During the summer of 1793, the food situation was still dramatic despite the law. The price of bread was indeed frozen at 3 sous per pound, but the shortage was general because of the decrease and then the near cessation of wheat deliveries. This tense situation makes it necessary to guard the bakeries from July 20. On July 26, the Convention adopts the law on hoarding and speculation (claimed since June by Jacques Roux, leader of the Enragés) which condemns to death the hoarders qualified as starvers of the people, but the elites in power still aim at the abolition of the anti-liberal law of May 4. As early as July 1, 1793, the Committee of Public Salvation and the Committee of Agriculture passed a decree that authorized the administrations of the departments and districts to make purchases directly from individuals and no longer from the markets as the law required. This decree, which was a very hard blow to the maximum, was voted without debate. The same authorization to buy outside the markets was given on July 5 to the administrators of military supplies, and, the same day, a new decree lifted all the export bans that the departments had promulgated, under the pretext that their censuses were not finished. From then on, the whole edifice of the law of May 4 collapsed"[231]. On August 9, the Convention accepted a plan to create "granaries of abundance" in each department to buy up surpluses.

Jean Jaurès, in his great *Socialist History of the French Revolution*, had already pointed out that the leaders of the Paris Commune had rallied "without enthusiasm" to the movement for the establishment of the maximum. Historians have long been divided on the meaning to be given to the attempt to create in July 1793, alongside the General Council, a

---

231. Albert MATHIEZ, *La vie chère et le mouvement social sous la Terreur*, Paris, Payot, 1927 (reed. in 2 vols., "le regard de l'histoire", Payot, 1973), chap. VII "La mort de Marat et le vote de la loi sur l'accaparement (juillet 1793)", § "Les décrets des 1er et 5 juillet 1793", *loc. cit.*, p. 242-243.

Union of Parisian sections that was largely responsible for the sectional movement of August 1793. According to some, such as Henri Calvet (who studied the departmental committee of public salvation[232]), this was an authentic popular movement of the sans-culottes... According to others, such as Albert Mathiez, this movement was a maneuver by moderates fighting against the revolutionary policies of the Jacobin convention. Mathiez concedes that the history of the August movement is "very muddled and confused. The characters are obscure. Their acts are poorly known and even worse their intentions. It is a continuous ebb and flow of petitions, demonstrations, troubles and intrigues"[233].

Are we therefore authorized to conclude that this sectional movement of August 1793 was fundamentally "counter-revolutionary"? Babeuf evokes, at the beginning of the Thermidorian reaction, his participation in the sectional movement (in *Du système de dépopulation*). He accuses (admittedly wrongly): "There existed, in 1793, a serious plan of famine against Paris... The directors were this Committee of Public Salvation, Barère especially, the Minister of the Interior Garat and Mayor Pache." Granting himself (rightly or wrongly) the fine role, Babeuf adds: "Those who foiled this plot were Garin, administrator of the commune's supplies, and me..." It is known that the 48 sections of Paris appointed "a commission to examine who the guilty authors of the famine that the city was close to experiencing might be [...] I made the most developed report to the commission, in which I was not afraid to formally denounce Pache, Garat, Barère, and the entire Committee of Public Safety. This commission issued a decree placing Garin and Babeuf under the protection of the 48 sections of Paris and ordered his report to be printed. Babeuf thus took an active part in the August movement and spoke in particular before the assembly of the section commissioners at the Bishop's Palace. The thesis of the "rolandist" character of the August movement does not hold... The movement did indeed start from the Beaurepaire section, which was very quickly accused by the Robespierrists of being a den of moderates and counter-revolutionaries, but it was nevertheless from it (and not from his own section of the Champs-Élysées) that Babeuf, after his arrest at the end of 1793, looked for a certificate of patriotism

---

232. Although there was officially only one Committee of Public Salvation at the national level, it seems that some surveillance committees, including the one in Paris, also chose to call themselves "committees of public salvation", see Henri CALVET, *Un instrument de la Terreur à Paris : le comité de salut public ou de surveillance du département de Paris (8 juin 1793-21 messidor an II)*. Paris, Librairie Nizet et Bastard, 1941.
233. Albert MATHIEZ, *La vie chère et le mouvement social sous la Terreur, op. cit.* chapter VIII, "L'agitation sectionnaire à Paris en août 1793. L'affaire Cauchois," pp. 258-290.

   A political history of food. From the Pateolithic to our days

capable of convincing the Paris revolutionary police of the righteousness of his commitment to revolution.

The Convention eventually gave in to the demands of the Enragés when the Commune defected under pressure from the sections in September 1793. The sectional movement was certainly directed against the Convention, the Comité de salut public and the mayor of Paris, but it was not fundamentally counter-revolutionary. This sectional movement of August was, moreover, the prelude to that of September.

The days of September 4 and 5, 1793

These two Parisian days constitute a decisive stage in the implementation of a policy of terror desired by the sans-culottes and the people. Albert Mathiez describes these two days as the "inauguration of terror" and speaks of an offensive by the Hebertist revolutionary avant-garde. These two days constitute a real revenge of the sections against the Commune and the Convention who had pronounced on August 25, 1793 the dissolution of their commission of inquiry on subsistence (Albert Mathiez, *La vie chère...* 1927, *op. cit.* Chapter X, "The Inauguration of the Terror", § "The Consequences", p. 337). Albert Soboul also describes these two days as "an unequivocal expression of the urban popular movement, that of the sans-culottes. He adds: "The working-class origin of the movement is indisputable: it came out of the most proletarian layers of the sans-culotterie"[234]. Robespierre still defends the mayor of Paris, besieged in his town hall, from the day of September 4: "One assures that in this moment Pache is besieged not by the people, but by some intriguers who insult him, insult him, threaten him... The scoundrels wanted to slit the throat of the National Convention, of the Jacobins, of the patriots." Pache and Robespierre will in fact submit to the will of the Parisian sections as evidenced by two decisions, that of September 11 which fixes the maximum at 14 pounds per quintal for all of France and that of September 29 known as the "law of the general maximum" which fixes the tariffs for many subsistence items but also for wages. This law set maximum prices for fresh meat, salted meat, bacon, butter, oil, salted fish, wine, vinegar, brandy, beer, firewood, while blocking wages. Anyone selling or buying above the maximum was fined and his or her name was put on the list of suspects. This attempt at a controlled economy had positive effects on food at first, but then the wealthy peasants began to hide their crops so as

---

234. Albert Soboul, *Les sans-culottes parisiens en l'an II*, Paris, Librairie Clavreuil, 1958, p. 166 and p. 267, quoted in Daniel Guérin, "D'une nouvelle interprétation de la Révolution française", in *Annales. Économies, Sociétés, Civilisations*, 20ᵉ année, n° 1, 1965, p. 84-94.

not to sell them at low prices. Rationing was organized in the cities, as well as a system of denunciation.

Babeuf took part in the September days as well as in the August movement. However, he did so without having any direct link with the leaders of the Enragés[235]. The fall of the Jacobins after 9 Thermidor marked the triumph of liberalism and the return to "economic liberty" in August and September 1794. The first consequence will be the soaring of prices, the fall of the value of assignats, the bankruptcy[236].

The insurrections of germinal and prairial year III

Between April and July 1794, the Committee of Public Salvation eliminates all the spokesmen of the Parisian sans-culotterie, the Enragés and then the hébertists, it dismisses the revolutionary army and abolishes the permanence of the sections, it authoritatively reduces the wages by a new maximum published on July 5. The workers will shout "Foutu maximum" on the passage of the cart that will lead Robespierre, Saint-Just and Couthon to the guillotine on the 10th of Thermidor.

The elimination of the Robespierrists will cause a clear degradation of the food situation of the Third and Fourth States. Thanks to the requisitions and taxes (all foodstuffs had been taxed in September 1793 at the price of 1790 plus a third and salaries at the value of 1790 plus a half), the people of Paris were eating their fill. The Thermidorians immediately reinforced the reactionary measures: they abolished the maximum on December 24, 1794, they suppressed the popular clubs and the allowances of the participants in the neighborhood meetings, they adopted on March 21 a law called "great police" punishing with death those who would declare themselves against the Convention and would incite to insurrection, They supported the "Golden Youth", the "Golden Bellies", several thousand young people from good families who, armed with clubs and canes, spread terror in the streets by hunting down "jacoquins" (a play on words with Jacobins), by attacking the sellers of the last Jacobin newspapers. These

---

235. After Thermidor, Babeuf affiliated himself with the Electoral Club, which held its meetings in the Bishop's Palace, a meeting of the "survivors" of the sectional movement of the second year, the Enragés, the Hebertists and all those who would soon be called Babouvistes.

236. See Guy LEMARCHAND, art. "Maximum" *in* Albert SOBOUL, *Dictionnaire historique de la Révolution française*, Jean-René SURATTEAU et François GENDRON (dirs), Paris, Presses universitaires de France, 1989; Guy LEMARCHAND, "Troubles populaires au xviiiᵉ siècle et conscience de classe : une préface à la Révolution française", art. Daniel GUÉRIN, *La lutte des classes ou la Première République, 1793-1797*, Gallimard, 1946, new edition in two volumes, revised and expanded, "La Suite des temps", Paris, Gallimard, 1968; Georges LEFEBVRE, *Questions agraires au temps de la Terreur*, Calmann-Lévy, 1968.

          A political history of food. From the Pateolithic to our days

muscadins destroyed the busts of Marat, object of a real popular cult, and scattered his ashes stolen from the Pantheon.

The death of Robespierre and the elimination of his relatives marked the beginning of a long deterioration of the food situation. Bread was still taxed at an affordable price, but it was not available. The new authorities argued that the poor harvest of 1794 and the terrible winter of 1794-1795 prevented the supply of grain from Denmark and the Netherlands because of frozen rivers, the blocking of ports, the state of the roads and food theft. The sans-culottes denounced the "accapareurs" and the politicians who had made a "pact of famine" against the people by freeing prices at the request of the big merchants and speculators. A decree of December 24, 1794 states: "All laws fixing a maximum are suppressed. The prices of foodstuffs increased much faster than wages. In four months, a pound of meat went from 34 to 140 sous.

This Thermidorian period will see the opposition between the "hollow bellies" and the "golden bellies" become stronger. Serge Bianchi reminds us that: "On one side, the nation of the 'golden bellies', of the 'fat pigs', prospers: they eat luxury products, the 100 cent buns; they party, and the cafés of the Palais-Royal are always full. Everything that reminds the egalitarian behavior of the year II is ridiculed. The red bonnets, the cockades are torn off, the passage of carmagnoles (short jackets worn by the sans-culottes), of pikes and sabots raises the quibibbles [...] On the other side suffers the nation of the 'hollow bellies', the tribe of the 'thin'"[237]. As Serge Bianchi notes, between these two "nations", the Thermidorian Convention made its choice: "Of course, it organized rationing and the distribution of food by an 'agency', to avoid unrest; the needy were counted and received meat and bread vouchers, according to the number of mouths to feed. But rations decreased rapidly: in February 1795, a forced laborer received 2 pounds of bread, an adult 1.5 pounds per day; in March, they dropped to 1.5 pounds and 1 pound respectively, and then to 500 grams for every adult. To supplement this, the 'agency' had some rice distributed (but with what fuel to cook it?) or potatoes, reputed at the time to be suitable only for pigs." These political choices in food could not remain without provoking popular riots.

On April 1, 1795 (12 germinal year III) a spontaneous demonstration broke out: processions including a good number of women formed from Notre-Dame and the ex-Bastille and converged towards the Tuileries

---

237. Serge BIANCHI, "Ventres creux contre ventres dorés. Insurrections of the year III" in *Gavroche*, n° 1, December 1981.

where the Convention was sitting: "Towards 1:30 pm, 20 000 demonstrators were massed in front of the Assembly; the tribunes were invaded in spite of the service of order. The occupation lasts five hours. The crowd marches shouting "Bread! Bread!" and booing the Conventionalists"[238]. The leader of the insurgents, Van Heck, former commander of the battalion of the Cité, came to the rostrum to expose the grievances of the demonstrators; he demanded bread, the Constitution of 1793 and the liberation of the political prisoners as well as the punishment of Fréron and his Golden Youth[239].

The Thermidorians mobilized the National Guard in the upper districts, but when these battalions of "golden bellies" reached the Convention at about 7 p.m., the crowd had already dispersed. The next day, Paris was placed under siege, and the command of the armed force was entrusted to Jean-Charles Pichegru (1761-1804), a general who had offered his services to the emigrants in Coblence, but had been rejected because of his modest social origin, and had become a republican out of spite: he was designated as the "savior of the fatherland" for his repression of the insurrection of the 12th and 13th of Germinal. He was arrested, judged and condemned to prison, from which he escaped before participating in other adventures with the Catholic counter-revolutionary army of the Vendée, to end up miserably strangled in his cell at the Temple on April 5, 1804.

The main leaders of the Montagnards were arrested and imprisoned. The sectional authorities were obliged to denounce all the participants in the day of 12 Germinal. 1,600 citizens were arrested, disarmed and deprived of their civil and political rights. Other hunger riots broke out in many cities, here they demanded "Bread and the Constitution of 1793", elsewhere "Bread and a King". Although the Thermidorian repression had calmed spirits, agitation resumed when the famine was transformed into famine because of the new reduction in rations, a quarter of a pound of bread per adult, then only two ounces (16 times less than the normal ration). On May 19, 1795, a call for insurrection was launched in the

---

238. *Id., ibid.*

239. Louis-Stanislas Fréron (1754-1802), a former far-left journalist close to Marat, deputy of Paris, denounced by Robespierre because, on the one hand, of his bloody actions to quell the federalist revolts of Marseille and Toulon, and, on the other hand, of his inability to justify the use of the funds entrusted to him by the Convention, he took part in the 9-Thermidor war against Robespierre, and he became the leader of the Muscadins, also known as the "Golden Youth. He was an important actor of the Thermidorian reaction, he took part in the hunt for the "jacoquins" and participated in the repression of the riots of the 12 and 13 germinal and the 1st prairial year III. He was also consul of Cagliari, then sub-prefect in Saint-Domingue where, pursued by his creditors, he died of yellow fever in 1802.

A political history of food. From the Pateolithic to our days

popular suburbs under the slogans "Insurrection of the people to obtain bread and reconquer their rights" and "Bread and the Constitution of 1793". On the morning of May 20, the tocsin sounded in all the working-class neighborhoods, groups of armed men and women invaded the premises of the sections and the national guard and invited or forced the authorities to march with them on the Convention. Serge Bianchi notes the essential role of the women: "Between 11 a.m. and 1 p.m., thousands of them march, preceded by drums; the men armed with rifles and pikes follow, with the inscription 'Bread or Death' on their hats. At 1 p.m., the first groups entered the Assembly's galleries and some even tried to break down the heavy cedar door that protected the deputies. The gendarmes resisted at first, cleared the accesses, and whipped the rioters. Around 3 p.m., the arrival of the battalions of the Faubourg Saint-Antoine changed the balance of power. At 3:33 p.m., sans-culottes armed with pikes blew up the door and the people in arms invaded, for the first (and only) time, the Chamber of Deputies to legislate in their place. The occupation goes on until midnight. The manifesto *"Insurrection du peuple..."* was read from the rostrum by a 25-year-old gunner, Duval. This manifesto distributed the day before in the popular suburbs whose full title is *Insurrection of the people to obtain bread and reconquer their rights* proclaims: "The people - Considering that the government is making them die inhumanely of hunger, that the promises it never ceases to make are deceptive and false [...] - Considering that a usurping and tyrannical government bases its criminal hopes and its strength only on the weakness, ignorance and misery of the people [...] - Considering that insurrection is for a whole people and for each portion of an oppressed people the most sacred of rights [...], resolves as follows. Article I - Today, without further delay, the citizens of Paris will go en masse to the National Convention to ask for: 1) bread; 2) the abolition of the revolutionary government, which each faction abuses in turn, to ruin, to starve and to enslave the people; 3) to ask the National Convention for the proclamation and the establishment on the spot of the democratic Constitution of 1793 [...] Article V - The immediate release of the citizens who are being detained for having asked for bread and for having expressed their opinion with frankness. Article VI - All power not emanating from the people is suspended. Article X - The rallying word of the people is "Bread and the democratic Constitution of 1793". Whoever during the insurrection does not wear this rallying word written with chalk on his hat will be considered as a public starver and an enemy of the people. The representatives of the demonstrators and some Montagnard deputies had measures voted in accordance with the program: release and arming of all detained patriots and the making of a "bread of equality"... Serge Bianchi goes on to note that the demonstrators were going to be reluctant to take power because of an ultimate respect for parliamentary legality, so they let the Conventionals withdraw and prepare the riposte, they even ended up dispersing themselves. As on Germinal 12, the National Guard of the "beaux quartiers" was assembled under the direction of Barras, and drove out the last insurgents present on the scene, took over the Convention without difficulty, and arrested the leaders and the last deputies of the Montagnards... The repression was terrible, and it took three days to finish off the people, in spite of the intervention in Paris (for the first time since 1789) of a 40,000-strong army, led by General Menou and assisted by the National Guards of "beaux quartiers". For three days the army faced 60,000 men and women entrenched behind barricades protected by cannons. The massacre will not take place because the barricades will surrender one after the other. 36 death sentences will be pronounced... Women are particularly targeted by the reaction, a decree of May 24 forbids them to attend any public meeting even from the stands, they lose the right to sign petitions, they cannot assemble more than five in the streets, etc. *The Messenger* of the 25th of Prairial exults: "It is from this day only that we can be assured of the respect that one will have for the persons and the properties. Serge Bianchi concludes: "For a few months the misery gets worse. In September 1795, the prices are multiplied by 30, the scrip is worth nothing, 'one feeds on the blood of the animals'. But calm reigns. The 'honest people' can breathe and consume in peace, rid of the 'famished rabbits, harpies, debauched'. The nation of the notables put an end to the movement of the 'hollow bellies' and consolidated its power durably by disarming those without whom the Revolution could not have triumphed".

The table of the Enlightenment and the Revolution

The revolutionary table, like the republican table, is not only a matter of nutritional logic but also social, cultural and political. The revolutionary table as well as the republican table respond to a vision of society, to a conception of society and particularly of the lower classes. The choice of food as well as the structuring of the table are essential issues in which the political priorities of an era can be read.

We can sketch out what the revolutionary table could have been if it had followed its own political logic aimed at considering food as a common good escaping the laws of the market, subject to a logic of public service with the creation of "granaries of abundance", with the most decentralized democratic control possible in terms of food policies, and therefore also in terms of agricultural policies...

The French Revolution is the daughter of the Enlightenment philosophy as much as it is of the subsistence troubles that mark this long period. I would like to show that the republican table is also the child of the Enlightenment against the clerical conception of food. Taine defines the eighteenth century as the century of the Enlightenment, it corresponds to an age of reason of humanity, to the passage from the light of faith to the light of reason. The table of the Enlightenment must therefore be structured and organized to allow this work of reason. The "old French-style service" (which allows you to flutter around and enjoy yourself, which is therefore "good for the mouth" but less so for the head) will be replaced by the "Russian-style service" (a succession of dishes that the cook can organize according to his will); we will adopt the ternary system (starter, main course, dessert) much simpler to think and structure; we will do away with the cuisine of mixtures and tepid (because it is less thought than binary oppositions); we will return to a classification of flavors and to a scale of taste that we can reason, etc. The Enlightenment is, according to Fontenelle's image (*Discourse on the nature of the eglogue*, 1688), the fruit of experience, it accumulates in the course of centuries, it is based on an apprenticeship. Thus, the schoolmaster's mission will be to learn to read and write (which is new because it was enough to know how to read orders), to learn to count and to learn to differentiate flavors (sweet, sour, salty, bitter, according to Adolf Fick's classification established in the 19th century). The table would thus be, like humanity itself, entering adulthood, or at least it could. For this, the philosophers of the Enlightenment expect everything from the bourgeoisie and nothing from the people, even if Condorcet appears less pessimistic than Diderot: "The nineteen twentieths of a nation are condemned to ignorance by their state and their imbecility. The other twentieth is now very enlightened and is so without effect" (Diderot). The philosophy of the Enlightenment, adapted to the table, inclines however more on the side of the empiricists than of the partisans of the pure reason, it is a question of creating perceptions which will be able to be organized in conscious thought. The menu will serve to express this unity and the direction of the meal. It is the ordering of the dishes themselves and the marriage of the dishes and the words that will deliver this message. The eater must lose in freedom what he gains in intelligence, because there is no question of questioning by disordered movements what has been (well) thought by the cook. A meal has obligatory standard steps. The cook is therefore the equivalent of a great watchmaker. He too assembles parts according to an organized plan. He too builds a marvelous machine which must allow to live well, and to eat and drink well. We discover, with the authors of the 19th century, including Brillat-Savarin and his *Physiology of Taste*, a faith in a determinism that is more physical and chemical than social. The moral and social forces dormant in humanity can be developed by good government, good education and good nutrition. We must not forget that the philosophers of the Enlightenment will never question the idea of absolute power, but that they wish for an enlightened despot, acting as a philosopher and not as a representative of God on earth, this is also true for the cook.

Food in the Encyclopedia

We can start from Diderot and d'Alembert's *Encyclopedia* to better understand how the Enlightenment thought about food. We are fortunate in that all the sections concerning our subject were written by the same author, the Chevalier Louis de Jaucourt (1704-1779), whom Diderot called "the slave of the Encyclopedia" since he supervised all the texts and wrote a significant part of them himself[240]. We are thus dealing with a homogeneous and solid thought. Jean-Claude Bonnet proposes to look for in the "culinary network" of the Encyclopedia "the advent of a new collective subject, the proof of a historical transformation of the forms of desire and of the status of the body, the affirmation of an orality characte-ristic of the dynamics of the century"[241]. Jaucourt's great thesis is that of a progressive complication of food: the food of the first peoples of the world (dairy products, fruits of the earth, honey, vegetables, breads cooked under the ashes, etc.) is certainly without refinement, but that is why it ensures robustness and health *(sic)*. This "miraculous state" would have been broken because of a psychic gear, the disgust, born by the habit, would have indeed made the humanity curious of new experiences. Commerce would also have contributed to the blurring of habits. This imbalance is the cause of the present poor health. The maximum aberration is pica, defined in *The Encyclopedia* (art. "pica") as "a violent appetite for absurd, harmful, and in no way nourishing things"; the article continues: "[...] the etymologists claim that it was given this name which in the natural sense means 'magpie', because as this bird is very varied in its words and

---

240. Georges A. PERLA, "La philosophie de Jaucourt dans *L'Encyclopédie*" in *Revue de l'histoire des religions*, vol. 197, n° 1, 1980, p. 59-78.
241. Jean-Claude BONNET "Le réseau culinaire dans *L'Encyclopédie*" in *Annales. Economies, Societies, Civilizations*. 31st year, n° 5, 1976, p. 891-914.

　　　　A political history of food. From the Pateolithic to our days

plumage, so the depraved appetite of this species of sick person extends to many different things and diversifies infinitely; could we not have found a more sensitive and striking respect between this bird remarkable by its chatter and the persons of the sex, which are the ordinary subjects of this disease" (*The Encyclopaedia*, 1st edition, 1751, volume XII, p. 544-547). 544-547). However, the criticism goes further than that of excesses and wastefulness harmful to oneself and to others.

Jaucourt believes that the history of cooking is a long falsification of flavors, thus a loss of taste. A table of the Enlightenment must make it its mission to return to a simple range of flavors so that it is intelligible. The elaboration of a table of flavors would be necessary. Jaucourt opposes to the deceptions of the Roman table the cooking of the "sober or poor" people which is "the most common art of preparing food to satisfy the needs of life". Jean-Claude Bonnet concludes that "the history of cooking is thus marked by the moral antithesis of a simple cuisine of nature and the unbridled developments of a fallacious art". Apicius symbolizes this distorted cuisine. However, Jaucourt draws up a more balanced balance sheet because the history of cooking is also that of constant progress insofar as the senses and knowledge are reconciled since it is in the same movement that man discovers new pleasures and new useful knowledge: "The habit of eating always the same things, more or less prepared in the same way, gave birth to disgust, disgust gave birth to curiosity, curiosity gave birth to experiments, experimentation brought about sensuality; man tasted, tried, diversified, chose, succeeded in making an art of the simplest, most natural action." *The Encyclopedia* is, of course, subjugated by the splendor of the technique and culinary production. We will see later that it shares the hatred of the stew, considered as what constantly revives the appetite. Jean-Claude Bonnet notes that Jaucourt makes pastry the emblem of a peaceful civilization and that he opposes to it the consumption of meat, symbol of violence. In *the Encyclopaedia* one does not find a word against coffee and sugar which have made the misfortune of Africa and America according to the formula of Bernardin de Saint-Pierre.

Revolutionary banquets

The Revolution is, in many memories, associated with the organization of great revolutionary festivals in which public banquets occupy an important place. This history being already well known, I will go to the essential. Mona Ozouf reminds us that we do not know what the citizens who were assembled in this way ate: "The menus that adorned the minutes of the

Federation have disappeared from them [...] at least they drank from the same bowl as "true sans-culottes"[242].

Pierre Birnbaum denounced the systematic consumption of pork, wanting to see in it, as under the monarchy, a manifestation of anti-Semitism[243]. This analysis is not convincing on this point, because these popular agapes do not take as their model (or counter-model) the religious tables, but follow other logics and motivations that have more to do with the symbolism of pork in the national political history since the Gauls. Not every pork eater is necessarily an anti-Semite, even if one cannot ignore the importance of the polemics that shook the nation at the time concerning the integration of the Jews. Pierre Birnbaum rightly reminds us that for the revolutionaries "the banquet tables could not be separated, distanced from each other [...] The fusion of the national body is translated by commensality." The banquet expresses indeed the political utopia of reconciled citizens.

The organization of the banquets does not rest more than the other aspects of the revolutionary festivals on the chance, all is learnedly constructed. These banquets, like the festivals, are inscribed in the will to take the opposite side of the absolute monarchy, under which the Church has, during the 18th century, suppressed numerous festivals, because the idleness begets the debauchery (*sic*). These festivals are also revolutionary in the sense that it is no longer for the people to simply attend, but to participate actively. One develops an art of the procession, the costume, the music, the songs, the dances, the meals, etc.

The Marquis Charles de Villette (1736-1793), who burned his titles of nobility, is certainly less known than the painter David, the great organizer of the revolutionary parties, but he nevertheless plays an essential role in the conception and organization of the great banquets. He proposed different types of banquets. He foresees four national feasts, one per season: the banquet of May 1 would be a festival dedicated to the troops of line to which one would offer the tree of the freedom; that of July 14 would be the festival of the national guards, i.e. of all the children of the "empire" (Villette wishing to create a "French empire"); the one in autumn would be the festival of free nations, during which the statue of Liberty would be erected, followed by Abundance, of which grapes, sheaves of wheat, baskets of flowers and fruits would be the emblems; the one in winter, the season of weddings, would be the occasion to celebrate morals,

---

242. Mona OZOUF [1976], *La Fête révolutionnaire (1789-1799)*, Paris, "Folio histoire" (n° 22), Paris, Gallimard, 1988.
243. Pierre BIRNBAUM, *The Republic and the Pig*, Paris, Éditions du Seuil, 2013.

   A political history of food. From the Pateolithic to our days

forgetting about hatreds between citizens and divisions between relatives. Villette describes the banquet sealing the recovered unity of the nation: "I would like that one institutes a national festival at the day which makes the time of our resurrection. I would like all the bourgeois of Paris to have their tables set up in public and to have their meals in front of their houses. The rich and the poor would be united and all ranks would be confused [...] The rich and the poor would be united and all ranks would be confused [...], the capital, from one end to the other, would form only one immense family; one would see a million people seated at the same table; the toasts would be carried to the care of all the bells, to the noise of a hundred shots of cannons, of musketry salvos, at the same moment in all the districts of Paris, and this day, the nation would hold its great table setting" (in *Lettres Choisies* de Charles Villette *sur les principaux événements de la Révolution*, Paris, 1792). This proposal inspires the organization of the banquet offered, in the park of the Muette, to the delegates of all the nation, other meals being organized in parallel in each district.

David, charged with presenting, on July 11, 1793, a report to the Convention for the organization of the feast of the nation, proposes the gathering of all the commissioners (delegates), place de la Bastille, so that they "drink one after the other in the same cup the pure and salutary water which comes out of the fountain of the Regeneration." He adds that "the end of these ceremonies will be a frugal banquet. The people, seated fraternally on the grass and under the tents made for this purpose around the enclosure, will share with their brothers the food they have brought"[244].

Let us also mention the project of construction in the Champ-de-Mars of a permanent national circus for the great festivals, formed of 48 immense tents that can contain each one 2 200 citizens. We also see a rise in banquets organized by the sections, then their decline from germinal year II, as the people are eliminated from the festivities and from the Revolution. Louis-Sébastien Mercier will have very hard words to depict these sectional banquets: "Each one under penalty of being suspected, under penalty of declaring himself the enemy of equality, comes to eat in family beside the man whom he hated or despised. The rich man impoverished as much as he could the luxury of his table; the poor man ruined himself to hide his misery; and while he had consumed by pride all the product of his week, his modest meal had made him blush with the one who believed to have been sans-culottised"[245]. The researcher Olivier Ihl has hardly more

---

244. Marie Louise Biver, *Fêtes révolutionnaires à Paris*, Paris, Presses universitaires de France, 1985.
245. Louis-Sébastien Mercier, *Paris pendant la Révolution ou le Nouveau Paris*, Paris, Poulet-Malassis, 2 vols, 1862.

friendly words: "These supposedly fraternal meals show the impossibility of an equality of places and manners [...] *a fortiori* when on the tables of the streets of revolutionary Paris, beside the patriotic emblems and the wreaths of flowers, the silverware rubbed shoulders with the pewter cutlery, the porcelain and the crystal with the coarsest crockery"[246].

The affair of the patriotic banquets of 1794[247]

The affair of the patriotic banquets broke out during the summer of 1794: the sections of Paris organized civic meals or fraternal banquets[248] to celebrate military victories after the victory of Fleurus, on 8 Messidor, and even more so on the anniversary of the storming of the Bastille, on 26. Historians agree that the moderates found in this popular initiative an opportunity to reappear. By drinking to the victory and the forthcoming peace, they implicitly wished for the end of the exceptional measures and thus the end of the revolutionary government. On 22 Messidor, a new banquet was organized by the section of the Friends of the Fatherland, which included supporters of Danton and Desmoulins who had been executed two months earlier. The revolutionary government could not tolerate it. On the 24th, Payan intervened in the General Council of the Commune: "It is the enemies of the fatherland who have propagated these meals. Who is the one who, after having drunk to the health of the Republic with the moderates, will denounce them tomorrow with as much courage? His arguments are taken up on the 28th at the tribune of the Convention by Barère who maintains that these sectional meals, diverted from their primitive goal, were "only a premature amnesty, an early proclamation of peace and a dangerous fusion of pure feelings and perfidious intentions, of republican actions and counter-revolutionary principles". And Barère continues: "There can be nothing in common between the opulent egoist, who longs for inequality and kings, and the frank sans-culotte who loves only the republic and equality." The Convention did not, however, issue any decree of prohibition, Barère having explained that "civic defense is the best article of decree to proscribe these so-called fraternal banquets, and, at this moment, the Convention refers the execution of this moral decree to

---

246. Olivier IHL, "De bouche à oreille. Sur les pratiques de commensalité dans la tradition républicaine du cérémonial de table" in *Revue française de science politique*, 48ᵉ année, n° 3-4, 1998, p. 387-408.
247. See on this question Hans-Ulrich THAMER, "Entre unanimité et conflit : la politisation des banquets publics, 1789-1799" *in* Natalie SCHOLTZ et Christina SCHRÖER (dirs), *Représentation et pouvoir. La politique symbolique en France (1789-1830)*, Rennes, Presses universitaires de Rennes, 2007, pp. 93-100.
248. See Albert SOBOUL, *Les sans-culottes parisiens... op. cit.*, p. 980-985.

    A political history of food. From the Pateolithic to our days

the revolutionary tribunal of public opinion" (*Moniteur*, XXI, 233). The same evening in the Jacobins, Barère reads his report, the printing of which has been decided by the Convention.

The movement of the banquets will decline before being reborn at the time of the anniversary of the capture of the Bastille. Robespierre will return on these banquets in one of his last speeches (July 16, 1794/28 messidor year II): "The momentary success of the alleged patriotic banquets had its source in the general feeling of civism which animates the whole people. The first attempts came from the perversity of the intriguers who have perfidious views, such as that of softening the public opinion and of putting to sleep the friends of liberty; how indeed could one distrust a man with whom one drank from the same cup, on whose lips one found the language of patriotism, and whose glance presented only the image of friendship? The calumnies against the revolutionary Government, and also against the Revolutionary Court, the persecutions directed against the energetic and honest patriots, have an intimate relationship with these banquets: skilful intriguers wanted to slip into them and to bring about, if it had been possible, an amnesty for the conspirators [...]"[249].

The robespierrists therefore said that they feared a contamination of the good people. How to understand such a lack of confidence in the sans-culottes? Is it not first of all a fear which finds its origin in the little attraction that Robespierre and his close relations carried to the form banquet in itself? As Maxime Rosso noted, Robespierre sorted out among the ancient institutions intended to weld the citizens around the common good, and this apart from the gravity of the situation and the counter-revolutionary threats: "Thus he rejects the idea of the republican meals, the Spartan *Syssities* or *Phidities*. The mistrust takes here the top on his unifying will"[250]. Could it not also be because of the conception of virtue that Robespierre defends, a conception that breaks with the old Christian virtue but that privileges too much the martial virtues to the detriment of the other forms? I do not believe that someone as knowledgeable as he is in history can speak of softening without thinking of the softness denounced by the Ancients[251]. It is also that if Robespierre intends to make the whole people participate

---

249. Maximilien ROBESPIERRE, *Œuvres complètes*, tome 10, *Discourses (27 July 1793-27 July 1794)*, Publications de la Société des études robespierristes, Ivry, Phénix Éditions, 2000, p. 533-535.

250. Maxime ROSSO, "Les réminiscences spartiates dans les discours et la politique de Robespierre de 1789 à thermidor", *Annales historiques de la Révolution française*, n° 349, 2007, p. 51-77.

251. Cf. *above* "The Roman conception of the table", in particular the paragraph "The soft and the hard".

in the national celebrations, he does not intend to rely on his creativity and prefers choreographies: "You will be there, brave defenders of the fatherland which decorate glorious scars. You will be there, venerable old men that the happiness prepared for your posterity must console a long life spent under despotism. You will be there, tender pupils of the fatherland who grow to extend its glory and to collect the fruit of our works. You will be there, young citizens to whom the victory must soon bring back brothers and lovers worthy of you. You will be there, mothers of family whose husbands and sons raise trophies to the Republic with the debris of thrones"[252].

Robespierre intended to educate the people as an instructor and not as a midwife who would simply awaken an "already there" that would exist in sharing. As a result, not only was he wary of overly spontaneous agape, but his feast of the Supreme Being, celebrated on the 20th of Prairial Year II (June 8, 1794), was, according to all accounts, totally out of step with the feelings of the people. The scenography is as always brilliant but leaves no room for initiative: the participants gather around a round basin at the end of the Tuileries garden. On this basin, a pyramid represents a monster, Atheism, surrounded by Ambition, Selfishness and false Simplicity. Robespierre appears dressed in a celestial blue suit with a tricolor scarf. He holds in his hand a bouquet of flowers and ears of corn. He sets fire to this ensemble which unmasks, once burned, a statue of Wisdom. The crowd, in particular that of the deputies of the Convention, will make fun of the (too) pedagogical character of this spectacle and will even refuse to march in step.

Robespierre and the search for happiness

However, Robespierre is unquestionably on the side of the search for happiness. To be convinced of this, it is sufficient to reread his speech on the Constitution of 1793: "Man was born for happiness and freedom, and everywhere he is a slave and unhappy. The purpose of society is the preservation of his rights and the perfection of his being; and everywhere society degrades and oppresses him." Article 1 of the Constitution states: "The purpose of society is the common happiness". Saint-Just will launch, from the same tribune of the Convention, one year later, on March 3, 1794, the famous formula: "Happiness is a new idea in Europe."

One cannot reproach the robespierrists for having remained with pious wishes. They multiply concrete measures in the economic and social field.

---

252. Maximilien ROBESPIERRE, *Œuvres complètes*, tome 10, *Discourses (July 27, 1793-July 27, 1794*, *op. cit.* p. 442-464: *Sur les rapports des idées religieuses et morales avec les principes républicains, et sur les fêtes nationales*, rapport présenté par Robespierre à la Convention au nom du Comité de salut public, le 18 floréal an II (7 mai 1794), *loc. cit.*, p. 461.

                A political history of food. From the Pateolithic to our days

Robespierre spoke out in favor of limiting the freedom of trade that starved the people ("Let us make laws that bring the price of foodstuffs closer to that of the industry of the poor"), he denounced the egoism of the powerful ("the first social law is the one that guarantees all members of society the means to exist"), He spoke out against the death penalty, against martial law, against the war of conquest ("No one likes armed missionaries"), against slavery in the colonies ("Let the colonies perish rather than a principle"), he finally sided with the sans-culottes in having the general maximum adopted and in trying to have it respected. This recognition of the right to happiness is not self-evident because it breaks with centuries of religious domination based on the renunciation of pleasures. The robespierrists, logical with themselves, therefore look to Antiquity, to its various conceptions of the good life (εὐδαιμονία, *eudaimonia*).

Robespierre as Saint-Just belongs however more to the Portico than to the garden, they are more stoics than epicureans[253]. Let us listen to Robespierre speak, in his speech of 18 Floréal Year II *On the relationship of religious and moral ideas with republican principles, and on national holidays*, of the "sublime sect of the Stoics, who had such high ideas of the dignity of man, who pushed so far the enthusiasm of virtue that only outraged heroism. Stoicism gave birth to emulators of Brutus and Cato until the terrible centuries which followed the loss of the Roman freedom. Stoicism saved the honor of the human nature degraded by the vices of the successors of Caesar, and especially not the patience of the people..."

The revolutionary virtue, in the sense that Robespierre understands it, is no longer that of the Church, which despises earthly pleasures that are always considered guilty, nor is it that of Kant, for whom Duty would be opposed to Happiness in the name of the Sovereign Good, but it is not that of the first materialists either (including Epicurus). As Paule Becquaert indicates, virtue for Robespierre is, of course, public virtue, "a virtue that would be nothing other than the love of the country and its laws", but it is also the necessity to live in accordance with reason, to "live in accordance with nature", which means that if virtue is declined according to the circumstances and the characters, prudence for some, wisdom, justice, courage, temperance, self-control, good advice, patience, for others, all these points of view lead to the same result which is "to escape the charm of the seductive representations, the perverting influences which emanate from the society. Seduction, perversion, therefore evil. Indeed, in front of the virtue is the vice, without intermediary". Consequence: the people

---

253. Epicureanism must not be confused with the enjoyment-without-entrails easily recoverable by capitalism. Epicureanism was one of the first materialist conceptions of the world in the face of the Stoic idealist current.

possesses certainly "naturally" the virtue ("the virtues are simple, modest, poor and often ignorant, sometimes coarse; they are the prerogative of the unhappy ones and the inheritance of the people"; "to like justice and equality, the people does not need a great virtue; it is enough for him to like itself"), but it is undoubtedly about a fantasized, imaginary people. It is not a question of disputing that virtue must be acquired and preserved and that it requires vigilance and rigor, to use Robespierre's words, but this conception of virtue inclines to what we call sad passions.

Robespierre will thus never break with the idea of a necessary sacrifice and not only because of the revolutionary and in particular military situation, he will never perceive that any call to sacrifice in the name of a future happiness (terrestrial or celestial) always calls for an ideological and repressive apparatus. The right to happiness does not suffer in Robespierre from a lack of democracy but from his tenacious refusal to aim at de facto equality. He is systematically on the side of a more democracy by maintaining that "never the evils of the society come from the people, but from the government", that "it is not the anarchy which is the disease of the political bodies, but the despotism and the aristocracy", that's why he proposes here again (as in economy) concrete solutions, as the limitation of the duration and the number of mandates, as short legislatures (one year), as the adoption of the universal suffrage against the censal suffrage, as a numerous deputation to reduce the intrigues, as the freedom of the press, as a popular judgment on the respect (or not) of promises at the end of the mandate in exchange for parliamentary immunity, as the right to petition, as the immediate non-reeligibility of outgoing deputies, as the payment of allowances to those who serve the public thing to democratize elective functions and to allow the poor to participate in meetings, as the impossibility of exercising at the same time several magistratures, as the choice of a maximum decentralization by leaving "in the departments and under the hand of the people the portion of the public tributes that it will not be necessary to pour in the general fund", by fleeing "the old mania of the governments to want to govern too much: leave to individuals, leave to families the right to do what does not harm others; leave to the communes the power to regulate their own affairs [...] In a word, give back to individual liberty all that does not naturally belong to the public authority, and you will have left all the less room for ambition and arbitrariness" (May 10, 1793).

On the other hand, the right to happiness suffers in Robespierre's case from his refusal of de facto equality, which is combined with his praise of poverty (which is not misery), which is not to be found in Mably (1709-1785), precursor of utopian socialism and the Revolution, nor in the Enragés,

A political history of food. From the Pateolithic to our days

nor in the Hebertists, nor, of course, in the first communists Babeuf and Buonarroti: "If I deigned to answer absurd and barbarous prejudices, I would observe that it is power and opulence that give birth to pride and all vices; that it is work, mediocrity, poverty that is the guardian of virtue" (Robespierre's speech to the Convention, *On the Constitution*, May 10, 1793).

Robespierre never hid the fact that he did not wish to go any further than a different distribution of wealth without calling into question the principle of inequality. He explained during his project for a new Declaration of Rights in April 1793: "No doubt a revolution was not necessary to teach the world that the extreme disproportion of fortunes is the source of many evils and many crimes; but we are no less convinced that the equality of goods is a chimera. As far as I am concerned, I believe that it is even less necessary for private happiness than for public happiness: it is much more a question of making poverty honorable than of proscribing opulence" (*On the new Declaration of Rights*, April 24, 1793). Some have not failed to speak of the opportunistic character of his "socialism", he who was a defender of private property and economic liberalism.

Louis-Sébastien Mercier does not show himself to be a friend of equality either, drawing up vitriolic portraits of the little people in *Le tableau de Paris*: "The butchers are men whose faces bear a ferocious and bloody imprint, their arms bare, their collars swollen, their eyes red, their legs dirty, their aprons bloody, their hands gnarled and massive and always ready for the brawls of which they are avid. The blood they spill seems to light up their faces and their tempers. A coarse and furious lust distinguishes them, and there are streets near the butcher's shops, from which exhales a cadaverous odor, where vile prostitutes, sitting on bollards in the middle of the day, publicly display their debauchery. It is not attractive: these speckled, farded females, monstrous and disgusting objects, always massive and thick, have the look harder than that of the bulls; and they are pleasant beauties to these men of blood who go to seek the voluptuousness in the arms of these Pariphaés"[254].

This refusal of pleasures was already what led the encyclopedist Jaucourt to demonize the "culinary" understood under the generic term of stew and which he defined as "sauce or seasoning to tickle or excite the appetite when it is blunted"[255], in short, as a true perversion of nature. This

---

254. Writer, journalist, he lived during the Revolution with Olympe de Gouges, he founded the *Annales patriotiques et littéraires* in 1789 to propagate the revolutionary ideas. He was arrested under the Terror, and was released by the 9-Thermidor. He took a stand against Descartes, accused of having invented the freedom of thought, responsible for the Terror, and against Voltaire, whom he accused of having destroyed morality. He will end up teaching history in the central schools.
255. Cf. article "ragoût" by Jaucourt in *L'Encyclopédie*.

refusal of pleasures will be also what will lead Louis-Sébastien Mercier, companion of Olympe de Gouges, to vomit the popular manners and in particular the taste of the people for the boiled[256].

How can we not draw a parallel between the conception of the good life nourished by stoicism, the praise of frugality and poverty, and the educational choices that Robespierre will make by choosing as a model (instead of the schools directed by the Jesuits expelled by Louis XV in 1764) the *Plan of civic and national education* written by Michel Le Peletier de Saint-Fargeau, shortly before his assassination, on January 20, 1793, and that his brother Félix presented to the Jacobins on July 19, 1793. Although this *Plan was* favored by Robespierre, who read it to the Convention, it was never implemented. If it had been, it should have - at least it was his ambition - ensured the primacy of moral training, since it was no longer a question of training "gentlemen" but citizens, men of all states. Le Peletier de Saint-Fargeau's *plan* considered children as a malleable raw material and public education as a mold. Boys from 5 to 12 years old and girls from 5 to 11 years old were to be "continually under the eye and in the hand of an active supervision. Maximo Rosso indicates that the life of these children is marked by the seal of frugality: "I desire that for the ordinary needs of life, the children deprived of any kind of superfluity, be restricted to the absolute necessities. They will be put to bed harshly, their food will be healthy but frugal, their clothing comfortable but coarse"[257]. Everything is said: to give to the children a healthy and frugal food to give birth to frugal and honest citizens!

Robespierre was arrested on July 27, 1794 and executed on July 28. It is the beginning of the very long Thermidorian reaction, of the revenge of the owners. July 28 will be the bloodiest day of the Revolution: 108 people were the victims of this legal plot of Robespierre's enemies. Saint-Just had been right when he declared shortly before: "The Revolution is frozen, all principles are weakened, only the red bonnets worn by intrigue remain. The exercise of the Terror has blighted crime as strong liquors blight the palate." The French Revolution is well over! The historian Louis Saurel lists the five main effects of the fall of Robespierre[258] : the return to power of the business bourgeoisie; the end of the democratic and egalitarian Republic, with in particular the replacement of universal suffrage by censal suffrage; the end of state supervision of commerce and industry; the resurrection of

---

256. *Écrits féministes, de Christine de Pizan à Simone de Beauvoir,* anthology presented by Nicole Pellegrin, Paris, "Champs classiques", Flammarion, 2010.
257. Maxime Rosso, "Les réminiscences spartiates dans les discours et la politique de Robespierre de 1789 à thermidor", art. cit.
258. Louis Saurel, *La Révolution française,* Paris, Éditions Fernand Nathan, 1939.

     A political history of food. From the Pateolithic to our days

the royalist party; the slide towards Caesarism: Bonaparte was already in the antechamber of power... Some "diehards" continued every January 21 to commemorate the beheading of Louis Capet by sharing a pig's head, then, since 1848, a calf's head. One of the explanations of this culinary shift is the adoption of the British model, since banquets commemorate every January 30 the beheading, in 1649, of Charles I, during which we consume calf's head washed down with red wine long drunk in calf's skulls, while toasting the end of the Stuart.

Cyril Triolaire notes a rapid decline in the frequency of "fraternal" meals from Thermidor onwards, and even more so after Napoleon's coronation: banquets also became less popular because of their confinement to rooms, the virtual disappearance of popular songs, and the replacement of the planting of the tree of liberty with the release of an aerostat: "The balloon's flight attracts almost all eyes to Heaven, where Napoleon's only transcendence now resides"[259].

The chestnut: a Christian stifler

With the fall of Robespierre, the Revolution in its popular and democratic aspects was defeated and the sans-culottes were condemned to silence. The triumphant bourgeoisie can once again, under the successive features of the Directory, the Consulate, the Empire and the Restoration, assume the continuity with the absolute monarchy in its ardor to cut down the chestnut trees, symbol of a food generating idlers. Today, it is difficult to imagine not only the motives, but also the violence of this hatred of the poor. In many regions, the working classes are first of all chestnut eaters, before being, according to the ideology, bread eaters.

Chestnut groves have been very important since the 10th and 11th centuries thanks to the action of Benedictine monks[260]. The consumption

---

259. Cyril TRIOLAIRE, "Célébrer Napoléon après la République : les héritages commémoratifs révolutionnaires au crible de la fête napoléonienne" in *Annales historiques de la Révolution française*, n° 346, octobre-décembre 2006, p. 75-96.

260. Ariane BRUNETON-GOVERNATORI, "Alimentation et idéologie : le cas de la châtaigne" in *Annales. Économies, Sociétés, Civilisations.* 39ᵉ année, n° 6, 1984, p. 1161-1189 ; A. GUILLAUME, "La récolte, le traitement et la conservation des châtaignes en France" in *Revue de botanique appliquée et d'agriculture coloniale*, 22ᵉ année, bulletin n° 249-250, mai-juin 1942, p. 259-263 ; Peter J. PERRY "L'arbre à pain : le châtaignier en Corse" in *Annales du Midi : revue archéologique, historique et philologique de la France méridionale*, vol. 96, n° 165, 1984, thematic issue: *À travers les campagnes méridionales*, p. 71-84; Diego MORENO, Lada HORDYNSKY-CAILLAT, Odile REDON and Silvano SERVENTI, "Châtaigneraie 'historique' et châtaigneraie 'traditionnelle'. Notes pour l'identification d'une pratique culturale" in *Médiévales*, n° 16-17, 1989, thematic issue: *Plantes, mets et mots. Dialogues with André-Georges Haudricourt*, p. 147-161.

still grows in the 16th century because of the royal gratifications offered for any plantation. The rich ate them roasted, the poor boiled. Joseph du Chesne (1606) classifies the chestnut as a bread. The decline begins in the 18th century when the contempt for a food of poor and lazy people is displayed. It is refused the quality of a product of human work, therefore of a culture, by assimilating it to the gathering. Montesquieu ranks in the camp of the "anti-chestnut", even if he is obliged to recognize that the density of the population goes with the chestnut. The ethnologist Ariane Bruneton-Governatori, author of a marvelous history of wood bread, notes that the main objection to the chestnut is moral: "It is a production that makes one lazy and constitutes a handicap to progress"[261]. The chestnut tree would also have "a harmful influence on morale by not stimulating the development of its industry, since it requires no other cultivation care, after its planting and pruning, than the harvesting of its fruits" (Bosc and Baudrillart, *Dictionnaire de la culture des arbres et de l'aménagement des forêts*, 2 vols. 1821 and 1823). This hatred was then commonplace. Alexandre Moreau de Jonnès (1778-1870), a senior civil servant and head of the General Statistics Department, wrote in 1848: "This production is a vestige of the times when people lived off the spontaneous fruits of the earth, and those that require neither care nor intelligence to provide a stodgy and coarse food"[262].

Adrien de Gasparin (1783-1862), a senior civil servant, author of a famous agricultural course for the Royal Agricultural Society, who was made a peer of France in 1834, thundered: "A population fed almost exclusively by the fruits of a tree is necessarily in a stationary state"; he continued: "A diet that is believed to be assured disgusts man from hard work; it is the chair that becomes his favorite occupation, with it [...] the character becomes bitter, becomes fierce, violent passions fill the heart." Choiseul proposes to cut down all the chestnut trees in Corsica and to substitute them with the cultivation of wheat, which, by dissipating idleness, would put an end to the revolt. This culture would be prejudicial to all the social classes because the chestnut would support the autarky: "Also one does not notice in the higher class any search for comfort; the lower class lives miserably being satisfied with a dwelling and a food also rudimentary. Jacques-Christophe Valmont de Bomare (1731-1807), a great French naturalist and member of the Institute, explains in his *Dictionnaire raisonné universel d'histoire naturelle* (1775) that "it is claimed that all these

---

261. Ariane BRUNETON-GOVERNATORI, *Le pain de bois : ethnohistoire de la châtaigne et du châtaignier* , work published with the assistance of the CNRS, Toulouse, Éditions Eché, 1984.
262. *Id.* Food and ideology: the case of the chestnut", art. cit.

                    A political history of food. From the Pateolithic to our days

peoples have a yellow complexion, an effect produced by this bad food." Edmond Demolins (1852-1907), a disciple of Frédéric Le Play, a great figure of social Catholicism, a virulent anti-socialist, editor of *La Réforme sociale*, patron of the Société pour le développement de l'initiative privée et la vulgarisation de la science sociale, explains that if the Limousins are what they are, it is because "the product of the chestnut tree is obtained without any prior work" and "consequently does not develop effort or initiative." He adds that the chestnut does not arouse the spirit of competition either: "The more capable or more industrious or more far-sighted individuals do not have in the exploitation of this product any fundamental superiority over the others since this quite spontaneous production is not in proportion to the capacity of the preliminary work or the foresight."

The chestnut would also undermine the legitimate male superiority: "For the harvest and the daily peeling of the chestnut [...] women, old people, children are as useful as men made because the work does not require the expenditure of force." Another argument is asserted: the chestnut develops "a community spirit" and "leads the family to live under the regime of the community". Another way to keep the interest of chestnuts quiet is to choose not to talk about them. Thus, the 1784 survey by Abbé Tessier and the 1786 survey by Abbé Lefebvre totally ignore chestnuts. The King's Council forbids, on several occasions, the planting of chestnut trees in cereal lands, but the resistance leads, including Turgot, to back down. Turgot, who could have said of the chestnut that it was a Christian stifler (if the word had existed in his time), because it eliminated the need to work, will have meanwhile torn out the chestnut trees of Limousin to plant potatoes in their place, accusing in passing the peasants of being fools: "The peasants of the country are naturally lazy and indocilious, because they are accustomed to live on chestnuts which provide them with a livelihood without cultivation or work. It will have been noted, Turgot puts himself resolutely on the side of the rich producers against the humble.

The defenders of the chestnut are however numerous, they explain, at first, that it is a gift of nature, that it does not exhaust the grounds, then, trying to turn over the theses of their adversaries, they argue that it would be a good food for the peasants who have a too lively blood, too spread out, too volatile (Hecquet, *The treaty of the dispensations of Lent*, 1709), in short that it would be a heavy food suitable for the heavy and miserable people!

The Revolution will thus succeed where the monarchy failed: the production falls of seven times in one century. The chestnut remains a challenge to the divine curse: "He who does not work, let him not eat" (Saint Paul). Le Roy Ladurie still speaks in 1966 of an International of misery and chestnuts. Fernand Braudel makes an exception by noting that the chestnut had a more important role in the 19th century than one might think. Ariane Bruneton-Governatori describes the many ways of cooking this wooden bread: raw chestnuts, cooked in ashes, roasted, boiled, bleached, dried, ground into flour, consumed in the form of cakes, bread, etc. In conclusion, we can only agree with his analysis: "Chestnut countries were densely populated countries, allowing their population to multiply and live on the spot. This phenomenon, in the 19th century, few want to see it, striving to associate misery, poverty and chestnut [...] the idea that emerges is that it is not appropriate that the same food is shared by the rich and the poor and that it is not appropriate to apply to a resource of the poor this beautiful name of bread"[263].

Is the potato republican?

The famous potato patch in the garden of Versailles, kept only during the day so that the plants would be stolen at night, is a late myth of the hussars of the Third Republic. The political power congratulates itself and its intelligence in front of the silliness of the people. The history is however less to its glory.

The history of the potato is emblematic of the relationship between power, people and food. First, the notables refused the potato because they considered it too productive, and therefore "morally harmful"; then, these same notables delayed its use by insisting on making bread with it, considering that bread was the most popular food; and these same notables used it as a weapon of mass destruction against the popular crops of rye and buckwheat. Let us specify that the potato of the 18th century is not ours, and its bitter taste is unpleasant because of a large quantity of solanine[264].

Potatoes: food for animals and the poor
Charles de l'Écluse, Latinized as Carolus Clusius, a great botanist of the 16th century, is officially charged with examining a new unknown

---

263. *Id., ibid.*
264. Lucien FEBVRE, "Les aliments : patates et pommes de terre" in *Annales d'histoire sociale*. 2ᵉ année, n° 2, 1940, p. 135-136 ; Marcel MORINEAU, "La pomme de terre au XVIIIᵉ siècle", in *Annales. Économies, Sociétés, Civilisations*, 25ᵉ année, n° 6, 1970, p. 1767-1785 ; Pierre JULIEN, "Notes autour de Parmentier" in *Revue d'histoire de la pharmacie*, 75ᵉ année, n° 275, 1987, p. 307-318.

plant[265]. It seems to be related to the mandrake cultivated in vegetable gardens but which has a bad reputation and is called "witch plant": "The potato starts its scientific career badly: fruit of the deep earth, it shares the bad reputation of underground plants. They all have this defect "to generate phlegm", these cold and aqueous humours which come, it is believed, from the fact that they grow far from the air and the sun in the cold and wet ground"[266].

Clusius therefore officially classifies the potato as an edible product, but nothing more. Contrary to its legend, the potato was first adopted, then rejected between 1650 and 1760. Madeleine Ferrières wonders: "Why, after the Thirty Years' War (1618-1648), did the potato stop in its conquering expansion? In 1613, was it not included as "king's meat" at the table of Louis XIII? Resistance came first from many local parliaments that forbade its cultivation in the 17th century, because it was accused of being a factor of leprosy, like all high-yielding products. Philippe le Hardi (1342-1404) also forbade the planting of Gamay, because it provided a grape juice that was too abundant, and therefore evil. The issue was primarily theological and political: by banning the potato, the aim was to tell the little people that there would be no return to the Golden Age, that bread would always be earned by the sweat of one's brow, and that there would never be a land of plenty. The potato thus benefits from the same bad treatment as the chestnut.

The question is to understand why the powerful suddenly chose to promote potatoes against other crops? If we look closely, the person responsible for this change is not so much Parmentier as Louis XVI's minister, Turgot, and even before he was a minister, when he was intendant of Limousin, from 1761 to 1774. The potato will serve as a laboratory for the political and economic theses of the physiocrats[267]. They will try to prove that through this product the agricultural revolution will come from "sensible men" and "zealous citizens", that is to say, good people, the owners. Turgot explains that "the state of misery and stupefaction in which

---

265. Jean-Marie PELT, "Charles de l'Écluse, prince des descripteurs" in *La Cannelle et le panda : les grands naturalistes explorateurs autour du monde*, Paris, Fayard, 1999; F.W.T. HUNGER, *Charles de l'Escluse (Carolus Clusius), Nederlandsch Kruidkundige, 1526-1609*, Martinus NijHoff,s' Gravenhage (The Hague), 1927.
266. Madeleine FERRIÈRES, *Histoire des peurs alimentaires. From the Middle Ages to the dawn of the 20th century, op. cit*; André DUBUC, "La culture de la pomme de terre en Normandie avant et depuis Parmentier" in *Annales de Normandie*, 3rd year, n° 1, 1953, p. 50-68.
267. Yves CHARBIT, "L'échec politique d'une théorie économique : la physiocratie" in *Population*, 57ᵉ année, n° 6, 2002, p. 849-878 ; Marie-Claire LAVAL-REVIGLIO, "Les conceptions politiques des physiocrates" in *Revue française de science politique*, 37ᵉ année, n° 2, 1987, p. 181-213.

---

the farmers in our provinces are could only be fought by the expenses and the intelligence of the rich and educated owners"[268].

Turgot obliged landlords to insert in their leases that tenant farmers had to devote plots to potatoes. The authors note that Turgot is, in this, very close to the colonial method, that which the English *landlords* put into practice in Ireland, or that of the planters of the West Indies imposing manioc as a compulsory food crop. The people are therefore opposed to plantations when they understand that it is not a question of bringing in a new foodstuff but of substituting it for what they live on. It is also a question of reinforcing the power of the notables.

Contrary to the legend, the notables did not set an example because the rich were in favor of potatoes for the poor. They do not eat them, explaining that it is a product unworthy of a good man. The English, who refuse potatoes for themselves, considering that it is a food for pigs, want to feed them to the poor Irish Catholics (who accumulate three defects). Madeleine Ferrières reminds us that the main protagonists of the potato were first recruited within the royal family. Marie-Antoinette ordered hats decorated with potato flowers from Rose Bertin, the milliner. The supporters of the royalist potato were not really helped by the editors of *the Encyclopedia*, since the author of the article devoted to the potato concludes that it is a bad food but suitable for beggars: "This root, however it is prepared, is bland and mealy. It cannot be counted among the pleasant foods; but it provides abundant food and quite salutary to men who only want to eat. The potato is rightly reproached for being windy: but what are winds to the so vigorous organs of peasants and laborers" (art. "pomme de terre", written by Gabriel-François Venel, doctor of medicine and friend of Diderot).

The "good society" agrees to potatoes only after the people and after having tried them on its own domestic staff. Parmentier experimented with potatoes on poor hospitalized people, provoking a violent conflict with the Sisters of Charity.

Parmentier will take over from Turgot, but by focusing on the image of the product. He explains before the Royal Agricultural Society: "Accustom your vassals to it by all sorts of means, except authority, but above all preach the example..." Parmentier indeed discovered with amazement that the poor also have taste and that they do not wish "to eat like pigs". The potato is only successful where pigs do not eat it... Alsace distinguishes

---

268. Quoted by Jean-Michel KIENER and Jean-Claude PEYRONNET, *Quand Turgot régnait en Limousin*, Paris, Fayard, 1979, p. 172.

                    A political history of food. From the Pateolithic to our days

between the human and animal varieties and gives these (quite similar...) different names: the potato for animals is called *Erdäpfel* and the "pear" for humans is called *Grumbeer* (from the German *Grundbirn*). Does this mean that the success of the potato owes everything to the marketing genius of Parmentier?

The provincial Mustel against the Parisian Parmentier
The first crops were grown in Normandy by François Georges Mustel, in 1765-1766, well before Parmentier (1788)[269]. Mustel was a former member of the military order of Saint Louis, which allowed him to be called "knight". He received a large pension, which allowed him to devote himself to his hobbies: botany and agriculture. He travels to Germany where this tuber is already a common vegetable. In 1767, he published a *Mémoire sur les pommes de terre et sur le pain économique,* presented to the Société royale d'agriculture de Rouen, in which he described the potato as both a vegetable and a flour. He brought tubers from England and planted six bushels on a plot of land in Saint-Sever. This first harvest is entirely distributed as seed to local farmers. Gabriel de Clieu, known for his acclimatization of the coffee tree in Martinique, declares: "You are doing for the cultivation of potatoes what I have done for coffee." Mustel produced before the Royal Agricultural Society of Rouen four leavened breads, called "economic bread", made with potatoes. The potato had undoubtedly other discoverers before Mustel, as Duhamel de Monceau experimented five years before him. It is him who invented the name of the potato, which used to be called differently depending on the region. How then can we understand Mustel's failure? His opponents were numerous within the Royal Agricultural Society of Rouen, in particular Louis-Alexandre Dambourney, steward of the botanical garden of Rouen, who was at one time a member of parliament and above all an advocate of madder cultivation. Mustel did not manage to make up for the French delay in this field, even if in some pioneer regions (Normandy, Alsace, Franche-Comté, Dauphiné) the success is now undeniable. Many local experiments were carried out, for example in Normandy, at Saint-Denis-sur-Sarthon, at Saint-Aubin-de-Scellon, after the publication of a laudatory article in the *Annals of Normandy.* In 1769, the parish priest of Saint-Roch distributed a potato soup called "economic rice" described in *La cuisine des pauvres* published in 1772 under the signature of Varenne de Beost. All these

---

269. André Dubuc, "La culture de la pomme de terre en Normandie avant et depuis Parmentier", art. cit.

experimenters had only one idea in mind, to make a bread or a rice called "economical". Even Voltaire took up this question: "When one would only put a third of these potatoes, it would always be a third of flour saved. But it requires a little effort to knead it well, and perhaps the bakers did not want to take this trouble." Of course, the bakers are not to blame, for the technical problem lies in the difficulties of breading the potato and the political problem in the inability of the powerful to conceive of a popular diet other than in the form of bread or even porridge.

Anticipating what will happen next, it is worth remembering that Parmentier had an epistolary exchange for ten years with Mustel, before claiming to be the sole inventor of "potato bread". Mustel replies: "This man puts me in the necessity to judge him of bad faith and to look at him as an intriguer who wants to appropriate my work and to surprise the government in order to take some advantage.

The success of Parmentier

After his death, Parmentier became a national myth that glorified the alliance between the powerful and science, in the name of Reason, against the people. In 1757, during the Seven Years' War, Antoine-Augustin Parmentier (1737-1813), just 20 years old, was sent to Hanover as a military pharmacist for an inspection tour. Legend has it that when he was taken prisoner (for three weeks), his only food was potato porridge: "Tightly confined for a long time in a narrow prison, fed only with potatoes and juniper brandy, he formed the project of multiplying in France this first edible, whose excellence he was able to appreciate and whose use he has since spread by destroying the prejudices that were opposed to its introduction. This is how, still young, he developed his beneficent and observant genius; this is how he knew how to make his own misfortunes useful to his country and to humanity" (Silvestre, *Report* of June 27, 1793 *on the work of A.-A. Parmentier*)[270].

Back to France in 1763, Parmentier became three years later pharmacist at the Maison royale des Invalides. During the famine of 1769-1770, he conducted experiments in the garden of the Invalides, including one with potatoes. In 1771, he responded to the competition organized by the Academy of Besançon. The Parliament of Besançon was one of those who had justly banned potatoes... already consumed. The subject mentions: "To indicate the plants which could replace in time of shortage

---

270. Henri BONNEMAIN, "Parmentier et la dignité de la pomme de terre", review of Ernest Kahane's book, *Parmentier ou la dignité de la pomme de terre. Essai sur la famine*, in *Revue d'histoire de la pharmacie*, 67ᵉ année, n° 242, 1979, p. 227-229.

A political history of food. From the Pateolithic to our days

those which one employs commonly with the food of the men and which should be the preparation of it". The six other candidates also mention the merits of the potato. However, Parmentier received the prize in 1772 for the quality of his chemical demonstration. That same year, the National Academy of Medicine lifted its 1748 ban on this plant. Meanwhile, Parmentier continued his work on many other products: in 1781, he listed 90 "uncultivated" plants that could be useful. Concerning the potato, his objective is to use its starch to make economical bread.

Parmentier did not become interested in potatoes as a vegetable until fifteen years later, in 1786, with his experiment on the Plaine des Sablons in Neuilly, a military field put at his disposal by Louis XVI, after the nuns had forbidden him to continue his cultivation on their land, because of his experiments on sick people. Parmentier visited the royal couple in Versailles on August 24, 1786, to offer them the first flowers of his potato crop. Legend has it that the royal couple wore them in their lapel after Louis XVI had proclaimed that "France will thank you one day for having found the bread of the poor". Much emphasis is placed on the brilliant idea (repeated for other contentious products such as horse meat) of organizing ceremonial meals in the world of scholars, where up to twenty potato-based dishes could be served, to show how much variety there was in the way this tuber could be eaten[271] (in soup, in matelote, in purée, in croquettes, in soufflés, in fritters, in cakes, in jam, in tarts, etc.). It is less said that Parmentier benefited from the active support of the whole state apparatus of the monarchy: the Minister of the Navy put at his disposal a ship to import plants from America, the Minister of the Interior asked his intendants to distribute potato plants in the departments to the "best farmers". Parmentier's first advantage was that he belonged to the "good society" of Paris, that he was a man of networks and that he benefited from the support of men of power, such as the governor of Espignac, the lieutenant general of police Le Noir, and Turgot.

The royalist potato could have disappeared into the dustbin of history for a while, but the Revolution turned it into a republican potato, and soon into an egalitarian one, despite Parmentier's compromising past in the eyes of the men of 1789. Declared a suspect in 1793, he was sent on a mission to the south of France by his protectors and thus escaped the guillotine. The republican potato would later become imperial, when Napoleon appointed him first pharmacist of the armies in 1800 and imposed the consumption of potatoes in the army.

---

271. *Id., ibid.*

The egalitarian potato

The Convention develops an important work to generalize its culture[272]. In the year II, the administration of the department of Loir-et-Cher prints and distributes an "Instruction for the manufacture of "mixed bread" of potato" with one third of wheat flour, one third of rye flour, one third of potatoes. A decree of 21 ventôse year III qualifies it as an "egalitarian vegetable". Madeleine Ferrières notes that the Sociétés populaires d'émulation demand that its cultivation be made compulsory on one twentieth of the cultivable surface and that local administrators prescribe that one hundredth of the land be sown with potatoes. The Minister of the Interior asks his agents to know the state of potato cultivation everywhere in France. Madeleine Ferrières speaks of a conference held in Saint-Laurent-en-Caux: "A citizen observed that the English had only come to the end of their revolution by the help of the potato. It can be called the plant of the free man, because it does not require constant care and consequently leaves to the farmer the necessary leisure to occupy himself with the great interests of the Republic [...] But one does not dissimulate that the lights are so little spread among the farmers that the authority of the government is absolutely necessary to spread this culture as much as it can be. In 1793, the first cookbook written by a woman, a certain Mme. Mérigot, appeared under the title *La Cuisinière républicaine*, entirely devoted to the potato (31 recipes on 42 pages)[273]. Germain Chevet, a horticulturist in Bagnolet, rose supplier to the court, arrested in 1793, pardoned because of his 17 children, was obliged to uproot his roses, the flowers of aristocrats, and to plant potatoes.

The Republican mystique of the potato

For a long time, it has been argued that the demographic boom of the 19th century was a consequence of the cultivation of the potato. More recent studies show that the results are, to say the least, rather mixed: the mystique of the progressive potato is an absurdity. Already because, as Marcel Morineau notes: "Everywhere and always, the potato arrived in the suburbs of misery [...], its chosen lands were the poor areas [...] The potato was a substitute, the ersatz of a better food that was lacking; sometimes, as soon as abundance returned, it was abandoned [...] sufficient consumption of potatoes to replace bread only made sense and was only real in the context of self-subsistence on the farm of the producers; for the same

---

272. André DUBUC, "La culture de la pomme de terre en Normandie avant et depuis Parmentier", art. cit.
273. https://openlibrary.org/books/OL20856334M/La_Cuisinie%CC%80re_re%CC%81publicaine

          A political history of food. From the Pateolithic to our days

calorific value, the commodity was expensive on the market"[274]. Secondly, because, as the historian analyzes, a relative pauperization is indeed linked to the propagation of the potato in the 18th century. Guillaume-Charles Faipoult (1752-1817) wondered whether it was appropriate to expand potato cultivation since "abundance is less constant in potatoes than it is in rye and wheat; two months of drought are enough to render the harvest of a potato field almost nil." And Faipoult announced "the frequent distress of a population that would have based its means of subsistence solely on an uncertain product."

The legend of Parmentier, the genius inventor of the potato, was established long after his death. His own 1773 *Treatise* re-establishes this truth: "The use of this food plant has been adapted for a century [...] It has spread so widely that there are provinces where potatoes have become a part of the food of the poor people."

The legend of Parmentier has at least the great merit of making children believe that the powerful are concerned about feeding the humble, despite their own obscurantism. As Henri Bonnemain analyzes: "Parmentier's great illusion, common to all his contemporaries and to some of ours, was to believe in the possibility of solving the problem of hunger by technical means"[275].

---

274. Marcel Morineau, "La pomme de terre au xviiie siècle", art. cit.
275. Henri Bonnemain, "Parmentier et la dignité de la pomme de terre" art. cit.

Twelfth service : The bourgeois table

Thermidor gave birth to a conservative counter-revolution that led to a new social separatism, no longer based on the old legends about the Trojan origin of the nobility, but on economic liberalism, contempt for the common people and the spirit of revenge. I have chosen to speak of the bourgeois table because this period is that of the triumph of the bourgeoisie, beyond the political regimes, and of its capacity to impose its vision of food, including within the working class, especially in urban areas.

Historians have largely questioned the golden legend of 19th century gastronomy, because this period was only gourmet for the upper middle class - and for the lower middle class, which tried to raise itself on its toes in order to access pleasures that were previously forbidden to it. This bourgeois cuisine makes something new out of something old, because if it takes on certain features of the service of the Ancien Régime, it invents a thrifty cuisine, more in keeping with its shopkeeper spirit. The people are not abandoned to their bad fate, because they would know how to do otherwise, but forced to be satisfied with little and bad : It is no longer only food judged unsuitable for them that they must do without, in accordance with the hierarchy of foods, but the right to eat unadulterated food, because this period of excessive industrialization, to which the Saint-Simonian enthusiasm and its successors testify, is the one that will see the birth of the abominable idea of feeding the people with bones, false bread, by-products, waste, etc. We must not let ourselves be fooled by the epinal image of the richness of regional tables, because this last one does not exist, if at all, for the majority of the French men and women[276].

---

276. Philippe MEYZIE, *La table du Sud-Ouest 1700-1850*, Rennes, Presses universitaires de Rennes, 2007.

The people delivered to the appetites of the big

The French Revolution brought new ways of despising the ordinary people, as the "big" ones replaced the "big" ones. The people are sacrificed to the little and the poorly eaten. Hunger is endemic among the working classes, especially the agricultural workers. We have a symptom of it in the succession of food troubles and in particular with the famine which strikes, in 1817, under the Restoration, that is to say in full Saint-Simonian industrialism, a famine which reminds that of the Old Regime, since it is the basic cereals which miss, and which, therefore, increase the most. This is the consequence of the choice, constantly reaffirmed, of the centrality of bread[277]. This centrality was reinforced in the 19th century, because, as Fernand Braudel argues, that century saw the replacement of rye bread by wheat bread, a sign not so much of an increase in purchasing power as of the submission of the people to bourgeois standards. The people lost out even more because white bread was not taxed, unlike the others. This mystique of white bread, Braudel tells us, is to be put in relation with the self-censorship of the bourgeoisie, the famous "Enrich yourself!" of Guizot. White bread is the anti-chaestnut par excellence, it is the retreat of popular cultures. As a consequence, the people of the countryside are forced, in the face of crises, to feed themselves (badly) with cereals intended for animals. Historians have measured the caloric rations establishing the decrease of the contributions as the country modernizes, in particular within the rural world, first victim of the economic liberalism[278].

The statistics of the Ministry of Agriculture's Subsistence Office specify the changes. It should be noted that for the purposes of these statistics, all plant products (potatoes, chestnuts) are given in "grain equivalent. The average annual production of cereals decreased from 85 to 90 million quintals before the Revolution to 70 million quintals around 1810-1813, mainly due to the substitution of potatoes for other foods (cereals, chestnuts). Despite the considerable increase in production, these political choices had the effect of multiplying the price of the potato by six, making it impossible to replace the products it was supposed to replace!

Meat production increased, but mainly for the wealthy, with a strong increase in sheep and lamb, a (later) increase in cattle, and a very strong decrease in pork, except in some rural areas (in the east, in the northeast of

---

277. Paul Leuilliot, "De la disette de 1816-1817 à la famine du coton (1867) [Les crises économiques du xixe siècle en France]" in *Annales. Économies, Sociétés, Civilisations*, 12e année, n° 2, 1957, p. 317-325.
278. Donald M. G. Sutherland and Tim J. A. Le Goff, "The French Revolution and the Rural Economy" in *History & Measurement*, vol. 14, no. 1-2, 1999, thematic issue: *Varia*, pp. 79-120.

France, and in the southern regions). Jean-Paul Aron notes that between 1789 and 1846, annual per capita consumption in France fell from 67 kilos to 50 kilos. Yvan Lepage specifies that the meat consumption of a rural person is a third of that of an urban person, despite the presence of a farmyard, and that a farm worker eats six times less meat than an urban person. On the other hand, it shows an increase in the average consumption of meat, including popular meat, in the second half of the 19th century, a situation that contrasts sharply with the situation in other countries[279]. In Europe, average per capita consumption rose from 19 kilos per year in 1803-1812 to 22.6 kilos in 1834-1844, reaching 40 kilos around 1900. Pork, which represented 40% of consumption between 1789 and 1862, then declined in favor of beef[280]. However, Yvan Lepage invites caution. How can we avoid the trap of ratios that measure the quantities consumed in TCE (tonne-equivalent-carcass) and divide the total weight of slaughtered animals by the number of inhabitants? This measure overestimates the consumption since it "eats" the bones, hooves and fat. It does not take into account the quality of the meat consumed (good or bad). These averages also hide, of course, considerable social and regional disparities: for example, Louis René Villermé describes meat consumption in the first half of the 19th century as exceptional among textile workers, while Heinz-Gerhard Haupt dates the beginning of popular meat consumption to the 1870s. Finally, Yvan Lepage insists on the decrease of family self-production with urbanization. We can therefore think, with him, that if "the bourgeoisie of the 19th century stuffed themselves [...] the working masses [adopted] frugality more by constraint than by conviction"[281]. The people (in the countryside as well as in the cities) were therefore haunted by the question of food, especially since the time spent preparing and eating meals varied in inverse proportion to income: the higher the income, the more time was spent eating, and the less time was spent preparing meals. Conversely, the lower the income, the less time is spent eating and the more time is spent preparing menus.

Throughout the 19th century, the table of the working class suffered from a crying insufficiency, coupled with a distressing monotony, consequences of the agricultural and food choices imposed by capitalism. This

---

279. Jean-Paul ARON, *Le mangeur du XIXᵉ siècle*, Paris, "Petite Bibliothèque Payot" (n° 8), Payot, 1989.
280. Yvan LEPAGE, "Évolution de la consommation d'aliments carnés aux XIXᵉ et XXᵉ siècles en Europe occidentale" in *Revue belge de philologie et d'histoire*, vol. 80, n° 4, 2002, thematic issue: *Histoire médiévale, moderne et contemporaine*, p. 1459-1468.
281. *Id., ibid.*

frugality is all the more important that it is reinforced by religious and scientific discourses, hygienists, which condemn the pleasures of cafés and cabarets. Robert Beck, author of *Histoire du dimanche de 1700 à nos jours* (Paris, Éditions de l'Atelier, 1997) shows that this tradition is recent and that the clergy, for a long time reticent, accepted this institution only because they saw it as a way to divert the people from the cafés. The Sublimes, the most qualified workers of the late 19th century, called for the celebration of "St. Monday" and thus for refusing to work on that day, because the cabarets were open.

A century of abandonment

In the name of the sacrosanct laws of the market, the State is progressively dismantling the old systems of consumer protection which, although insufficient, showed a mistrust of food professionals and led to the regulation of supplies. We will only give a few examples, as a whole book would not be enough to list everything.

Bourgeois society (republican, imperial, monarchist, then republican again) abandoned the old system of meat control, which was based on the existence of several distribution networks ranging from good meat to foul meat, in the name of the interest of industry and with the endorsement of scientific institutions. Sick animals, such as sickly pigs and tuberculous cows, were thus sold over the counter[282]. The State added to this, with Reynal's authoritative *Traité de police sanitaire*, explaining that consumers would have nothing to fear from eating tubercular meat, because it would be enough to remove the lungs. The consequence is unfortunately known: the French livestock will be the most seriously ill! Several arguments have been put forward to explain this delay, if not this criminal blindness: the choice of a "liberal" model, the blissful faith in industrial progress and in science. I think that one cannot exclude a class tropism: it doesn't matter what the people eat as long as they are fit for work and war.

The French livestock crisis

The bourgeoisie combines two positions more complementary than contradictory. The founding fathers of gastronomy, such as Brillat-Savarin, Grimod de La Reynière, Alexandre Dumas, Carême, etc., did not give a damn about the people and said so. Those who are in charge of them have a particularly unhealthy attitude towards the people, with the decrease of

---

282. Henri Picheral, "La brucellose en France. Essai de géographie médicale" in *Annales de géographie*, vol. 78, n° 426, 1969, p. 189-205.

food controls, the denial of the diseases that affect the French livestock, the vogue of food substitutes and "economical" products intended to feed the people. This choice of blindness and this spirit of revenge of the elites, after the "great fear" that the Revolution had given rise to, would make tuberculosis a success. Madeleine Ferrières, analyzing the French delay compared to other nations such as Germany and England, maintains that "in France, concerning animal diseases, the regulatory work stops between the Revolution and 1881"[283]. The poor quality of human food, especially meat, is the consequence of economic policies[284]. The State only recognized its competence in one area: the manufacture of sweets, with a protective law that Madeleine Ferrières analyzed as a compensation for the culpable inertia that reigned everywhere else. I add that if the law of July 21, 1881 obliges the breeders to declare, with much delay compared to the other countries, the contagious diseases which strike their herds (rinderpest, glanders, sheep pox, foot-and-mouth disease), the intention is first to take advantage of it to prohibit the American and German pigs, suspected of trichinosis. The State refuses to include bovine tuberculosis, because the French herd is less competitive. It was necessary to wait a few more years and a decree in 1888 to make the slaughter of sick animals mandatory, but since no mandatory screening was wanted, this text had no effect. The tuberculosis test was not made compulsory until 1935, "when the Frenchman was twice as likely to die of tuberculosis as any other European"[285].

The public authorities will never stop hiding the reality by explaining that in France only one horned animal out of 100 is contaminated whereas the contamination affected 20% of the bovine herd in Brittany, 40% in the Vosges, 50% in the Pyrenees. It is true that these same public authorities maintain that this disease is English and therefore does not concern us. Madeleine Ferrières points out a guilty contradiction in the theses supported by the State with the support of scientific institutions: "The Republican elites have kept, even accentuated, a certain vision of the citizen-eater. This adult man, capable of making a free and rational choice on the market, would be incapable of making good use of information

---

283. Madeleine Ferrières, *Histoire des peurs alimentaires. Du Moyen Âge à l'aube du XXᵉ siècle*, *op. cit.*

284. Yvette Maurin, "La crise de l'élevage ovin en Languedoc méditerranéen dans la première moitié du XIXᵉ siècle" in *Cahiers de la Méditerranée*, hors série n° 2, 1977, *Typologie des crises dans les pays méditerranéens (XVIᵉ-XXᵉ siècles)*. Actes des journées d'études Bendor, 13, 14 et 15 mai 1976, p. 55-74.

285. Madeleine Ferrières, *Histoire des peurs alimentaires. Du Moyen Âge à l'aube du XXᵉ siècle*, *op. cit.*

on risk"[286]. This contradiction does not in fact exist for the heirs of the physiocrats, who consider that only good people can access rationality. The people are not capable of thinking for themselves. It is enough to look at the "great projects" that this century of the triumphant bourgeoisie gave rise to to see that it was more a century of counter-utopias than of generous utopias.

The food counter-utopias

One often contrasts, as in the *Encyclopædia Universalis*, the Malthus who wrote in 1796 *The Crisis* (unpublished text), in which he proposed the creation of hospices to take in the destitute, and the Malthus who wrote two years later his famous treatise (*Essay on the Principle of Population*) in which he explained that the multiplying power of population would be infinitely greater than the power of the Earth to produce man's subsistence. This apparent contradiction clears the progressive camp of any anti-social ulterior motive. On the one hand, there are the nasty Malthusians who explain that "the alleged right of the poor to be maintained at the expense of society must be publicly disavowed", in the continuation of the apologue of the banquet: "A man who is born into a world already possessed, if it is not possible for him to obtain from his parents the sustenance which he can justly ask of them, and if society has no need of his labor, has no right to claim the least share of food, and, in reality, he is too much. At the great banquet of nature, there is no empty place for him; she orders him to leave, and she will not delay in carrying out her order herself, if he cannot have recourse to the compassion of some of the guests at the banquet. If they squeeze in to make room for him, other intruders immediately appear, claiming the same favors. The news that there is food for all those who arrive fills the room with many applicants. The order and harmony of the feast are disturbed, the abundance that previously prevailed turns into dearth, and the joy of the guests is destroyed by the spectacle of misery and scarcity in all parts of the room and by the importunate clamor of those who are rightly furious at not finding the food they had been led to expect."[287], and on the other hand, the "nice" humanists are constantly trying to find technical solutions to feed humanity. If the truth about Malthus has been established since Proudhon: "There is only one man

---

286. *Id., ibid.*
287. See the site Dictionary - Thomas Malthus, *Essay on the Principle of Population* at: http://www.farreny.net/dictionnaire/oeuvre/250/Essai-sur-le-principe-de-population/Thomas-Malthus

          A political history of food. From the Pateolithic to our days

too many on earth, and that is Malthus"[288], things remain much more complex with the humanists of the 19th century...

This is the era of these counter-utopias, always presented under philanthropic pretexts. The same desire to invent a "kitchen for the poor", made of all the by-products and scraps, has accompanied capitalism since the 17th century. I don't see such a big difference between the Malthusian idea that we can't feed all the poor and the idea of the "good bourgeois" and scholars of the 16th and 19th centuries who maintain that we can't feed them with real food, but only with substitutes.

These counter-utopias adorned with good feelings
Let's put aside the situations of war, although the food situation of the population seems less thoughtful in the 16th and 19th centuries than in the 2nd century BC in Greece. If during the siege of Paris in 1590, the worst of those that the city knew under the League (1589-1594), dogs and cats were boiled in huge cauldrons from which a broth was distributed to the poor and needy, in 1870, during the Franco-Prussian war, a new category of butcheries was opened for the meat of cats, dogs and rats.

I would like to establish a link between this strategy of the powerful and what Jean-Paul Aron calls the "disease of rationalism" in the 19th century with regard to the desire to reduce everything to unity. Jean-Jacques Virey (1775-1846), author of the article "Aliments" in *Le Nouveau Dictionnaire d'histoire naturelle, appliquée aux arts, à l'agriculture, à l'économie rurale et domestique, à la médecine* (published by Deterville over several years at the beginning of the 19th century), is a good prototype: "Just as Lamarck, Cuvier, etc., Geoffroy Saint-Hilaire, in different languages and from different perspectives, reduces the phenomenal diversity of living nature to the unity of the planes of organization; it is observed that there is only one food, if there is a multiplicity of foods [...] in the midst of these innumerable species of vegetable and animal foods, we find common principles. For example, every animal is composed in general of nitrogen, carbon, hydrogen and oxygen, in various proportions and with some varieties [...] Thus foods are of an infinite number of species, but they are similar in one respect. There are many foods but only one food. Whether a man lives on bread, flesh, milk, herbs, vegetables, fish, etc., he always derives from it only one matter capable of being transformed into his own organs."

---

288. Pierre-Joseph PROUDHON [1846], *System of Economic Contradictions or Philosophy of Misery*, Paris, "Le Monde en 10-18", Union Générale d'Éditions, 1964.

I would add that Geoffroy Saint-Hilaire, this protégé of Parmentier, also a military pharmacist, was a follower of the vitalist current which praised war between nations because it would develop the vital impulse. For the same reasons, he vomited the idle and the people, and set his sights on the industrious middle classes. This thought, both scientistic and productivist, could not find anything wrong with food substitutes[289].

Making the people eat bones

Ossein, gelatin, meat broths, false bread: so many substitutes in competition with each other, which made the glory and fortune of many scientists and industrialists between the 17th and 19th centuries, without improving the table of the poor[290]. To understand the spirit of the 19th century, we must go back to the 17th century[291].

Denis Papin, inventor of the pressure cooker (which he called the "digester") or pressure cooker, published, in 1682, *Manière d'amollir les os et de faire cuire toutes sortes de viandes en fort de temps, et à peu de frais*. He proposed to Charles II, King of England, Scotland and Ireland, to supply poorhouses and hospices, in order to feed the poor in an economical way. Michel Lévy tells in his *Traité d'hygiène publique et privée* (1869) that "some jokers attached to the neck of the dogs of the king's pack a request to keep the privilege of eating bones to the dogs, and Papin's offer was rejected". Papin, a Protestant, before the revocation of the Edict of Nantes, took refuge in London in 1675 and then moved to Germany in 1688, where he held a chair of mathematics. His ideas were immediately taken up by a canon of Rouen, again to feed the "poor". These experiments, neglected for a century, were rediscovered by François-David Hérissant and, above all, by Joseph-Louis Proust (1754-1826). In 1758, Jean d'Arcet presented a report to the Academy, which was followed by another one in 1775, this time signed by the Abbé Changeux, still on the methods of extracting gelatin from bones. A new report was presented in 1799, under the title *Extrait des recherches sur les moyens d'améliorer la subsistance du soldat*. It is explained that it is a question of "a food which does not cost anything to

---

289. The 20th century will undeniably mark a retreat of these "counter-utopias" because of the construction of different power relations between the "enriched" and the "impoverished", we see, however, again, such projects appearing, always because of new power relations, this time, more unfavorable to the "impoverished".
290. Michel BONNEAU, *La table des pauvres. Cooking in Industrial Cities and Towns (1780-1950)*, Rennes, "Histoire", Presses universitaires de Rennes, 2013.
291. Claude VIEL and Josette FOURNIER, "Histoire des procédés d'extraction de la gelatine et débats des commissions académiques (XIXe siècle)" in *Revue d'histoire de la pharmacie*, 94e année, n° 349, 2006. p. 7-28.

            A political history of food. From the Pateolithic to our days

the State, but which does not depend even on the superfluity of the rich, or on the commiseration of the well-to-do man".

The 19th century began with the collective work of Cadet de Vaux, Candolle, Delessert, Money and Parmentier, published in 1801 under the title *Recueil de rapports, de mémoires et d'expériences sur les soupes économiques et les fourneaux à la Rumford (Collection of reports, memoirs and experiments on economical soups and Rumford stoves), followed by two memoirs on the substitution of hulled and grooved barley for rice.* This work, which takes up the previous works, is supported by a committee called "Republican Brotherhood" composed of François de Neufchâteau, Parmentier, Thouret, Say. Among the subscribers there are few proletarians but the (very) good society like Bonaparte and Cambaceres. The pretext for this publication is the experiment carried out by Benjamin Thompson, who will be ennobled and will bear the title of Count of Rumford. This American chemist made a career in the European courts, in particular with the king of Bavaria Joseph I. He reorganized the army, established workshops, and prohibited begging. Numerous so-called "charity" establishments were then built on the model of the "furnaces" he had established in Rumford. The first one, which opened in Paris in 1800, distributed 300 soups a day... Scientists like Parmentier and philanthropists like Cadet de Vaux (member of the Philanthropic Society, president of the Association of Economic Soups) multiplied the initiatives. Parmentier submits a report to the Minister of the Interior on vegetable soups, then another one on the substitution of hulled barley for rice. Cadet de Vaux also submitted a report on the substitution of barley gruel for rice, and in 1802, at the request of the government, he wrote a complete report on bone gelatin in which he established a parallel between its consumption by dogs and humans. In 1818, he wrote a new report entitled *De la gélatine des os et de son bouillon, dedicated to Monseigneur le duc de Berry,* his successor on the board of directors of the Société philanthropique. He explains that gelatin constitutes "the philosopher's stone" and claims the friendship of the Holy Father, who owns 11 bone broth establishments. During the siege of Paris in 1870, a certain Dumas (not Alexandre), a member of the Gelatine Commission, in charge of the dossier, recalled the work of the Commission from 1831 to 1841 as well as its numerous reports. On October 31, Fremy proposes the use of ossein as a replacement food, judging that the nutritional properties of gelatin should be re-examined. Chevreul contests the nutritional power of ossein but qualifies gelatin as a perfect food (*sic*) and assures of the "good health of dogs fed with bones". The government then requisitioned all butcher's bones... One could mention the use of muriatic acid to dissolve the calcareous part of the bones, leaving all the gelatin in it. In the 19th century, Baron Justus von Liebig marketed gelatin under the name of "meat extract", a kind of broth as a meat substitute for the poor. In 1884, the city of Paris, which organized a collection of food for the charity offices, asked itself: "Couldn't we conceive of a food for the humble, a food appropriate to them, probably not tasty, but nutritious nevertheless?

The 19th century, the golden age of forgeries

Alexis-François Aulagnier published in 1830 his *Dictionnaire des substances alimentaires et de leurs propriétés*, a true inventory of falsifications. Paul Lafargue, Marx's son-in-law, is better known for his famous *Right to Laziness* than for his denunciation of adulteration. However, he is the one who best theorizes this period, relating it to the bourgeois age of appearance.

Economic bread

The 19th century was no exception, adding an inglorious page to the history of bread[292]. The powerful, after having imposed the assimilation between popular food and bread, noticed that the "all cereals", in particular the "all wheat", endangered the supply. The triumphant bourgeoisie will therefore want to make flour of any plant... to try to invent an economical bread for the people. Of course, one of the main instigators of this campaign is Parmentier who sees the opportunity to establish the reign of the potato. So, after the 9th Termidor, he resumed his propaganda and his work to invent an economical bread based on his booklet *Manière de faire le pain de pommes de terre sans mélange de farine*. Many cities, including Marseille, bought large quantities of this tuber to try to make bread with it. The Thermidorian Committee of Public Safety (nivôse year III) publishes the following notice: "In several communes, experiments have been made with a bread-making process of two thirds of wheat flour and one third of potatoes, or of one third of wheat flour, one third of rye flour and one third of potatoes: these experiments have been perfectly successful: the result is a very white bread, very nourishing and which keeps fresh for a long time [...] By this manipulation one will decrease the consumption of grains [...] The consumption of potatoes should be encouraged (in *Journal*

---

292. On the mystique of bread: Jean Bure (dir), *Le pain. Recueil des usages concernant les pains de France*. Actes du colloque du CNERNA à Paris, novembre 1977, Paris, Éditions du CNRS, 1979.

A political history of food. From the Pateolithic to our days

des Débats, 21 nivôse an III)[293]. Other specialists will make economic bread with cabbage, pumpkins, pumpkin...

Grape sugar versus beet sugar

Parmentier indirectly took a position in the great conflict that opposed, at the beginning of the 19th century, the supporters of cane sugar and slavery to the supporters of beet sugar and the abolition of slavery[294]. He proposed to Napoleon to opt for a transitional solution which consisted in retaliating against the blockade preventing France from importing sugar from its colonies by exploiting a substitute derived from grapes[295]. In 1808, Napoleon asked him to write an *Instruction on the means of substituting sugar*, in which he explained how to obtain a sweetening substance from grapes. In 1809, he wrote an *Instruction on grape syrups*, followed the next year by a *Treatise on the art of making grape syrups and preserves, intended to replace sugar in the colonies in the main uses of the domestic economy*. In 1812, he reports on the experiments carried out in about fifteen departments in a pamphlet entitled *Overview of the results obtained from the manufacture of syrups and preserves of grapes during the years 1810 and 1811*.

France chose to lose two decades, when it had already lost two centuries, since the principle of extracting sugar from beet was discovered as early as 1600 by Olivier de Serres, then forgotten under the pressure of the sugar cane lobby, then rediscovered in 1799 by Achard, after having passed through Germany. Augustin-Pierre Dubrunfaut revived the debate in 1825 with his *Art de fabriquer le sucre de betterave* and his *Notice sur la fabrication des alcools dits fins, fins fécule, fins betterave, ou autres*[296]. Timothée Dehay replied in 1839 with *Les colonies et la métropole, le sucre exotique et le sucre indigène*[297]. He writes: "The colonies shouted at us: "Death to indigenous sugar!" We will answer: "Prosperity to the indigenous sugar and let us save our colonies!" "The solution is only unblocked politically when some large cannasucriers also become the main sugar beet farmers. Thus, the Marquis de Forbin-Janson, owner of the most important European cane sugar factory and operator of one of the main cane sugar refineries, published in 1840 an *impartial Examen et solution de toutes les questions qui se*

---

293. https://books.google.fr/books?id=pzhEAAAAcAAJ
294. François CHAST, Pierre JULIEN and Anne MURATORI-PHILIP, "Parmentier et le sucre de raisin" in *Revue d'histoire de la pharmacie*, 89ᵉ année, n° 330, 2001, p. 149-168.
295. Claude VIEL, "À propos de la fabrication du sucre de raisin sous l'Empire" in *Revue d'histoire de la pharmacie*, 76ᵉ année, n° 276, 1988, p. 59-62.
296. http://gallica.bnf.fr/ark:/12148/bpt6k28160f
297. http://gallica.bnf.fr/ark:/12148/bpt6k5790502q.

---

rattachent à la loi des sucres[298]. In the same vein, Louis Napoleon Bonaparte distributed in 1842 to all the members of the general councils his *Analyse de la question des sucres (Analysis of the sugar issue)*[299] , a pamphlet written by followers of Saint-Simonism, in which he proclaimed: "I am a citizen before being a Bonaparte", recalling that his colonial grandmother was a cane sugar producer.

The falsification of wine

Wine is no longer just a drink when it contributes to the calorie intake. One liter of wine at 10° is equivalent to 800 calories, or the equivalent of 1 pound of bread or meat or 1 kilogram of potatoes. Therefore, there will be no shortage of specialists seeking to create a nourishing wine without grapes. This economical wine is presented as an indispensable complement for the people. This vogue for fake wines was launched in 1824 by the *Traité théorique et pratique de vinification, or the art of making wine with all fermentable substances, at all times and in all climates*. Joseph Audibert also published *The Art of Making Wine with Raisins* in 1881. Ernest de Neyremand published *L'Art de frelater les vins* in 1889.

Vegetarianism to discipline the people

Vegetarianism is not at issue in my analysis but the reasons that led some people to advocate it to the people[300]. Vegetarianism in the 17th, 18th and 19th centuries had two faces. First, it was promoted in England within religious sects as a means of saving souls. However, a rationalist and philanthropic vegetarianism succeeded this spiritualist vegetarianism in the 19th century[301].

Jakob Böhme (1575-1624) sees in the consumption of meat one of the reasons for the supremacy of reason over the heart, since to kill animals is to erect barriers between the soul and God, and thus to profane creation[302]. The great merit of this first vegetarianism is to break with any dolorous

---

298. http://www.manioc.org/patrimon/HASH01bc793dfde8b605e8fe0cab

299. Louis Napoleon Bonaparte, *Analyse de la question des sucres*, Paris, Administration de librairie, 2nd ed. 1843.

300. Renan Larue, *Vegetarianism and its Enemies. Vingt-cinq siècles de débats*, Paris, Presses universitaires de France, 2015.

301. Arouna P. Ouédraogo, "De la secte religieuse à l'utopie philanthropique. Genèse sociale du végétarisme occidental" in *Annales. Histoire, Sciences Sociales*, 55ᵉ année, n° 4, 2000, p. 825-843.

302. http://gallica.bnf.fr/ark:/12148/bpt6k77909p

   A political history of food. From the Pateolithic to our days

vision linked to the myth of original sin, since it is enough to change one's diet to save oneself.

Jakob Böhme's successors, such as Thomas Tryon (1634-1703), made a first ideological shift because they abandoned the objective of transforming society by relying on the working classes to put forward the animal question and by opening up more to the rich. It is no longer a question of opposing the consumption of meat to a more fraternal and egalitarian society, but a society based on work, sexual abstinence and the cult of effort. This new trend was reinforced by the work of the London physician George Cheyne (1671-1743). Deploring the "invasion of sensuality" in society, which produces "vitiated souls and putrefied bodies", he exalts the return to the "ancient regime of natural and moral simplicity", the monastic and military institutions serving him as models[303]. He forbids the consumption of strong alcohol as well as the search for new foods and prescribes a simple and frugal diet, made of vegetables, preferably raw, milk and water, he recommends to multiply fasts with the aim in particular to provide the notables with a "solid body" guaranteeing their professional performance (*sic*). Cheyne multiplied his disciples among the British aristocracy, and thus converted to vegetarianism the Reverend John Wesley, founder of Methodism. It was the latter who, paradoxically, provided vegetarianism with its "rational" and "scientific" argument by explaining that a diet that excluded meat and favored potatoes, oatmeal, water and milk would produce solid workers who respected the values of order and discipline necessary for capitalism.

These theses became popular, especially in the United States, where they were taken up by the Christian Bible Church. Its leaders, distraught by the French Revolution, called for the replacement of bread by potatoes. They multiplied philanthropic societies that called on the people to change their eating habits, to adopt simple and frugal food, to become thrifty and provident rather than unruly and rebellious. In 1795, William Cowherd (1763-1816) preached vegetarianism, explaining, "Be not of those seditious [readers of Thomas Paine's *The Rights of Man* (1791)]. Meat makes man stumble, it does not lead us to God." This current adopts a double discourse calling both on the powerful to accept social reform to avoid revolutionary contamination and preaching submission to the poor. Edmund Burke said no less: "Patience, labor, sobriety, frugality, and religion are to be recommended to the workers: all the rest is deceit."

---

303. Arouna P. OUÉDRAOGO, "De la secte religieuse à l'utopie philanthropique. Genèse sociale du végétarisme occidental", *loc. cit.*, p. 829.

This vegetarianism goes hand in hand with the fight to substitute bread (which had become too expensive and caused many revolts) with potatoes served in popular soups. The English religious will then get closer to the American religious, in particular to the Presbyterians of Sylvester Graham (1794-1851) and the Seventh Day Adventists. The latter included among their followers the Kellogg brothers... who had the genius to disguise their religious and commercial struggle as a hygienic approach, thus ensuring the success of their multinational cereal company. This success of the hygienic vegetarianism on the other side of the Atlantic will have repercussions first in England and then in France. The Christian Bible Church called for the foundation of the Vegetarian Society and then created a coalition between this society, the Bible Church and a liberal fraction of the employers. Vegetarianism is defended as the best rampart against the propagation of revolutionary ideas, because it would allow to reduce misery without upheaval. Arouna P. Ouédraogo observes that "vegetarianism is, in the opinion of the leaders of the Vegetarian Society, the most efficient way to produce healthy, pure, vigorous, hard-working and respectable industrial workers, all qualities required by the new discipline of factory and industrial work. They extol the economic, moral and health virtues of vegetarianism and use all the protest arguments fashionable in the 1850s, such as the adulteration of industrially produced food, poor sanitary conditions, poverty and air pollution in industrial cities." Arouna P. Ouédraogo concludes by noting that the figure of the worker exalted by "the leaders of the [Vegetarian] Society was the antithesis of the idea they had of the peasant. Thus, they opposed the intelligence, agility and acuity of the city-dweller and industrial worker to the heaviness and slowness of the rural and peasant". I would qualify this analysis by recalling that, in parallel with the importation of this vegetarianism into France around 1880, other currents of more or less anarchist obedience tried to organize a return to primitive forms of life by giving a beautiful part to vegetarianism, to crugitovorism... without the support of the employers or the Church. The "sauvagists" pushed to the extreme the conceptions of the naturists by trying a return to the kind of prehistoric life[304].

---

304. Jean MAITRON, *Le mouvement anarchiste en France*, tome 1 : *Des origines à 1914*, Paris, Maspéro, 1982, reedition Paris, "Tel", Gallimard, 1992.

Horse meat to feed the people

It is not the horse meat that is at issue in my analysis, but the reasons that may have led to its consumption. The scientific world and the bourgeoisie began to take an interest in horse meat in the middle of the 19th century with the aim of feeding the people in an "economic" way, that is to say for the same reasons that others want them to be vegetarians[305]. I remind you that the consumption of horse meat was forbidden for a long time, except in times of famine, for religious reasons, but also, I think, for political reasons. The horse, for a long time object of prestige of the powerful, symbol of the warriors, could not be the meat of the poor...

Alexandre Parent du Châtelet, a famous physician, wrote a first report to the Paris police prefecture on the removal and use of dead horses, in which he recommended their consumption by the poor[306]. Eric Pierre shows, however, that the decisive offensive came, at the beginning of the Second Empire, from the National Museum of Natural History, in the person of Isidore Geoffroy Saint-Hilaire, who published, in 1855, *Lettres sur les substances alimentaires et particulièrement sur la viande de cheval*[307]. Those who advocated the consumption of horse meat, remembering the famous potato banquet, organized hippophagic meals such as the one during which Professor Renault of the Veterinary School of Alfort, invited 11 personalities (doctors, journalists, civil servants of the Ministry of Agriculture, etc.) to consume, in three forms, an old paralytic horse. We owe to Eric Pierre's work a good knowledge of the backgrounds of this battle that will oppose, for a decade, supporters and opponents of horse meat[308].

On the side of the opponents, one finds mainly "radical" militants, whose leader is Dr. Robinet, popular obstetrician, future Republican mayor during the siege of Paris and under the Commune, active member of the positivist school. He explains that the introduction of horse meat

---

305. Éric Pierre, "L'hippophagie au secours des classes laborieuses" in *Communications*, 74-1, 2003, thematic issue: *Bienfaisante nature*, under the direction of Françoise Dubost and Bernadette Lizet, p. 177-200.

306. Alexandre Parent du Châtelet, *Recherches et Considérations sur l'enlèvement et l'emploi des chevaux morts et sur la nécessité d'établir à Paris un clos central d'écarrissage* [sic]... Paris, Bachelier, 1827: "The indigent class would thus find at its will a resource that it lacks now, and would soon put aside all prevention, when it would be assured of the supervision of the authority, and when it would have the advantage of low price and good quality. We hope that this question will be carefully examined and that the opportunity will be taken to take advantage of healthy, abundant, cheap foodstuffs, the use of which has not hitherto benefited the indigent class", quoted by Éric Pierre, "L'hippophagie au secours des classes laborieuses", art.cit. *loc. cit.*, p. 178.

307. Éric Pierre, "L'hippophagie au secours des classes laborieuses", art.cit. *loc. cit.*, p. 179-182.

308. *Id., ibid.*

---

would lead to a regression of civilization by bringing man back to the rank of the carnivore: "It is neither by economic ignorance nor by physical disgust that man has stopped eating such and such animals, and the horse in particular, but because as he has moved further away from primitive brutality, he has become repulsed by devouring the companion of his work as the price of his services...". Robinet explains that after the horse would come the turn of the dog.

On the side of the supporters, we find, first of all, the "good society", and in particular the leaders of the SPA, of which Geoffroy Saint-Hilaire, who all hope thus to protect the old horses, then, his successor, the military veterinarian Émile Decroix. The latter made it his great fight: He writes propaganda brochures, he finances the distribution of horse meat to the poor illegally, he intends to demonstrate that sick horses are still edible, he gives a report to the Academy of Medicine where he reports his experience of having fed on the flesh of horses suffering from glanders and farcin, pneumonia, lesions and various concussions, but also feverish, phthisic, typhus or plague-ridden oxen, pestiferous pigs and sheep, cholera chickens, etc. He even consumed the raw flesh of rabid dogs. Émile Decroix was also the founder of the Society Against Tobacco Abuse and the Society Against Alcohol Abuse. However, the anti-hippophagy camp progressed within the SPA.

Eric Pierre explains that those who oppose the consumption of horse meat are recruited among the nobility and the clergy, while those who are in favor of it come from scientific circles, especially medical ones. However, the Catholic Church lifted its ban in 1816. The hippophagi broke away and created the Committee for the Propagation of Horsemeat and resumed their free and illegal distribution of horsemeat, their publications and conferences, and the organization of banquets such as the one held on February 6, 1865, at the Grand Hotel: this "select assembly, composed of 132 guests, tasted three old horses in the most refined forms..."

The campaign was sufficiently effective in the media that the Prefect of Police of Paris authorized the sale of horse meat in 1866. The only concession to the opponents was that it was only available in horse butcher shops.

Gastronomy, the language of revenge

We underestimate today what was the conservative counter-revolution that swept Europe and America after 1789. We also underestimate the spirit of revenge that will be felt by all those who were afraid in 1789, in 1848, in 1871... This century of revolutions needed its antidote: the invention of gastronomy is not an extension of ancient tables but of the

A political history of food. From the Pateolithic to our days

Ancien Régime, offered as a model to the new rich... Joseph Berchoux is not mistaken when he calls for an end to the Greeks and Romans in order to better appreciate the delights of a Restoration that is still desired. The founding fathers of gastronomy not only put themselves at the service of the new fat people seeking to copy the old Great ones, they do not only abandon the medical discourse for a promise of abundance and appearance, they contribute to the conservative counter-revolution by their contempt of the people and by their capacity to reinvent in the middle of the 19th century a language which reminds that of the Old Regime. All these inventors of French gastronomy are reactionaries, not only because they put themselves at the service of those who pay them, but because, as defenders of haute cuisine, they can only support an inegalitarian society (according to Jack Goody's thesis[309]), incapable of imagining a popular gourmandise.

These great counter-revolutionary cooks
Jean Anthelme Brillat-Savarin (1755-1826) is emblematic of this movement. He was a deputy to the States General in 1789 and went into exile in the United States in 1793 to escape the Terror and the Revolutionary Court, which prosecuted him as a federalist. Returning to France in 1796, he was reinstated as a judge at the Cour de cassation. In 1801, he published *Vues et projets d'économie politique par le citoyen Brillat-Savarin, ex-Constituant, member of the Tribunal de cassation*, a work he dedicated to Napoleon, First Consul. He also published a *historical and critical essay on the duel* in 1819, this time dedicated to King Louis XVIII "for the triple benefit of the Charter, external peace and public tranquility. He explains that "the duel contributes to the maintenance of the respect that one owes each other in society" (*sic*). The *Physiology of Taste*[310] , a book he printed at his own expense in only 500 copies, was published in 1826, two months before Brillat-Savarin died, victim of pneumonia caught in a church where the death of Louis XVI was commemorated. This work later became a classic for political rather than gastronomic reasons. Brillat-Savarin was mocked during his lifetime. Alexandre Dumas, referring to his heavy gait, his vulgar air, his costume ten years behind the fashion, qualified him as a drum major of the Court of Cassation. Baudelaire made fun of him and

---

309. See Jack GOODY, *Cooking, Cuisine and Class. A Study in Comparative Sociology*, Cambridge, Cambridge University Press, 1982 and the review of this book by Jean-Louis FLANDRIN, in the journal *Annales. Économie, Sociétés, Civilisations*, 42ᵉ année, n° 3, 1987, p. 645-651.
310. Jean Anthelme BRILLAT-SAVARIN, *Physiology of Taste*, Paris, "Champs classiques", Flammarion, 2009, gallica.bnf.fr/ark:/12148/bpt6k5455011p

compared him to a "big bun". Carême repeated that he had never known how to eat and that he filled his stomach...

Alexandre Balthazar Laurent Grimod de La Reynière (1758-1827) does not hide his nostalgia for the Ancien Régime either. Son of a rich farmer general, he invented gastronomic journalism, which he elevated to the rank of a class ideology. He first published eight issues of his *Almanach des gourmands*[311] (1803-1812), then his *Manuel des amphitryons*[312] (1808) conceived as a catechism "in the art of living well and making others live well". This exposition of good manners is no longer, in the manner of Erasmus, a generous appeal to humanism and shared pleasure, but an opportunity to display an aristocratic contempt for everything that deviates from the old rules of life. He pursues only one objective: to convince the new elites to learn the codes of the Ancien Régime. This is why he praises good taste and the palate against the belly, in order to make that of the aristocracy against the new rich. Grimod de La Reynière is not interested in the people. As a supporter of this social separatism, he advocated not only the prohibition of political discussion in front of the servants, but also their exclusion at the time of the desserts, hence the generalization of the bell to call them. The Marquis de Rouillac will extend this exclusion of servants to the entire meal.

Marie-Antoine Carême (1784-1833) is considered to be the main architect of the French "grande cuisine" of the 19th century. His work is inseparable from that of Grimod de La Reynière and Brillat-Savarin. He is often presented as the man of the transition between the old monarchic cuisine and the bourgeois cuisine. This usual presentation is certainly accurate but it hides the essential. If he indeed founded the bourgeois cuisine of the 19th century, he did so with the desire to be part of the monarchic tradition. We do not take seriously enough the fact that he is first and foremost a pastry chef and not a cook or a maître d'hôtel. His kitchen is not only decorative but monumental. It must serve (especially his pastry) to express omnipotence. Carême is an ideologist who puts his art at the service of the powerful.

This is why Talleyrand knew how to make Carême, who was already in charge of the Baron de Rothschild's dinners at the Château de Boulogne, the instrument of the great splendors of the Empire. On Napoleon's

---

311. Alexandre Balthazar Laurent Grimod de La Reynière, *Almanach des gourmands*, Paris, Maradan, 1806, gallica.bnf.fr/ark:/12148/cb343982165/date; reprinted Chartres, Éditions Menu Fretin, 2012.
312. *Id.*, *Manuel des amphitryons*, gallica.bnf.fr/ark:/12148/btv1b8622142d/f1.image; reprinted in "Archives nutritives", Chartres, Éditions Menu Fretin, 2014.

orders, Talleyrand gave, from 1808, four gala dinners a week to seduce and reassure the monarchist powers of Europe, copying the old rituals. The etiquette of the imperial palace adopted in 1808 to reorganize Napoleon's table service takes up the Ordinances of Louis XIV by reintroducing the same symbols (the nave, the padlock), the same methods of service and the same organization with the hall usher, the head of the goblet, the comptroller general, the pages, etc. Carême, aware of his function, dedicated his book *Le Pâtissier national parisien* (note that the pastry chef, from *national* under the Empire, became *royal* under the Restoration) to the general controller of the house of the prince of Talleyrand-Périgord.

This is why Carême published in 1821 two rather unexpected architectural works aimed at beautifying cities to celebrate the glory of the powerful: his *Projets d'architecture dédiés à Alexandre Ier, tsar de toutes les Russies* and his *Projet d'architecture pour les embellissements de* Paris[313]. Each of his works testifies to both his love of the monarchy and his conviction that the good times will not return (*L'Art de la cuisine française au* XIXE *siècle, Le Pâtissier royal parisien, Le Pâtissier pittoresque, Le Maître d'hôtel français* (comparison between the ordering of the old and the new service according to the four seasons), *Le Cuisinier parisien, L'Art de la cuisine française,* etc). Carême writes in *Le Pâtissier royal parisien*: "The extreme good taste of the court of Louis XV had a singular influence on the civilization of all classes of society, but particularly on good men, who, at that time, were rightly considered as Great : also there was not a cook of a lord who did not have himself the turn and manners of a man of good tone: the embroidered suit, lace cuffs and diamond buckles were their adornment; the sword was their ornament, and they knew how to carry it." Carême signed his creations with famous names according to the tradition of the Ancien Régime: "The dishes of French cuisine bear the most illustrious names of the nobility of France: à la reine, à la dauphine, à la royale, à la d'Artois, à la Xavier, à la Condé, à la d'Orléans, à la Chartres, à la Penthièvre, à la Soubise, etc."[314]. He qualifies the new appellations of "barbaric" because without nobility. The last straw was the popular names such as "pets-de-nonne". Carême deplores that "the cooks of our days are not always appreciated in France" to the point of obliging them "to work with the kitchen girls". He cannot help but sprinkle his numerous works with political sentences marking his contempt for the people and his attachment to the (splendors) of the

---

313. Marie-Antoine CARÊME, *Projets d'architecture dédiés à Alexandre Ier, tsar de toutes les Russies,* Paris, Firmin-Didot Père et Fils, 1821; gallica.bnf.fr/ark:/12148/bpt6k6281582s.r=
314. *Id. Le Pâtissier royal parisien ou Traité élémentaire et pratique de la pâtisserie ancienne et moderne...,* Paris, J. G. Dentu, imprimeur-libraire, 1815; http://gallica.bnf.fr/ark:/12148/bpt6k852237p

powerful. Carême is convinced that "gastronomy walks like a sovereign at the head of civilization, but it vegetates in times of revolution". Savoring the aphorisms, he adds: "The rich and beneficent man is a God on Earth, his name is blessed by the unfortunate. The rich man without defiance deserves to be nobly loved"; "The servant who believes himself the equal of his master is a fool...". Receptive to the Revolution of 1789, he does not appreciate the one of 1848 either, against which he writes his *Trait de dévouement d'un domestique*. Carême is however soluble in all the regimes because drawing from the oldest traditions, he maintains that "France is the mother country of the amphitryons; its kitchen and its wines make the triumph of the gastronomy. It is the only country in the world for good food; foreigners are convinced of these truths". This nationalism is as much monarchist, imperial as republican.

We could continue the demonstration with so many other great cooks and with most of the gastronomic critics. André Viard, a precursor of Carême, published the same work under different titles: *Le Cuisinier impérial*[315] (1806) becomes *Le Cuisinier royal*[316] under the Restoration, it then becomes *national* to become *imperial* again in 1854... Joseph Berchoux, author of the famous poem *La Gastronomie*, displays his royalism[317]. He published in 1800 (?) *La Gastronomie ou l'Homme des champs à table* to which Jean-Baptiste Gouriet's book, *L'Antigastronomie ou l'Homme de ville sortant de table* (1806), responds with the famous metaphor of the dove, victim of the experiments of a gastronome[318].

The only character to stand out is Nicolas Appert (1749-1841), the inventor of the tin can. This follower of Rousseau became involved in the heart of the Revolution: on July 13, he was charged by his district to go and get weapons from the Invalides. He will be the president of the section of the Lombards. As a delegate, he attended the execution of Louis XVI. Impeached after the fall of the Girondins, he was released only after the 9-Thermidor. In 1795, the government, in order to fight scurvy which was weakening its armies, promised a reward for a process that would keep food healthy and fresh. He invented the process known as "appertization", that is to say the can. He immediately opened a workshop whose first

---

315. *Id.* Le Cuisinier parisien, on the website http://gallica.bnf.fr/ark:/12148/bpt6k110705g.r=
316. André VIARD (and Fouret) [1806], *Le Cuisinier royal ou l'Art de faire la cuisine, la patisserie et tout ce qui concerne l'office...*, Paris, J.-N. Barba libraire, 11th edition, 1821; http://gallica.bnf.fr/ark:/12148/bpt6k54559267
317. Joseph BERCHOUX, *La Gastronomie ou l'Homme des champs à table* ; http://gallica.bnf.fr/ark:/12148/bpt6k1170282/f23.image
318. Jean-Baptiste GOURIET, *L'Antigastronomie ou l'Homme de ville sortant de table*, Paris, chez Huber et Cie, Imp.-Lib., 1806; http://gallica.bnf.fr/ark:/12148/bpt6k55353137

                    A political history of food. From the Pateolithic to our days

client was the Ministry of the Navy. In September 1806, he participated in the Salon de l'industrie and submitted his invention to the jury, which included Bourrat and Parmentier. Not only did he not receive any prize, but his invention was not mentioned in the press. He did not get discouraged and in 1810 published a work that would revolutionize cooking, *The Art of preserving animal and vegetable substances for several years*[319], a work that was immediately well received, 6,000 copies were quickly sold. The government orders 200 copies and 71 prefects receive a copy with the mission to popularize his discovery as soon as possible, notably through learned societies... The government proposes him either to register a patent or to offer his invention to humanity and to receive a government prize. Nicolas Appert refused to register a patent to allow everyone to use his process. The English and the Americans will do it in his place. Appert is buried in a common grave.

At the table of the bourgeois!

Madeleine Ferrières believes that four key words characterize the table in the 19th century: taste, flavor, pleasure and conviviality. We can only agree with Jean-Paul Aron that this is only true for the bourgeoisie, which makes the table, according to his formula, its elective instrument. Jean-Paul Aron starts the pact between the bourgeoisie and gastronomy before the Revolution and gives it as its birth date 1783, the year of the macabre agape organized by Grimod de La Reynière. Aron describes this banquet as "Death played out, death as a symbol, an outlet for the unconscious, for the ferocious impulses of a culture". Something is set up from this time of rise of the capitalism which does not link any more "good food" and sensuality (sexuality), but "good food" and expression of a morbid omnipotence. I would like to point out as a symptom another observation that Aron establishes and which concerns the exclusion of women. While the aristocracy of the Ancien Régime would never have thought of dining without ladies, preferably beautiful ones, the bourgeois republic locks up wives and only shows off in restaurants accompanied by women, except for romantic dinners. Jean-Paul Aron finally insists on the new constraint of silence: freedom of speech is found only at dessert and especially during the passage in the library. The guests must therefore remain silent during the first service, and especially during the soup: "The guest who knows his world will never start a conversation before the end of the first service;

---

319. Paris, Patris, 1810, reprinted by Gutemberg, 1980.

until then, dinner is a serious matter from which it would be impudent to distract the assembly" (Horace Raisson, *Code gourmand*, 1828). I would like to add an additional rule that is characteristic of the 19th century bourgeois table: its concern for economy. This desire can be seen in numerous works such as *La Cuisinière de la campagne et de la ville or Nouvelle Cuisine économique*[320]. This concern for economy explains many changes in service, such as the two or even one service meals, the invention of "flying plates" (or "revolving plates") that allow for extras to be offered to those who want them but do not have enough for everyone, and, of course, the invention of the so-called "Russian" service.

The table service "à la bourgeoise"

The dining room has become an essential part of "good society". The rule is now to leave 60 centimeters between each guest who also has his or her own cutlery. A wool carpet is laid under the table for comfort. The use of the crumb brush before the third service made it compulsory to do away with the placemat. The spoon is now placed on the right side of the plate, the knife, knife rest and fork on the left. The napkin is carefully folded and the bread is placed in its fold. Each guest has an ordinary glass for water and different stemmed glasses for different types of wine. This period saw the development of the one-serve meal called "ambiguous" because everything was mixed together, i.e. placed on the table beforehand. This allows not to be disturbed by the servants, to eat faster at noon or in the middle of the ball... We also see the development of the two course meal, more economical than the traditional three course meal. The soup tureen was no longer placed on the table, but soup was distributed from the serving table. This concern for economy is compensated by the fact that extras are offered in the form of "flying plates" (or "revolving plates") which guarantee the same abundance in the bellies without imposing waste during the service. Cookery books always insist on the importance of the "table's main", also called "the dormant", but explain that it allows to garnish the table... with much less dishes, therefore money. The "Russian-style" service will save even more money, because the hot dishes are cut up in the kitchen and placed on the plates. However, two objections are raised: it is less flattering to the eyes and it does not allow for the distribution of "unequal" pieces, because the very nature of "Russian-style" service is to make identical cuts.

---

320. Louis-Eustache AUDOT, *La Cuisinière de la campagne et de la ville ou nouvelle cuisine économique*, by the author, 1818; http://gallica.bnf.fr/ark:/12148/bpt6k54008652/f425.image

The great meal "à la française" remains structured in three stages, therefore in three successive services. The first two are the responsibility of the kitchen, the last of the pantry. The first service must be prepared before the guests are seated. The hot dishes risk becoming lukewarm, so rechauds are used, and the dishes are left cloche until the last moment. This service concerns the starters with soups, the soups statements, the hors d'oeuvres, etc. Among the entrees, boiled beef decorated with parsley is a must; for the starters, meat, game, poultry, fish with sauce, stews, purées, etc. are served. Stoves (with candles) are placed under the hot dishes and also under the cold dishes (without lighting them) for symmetry on the table. The second service consists of a number of dishes identical to the first but of a smaller capacity, it is devoted to the rôts and the hot or cold entremets as well as the salads. These desserts are lighter than the starters (fish, vegetables, eggs, etc.). The third service, the desserts, should be brought only after the second service has been cleared: first the salt shaker and cutlery are removed, then the plate, and then the table is swept with the crumb brush. Only then are the dessert plates brought in, which must be smaller than the others, on which the dessert cutlery has already been placed. Only then do the staff remove the dishes and the stoves used for the second service. This last service includes cheese, fruit, ice cream and candy.

The adoption of the "Russian-style" service

Jean-Paul Aron clearly saw how the transition from service "à la française" to service "à la russe" occurred in the decade 1850-1860, that is, shortly after the revolution of 1848, with the return of republican ideas. He believes that this "war of services" is won around 1890: "It fulfills the wish of a Jacobin society, rebellious to differences, it fulfills its egalitarian projects." So be it. However, I would like to qualify this statement. This egalitarian ideal concerns only the bourgeoisie which, contrary to the aristocracy always preoccupied by the questions of rank, can think its members as equal as good men, i.e. as owners. This equality of the bourgeoisie, symbolized by the Russian-style service (let us recall that if the ideas of the bourgeois humanists had little effect among the nobles in France, they were received with enthusiasm at the court of Catherine of Russia or in Prussia), was only possible by excluding from this equality all those who were not property owners. The passage from French-style service to Russian-style service is therefore not (and Jean-Paul Aron is right on this point) a phenomenon of modernity, and even less of fashion, but the sign of a political evolution which is not, in my opinion, the victory of the Republic, but that of the bourgeois Republic which hates the people.

The bourgeoisie needs a new language to express, certainly, its class unity, but also to express its desire for reinforced domination. On this point, we refer to the famous work *La cuisine classique: études raisonnées et démonstratives de l'école française appliquée au service à la russe*, published in 1868 by Urbain Dubois and Emile Bernard, chefs de bouche of William I, King of Prussia and Emperor of Germany[321]. This work, no more than those of Carême, another follower of the Russian-style service, does not show an egalitarian bias. To the multiple inequalities, notably of birth, but also of fortune or function, which characterized the society of the Ancien Régime and which its table service translated by producing inequality between the guests, on the one hand, and between the servants, on the other hand, succeeds a new regime which only wants to see one type of inequality, that created by money, which distinguishes the possessors from the non-possessors. Carême himself will complain about this, now obliged to work with the kitchen girls, downgraded, despite his genius, to the rank of the unlucky, obliged to recognize that even the greatest chefs are no longer recognized as they used to be, and confessing that he only continues to work for the love of his art: "The cooks of our days are no longer always appreciated in France; the love of science alone sustains them in practice" (*in* Antonin Carême, *L'Art de la cuisine française au dix-neuvième siècle...*, t. 2, 1847). The equality of the bourgeois guests exists only to better mark the inequality with the non-bourgeois guests. The great republican banquets testify to this.

The banquets of the 19th century: a conflict of memory

Several works have brought the banquet back to the center of memory[322]

This memory of the reformist banquets is important but also contributes to occult that of the fat banquets, the meals of the secret societies, of the charcoal industry then of the blanquist organizations, (of the heirs) of the Commune, of the first trade unionists, of the anarchist picnics, of

---

321. Urbain Dubois and Émile Bernard [1868], *La cuisine classique : études pratiques, raisonnées et démonstratives,* tome 1: *De l'école française appliquée au service à la russe,* Paris, "Savoirs et Traditions", Hachette Livre/BnF, 2013.

322. Vincent Robert, *Le temps des banquets. Politique et symbolique d'une génération 1818-1848,* Paris, Publications de la Sorbonne, 2010; Jean-Clément Martin and Olivier Ihl, *La Fête républicaine, Annales. Histoire, Sciences Sociales,* vol. 54, n° 6, 1999, p. 1399-1402 ; Olivier Ihl, "Socialisation et événements politiques" in *Revue française de science politique,* 52ᵉ année, n° 2-3, 2002, numéro thématique : *Dimension de la socialisation politique,* p. 125-144 ; Yves Schemeil, "Déjeuner en paix : banquets et citoyenneté en Méditerranée orientale", in *Revue française de science politique,* 48ᵉ année, n° 3-4, 1998, numéro thématique : *Cuisine, manière de table et politique,* pp. 349-375.

A political history of food. From the Pateolithic to our days

the mutualist and cooperative movements, of the old "popular bombings" organized and financed by the villages and that the State will end up prohibiting under pretext of illegality. The republican banquets do not innovate: they return to the profit of the opposition a form of meeting practised for a long time by the powerful. These reformist banquets which will lead (in spite of them) to the revolution of 1848 are not popular banquets, but banquets of owners. These banquets (except exception) do not intend only to marginalize the people but to exclude it, with the fear of its always possible, always dreaded irruption.

This fear of the irruption of the people, whether physical or moral, is still present in the 19th century as it was in the 18th. We remember the buffets invaded by the "rabble" during the banquet organized in 1745 by the provost of the merchants of Paris to celebrate the marriage of the Dauphin to which the good bourgeois were invited in seven public rooms. Johann Blondel wrote in 1880, in a text entitled *Saute Marianne !* That long tables be set up in all the squares where the good people could drink large blue wine and get drunk at their ease. Let there be these days of immense democratic banquets where the republican calf will be served with the cervelas with garlic: the people have only the festivals which they deserve"[323]. For a long time, the good society laughed at the popular agape, at those they called the "saucialists" (*sic*). What indeed has in common between the campaign of the reformist banquets, the fat banquets, the revolutionary banquets, the anarchist picnics. What is common between the big banquet organized in 1871 in Versailles to drink to the death of the Commune and the one which is held in 1874 in margin of the congress of the First International.

The campaign of the reformist banquets

It is difficult for the younger generation to understand that the revolution of 1848 was born from the prohibition of a banquet, the last of a campaign. Since the Penal Code forbade political associations, "it was necessary to have recourse to new instruments to make use of the number and its representation against the established order: commemorative parades, national petitions, funerals of prominent personalities, university forums, posters and almanacs... The banquet was one of these means"[324]. The idea germinated at Prosper Duvergier de Hauranne to create a political

---

323. Quoted by Olivier IHL, "De bouche à oreille. Sur les pratiques de commensalité dans la tradition républicaine du cérémonial de table". in *Revue française de science politique*, 48ᵉ année, n°3-4, 1998, p. 387-408.
324. *Id., ibid.*, p. 389.

agitation by means of a campaign of banquets. A central committee of the banquets is created at the republican publisher Laurent-Antoine Pagnerre and Elias Regnault is designated as general secretary. The objective is to obtain a reform to prevent a new revolution. The people will be kept away if only by the price. The first of these banquets takes place on July 10, 1847 in a garden of Montmartre, the Château-Rouge. Garnier-Pagès describes it: "On the day indicated, twelve hundred people came to sit at this great agape of the revolution. Electors, deputies, journalists, all the nuances of the opposition except the legitimists met there, all freed from the memory of the previous dissidences... Around fourteen tables, unrolled under a vast tent, the assembly was pressed, moved, happy of a great begun duty, raised in its own eyes by the conscience of its moral greatness... The music, throwing to the evening winds the most beautiful songs of the revolution, celebrated this double festival of the nature and the thought"[325].

Other banquets followed all over France during which the guests (but not all) made toasts: "To national sovereignty!"; "To the revolution of 1830!"; "To electoral reform!" Disagreement soon arises over whether the obligation to make a traditional toast to the king is respected. Olivier Ihl summarizes the issue: to give a toast to the king is to commit oneself to the camp of reform, to forget it is to take sides with the revolution: "Hence the opposition at the banquet in Lille between Odilon Barrot, who demanded that this gesture of allegiance be preserved, and Ledru-Rollin, who stubbornly refused to do so; having gained the upper hand, the latter obliged Odilon Barrot to leave the table of the guests with a flourish." This polemic testifies to the fact that the campaign of the banquets amalgamates contrasting social interests: is it necessary "the equality of the bourgeois between them" (Jules Simon) or "the equality of the people with the bourgeois" (which supposes the refusal of the censal suffrage).

The banning of the last banquet of the National Guard in the 12th arrondissement of Paris, on February 22, 1848, led to the insurrection, the fall of Louis-Philippe, the establishment of the Second Republic... The revolution of 1848 was the result of a campaign of banquets that would have brought together about 17,000 citizens. Olivier Ihl shows that these banquets were organized in such a way as to create a double exclusion, that of the people and that of women and children. "This is the meaning of the call for subscriptions, a very widespread mode of financing meals which nevertheless exercises - let us not be mistaken

---

325. Louis GARNIER-PAGÈS, *Histoire de la révolution de 1848*, Paris, Pagnerre, 1851, p. 106 and 108, quoted by Olivier Ihl, "De bouche à oreille. On the practices of commensality in the republican tradition of table ceremonial", art. cit. , p. 389-390.

　A political history of food. From the Pateolithic to our days

- other forms of segregation. Higher than two or three francs, the fee is a promise of abundance but, at this price, the most modest purses are closed and the banquet exerts a discrimination; at 25 centimes, as in the "popular" banquet to which the newspaper *Le Père Duchesne* called at the beginning of June 1848, the guests are innumerable but the tables, less furnished, risk stimulating the frustrations"[326]. The banquets reformers by choosing to mobilize only voters, thus men owners, excluded voluntarily the popular circles. The revolutionary people imposed their presence only in rare cities, provoking scuffles.

Divide and conquer: the banquet of the mayors of France

In 1900, in Paris, on the occasion of the Universal Exhibition, the banquet of the mayors of France gathered nearly 23,000 guests on September 22, the anniversary of the proclamation of the Republic, 108 years earlier. I use this event to illustrate an essential political mechanism that is a common thread in this journey through the political history of the table. We have discovered, from the banquets of prehistory to those of Antiquity, and then going back through the history of France and partly through religious history, that it is never possible to gather guests without immediately excluding others, not all have a share in the banquet, and among those who have a right to the banquet, it is necessary to differentiate the shares. Politics is always an operation of division which consists in drawing two borders, a first border separates the friends from the enemies, those who are admitted to the banquet from all the others, a second border separates then the brothers from the half-brothers. All are guests, but not all are guests, or not to the same degree, not in the same way. The banquet of the mayors of France of September 1900 is thus obliged to distribute the mayors according to two orders, alphabetical and geographical, in order to stage the single and indivisible character of the Republic. The provinces were not allowed, nor were the parties or other chapels. This staging of the unity of the Republic supposes however to draw a border between those who are invited, the representatives of the people, and those who are represented. A second border separates then those who have right only to the agapes and those who reach through the toasts the monopoly of the authorized word. In the same way that the reformist banquets of 1847-1848 were banquets of owners excluding the poor, the women, the children, the republican banquet institutes a republic of notables. We no longer know how to allow the anonymous

---

326. *Id., ibid.,* p. 392.

to take part, to bring their share, to receive their share, which is however at the very foundation of democracy. Jules Vallès was one of those who took a stand against this political separatism that accompanied social separatism, a sign of the inability to build a social democracy that would recognize the competence of the parochial and the incompetent (see "Les banquets" in *Le Cri du peuple*, 21 March 1884).

The 19th century, which was the century of food counter-utopias, perhaps anticipates our century. This black century was also the one of hopes and fights to grant to each one the right to the banquet and to give him a share which makes him want to live. These food utopias are still ours. We will find them in "Exit from the table", but first we will have to go through the not very engaging industrial tables of the TWENTIETH century and the beginning of the 20th century, whose trial we have to investigate.

Thirteenth service: Industrial tables of the 20th and early 21st centuries

Agriculture underwent a fundamental change during the second half of the 20th century. Was it the same for the table (what do we eat? how do we eat?). At the beginning of the 21st century, agriculture is about to undergo a new mutation: will it be even more fundamental? What will soon happen to the content and conception of the table? The 20th century has given the lie to Fernand Braudel's famous phrase about history standing still[327] , since between 1950 and 1980, the agricultural system underwent a revolution that is unprecedented in history.

The time has come to take stock and we know that we are paying dearly for this crazy race for productivity, because if it has undoubtedly allowed us to feed those who made the Glorious Thirty (which does not mean that it would have been impossible to do it otherwise), it has also destroyed the soil, damaged the ecosystems, created new food pathologies, reinforced the mistrust towards our food and generated what Daniel Tacet denounced in his 1992 book, *Un monde sans paysans* (Hachette) In 1950, 8 million farmers fed 40 million French people, i.e. 5 mouths per farmer. The number of farmers has been divided by 10 and one farmer feeds 100 people. France should soon lose half of the 800,000 surviving farmers.

However, the 21st century will not only be the continuation of the previous century, because if the latter was characterized (as we will see later) by the invention of a productivist agriculture based on an extractivist model that is totally unsustainable in the long term and giving rise to what I will call petro-foods because of their energy content, the 21st century will be the century of food biotechnologies that promise to go much further

---

327. Fernand BRAUDEL [1949], *La Méditerranée et le monde méditerranéen à l'époque de Philippe II*, Paris, Armand Colin, 2 volumes, 1985, "Préface", volume 1, p. 13-14.

than GMOs, cloned meat, nano-foods and irradiated foods! If the 20th century put an end to several million years of gathering, hunting and soon fishing (to the benefit of industrial forestry), the 21st century is already imagining what will be an agriculture without livestock (thanks to meat substitutes) and even a food without agriculture, i.e. without any relation to the land, thanks to biotechnologies. This evolution seems to many to be inevitable in order to be able to feed 10 billion people, but some specialists such as Jean Ziegler and Olivier De Schutter, both special rapporteurs for the United Nations on the right to food[328] , or Bruno Parmentier, former director of the ESA Group (École supérieure d'agriculture d'Angers), argue that the current abundance and relative quality will probably constitute a parenthesis in history, not because of the increase in the human population, but because of the failure of a mistaken productivist system that is collectively leading us into the wall[329]. The question is whether humanity can jump over this wall by relying on "biotech", as the companies wish, or whether it is not more promising to listen to the multiple alternatives that billions of humans are already experimenting with[330].

Of two theses I would like to convince the reader:

If humanity has been able to humanize itself by humanizing its table, it could dehumanize itself by dehumanizing its table: an overview of the current mutations will show that what threatens is the birth of a world without breeding, without agriculture and without food worthy of the name. I announced this in *La Fin des mangeurs*, in 1997[331] , a book in which I analyzed the metamorphosis of the table. I have no reason to question this judgement because the indictment is even heavier. This is why I believe it is necessary to enrich this analysis by arguing that no solution is credible if we do not invent food policies alongside agricultural policies.

Of course, the metamorphoses of the table in the 20th and 21st centuries are rooted in the socio-economic changes linked to the great transformations of the contemporary world: urbanization, industrialization, the disappearance of self-production functions, but the essential point seems to me to be the weight of the transnational corporations that govern

328. Jean Ziegler, *Mass Destruction. Géopolitique de la faim*, Paris, Éditions du Seuil, 2011, republished in paperback, Paris, "Points Documents", Points, 2012 ; Olivier De Schutter, *La faim, un choix politique ?* Brussels, Éditions André Versaille, 2010.

329. Bruno Parmentier, *Nourrir l'humanité. Les grands problèmes de l'agriculture mondiale au XXIe siècle*, preface by Edgar Pisani, Paris, "La Découverte Poche/Essais" (n° 296), La Découverte, 2011; *id. Faim Zéro. En finir avec la faim dans le monde*, Paris, "Cahiers libres", La Découverte, 2014.

330. Isabelle Saporta, *Le livre noir de l'agriculture. Comment on assassine nos paysans, notre santé et l'environnement*, Fayard, Paris, 2011.

331. Paul Ariès, *La Fin des mangeurs*, Paris, Desclée de Brouwer, 1997.

     A political history of food. From the Pateolithic to our days

agriculture and food: economic weight, since a few firms control the seed market and sometimes more than a quarter of a world's agricultural production; ideological weight, since this agribusiness lobby has replaced, via marketing, the Churches as the food prescriber; political weight, since this agribusiness lobby largely manages to impose the rules of the game.

From the fear of withdrawal to the fear of eating poorly

In the 20th century, the West has undoubtedly seen an improvement in food security (outside the context of war) and even an increase in basic health security: people no longer die massively from food poisoning in France as was still the case in the 19th century[332]. This improvement is undeniable (despite all the health scandals), althoughit was obtained at the price of an extractivist model responsible for the plundering of natural resources, the destruction of ecosystems and, above all, the fertility of the soil[333]. We could therefore have expected the gradual disappearance of the feeling of anxiety linked to food, but instead we are witnessing the explosion of new behavioral disorders (anorexia, bulimia, orthopraxia). The fear of eating too much or badly has replaced the ancestral fear of lack. This is a good opportunity to remember that eating is always a way of making oneself out of the other, since it means incorporating something that is foreign to us. In short, eating is always a risky operation, not only on the biological level, but also on the cultural, religious, social or political level. Food fears are the consequence of the fact that food should not only be good to eat, but, as the sociologist Claude Fischler says, "good to think about". It is because we feel that we are no longer eating in an anthropologically satisfactory way that we wish ourselves - I borrow this phrase from Pierre Rahbi - "good luck" when we sit down to eat! This is why I think that Bruno Parmentier is only half way through when he explains that after having produced a lot with more and more, we will have to learn to produce even more, this time with much less (water, soil, energy, chemistry, farmers), because this challenge can only be met if we eat with "much" more culture (rituals and symbols).

The easiest part of the answer is in agriculture, since 70% of human beings still eat outside the logic of the productivist agricultural model. The worst conviction, because it would be hopeless, would be to believe

---

332. Madeleine FERRIÈRES, *Une histoire des peurs alimentaires. Du Moyen Âge à l'aube du xxᵉ siècle*, Paris "L'Univers historique", Éditions du Seuil, 2002.
333. Patricia TOUYRE, *Le sol, un monde vivant. Formation, faune, flore*, Paris, Delachaux et Niestlé, 2015; Claude and Lydia BOURGUIGNON, *Le sol, la terre et les champs*, Paris, "Dossiers écologie", Éditions Sang de la Terre, 2015.

that the productivist system is the only one, when it only concerns a tiny minority of farmers: 28 million have tractors, large surfaces, industrial seeds, sufficient water, fertilizers, etc.; 250 million use animal traction alone (oxen, horses, mules, buffaloes, zebras, etc.); 1 billion farmers have only their muscle power. Of course, it is not a question of idealizing these other forms of agriculture, especially since these small farmers remain the first victims of hunger in the world and their farming techniques can sometimes be destructive of local ecosystems (slash-and-burn agriculture). However, this peasant knowledge constitutes a reservoir of good practices for the future.

The other part of the answer concerns food in its anthropological dimensions. The worst conviction would be to believe that the Western conception would make all humans dream. These other ways of conceiving food and eating constitute a reservoir of popular traditions that will be useful in meeting the challenge of feeding 10 billion people[334]. The 21st century already signals the end of Western food standards. The question is to know what the new standards will be: are we moving towards a biotechnological food, with an increasingly tenuous relationship with agriculture? Are we moving towards a food conceived solely from the point of view of nutrition and ignoring the other dimensions of the table (including sometimes within the so-called "alternative" models)? Are we heading towards the end of the grammar of food forms that have more or less allowed humanity to know for thousands of years what eating means beyond nutrition, or will we be able to reform this grammar to make the table a language?

The revolution of the content of the plate

Our children will not eat like us, just as we ourselves did not eat like our parents. What is new, therefore, is not the change in the content of the plate, but the pace and the motor of the evolution. Specialists argue about the actual rate of renewal (from 70 to 90%), but these debates often mask the essential because eating the same product in appearance can hide considerable differences: thus we consume much less bread, but it is no longer the same and its symbolism has changed. The table is no longer evolving primarily for climatic, religious, economic, social and political

---

334. François Couplan, *Le régal végétal. Plantes sauvages comestibles*, Paris, Éditions Sang de la Terre, 2009; *id. La cuisine sauvage. Accommodating a thousand forgotten plants*, Paris, Éditions Sang de la Terre, 2010.

 A political history of food. From the Pateolithic to our days

reasons, but because of the weight of technoscience and the strategic choices of companies.

The French table of the 20th century is first characterized by the end of the cereal model that had been progressively imposed until it became dominant, in favor of a much more diversified model (wheat and corn, always, but also milk, meat, fruits and vegetables). The breakthrough came in the 1950s with a sharp increase in the consumption of these products considered "rich". Bruno Parmentier provides some precise benchmarks: fruit: 65 kilos per year per person in 2000, compared to 38 kilos in 1950; vegetables: 116 kilos compared to 60; meat: 85 kilos compared to 44; fish: 25 kilos compared to 10; cheese: 18 kilos compared to 5; vegetable oils: 14 kilos compared to 5[335]. I would add that the decreases in other foodstuffs are just as significant: bread: 60 kilos against 121; potatoes: 65 kilos against 153; wine: 67 liters against 143.

What do we eat today?

On November 16, 2010, France has seen its gastronomy listed as a World Heritage Site. This recognition is good news because it means that, like exceptional natural or historical sites, the "gastronomic meal of the French" should be valued and protected. The Center for Studies and Forecasting took the opportunity to publish a report on the evolution of food in France during the 20th century and early 21st century. This study, signed in 2011 by Céline Laisney, is full of lessons[336]. It confirms that, contrary to popular belief, the French are still consuming more food in absolute terms and that it is only the relative share of the overall budget that is tending to decrease. On average, we spend 13.6% of our income on food. In fact, the French are the ones who spend the most on food in absolute terms, with the exception of the wealthy Swiss and Luxembourgers, and the Icelanders who are far from the sources of supply. These averages are misleading, however, because working-class people spend much more and always give preference to food over leisure expenditure: "The share of the budget devoted to food (food and non-alcoholic beverages excluding catering) for executives was 12.4% in 2006, while that of workers was 16%. It reached 50% for the poorest households. The figures for the

---

335. Bruno Parmentier, *Nourrir l'humanité. Les grands problèmes de l'agriculture mondiale au xxie siècle, op. cit, loc. cit.* , p. 35.
336. Céline Laisney, *L'évolution de l'alimentation en France, Futuribles* magazine, No. 371 and 372, February and March 2011; this report can also be consulted on the website of the Service de la statistique et de la prospective of the Ministry of Agriculture, Food, Fisheries, Rural Affairs and Land Management: http://agreste.agriculture.gouv.fr/IMG/pdf/doctravail50112.pdf

---

composition of meals at the beginning of the 21st century extend those put forward by Bruno Parmentier for the previous period. It is not a matter of fashion (fashion is what goes out of fashion) but of structural changes: "The composition of the average household basket has changed. Thus, between 1970 and 2008, according to INSEE, the average consumption of bread at home fell from 80 to 50 kilos per person per year, and that of potatoes from 95 to 68 kilos. At the same time, the consumption of fresh fruit and vegetables, from 70 kilos in 1970, reached 86 kilos in 2008. As for meat, beef has declined in favor of pork and poultry, and to a lesser extent eggs and fish."

Céline Laisney reports the latest figures from INSEE on beverages: "In terms of beverages, the French now drink only 51 liters of fresh milk per year (compared to 95 liters in 1970), but swallow nearly 22 kilos of yogurt (compared to only 8 kilos in 1970). The strongest increase, all products combined, is that of mineral and spring water, which has jumped from 40 liters per year to more than 150 liters over the same period. On the other hand, the consumption of ordinary wine has collapsed (from 96 to 22 liters), while that of AOC (appellation d'origine contrôlée) wines has increased (from 8 to 22 liters) to represent today half of the total consumption of wine, which, overall, has nevertheless decreased significantly. Wine is no longer systematically present on French tables: only a quarter of French people consume it on a regular basis (at least two to three times a week). In a few decades, it has gone from being a necessity to a pleasure, which explains why the French are also more demanding and why 80% of them are now looking for better quality wines.

The EPIC (European Prospective Investigation into Cancer and Nutrition) study allows us to refine the analysis by comparing the consumption of Europeans. It distinguishes between the diets of Greeks and Italians, characterized by high consumption of fruit and vegetables, and those of the Dutch and Germans, who eat more potatoes and meat. The French are in an intermediate position: with 87.8 kilos per person per year in 2009, they rank eighth in Europe for meat consumption (with the notable exception of beef, for which they rank first with 25.4 kilos compared to the European average of 15 kilos). The French are also the leading consumers of butter and second for wine and cheese. Céline Laisney's study also puts into perspective the discourse on the homogenization of the table: regional specificities and social differences remain and are even tending to become more marked. Thus, the north and south of France are separated in terms of fat consumption (more butter and margarine in the north, oil in the south). The north of France

    A political history of food. From the Pateolithic to our days

consumes more potatoes, pastries and pastries, and coffee; the south of France consumes more soups, vegetables and tea. The specificities of the eastern and western regions of the country appear in the processing of food: the west is characterized by higher consumption of unprocessed or slightly processed products and by a higher overall consumption. Social differences are reflected in the consumption of processed or more expensive products (seafood, fruit, vegetables) by the wealthy French, while the more modest buy cheap products (eggs, poultry) and consume processed foods containing inexpensive ingredients (sugar, cereals, potatoes, vegetable oils).

Thus, there are still middle-class foods (veal, beef, mutton, chicory) and more popular ones (pork, rabbit, working-class potatoes and peasant leeks). Senior executives buy more expensive products (fruit, butcher's meat, fish, cheese, fine wines) or more elaborate ones (prepared meals, frozen meals). They also buy products that are considered easier to use (coffee in capsules versus soluble coffee, soluble coffee versus ground coffee, ground coffee versus coffee beans, etc.) or that have a better brand image (wild rice versus other rice). Eating canned food is not enough to characterize a diet: canned vegetables are mainly used by young men in eastern France; canned fish is primarily consumed by "single campers" and "modern urbanites"; canned fruit is preferred by rural and elderly people. Frozen products are mainly aimed at the urban strata, even if the invention of the microwave oven has created a category of younger and less settled customers.

This reproduction of certain social markers should not mask the fact that the affluent society (not for everyone, as we shall see) has transformed social divisions to the point of making them unrecognizable. Households whose wives work outside the home consume twice as much for their food budget (17% versus 9%), regardless of social background, age or place of residence. The popular culture, described by Pierre Sansot, still exists in its main features, such as the cult of communal meals, "home-made" food, the choice of abundance and casualness (compared to the so-called "bourgeois" ways). However, this popular art of dining is less and less claimed as such. This denial is indicative of the establishment of a two-tiered food society where popular food becomes a by-product of bourgeois food. Whereas in the past we used to oppose the peasant rabbit, the working-class pig and the bourgeois veal, today everyone eats chicken: for a minority, it is farmhouse (or organic) chicken, for the others, battery poultry. Are we to conclude that popular cultures, once claimed with the same pride, have become by-products of the dominant culture, cultures "for want of anything better"? Specialists thus oppose popular "service foods" (80% of foodstuffs) to bourgeois "pleasure foods" (20% of foodstuffs), popular hypermarkets and discounters to local food shops, and low-end and high-end products. The industrialists are registering this change by proposing, next to commonplace dishes made with ever less expensive ingredients, products that are increasingly upmarket. Intermediate products, with the best quality/price ratio, tend to disappear from the shelves. The popular tables are therefore the first to suffer from the industrialization of food products.

What will we eat tomorrow?

The modes of production and transformation of our food are based on agro-industrial systems totally unbalanced and responsible for numerous crises[337]. Crops are more and more intensive and concern varieties selected for their yield potential, without taking into account the problem of the soil, which has been totally abandoned in favor of a simplified system based on the massive use of chemical inputs. At the same time, a new purely functional classification of products forbids to give a sense to one's table, it is a formatting of the consumer by a holy alliance of the food industry and changing dietary advice, it is new products which all tend to reinforce the artificialization of foodstuffs.

The eater no longer eats according to the seasons, the regions, his social environment or his religious or political convictions, but essentially according to the strategic choices of the big companies. The food market is in fact 80% in the hands of the big supermarkets, which are themselves linked to the giants of the food industry, themselves increasingly integrated into the medical-pharmaceutical complexes. The food industry is the leading industrial sector in France with a turnover of nearly 160 billion euros. Supermarkets account for 50% of food sales and up to 90% for certain basic foodstuffs (sugar, pasta, coffee, mineral water, aperitifs, etc.). This commercial structure has a direct influence on household demand by generating new requirements: extended product ranges, emphasis on top-of-the-range products, the disappearance of salespeople: grocers, bakers and very often butchers. Finally, this offer influences the way foodstuffs are classified, making it increasingly difficult to understand them.

---

337. This chapter takes up and extends the analyses proposed in my above-mentioned book *La Fin des mangeurs*.

     A political history of food. From the Pateolithic to our days

The new food classification

Mankind has always felt the need to classify its foods: are they edible or not? Do they taste good or bad? Are they pure or impure according to the religious questioning of Jews or Muslims? Do they correspond to the ordinary or to penance (Lenten oil and bacon on ordinary days) according to the Christian "revolutionary" food model? The French table of the 20th century first took up this old religious taxonomy by making ordinary or festive food its supreme distinction. However, today's eater learns less to symbolically "mark" his food (why eat such and such a dish in such and such a context) than to identify it according to purely financial or even technical criteria. If we no longer know why we eat a log at Christmas, the only way to celebrate is to splurge, to buy expensive products, to eat fresh rather than canned, etc. Professional cooks agree on the existence of five product ranges. This classification refers to functional dimensions that do not convey any conception of the world; with a first range grouping together fresh products, a second for industrial canned food, a third for industrial frozen food, a fourth for raw or cooked products, ready to use, vacuum-packed, dehydrated, freeze-dried or ionized, and the fifth for industrially cooked products... This classification means nothing apart from its own technological problems. It does not open on any sense allowing the consumers to understand their table. It corresponds to the invasion of technical-scientific thinking, first in the professional and then in the collective imagination.

A controlled eater

The 20th century eater is much less dependent on tradition and popular knowledge, but he is at the mercy of industry and subject to contradictory dietary injunctions. He ended up eating what he was told to eat, or even what he was given in a show or in a dream. This eater is also under surveillance: he is examined by sociologists, psychologists, economists, marketers and nutritionists. We are not only facing a formatting of behaviors by new religions, whether it is the one of the diet gurus or the one of the economic market with its places of worship (hypermarkets), its new credo (happiness is consumption), its high priests (economists, marketers and advertisers), its cult objects (department store or cafeteria shelves, shopping carts), its new temporality (with its promotions and sales), its grace actions (fair trade or ethical trade), its excommunications (those excluded from consumption), its heretics (followers of other ways of consuming, AMAP, organic, shared gardens, etc.).

Indeed, the formatting of the palate begins long before that of the mind. The industry has learned, with the techniques of sensory analysis, to classify the gustatory perceptions, in order to better be able to (re) produce them at will and in an increasingly artificial way. Sensory analysis measures the color, smell, aroma, flavor, texture and shape of food. It uses tests standardized at the international level by the AFNOR and the ISO (whose name alone makes one shudder: International Organization for Standardization) which use a technical language designed with the sole aim of objectifying sensations in order to measure them and then reproduce them. This ensures that the sensory profile of a food complies with the test results. We then check that its organoleptic qualities are maintained throughout its life cycle. Standard products are created to serve as organoleptic strains for subsequent production. Biotechnology is used to create "truer" sensations than natural. The strawberry-flavored product ends up surpassing the natural strawberry in organoleptic perfection. The natural product thus risks becoming a derivative of an industrial artifact. The flavor itself appears as an artifice in its own right, developed in isolation and industrially. Taste becomes, thanks to the generalization of enhancers, an industrial element like any other. The 21st century eater has thus entered the era of organoleptic lure. These additives, derived from chemical processes or biotechnologies, fulfill three functions. They dominate nature by preserving foodstuffs from microbial and enzymatic degradation. They overcome time by making the product easier to use, or even available out of season. Finally, they help to overcome monotony by varying the taste, texture and color. How can we not wonder about the consequences of this explosion of additives on taste formation? The (re)colored, (re)flavored, (re)texturized food biases each mental operation of the (young) consumer: will the child lured into learning about food develop in an appropriate way the complex biocultural phenomena that are at the origin of taste and disgust perceptions? Is there not a risk of provoking classificatory disorders that will no longer allow the child to truly live with food, i.e. to understand it? Doesn't this evolution deprive the individual of the true exercise of his ability to judge, since food is designed to directly satisfy the most immediate sensations? One could thus eventually promote a (artificial) food associated with a particular aroma in order to make it benefit from previous positive metabolic experiences. This would be a dangerous drift that would allow us to orient the taste of consumers at will. Why not play on the cerebral mechanisms that control gluttony to direct it towards particularly profitable products?

                    A political history of food. From the Pateolithic to our days

The concept of petro-foods

The vocabulary of agriculture and food is made up of big words that sometimes prevent us from thinking. So-called "sustainable" agriculture at the beginning of the 21st century is a poisonous word that intoxicates thought because it obscures rather than illuminates the major issues of the period. So-called "reasoned" agriculture is in fact only a way to pollute a little less in order to continue to pollute longer. We therefore need our own big words to think about the fundamental characteristics of our food.

This is why we have been able to speak of *junkfood* by analogy with the concept of *junkspace* proposed by urban planners[338]. This notion of *junk food was* invented in 1972 by Michael F. Jacobson, director of the CSPI (Center for Science in the Public Interest), and was initially used to designate a whole series of products responsible for the increase in obesity (hamburgers, pizzas, sweets, potato chips, sodas, etc.). This concept was then extended to products that are not only too high in calories and low in nutrients, but also contribute to the undermining of taste (and therefore the ability to judge). *Junk food* has had its popular version under the name of junk food.

This is why I will also speak of petrofoods by analogy with the notion of petromedicines used internationally by the TRAMIL network, which scientifically studies the contribution of popular medicines, particularly in the West Indies[339]. To speak of petro-foods is to denounce the over-consumption of fertilizers and pesticides (major consumers of oil) and the waste of nitrogenous materials, but above all it is to denounce the fact that, for the first time in the history of humanity, agricultural production and food use more calories than they provide[340]. It now takes about 15 calories to produce a single calorie of food. In England, transporting one lettuce consumes 127 calories for 1 calorie of lettuce; in France, we consume 97 calories of oil for 1 calorie of Chilean asparagus, and 66 calories of gasoline for 1 calorie of African carrot. A bottle of South American wine transported by plane represents 5 kilos of CO_2 more than a local bottle. As for the lamb from New Zealand, it travels 18,000 kilometers, the steak from Argentina 12,000 kilometers and the yogurt pot (through each of its components) 9,115 kilometers. This model of agriculture is therefore

---

338. The concept of *junkspace* was proposed by Rem Koolhass to understand the mutations of the urban system. The architect explains how the model of the shopping mall has progressively devoured the whole city.

339. www.tramil.net/francais/Tramil.html

340. World energy consumption represents 13 million tons of oil equivalent (Mtoe) per year. Oil remains the primary source of energy and represents one third of the world's energy consumption.

---

totally unsustainable in terms of energy. However, everything proves that tomorrow's products, far from being less energy consuming, will be even more so, whether they are GMOs, alicaments, irradiated foods, cloned meat, new "meat" food substitutes or "all biotech".

Agro-extractivism

The concept of extractivism is quite recent but essential in the debates. This is why I had accepted, in 2014, to preface the book *Dette et extractivisme* (Éditions Utopia) by Nicolas Sersiron, president of CADTM-France (Committee for the Cancellation of Third World Debt), as it was the first synthesis in French language on the extractivist model, particularly in the agricultural and food field. This concept of extractivism was first used in South America to denounce the regime of agricultural and industrial monocultures. It was then extended to other activities, notably by the landless peasants of Brazil who opposed the construction of new hydraulic dams, believing that there was already enough energy to satisfy the needs of the population and that those who always wanted more were the large corporations and the enriched minority who lived at the expense of the majority.

This concept of extractivism (and therefore also of antiextractivism) in a way makes something new out of something old, since it recycles what Africans denounced in the early years of decolonization as "white elephants", i.e. pharaonic projects that benefit only a tiny minority. This concept of anti-extractivism has received its European translation with the mobilizations against the GP2I - Grand Useless Imposed Projects - notably in the agricultural domain. Extractivism is thus understood, in a general way, as the plundering of natural, human and financial resources for short-term financial profit[341]. We are justified in speaking of agro-extractivism as soon as the model of subsidized agricultural productivism threatens the food agriculture that still feeds 70% of humans. In 2014, the UNCTAD (United Nations Conference on Trade and Development) issued a warning to governments that if they did not react to provide real protection for small farms, they would be wiped out by future crises. Yet they are the solution to world hunger. The 1993 Alternative Nobel Prize winner, Indian economist Vandana Shiva, has established that productivity is on average two to three times higher, and the FAO estimates that training farmers in agro-ecological techniques would increase their yields by another 79%.

---

341. Anna BEDNIK, *Extractivism. Industrial exploitation of nature: logics, consequences, resistances*, Neuvy-en-Champagne (72240), Éditions Le passager clandestin, 2016.

   A political history of food. From the Pateolithic to our days

Shrimp has become the symbol of agro-extractivism. Its consumption has increased by 300% in ten years in both the United States and Europe, but the trawl fishery for wild shrimp is one of the most wasteful, since it alone results in the discarding of 27% of the by-catch of the entire commercial fishery, i.e. for every ton of shrimp, 4 to 10 tons of unintentional catch (fish, mollusks, crustaceans, small cetaceans, turtles) are discarded at sea.

However, the situation is more general, as the problem of nitrogen proves. The 20th century has certainly revolutionized agriculture by increasing yields, thanks to the massive use of nitrogen, but nitrogen that is not absorbed by crops presents considerable risks since it is diffused in the environment. In Europe, since the beginning of the 1990s, the total consumption of nitrogen fertilizers exceeds that of potash and phosphate combined. The nitrogen contained in commercial mineral fertilizers is particularly soluble in order to facilitate its assimilation by crops, which exposes it to runoff after heavy rainfall and leaching to groundwater. After five years of work, 200 researchers from the European Science Foundation and the European NitroEurope project have estimated the cost of nitrogen at between 70 and 320 billion euros per year (air, water and soil pollution, increased greenhouse gases and impact on ecosystems). The problem of nitrogen is therefore considerable but not unique. Europe has chosen to feed its livestock to the detriment of the food of the populations of the South: it imports each year the equivalent of 15 million hectares of soybeans, manioc, peanuts... Olivier De Schutter estimates that these extractivist policies have already caused the loss of 30 million hectares of cultivated land (the equivalent of Italy) due to environmental degradation and urbanization[342].

The famines of the 21st century

The beginning of the 21st century has thus been marked by the return of major famines, in addition to the 35 million people who die of hunger each year and the nearly 1 billion others who are permanently undernourished. Everyone remembers the food price hike of 2007 and especially, in 2008, the hunger revolts. Economists, such as Aurélie Trouvé, have been able to prove that stock market speculation was to blame, as speculative funds migrated with the financial crisis: they left the financial markets to throw themselves on the agricultural commodities market[343], like locusts

---

342. Figures given by Olivier De Schutter, United Nations Special Rapporteur on the Right to Food, October 21, 2010.
343. Aurélie Trouvé, *Le business est dans le pré. Les dérives de l'agro-industrie*, Paris, Fayard, 2015.

---

on Egypt. The consequences were immediate, with an explosion of prices for the three basic foods that represent 75% of human consumption (corn, wheat, rice). Thus, while climatic hazards were the main cause of famines in the Middle Ages, the cause of today's food shortages is, on the one hand, the stranglehold of multinationals on the world market for seeds, phytosanitary products and foodstuffs (a few firms control most of the trade in bananas, sugar and cereals), and on the other hand, stock market speculation.

The theft of the land

The World Bank estimates that more than 50 million hectares of arable land have been taken over since the beginning of the 21st century by investment funds and multinationals, causing the immediate expulsion and starvation of small farmers. Some have justified this land theft by the low productivity of African agriculture. The great problem of Africa is elsewhere[344]. Africa suffers first of all from a cruel lack of financial resources due to illegitimate debt and the undue enrichment of its leaders: 3.8% of the land is irrigated and there are only 250,000 draught animals and a few thousand tractors... Africa also suffers from the agricultural dumping practiced by the industrial states of the North, since rich countries subsidize their own farmers to the tune of 349 million dollars every year. The World Bank's policy has caused the share of support for agriculture in public spending to fall: for Africa, between 1980 and 2004, from 6.4% to 5%, for Latin America from 14.8% to 7.4%, for Asia from 8% to 2.7%. The theft of agricultural land is therefore a form of absolute extractivism.

The inventions of the Folamour of industrial food

The debate on GMOs and mutagenesis

Five transnational corporations control more than 80% of the world's seed industry. This process of monopolization has been accomplished in two stages: first, as part of the "green revolution," farmers delegated the art of making seeds to professionals, who produced increasingly specialized varieties adapted to industrial standards. At the same time, these new varieties require more inputs (fertilizers and pesticides).

---

344. *Les agricultures africaines, Recherches internationales* magazine, December 2007.

GMOs

The 21st century marks a new stage with the switch to GMOs and the "biotech" era[345]. GMOs arrived in Europe in 1995, just as the WTO agreements were coming into force. This transgenic technique constitutes a real breakthrough since the plant is transformed by integrating bits of DNA from various species (viruses, bacteria, animals, plants): the aim is therefore to free oneself from the reproductive barriers between species in order to create chimeras. For example, a gene for resistance to the cold is taken from a fish from frozen seas to introduce it into a strawberry in order to freeze it more easily for marketing. GMOs are a new step in the appropriation of living organisms through patenting. This technique is particularly developed for basic cereals (corn, soy and rice). Its development has been legitimized by the notion of "genetic progress" (plant improvement). Yields have certainly increased but not to the level announced and with failures. GMOs are pesticide plants since 98% of them concern plants manipulated so that they do not die when sprayed with herbicides. There is also a lot of collateral damage with the contamination of other crops and natural species. Finally, there is the question of the private appropriation of living organisms with the possibility of patenting them. More than 2,000 patents have already been granted by the European Patent Office, to the detriment of farmers' rights to renew their seeds in their own fields. It must be said that the European Commission is very much in favour of GMOs, while two thirds of Europeans are opposed to them... the so-called "terminator" biotechnology, which produced sterile seeds, has certainly been abandoned, but the industry is achieving the same result with the legislation on patents[346].

After GMOs, mutagenesis and cisgenesis

The agri-food industry is also developing other techniques such as mutagenesis, which consists in causing genetic mutations by shocks imposed on seeds or plants, by chemical or radioactive treatments or other aggressions, in order to produce strains resistant to herbicides (this concerns sunflower varieties planted in France). These mutations, because they do not fall within the legal framework of GMOs, are not subject to legislation and control. However, the FAO and the IAEA (International Atomic Energy Agency) list the varieties mutated by mutagenesis on the basis of voluntary declarations and thus already

---

345. Jacques TESTART, *À qui profitent les OGM ?* Paris, "Débats", Éditions du CNRS, 2013.
346. José BOVÉ (WITH the collaboration of Gilles LUNEAU), *Hold-up à Bruxelles, les lobbies au cœur de l'Europe*, Paris, "La Découverte Poche/Essais" (n° 429), La Découverte, 2015.

---

count more than 1,700 species and 3,000 varieties concerned. The associations therefore rightly speak of hidden GMOs and denounce the total lack of transparency.

Another "biotech" with a bright future is cisgenesis, which consists of transferring genes between organisms that could be crossed naturally. The result is cisgenic apples modified so that they do not turn brown when peeled, melons with delayed ripening, fruit trees genetically modified to better resist fire blight, etc. These genetically modified foods by cisgenesis are widely tolerated by the European Food Safety Agency (EFSA), which recommends a reduction in controls on them. The citizens' watchdog association, InfoOGM, has major reservations: "It would be misleading to say that cisgenesis - also called "intragenesis" - is different from trans-genesis in its principle and effects. In fact, as with transgenesis, the gene of interest inserted into cisgenic plants, even from the same species, must have a promoter and a terminator, like any transgene, and must be carried and traced. It therefore contains genetic elements from other species, such as bacterial DNA sequences used as vectors, viral sequences used as promoters, or selection genes (e.g. antibiotic resistance genes). Moreover, the uncertainties related to random insertion of the cisgene, and thus the extinction of native genes or the production of truncated proteins, are the same as those raised with transgenesis"[347].

Medicines, nutricosmetics and cosmeto-food

The food industry is constantly transforming its products to increase their added value and thus maintain its profitability. What better way to do this than to promise that food, far from simply providing the consumer with biological sustenance, will also bring him good health or allow him to increase his seduction thanks to a beautiful skin. Mankind has always wished to make its food its medicine according to the formula of Hippocrates, but the ideology of "perfect health", denounced by Lucien Sfez, reinforces this tendency. It doesn't matter that most medical or cosmetic indications are unfounded because, in this field, only faith saves and allows to reassure the consumer.

We can distinguish between nutraceuticals, which claim to provide good health, and *cosmeto-food* (also called "nutricosmetics"), even if the economic stakes are similar. The market for nutraceuticals is worth 6 billion dollars and that of nutricosmetics, 3 billion. French consumers spend the most per capita on nutricosmetic food supplements, among

---

347. http://www.infogm.org/la-cisgenese-techniquement-aussi-risquee-qu-une-transgenese

                    A political history of food. From the Pateolithic to our days

the 12 countries covered by a recent market study[348]. According to the magazine *Que choisir*[349] , nutricosmetics (or *cosmeto-food*) is the "latest marketing concept invented by the food industry" and "seems to have a bright future in our societies where the cult of appearance is king".

Food irradiation

The irradiation of food (called "ionization") is the very condition of its globalization. This technique is one of the applications of the principle "the atom in the service of peace" presented by President Eisenhower to the General Assembly of the United Nations on 8 December 1953. One can think that at the beginning it was initially a showcase for the nuclear industry aiming at exposing nuclear technologies that could save lives rather than destroy them. This food irradiation program was officially launched in 1961 by three UN agencies: the WHO, the FAO and the IAEA, the latter handling the scientific side of the issue... In 1982, this triumvirate questioned the need to choose a less stigmatizing name: "Any word or statement containing the word 'irradiation' (or 'irradiated') may inspire fear and cause rejection of the product." The delegate added, "We need to talk with experts in advertising and psychology to put consumers at ease and develop a more benign feeling about irradiation"[350]. The term "ionization" was eventually adopted.

Food irradiation is therefore a process used to decontaminate food by destroying microorganisms, slowing down ripening, inhibiting germination and conferring a better preservation. It consists in subjecting the products to a very high energy gamma radiation, directly from the cobalt, or to a very high energy electron beam. This nuclear technology is implemented in state-controlled facilities. Ionization is now presented as the best solution (or the least worst), it would be much better than the use of chemicals whose toxicity is proven, it would be much more flexible than freezing and without the risks associated with breaks in the cold chain, it would be much better than heat treatment which is impossible for some foods. The majors of this sector are American companies like Titan,

---

348. Report *Seaking Beauty Through Nutrition: Opportunities in Oral Beauty Products*, DataMonitor, May 2009.
349. Florence HUMBERT, *Cosmetofood. Fausses promesses*, on: http://www.quechoisir.org/alimentation/produit-alimentaire/actualite-cosmetofood-fausses-promesses, UFC-Que choisir, 29 September 2008.
350. [*L'irradiation des aliments, atôme, malbouffe et mondialisation*, work coordinated by the French Collective against Food Irradiation, preface by Paul Ariès, Villeurbanne, 2008, Éditions Golias, *loc. cit.* p. 25.

Isomedix/STERIS and the International Agency for Industrial Irradiation (now International Association for Irradiation).

The use of this technique has increased significantly since 1999, when the three UN agencies concluded that any food could be irradiated without any danger... Since then, about sixty countries have authorized this practice, initially obviously in the greatest silence. The situation became tense however when North American associations started to inform the public about the risks for the health which the irradiation of food presented, because of the induced losses in vitamins, of the development of the radioresistant bacteria, of the carcinogenesis and mutagenesis, of the risks related to the operation of the classified installations and to the transport of the nuclear materials, of the socio-economic risks, since the irradiation makes even easier the relocations of the sources of provisioning towards countries not very regardful on the social and ecological level.

Opponents won their first victory when the Bush administration sought to mandate the consumption of ionized foods in school cafeterias. Several cities passed ordinances banning the practice, including Los Angeles and Washington. At the same time, the U.S. government established the Framework Equivalency Work Plan (FEWP) to promote bilateral trade in irradiated foods. The first FEWP agreement signed between the United States and Thailand, in 2006, concerned mango, mangosteen, pineapple, rambutan and lychee... The second victory was won in 1988 when the European Commission tried to force the hand of the Parliament and the Council of Ministers, by proposing a draft directive clearly in favor of the development of irradiation... In 1999, a new attempt resulted in a half failure, since an extremely restrictive list was adopted. A third attempt in 2002 could not challenge the *status quo*, even if the States obtained the right to maintain the authorizations prior to 1999.

The French Collective against food irradiation (which federates today about twenty associations) was constituted in 2004 at the initiative of Public Citizen Europe and Food and Water Watch Europe with for objective to obtain the prohibition of food irradiation in France and in the world by application of the precautionary principle. The French situation is indeed worrying with regard to the volumes treated and the foods concerned. In terms of volume, France is the third European country (after Belgium and the Netherlands) with more than 4,000 tons of irradiated food. The decree of August 20, 2002 sets the list of categories of foods for which the treatment by irradiation is authorized: aromatic herbs, spices and condiments, onion, garlic, shallot, dried vegetables and fruits, flasks and germs of cereals for dairy products, rice flour, gum arabic, poultry, frozen frog legs, dried blood and plasma, shrimp, ovalbumin, casein and caseinates.

Nano-foods

Nano-foods concern the application of nanotechnologies to the food sector, one of the four branches of the "NBIC revolution" (nanotechnology, bacteriology, information and cognitive sciences) launched with a great deal of funding by the United States[351]. Our lifestyles and our food supply should be profoundly affected in the coming years. Nanomaterials are tiny particles of the order of one millionth of a millimeter. In agriculture, nano-technologies will be the next step towards the "smallest" (after GMOs and mutagenesis), moving from the manipulation of genes to that of atoms. The agri-food sector is the one in which the most important developments have been announced. The monthly magazine *Les Zindigné(e)s* is an alert thrower thanks to the Association de veille et d'information civique sur les enjeux des nanosciences et des nanotechnologies (AVICENN). Below, I have reproduced most of the information provided by AVICENN[352]. Several estimates of the world market for nanos in food have been made, proposing figures ranging from several hundred million to over 20 billion dollars. In agriculture, the manipulation of atoms makes it possible to reshape the deoxyribonucleic acid of seeds in order to obtain plants with new properties (smell, growth period, yield, etc.). In the food industry, the applications concern both packaging and foodstuffs.

Nano elements in contact with food

Most of the applications of nanotechnologies in the field of food today concern materials in contact with food: packaging, cutting surfaces, kitchen instruments, refrigerator walls, etc. - their purpose is to : to reinforce the solidity, rigidity and resistance to degradation of these mate-rials (titanium nano nitride to prevent scratches on plastic packaging); to increase their transparency; to allow a better preservation of food by protecting food or drinks against UV rays (titanium oxide (TiO2) nano-particles in plastic packaging, zinc oxide nanoparticles) ; to suppress the loss of flavors (titanium oxide nanoparticles in plastic bottles for beers in the United States, titanium nitride nanoparticles in PET (polyethylene terephthalate) packaging authorized in Europe); to regulate humidity and

---

351. Paul Ariès, *La simplicité volontaire contre le mythe de l'abondance*, Paris, La Découverte Poche/Essais (n° 350), La Découverte, 2007.
352. Association AVICENN, *Nanomaterials and risks to health and the environment*, Gap, Éditions Yves Michel, 2016.

---

oxygen (aluminum or aluminum oxide nanolayers used for chocolate bar packaging); to fight microbes, bacteria or fungi (nano zinc oxide (ZnO), nano titanium dioxide and nano silver found on the inner walls of some refrigerators, on cutting boards, on containers for food preservation : food trays, transparent films, etc.).

The AVICENN specifies that the fears relate to the possibility that nanomaterials migrate from packaging (or surface coatings of cooking instruments) to food: "The modalities of this transfer and the risks they could entail are still largely unknown and very variable because many factors are involved (temperature, duration of packaging, nature of the packaged food: liquid or solid, etc.)".

Nano elements in food

Nanomaterials can also be directly integrated in foodstuffs. AVICENN reminds that some applications are presented as innovative solutions to nutritional and/or sanitary problems (such as the reduction of fat, salt, calories or emulsifiers content in foods) or allowing a better assimilation of nutrients and food supplements. Other nanoelements are also used to modify the aromas, flavors, colors and textures of certain foods (nanoparticles of titanium dioxide are used as white pigment to make foods whiter or to decline a palette of colors by being associated with other food coloring), on the icing of pastries, for example. AVICENN adds that nanoparticles, especially nanosilicas, are added in some food products (frozen meals, ice cream, sauces for lasagna, instant noodles, various seasonings for ground meat and burrito, pancake, cream, roasted vegetables, etc.) in order to make their texture more homogeneous, smoother. The AVICENN also lists the research done to diffuse flavors, by progressive opening of nanocapsules - cocoa nanoaggregates would allow to increase the chocolate aroma thanks to the increase of the surface that comes in contact with the taste buds. Other nanoelements allow an extension of the shelf life of flavors (or set of sensations perceived from the mouth: tastes, smells...) through the integration of nanocapsules that gradually release preservative substances in foods: lemonades, fruit juices, cheeses, margarine, chewing gums, candies, chocolate bars, etc.) Platinum nanoparticles are also used to break down ethylene and slow down the ripening of fruits and vegetables, and a nano-silver coating is added to cut fruits to extend their shelf life... The ultimate goal is also to create "intelligent" foods that interact with the consumer to "personalize" foods, change the color, taste or nutrients on demand...

France is a leader in this field and does not want to lose this advantage. For example, the French National Research Agency has included in its call for "P2N" projects (i.e. nanotechnologies and nanosystems) a request to support research on "the protection and delivery of essential micronutrients through nanostructured foods", or on "new food additives or supplements in nanometric form". The members of the European Parliament debated, during the session of 23 to 26 April 2009, the potential dangers of nanofoods and asked for a risk assessment, thus opposing the positions of the Commission, which wanted to adopt a threshold of 50% of nanoparticles in a product to be called a nanofood. The European Parliament therefore rejected any idea of relaxing the labelling of foods modified with nanotechnology.

Cloned meat

Cloning techniques have existed since the early 1950s, but the cloning of Dolly the sheep in 1996 opened the debate on the consumption of cloned meat. Other animals soon followed: cows, pigs, cattle, rabbits, mares, etc. A step forward was taken at the end of the 20th century with so-called "second generation" cloning, which consists of cloning a clone, i.e. obtaining cloned organisms from other cloned organisms. The commercial exploitation of cloned meat is so far of no interest: firstly because only 5 to 10% of the eggs produced and reimplanted produce viable and healthy clones, secondly because the cloning of males is much more uncertain than that of females, and thirdly because the cost of a cloned animal remains prohibitive, except as a breeder. Europe does not believe in the feasibility of this technique, which is why legislation has been adopted prohibiting the cloning of animals for breeding and food purposes in the European Union, but also the importation into Europe of their descendants and of products derived from them (meat, milk, reproductive material, etc.). The European Commission, which had only proposed to ban animal cloning in Europe, but without banning the sale of meat or milk from their descendants, nor without ensuring the traceability of these products, followed suit. Europe seems to have listened to Europeans since, according to a 2008 survey, 58% of them say they are opposed to cloning for food production, for reasons related to animal welfare or for ethical issues, and 83% want meat and milk from the offspring of clones to be labelled as such. This refusal of cloned meat can thus be understood as a limit to the artificialization of meat, unless, for the same reasons invoked against cloning, notably animal welfare, the European Union continues to support totally artificial meat projects...

Agriculture without livestock

The great danger of the 21st century is the invention of an agriculture without livestock with the industrial development of substitutes for animal production (which is covered by the notion of "biotech" livestock). Thanks to the work of Jocelyne Porcher, a sociologist at INRA, the monthly magazine *Les Zindigné(e)s* has initiated a reflection on the end of livestock farming as a common good of humanity[353]. Since the beginning of the 21st century, there have been countless investments and patents filed to produce meat by cultivating chicken, beef or pig muscle cells in the laboratory, as is already done to produce beer or yoghurt. The promoters of this farming without breeding certainly do not lack arguments: to eliminate animal suffering, to reduce CO_2 emissions due to a meat diet, to provide the means to feed 10 billion humans by giving them the possibility to eat (fake) meat...

The promoters of this farming without breeding are recruited within the largest firms. The Bill Gates Foundation supports Beyond Meat and Hampton Greek Foods (Beyond Eggs), which offer ersatz chicken without chicken, beef without beef and eggs that are not eggs. The firm Cargill has patented a cheese substitute essentially composed of starch. A mayonnaise made without any eggs is also marketed. In 2011 and 2012, researchers announced that they had succeeded in making artificial meat from embryonic turkey stem cells and shellfish carapaces cut into microbeads, then from bovine stem cells cultivated for six weeks before adding breadcrumbs, salt, egg powder as well as beet juice and saffron to give a red color to the whole, all for a cost of... 250,000 euros (!) paid for by the co-founder of Google, Sergey Brin. In 2013, the first artificial burger entirely produced in a test tube from beef muscle stem cells was made by a Dutch laboratory for 290 000 euros (!!).

The big winners of this farming without breeding are first of all the soya producers. The first artificial meats could be introduced on the market in the form of carpaccio before "real fake" pieces produced *in vitro are* marketed in ten years. However, this solution, presented as miraculous, does raise some doubts: mass production of artificial meat would entail exorbitant costs and would require huge quantities of hormones to promote growth and antibiotics to avoid contamination. Jean-François Hocquette, director of research at INRA, reminds us that it is not "a real meat, a piece of striated, contractile red muscle. We are dealing with a simple cluster of

---

353. Jocelyne PORCHER, *Living with Animals. Une utopie pour le XXIe siècle*, Paris, "La Découverte Poche/Sciences humaines et sociales" (n° 401), La Découverte, Paris, 2014.

muscle fibers, but not meat, since the nerves, blood vessels and fat islands are missing", this fat being essential for the organoleptic qualities (taste) of the meat. The ecological argument is also questionable because "the 70% of agricultural land used for livestock (meat, but also dairy) does not correspond to the reality of average farms in Europe committed to ecological practices (grazing), unlike North American *"feedlot"* farming (where cattle do not graze grass but are fed at the trough), or that of South America where deforestation is practiced to practice extensive livestock farming. Jocelyne Porcher adds that imagining an agriculture without breeding is by nature anti-ecological. The researcher therefore puts forward the idea of creating new relationships with farm animals based on the logic of giving (good care) and receiving (meat). I would add that the most viable ecological solution is still to reduce our consumption of meat[354]. Livestock breeding is already an obsolete activity, but tomorrow it will be the whole of agriculture, since thanks to "biotech" we are being offered the possibility of inventing foodstuffs that have no link with the earth. Animal husbandry and agriculture would become niche activities for wealthy consumers...

Food without agriculture

The formula of Henri Mendras (1927-2003) predicting in 1967 *the end of the peasants* has struck the imagination, but it was often misunderstood. The sociologist predicted in fact the disappearance of the peasant civilization and its replacement by a technical civilization, he announced the end of the state of peasant and the emergence of the profession of farmer (of agricultural operator). Daniel Tacet, in his book *Un monde sans paysans*, confirms Mendras' analysis: 50 million peasants are disappearing every year... Thus, in France, we are witnessing an accentuation of the phenomenon of land concentration, since 50% of cultivated land is now in the hands of slightly less than 10% of farmers. The causes of this evolution are well known: the choice of a productivist agricultural model requiring considerable investments, the increase in the price of land (more than 5% per year on average), the consequences of the CAP (Common Agricultural Policy of the European Union) which grants 84% of aid to only 20% of farms.

This phenomenon of concentration and industrialization logically leads to the creation of giant farms, including the emblematic and caricatured "1,000-cow farm" - some thirty projects are currently being studied in

---

354. Catherine Thoyer, *Le Yin & le Yang*, with contributions from Jocelyne Porcher and photographs by Philippe Busset, "Des choses à dire", Montvicq (03170), Éditions du miroir, 2015.

France - but the situation is often worse elsewhere: the company El Tejar cultivates one million hectares in Brazil. This phenomenon of concentration and industrialization should therefore continue, but above all take on a new meaning with the rise of food biotechnologies... The "biotech" approach undermines the traditional link between land and agriculture (soil-less agriculture), and may even *ultimately call into* question the link between food and agriculture. The industry dreams of instrumentalizing the old ecological dream of the farm in the city, just as it already instrumentalizes the animal cause (animal welfare, including its vegan version). These biotechnologies do not only concern seeds but also the type of agriculture, with the rise of various forms of soil-less agriculture such as hydroponics, a plant culture carried out on a neutral and inert substrate (such as sand, clay balls, rock wool) irrigated by a stream of industrial solution providing the mineral salts and nutrients necessary for the plant; aeroponics, which replaces the inert substrate with a nutrient mist obtained by fogging with a nutrient solution and which should become widespread for potatoes; aquaculture, in which the roots are soaked in a modified water solution.

These techniques increase yields by, for example, modifying the nycthemeral rhythm (succession of day and night) in order to trick the plants into producing several harvests per year. These techniques are perfectly adapted to the realization of so-called "vertical farms" (or "vertical agriculture") which would cultivate food products in high-rise buildings (skyscrapers dedicated to agriculture). Dick Despommier, a pioneer in this field, proposed in 1999 a 30-story urban farm project capable of feeding 10,000 people. The first projects concern Singapore, China, Korea, Dubai, Abu Dhabi, the United States, Denmark... Capitalist groups put forward convenient arguments: only these vertical farms would be capable of feeding the planet in the 21st century, they would preserve land for other activities, they would develop organic and local food that would no longer be a niche for the wealthy population alone, etc. The choice is therefore between feeding the planet with a few hundred thousand agronomists of this type or with one and a half billion small farmers defending the principle of food sovereignty[355].

The principle of food sovereignty
Pascal Lamy, then Director General of the WTO, declared in the newspaper *Libération* on September 20, 2010 that human food can only

---

355. Gaspard d'ALLENS and Lucile LECLAIR, *Les néo-paysans*, Paris, "Reporterre", Éditions du Seuil, 2016.

 A political history of food. From the Pateolithic to our days

be ensured by the globalization of trade and that food sovereignty is an illusion; in short, according to him, the solution would be on the side of the defense of agro-industry, the reduction of cultivated diversity and the stigmatization of *locavores* who militate for the relocalization of agriculture and food. The international association MINGA immediately reacted by constructing *Responses to the WTO in the* form of a manifesto book, *Only Cultivated Diversity Can Feed the World* (with the participation of Stéphane Hessel, Edgar Pisani, former Minister of Agriculture, Vandana Shiva and some thirty other international contributors, including myself with a contribution on "Food and Ecology"[356]. The principle of "food sovereignty", introduced by the international peasant network Via Campesina at the 1996 World Food Summit, forms the backbone of this response to the WTO[357]. This principle has many concrete applications in terms of the effective recognition of the right to food, such as the right to produce one's own seeds (which presupposes the revival of peasant seeds and the questioning of mandatory registration in the seed inventory), the development of AMAPs (Associations for the Maintenance of Peasant Agriculture), the creation of municipal agricultural boards to supply school catering with "local organic" products (as in Mouans-Sartoux, in the Alpes-Maritimes region of France), etc. The objective of the principle of food sovereignty is to "guarantee in international law the possibility of implementing agricultural and food policies that are best suited to the population, with the possibility of border protection and without negative impacts on the populations of other countries.

The debate on farmers' seeds

The imposition of transgenic plants at the end of the 20th century, as the only horizon for tomorrow's crops, has made us fully aware of the major current issues[358]. We will not be able to feed the planet and succeed in the ecological transition with non-reproducible seeds. Also, after half a century of monopoly of industrial seeds linked to hyperproductivist agriculture, more than 80 organizations have joined the "farmers' seed network" which serves as the backbone of what constitutes a real social movement. The idea of a network of peasant seed producers, that is to say

---

356. [COLLECTIVE], *Only cultivated diversity can feed the world. Answers to the WTO*, Paris, Éditions du Linteau, 2011.
357. Alexandra STRICKNER, Gérard CHOPLIN and Aurélie TROUVÉ, *Souveraineté alimentaire… Que fait l'Europe?* Paris, Éditions Syllepse, 2009.
358. Robert Ali BRAC DE LA PERRIÈRE, *Peasant Seeds, Plants of Tomorrow*, Paris, "Dossier pour un débat", Éditions Charles Léopold Mayer, 2014.

a more autonomous mode of agriculture, both ecological and peasant, is based on the right of local communities and peoples to feed themselves with their own culturally adapted products, according to the principle of food sovereignty. The Peasant Seed Network promotes horizontal peer-to-peer exchanges (with the creation of exchange exchanges and Peasant Seed Houses).

These experiences lead to the differentiation of three types of seeds with their characteristics: industrial seeds, produced either from classical selection or from F1 hybrids, GMOs or mutated plants, which are perfectly standardized; farm seeds, which are seeds harvested from industrial seeds but multiplied by the farmer (cf. the National Coordination for the Defense of Farm Seeds); farmers' seeds, selected and reproduced by farmers directly in their fields, which are neither standardized nor stabilized because they are the result of non-transgressive natural selection methods and because they are adapted to the diversity and variability of terroirs, climates, farming practices and human needs However, in order to be marketable, all seeds must be registered in the "Official Catalogue of Varieties", which has existed since the beginning of the 20th century, but whose spirit the seed industry has managed to transform thanks to the decree of May 18, 1981, since it is no longer so much a question of fighting against the risks of fraud as of defending a certain conception of agriculture based on completely standardized and stabilized seeds. While all European countries, and many others in the world, have such catalogs, only France has chosen to use them as an instrument to fight against genetic diversity. Consequences: the conditions of compulsory registration are contrary to the nature of farmers' seeds, without even mentioning the question of cost (for a cereal variety: more than 6,000 euros, to which must be added more than 2,000 euros for the first ten years). The "Official Catalogue of Varieties" has thus become not only harmful to small farmers but also to the defense of cultivated biodiversity. The association Kokopelli talks about it as an "agricultural nuisance". The debate is therefore open and the question is whether the quality of botanical varieties and plants depends on the stability of varietal characteristics, and therefore on their level of standardization, or, on the contrary, on their adaptability to changing biotopes and contexts - which leads to a lesser degree of fixity of the characteristics of the variety in favor of a greater diversity. Will we not need a very flexible gene pool with climate change?

The revolution in the relationship with food

The revolution in the content of the plate too often masks a second revolution, just as important but unnoticed, a sign that we consider this evolution as normal. This second revolution concerns the relationship to food: how do we eat? This essential dimension explains why the poorest regions often produce the tastiest cuisines because they compensate for their initial handicap by the richness of their elaboration. However, the 21st century eater consumes more and more anything, anytime, anywhere, and in any way, reintroducing bodily manifestations that were previously censored, such as eating standing up, eating with one's hands, eating in disorder, making noise, stuffing oneself, etc. We could rejoice in this freedom that would finally allow us to eat without taboos, with anyone and for any reason. Unless, of course, this deculturation, desymbolization and de-ritualization of the table, ends up being perverted into anomie, that is to say, into the absence of norms allowing everyone to regulate their behavior.

If the key words concerning the evolution of the content of the plate are artificialization and denaturation, those concerning the relationship with food are destructuration and desymbolization. It is true that France is doing less badly than its Anglo-Saxon neighbors, but how can we maintain in 2012, as Céline Laisney does, that the French model is not (yet) threatened? We will see that everything depends on the questions we ask and that the changes underway do not only concern statistical measures, as important as they are: "In a very stable way since 1988, 8 households out of 10 still eat the same menu at dinner. Similarly, 57% of French people are busy eating at 12:30 p.m. compared to 38% of Belgians, 20% of Germans and 14% of British people. Non-meal consumption is half as important in France as in the United States (10% of daily energy intake versus 22%). Moreover, conviviality still plays an important role in the French food model: for 67% of households, getting together is the most important element during lunch at home. The international team led by Claude Fischler and Estelle Masson has worked on the issue of cultural differences and has shown that the French recognize themselves more in the portraits of the 'convivial eater' and the 'gourmet gourmand', contrary to the British and the Americans who lean towards the 'rational eater'"[359].

The Centre de recherche pour l'étude et l'observation des conditions de vie (CRÉDOC) published a comparative study in 2012 between the diets of the French and North Americans. Its conclusions are much less

---

359. Céline LAISNEY, *L'évolution de l'alimentation en France, op. cit.*

positive. It shows that while Americans eat more sugary overall, the intake of saturated fatty acids and cholesterol is higher in the French because of deli meats and cheese, and that the situation of young French people is worse than that of young Americans: young people aged 21 to 34 in France eat worse than Americans of the same age, multiplying sandwiches without consuming much fruit and vegetables. The study also reveals a sharp decline in diversity between 2007 and 2010 for those under 14 years old. Caloric intake has thus become identical in France and in the United States and the only thing that still explains why we suffer less from obesity is a better respect of chronobiology, a diet that remains more structured around daily meals.

Our model is therefore in danger, even if we can still rely on a few characteristics of the French diet, products of our history: three main meals a day; meals taken at relatively fixed times and common to all; a relatively high preparation time and duration of meals; a meal structured by two or three components taken in order; a great importance given to the taste of food, a know-how transmitted by experience[360].

Thus, we can argue that the eater of the beginning of the 21st century is at the crossroads, still between two tables, but, undoubtedly, he is becoming more and more solitary and falsely cosmopolitan, his table no longer really speaks to him; faced with a profusion of interchangeable dishes, the eater of today falls into indifference and sinks into apathy.

A table without a cook

The 21st century eater will do less and less cooking, just as his ancestors did in the 20th century with self-production, with the exception of DIY (vegetable gardening, sewing, knitting, etc.). Architects are even designing apartments without a "kitchenette", but for different reasons than the young Russia of the Soviets, which thought it possible to collectivize everything that contributed to the alienation of women (cleaning, childcare and education, cooking). The divorce between the cook and the eater is realized this time in favor of a new alliance between, on the one hand, the eater metamorphosed into a simple consumer and, on the other hand, the food products that have become, despite protests, commodities like any other.

The 20th century has seen the birth of the figure of the consumer in place of the ancestral figure of the eater. Consumption is not only another more modern way of qualifying uses. One is not born a consumer, and

---

360. *Id., ibid.*

   A political history of food. From the Pateolithic to our days

all historians recognize that it takes two generations to transform users who are masters of their uses into consumers. The consumer society is not first of all a society where one consumes more than in another, it does not come above all to fill a void, to satisfy a lack, it rests on the break-up of the popular traditional cultures, on the disappearance of the other ways of living, thinking and dreaming. This explains the strength of resistance, whether individual or collective, and why there are still regional, cultural and not only social specificities.

The current metamorphosis of the table is inseparable from the invention of new technologies that undermine the traditional relationship between cook and eater (even within families). This couple is experiencing a lasting crisis that could well lead to a divorce. The success of reality TV shows featuring amateur and professional cooks, as well as cooking classes given by professionals to amateurs trying to master a few dishes, are only derisory compensations in the face of these developments. The industry also relieves the consumer of his guilt by letting him finalize the industrial product: it is up to the consumer to pour on what he is about to eat the bag of spices, or the small bag of sauce, graciously provided with his vacuum-packed package or to heat it up in the microwave.

The assembly kitchen

The future of the cook (amateur or professional) is closely linked to the success of the food industry and in particular to the development of biotechnologies for production and preservation. In the 20th century, cooking has undergone a triple evolution with the emergence of semi-finished products, frozen foods and vacuum-packed foods. These new technologies have created a so-called "assembly" cuisine, a step towards the forthcoming generalization of totally ready-to-eat products. This assembly kitchen is already evolving towards a so-called "terminal" kitchen where it is sufficient to reheat industrially designed and manufactured dishes. This assembly kitchen does not simply undermine professional know-how, but the very meaning of what used to be cooking. It is now enough to assemble culinary bases that are cooked separately and then put together on the plate. The change in the professional vocabulary of the kitchen testifies to this profound mutation: whereas in the past we used the musical repertoire, we spoke of the chef, the piano (stove), scales, we said that we were adding a note (flavor), that we were composing a menu, etc., today we use the industrial repertoire (we never assembled a symphony, we compose it...) by speaking of cost calculation, efficiency, technical sheets, final cooking, etc. Moreover, this industrial cooking alters certain nutritional and organoleptic characteristics of the foodstuffs: one does not work in the same way with products that have undergone transformations of varying nature and intensity such as dehydration, freezing, inerting, etc. This sum of innovations initially included relatively few revolutionary products. This is why it went unnoticed for a long time before GMOs, nutraceuticals and other nano-foods. These new products were simple additions helping the cook in certain delicate phases of his work: the fifteen or so ingredients formerly necessary to make a bone-based sauce base in twenty-four hours have been replaced by an equivalent industrial product, directly usable and presenting no microbiological risk.

The serving methods themselves have been revolutionized to respond to this evolution. The placement of the guests, the order of the cutlery and glasses speak much less to the eaters. The generalization of service by the plate is not a new language that means anything, but simply a good way to reduce costs, to hire less qualified and therefore less paid staff, who no longer know how to cut up food in the dining room but who know how to carry a plate and lift a bell. The adoption of verrines is in the same vein, since it reduces the cost of materials even more by using waste products that were previously wasted.

Abundance versus choice

The food industry offers long ranges of deceptively diverse products. Supermarkets sell hundreds of different dairy products but only offer a few standard varieties of fruit, vegetables or legumes. The foodstuff thus disappears in its commercial form and is increasingly euphemisized: we eat salad, cheese, meat, but without being able to name the varieties, whereas we can name dozens of brands of food products or exotic dishes. This tendency must be taken very seriously because it leads to the reduction of the commodity to a material. This ephemeralization is also an industrial response to the transformation of the phenomena of taste and disgust as proven by fish marketed in an artificial form (sticks...) or meat accepted only if it has lost its exudates, its sinews, its apparent fat... The low cuts, which for a long time constituted a summit of the food, have almost totally disappeared from our plates: nipples (cow's udders), fat-double (yet essential to a good sapper's apron), brains..., as well as the butcher's cuts: pear (of beef), whiting (of beef), spider (of beef), mouse (of lamb)...

The food diversity that the industry offers us is largely only formal, it is therefore that of a false choice. In cafeterias (commercial or social catering), the customer has indeed the choice between several starters, several dishes, several desserts but, every day, he has the choice between the

A political history of food. From the Pateolithic to our days

same products, contrary to the forms of catering served at the table with a fixed menu... The majority of the children regularly eat only some basic foodstuffs (pasta, French fries, delicatessen...) Paradoxically, the large-scale distribution of food has led to great poverty. How many varieties of beans? How many types of cabbage or potatoes? Diversification is only reintroduced for commercial purposes, so bread has diversified in order not to disappear completely from our tables. This is why the bread menu is enriched as its consumption declines (Parisian bread, sandwich bread, country bread, rye bread, bran bread, wholemeal bread, nut bread, seaweed bread, cereal bread, onion bread, milk bread, raisin bread, sprout bread, cumin bread, poppy bread...). This modern bread has even regained some market shares by diverting an old technical constraint to appear (falsely) traditional: the flouring of the dough pieces has nowadays for only reason to be to give to bread a rustic aspect.

New relationships with time
In the past, cooking had multiple relationships with time: time of the seasons, time of choice, time of provisioning, time of preparation, time of consumption... Canned food has thus passed, from the 19th to the 21st century, from necessity to pleasure. While humanity had always had to store food to make the transition between two harvests, it has largely emancipated itself from time because of the artificialization of food products. The United Nations deplores the fact that the level of world food stocks is at its lowest. Modern methods of preservation certainly modify the organoleptic characteristics of foodstuffs much less, but the old techniques also had the advantage of creating new products: cold cuts, smoked fish, cod or salted bacon, sauerkraut, etc. The 20th century has led not only to an acceleration but also to a denaturation of time, with the primacy of short times over long times, of fast times over slow times, of long conservation, and even of deseasonalization, brought about by the new technologies. Food, as much on the side of the cook as on the side of the eater, is subjected to a constraint of instantaneousness, as witnessed by take-away, delivered, automatic and industrial restaurants.

Assembly cooking does not innovate by combining distinct elements, but by allowing them to be blended without any time constraint. It thus eliminates the time needed to achieve a progressive harmonization of the ingredients (one of the secrets of good cooking): a puree and a sauce base can now be prepared in a few seconds... Fast food (and why not fast love?) is an emblematic figure in this respect, since cooking times are fixed internationally and imposed electronically so that no one commits the heresy of substituting the eye of the cook for the precision of the clock. In the face of "nefarious food", the *Slow Food* movement was invented in Italy[361]...

The time of the eater is also changing, even if France is still an exception. The man who used to eat according to the sun has now moved on to eating at fixed times, independently of the rhythm of the seasons, but according to work schedules and television programs. This evolution concerns the time of the meal, its duration and its order. The eater consumes his food more and more at any time, but also in any order, respecting neither the specific time of the meal nor that of each food. In cafeterias, people eat their (still) hot dish before consuming their starter. This destructuring of the food temporality favors the "papillonnage", i.e. the multiplication of food intake (an average of 20 intakes per day in the United States). We end up not taking the time to eat, but we eat (and drink) constantly.

This destructuring of meal times has allowed for the development of eating patterns. Food fashions have always existed, but in a marginal and non-structural way. Today, the market and technology, after having abolished the natural rhythm of the seasons and of foodstuffs, impose their own rhythms as a new temporality, for example, that of the March beer, once a real technological necessity and today a banal marketing issue, or that of McDonald's, which only markets McTimber, McFarmer and McRancher at certain times of the year... thus creating false situations of scarcity and seasonality! Food is more willing to submit to the dictates of fashion because it must constantly renew itself to satisfy a demand for change that nature seems to leave unsatisfied. While he loses the pleasure of (re)discovering each season the first strawberry or the new potato, the 21st century eater is ecstatic about the latest artificial flavouring of a yoghurt or the latest technological innovation concerning the opening of a carton of milk! Food is also becoming more and more ephemeral as a result of dietary trends (with or without sugar, with or without bifidus, good or bad cholesterol, etc.) or technological trends (the pack, the carton, etc.). The so-called "themed" restaurant industry is chaining themes together at a frenetic pace, deceptively Japanese at noon, Tex-Mex in the evening, reducing exoticism to beautiful colors and powerful spices.

---

361. Carlo PETRINI, *Slow Food, manifesto for taste and biodiversity. La malbouffe ne passera pas*, Gap, Éditions Yves Michel, 2015; *id., Good, clean and fair. Éthique de la gastronomie et sauvegarde alimentaire*, Gap, Éditions Yves Michel, 2006; *id., Terra Madre. Renouer avec les chaînes vertueuses de l'alimentation*, Paris, "manifestô", Éditions Alternatives, 2011.

A political history of food. From the Pateolithic to our days

The food consumer of the 20th and 21st centuries is an exception to the long history of mankind, which firmly forbade eating alone, since it represented a transgression of our political, social and, therefore, moral dimension.

The system had to impose this reform, as shown by the popular resistance to the generalization of the continuous day, to the distance from the workplace and the family home, but also the invention of various forms of collective catering, including the famous canteen. Since man is what he eats, eating alone is therefore "eating solitude".

We know the harm in terms of acceleration of meal time, of less attention paid to what we eat and how we eat it (by actually sitting at the table), in terms of malnutrition, especially for the surviving spouse in elderly couples... Eating alone does not only have biological effects, but changes the very conception of the table by reinforcing the nutritional dimension to the detriment of other social functions, such as conviviality, among others. The person who eats alone fills up on nutrients, he eats mainly to feed himself.

This solitude contributes to the trivialization of food and, at best, to food fetishism, as if the essential was the content of the plate and not everything that is built around it. The shared meal certainly retains its place as the family's common place par excellence, but breakfast is systematically split up (in the time of the snack and in its composition), lunch is only exceptionally shared and dinner is only collective for one household out of two.

Joint eating does not necessarily mean that it is shared: families play "open fridge" and in restaurants everyone orders according to their own taste. As a result, there are fewer and fewer dishes for several people in restaurants and the unfortunate habit of not serving all the guests at the same time. We are definitely no longer in the era when lovers chose two different pizzas to exchange their promise of love with their half share. Eating alone is no longer experienced as a transgression (which could be pleasant at the time), like eating exceptionally from the pan or from the wrapping paper... The last bastions of shared social catering are giving way with the generalization of cafeterias and vending machines and with the great return of the lunchbox for employees. This evolution is facilitated by the invention of service products in individual portions. People meet up from time to time for a big meal, but everyone knows that real life is elsewhere.

The falsely cosmopolitan eater

The man of the end of the 20th century and the beginning of the 21st century would certainly eat in an unstructured way, but, in spite of everything, he would have more access to the cuisine of others. To believe this is to confuse what is a real discovery with a missed encounter! Eating Chinese food is not primarily about eating rice with chopsticks, but about understanding that each food means something in itself, depending on how it is prepared. For example, for a romantic meal, you should prefer dishes with rounded shapes because the sphere is the symbol of love, and for a birthday meal, elongated dishes as a promise of longevity. Eating Japanese means eating fresh food, not industrial sushi. Eating Indian food means knowing who prepared the meal according to their caste. Modernity has created a kind of food Esperanto for a humanity that no longer really knows what eating means and is content to reduce the cuisine of others to a sign. This shrinking of the world is already being cooked in the kitchens of the big food groups. This globalization of food presents two equally insipid faces. From Paris to Beijing, consumers are already accessing a new cuisine that is considered global. Certain dishes are being globalized, just as the dark suits of the leaders are being globalized. Certain drinks are globalized, just as the furniture in the rooms of international hotels is globalized, and apparently even the way people kiss, wax and make love... I have already shown that this globalization has a double logic, that of the lowest common denominator, but also that of the imperialism of certain Western codes. We also globalize certain dishes that are presented as typical or as born from the mixing of cultures, while we generally retain only a sign that we make work instead of the whole... This food globalization is based on a real folklorization of the table. How can you can a couscous, for example, without producing anything other than the original dish? The "fast-couscous" thus makes fun of the particularities of the indigenous couscous (with or without meat, eaten as a dish or as a dessert, sweet or salty, with honey or with grapes, etc.). It does not mention the way of eating (with the fingers but not in any way) and the social significance of this dish, in order to keep only a cheap exoticism. We already know that the condition of the globalization of pizza was its cultural impoverishment by the deprivation of what was (too) typical, the fresh garlic and basil, the fruity olive oil...

Let us not delude ourselves, this culinary impoverishment is indeed the condition of its globalization. We can dare to make a comparison with the globalization of the djembe (a real musical instrument of the Malinke people that allows them to play several hundred rhythms and

     A political history of food. From the Pateolithic to our days

even polyrhythms). The djembe has become a kind of binary tom-tom, marking the supremacy of rhythm over melody. Rhythm is the closest thing to the biological body (common to everyone) while melodic variations depend on cultural areas and long learning. Chinese opera, real flamenco, Breton chouchen, Alsatian white sausage (*brotwurscht*) are all earned. Fast food (of which McDonald's remains the paragon) allows us to understand the issues. This food is not a subculture but an infraculture insofar as the product is designed to target the basic organoleptic sensations (sweet, salty, crunchy, soft) and thus satisfy the greatest number of diners. This is why I said in 1997 in *Les Fils de McDo* that McDonald's did not taste bad in the mouth but in the head, because it is a food that prevents one from growing up, by satisfying the reptilian palate (as one could sometimes speak of a reptilian brain). This is why McDonald's is not the example of North American food, since its conception breaks with the traditions of the different cultures that make up the melting pot. If Portugal had been the most advanced country in globalization, McDonald's would have been Portuguese. The BigMac is the emblem of a culture that no longer really knows what eating means. Its "secret" is to have emptied each of its ingredients of its main characteristics: meat is no longer really meat because it is minced, overcooked, and has lost its resistance and exudates; bread is no longer really bread because of its consistency and the absence of crumbs; cheese and salad are reduced to an essentially decorative function... This is why we can legitimately draw a comparison with the candy stage: we know that sugar being immediately pleasant, we please a European, African, Asian, American child, but without forgetting that there are more refined gastronomic pleasures, therefore more educated.

This cosmopolitanism, which is at first only a subculture, ends up replacing the real kitchens. Here we are close to the theses developed by Umberto Eco in *The War of the False*. This blurring of reference points may become strong enough today for the 21st century eater to choose to eat the cuisine of his terroir in the same way that he eats that of his past, but also that of other cultures or imaginary tables, such as that of Venus or Mars. The cuisine of the terroir (currently in vogue) thus constitutes a true exoticism of the interior which also proceeds from the folklorization of the regional cultures and the local products. We see the emergence of falsely typical cuisines, just as falsely artisanal products are made, seeking the effect of reality instead of reality (Bonne Maman jam, Grand'Mère coffee). We invent biolegends (George Killian, Comtesse du Barry...) or a homeland (Cantalou). Saint-Moret evokes a charming little village, whereas its name was simply invented to give this product, launched in 1981, the image of a quiet village, which is good for France with its bell tower, intended to reassure buyers of its quality. When necessary, the dish is made rudimentary in the manner of "old-fashioned patinated" furniture. Ranges are launched for ugly fruits labeled "gueules cassées" (broken mouths), after having managed to market perfectly homogeneous products without any typicality. Without doubt, the 21st century eater eats (almost) everything, but he no longer digests anything, because he no longer has any reference points, if not a blurred one. The culinary adventure presupposes the maintenance of one's own culture, or at least of some rudiments.

The biologization of the eater
Mankind has always known that it had to account for its table both socially, and culturally, and economically, and religiously, and politically and, of course, already nutritionally and medically. However, the 20th century has undoubtedly given birth to a strong tendency towards the biologization of food. This biologization follows two main paths. The first one consists in making food a biological material that can be manipulated at will because it is devoid of any other intrinsic meaning. Man eats to fill his stomach and if he is opposed to GMOs, it is for health reasons. Raw material prevails over culture and pleasure, justifying the generalization of appetite suppressants. The other way consists in overloading food with nutritional or medical potentialities, to the point of making it a means of shaping man, i.e. denying his biological fatality. This falsely modern evolution is based on traditional representations. Among certain primitive peoples, warriors had to abstain from eating hare for fear of becoming fearful, women had to avoid pork in order to preserve the beauty of their offspring. In the 20th century, red meat was supposed to give strength. Some of the behaviors of the 21st century eater are still determined by similar analogies: trace elements or bifidus are still supposed to give good health, and the claims of "health foods" and *cosmeto-food* are, with some exceptions, largely illusory, even deceptive. This system of food beliefs is a magical thinking because it postulates the possibility of making the various levels of reality interact with each other. This magical thinking can coexist with scientific knowledge because they belong to different registers. This archaic culture has always been the basis of food utopias imagined to heal or improve the body but especially the soul of the otherwise sinful eater.

The 21st century eater is spontaneously a devotee of what Lucien Sfez called "the cult of perfect health," an ideology of "great health" that is doubly dangerous, dangerous already because it works to bring together nutritional, sanitary and social issues; dangerous also because it surfs on the

     A political history of food. From the Pateolithic to our days

refusal to be sick, to age and to die, which characterizes a humanity ready to give in to transhumanism and its promise of an augmented human. The success of light or enriched foods, light and enriched at the same time, the success of health foods, express the new food motto: "Eat to be in shape without the shape." Such food utopias are certainly not new. They had an important development at the end of the 19th century in certain hygienist movements ("a healthy mind in a healthy body"). These American *food movements* intended to reform man by modifying his diet and gave rise, for example, to the Kellogg's empire, named after John Harvey Kellog, a famous disciple of William Miller, pastor of the Seventh Day Adventist Church, and a veritable guru of a crusade against white bread, meat, spices and sugar, in favor of cereals, of course.

We will see in "Leaving the table" that these utopias have known other, much more coercive forms. The fact remains that this combination of nutritional, health and social issues is often perverse. The study of the relationship between types of food and certain social behaviors has come back into fashion. The aim is to determine which bad diet is responsible for bad people... "Hyperactive" children are the main target of research aimed at preventing social maladjustment. The current work focuses on the harmfulness of certain common foods but also on the favourable effects of other foods. For example, they support the existence of a strong relationship between excessive consumption of sugary foods and cereals and a high degree of aggressiveness. At the same time, they claim that a diet based on dairy products and vegetables characterizes the non-aggressive. Some of his experts in social objectification multiply the subcategories: they establish that fruit consumption is higher among prosocial aggressors than among others. First of all, it will be objected that these statistical correlations do not prove anything. It will then be noted that these works evacuate the social and political dimension of the observed phenomena in order to keep only a biologizing and psychologizing approach.

Dietetics or dietetics

We have not come across any food system that did not claim to contribute to good health, even when everyone had to eat according to his rank and refrain from desiring more. The Church, which refused the pleasures of *gula as* much as those of sex, was perhaps sincere. The current specialists in nutrition, by claiming to help us die in good health, are no exception, but they claim to base their discourse on science. Inspired by the famous couple science and scientism, I would like to oppose dietetics and dietetics. The dogmas of dietetics change quite often, systematically making a clean sweep of past precepts, but always speaking with the same authority of those who know: thus, bread is suppressed on Monday and restored on Tuesday, the merits of bifidus are praised on Wednesday, only to be blamed for their credulity, etc. Dietetics draws almost exclusively from certain fields of biology (anatomopathology and physiology) to the detriment of branches such as molecular biology, immunobiology or chronobiology. It does not take into account the capacity of individuals to resist and adapt and ignores intercellular communication. It privileges the notion of organization and the individual dimension of disease by reintroducing a deterministic vision, according to the principle of "one disease, one cause", exclusive of any probabilistic approach centered on the study of the interface between the individual and his environment. This fragmented vision of the human body underestimates the fact that it is above all an integrated and self-regulated system. This fragmented vision of the human body is, on the other hand, commercially fruitful, because each pathology can be matched by a "miracle product".

From hygiene to hygienism

The new homogeneous industrial standards eliminate the natural products that can be produced by farmers or directly by self-producers. Nettle manure, a symbol of this safety and hygienic drift, has only been saved by becoming a commodity. Beyond that, all natural products and popular knowledge about the care of plants and animals risk being gradually banned. The industrialization of the table scored points when the system succeeded in imposing the same rules of hygiene initially conceived for the big industry. The typical example of this drift is the HACCP method (*Hazard Analysis Critical Control Point*), invented by the North American army to secure the supply of space shuttles, and imposed on all forms of commercial or social catering. This deadly ideology of health risk control is responsible for the bankruptcy of many cheese dairies, delicatessens, farm or artisanal bakeries, local slaughterhouses, family poultry farms, etc. Moreover, by eliminating all forms of life, all microbes, all fungi, the industry creates a vacuum, and, as we know, since nature abhors a vacuum, the first organisms to colonize these virgin spaces are obviously pathogenic organisms. The only solution is then to use dangerous products to fight them (antibiotics, insecticides, fungicides, herbicides, vermicides, ovicides, vaccines of all kinds to eliminate any form of uncontrolled life that might remain). This hygienism, the food version of the security ideology, is also the pretext for the implementation of traceability not only of goods but also of livestock (marking by electronic chips).

A political history of food. From the Pateolithic to our days

The hatred of fat

The hatred of fat is one of the main characteristics of the modern diet. By hatred of fat, I naturally mean hatred of visible fat, since industrial products are infinitely richer in saturated fats (fast food, deli meats, etc.). By hatred of fat, I also mean hatred of obese or even fat people. This hatred of fat therefore deserved interdisciplinary research as it has become a symptom of the pathological nature of our table and our societies.

Two clues: more than one North American in three considers fat to be a toxin; more than one French woman in three follows a diet without any pathology... How could we turn the food of the ancient gods into a poison[362] ? How can we "eat well" if we forget that fat is the support of taste (as all wine lovers know)? Many North American researchers have been trying to understand, for years, what this demonization of fat might mean. We already know that this hatred of fat appeared in England in the 17th century, at the time of the religious reform. To put it simply, the Roman Catholics loved fat, just like the continental French, so the reformed islanders will have to start hating fat: "Historically speaking, the origins of this reaction can be traced back to 17th century England, when gluttony and lust, the infernal couple, were mortal sins. Gluttony was not only eating too much, but consuming too much fatty food [...] Four hundred years ago, rich food was almost forbidden in Britain because it was the preferred cuisine of the French, Italians and Catholics and was seen as a threat to English Protestantism"[363]. Hatred of fat was thus the form that the declaration of religious (Protestantism) and national (insularity) independence took.

We also know that the hatred of fat accompanied (and even, it seems, still accompanies) that of sensuality and sexuality. Linda Murray-Berzok was able to establish the importance of this link in English popular literature: a woman eating "fat" (an obese woman) is necessarily avid for sexuality, it would be a woman unable to control herself because dominated by her impulses. The historian adds: "It is eloquent that it is Mrs. Sprat (a central character in British popular literature), and not her husband Jack, who eats fat, remaining faithful to the image of women who, at least from Eve onwards, were lustful creatures with greedy sexual appetites." Linda Murray-Berzok is therefore right to point out that thinness was idealized

---

362. Georges Vigarello, *Les métamorphoses du gras. Histoire de l'obésité. Du Moyen Âge au XXe siècle*, Paris, "L'Univers historique", Éditions du Seuil, 2010, reed. in pocket, Paris, "Points histoire", Points, 2013.
363. Linda Murray-Berzok, "A Question of Morality", in *Malaise, Shame, Pleasure, Slow* magazine, 1994, p. 24

to better repress female sexual desire, unlike other cultures where opulent forms have always been the symbol of seduction and success. The ideal French woman of the 19th century was still the "femme-fruit" painted by Renoir. The example of success remained the petty bourgeois with a paunch..., his paunch showing that he had known how to "capitalize". The hatred of the fat is thus also a social stake and of power. Linda Murray-Berzok notes that "in American culture, women have always been taught to deny hunger and the desire for food and sex, but at the same time, and contradictorily, they are asked to give food and sexual pleasure to others!" Some feminists believe that these paradoxical injunctions are the cause of the high rate of sexual and eating disorders in women (anorexia, bulimia).

The globalization of the fat phobia would be linked to the domination of the Anglo-American model and I would add with the ideology of the sportiness of life. Sexist domination: all sociological surveys show that when confronted with simple paper silhouettes correlated with value judgments, people always judge fat people as less trustworthy and more fickle: "The 'skinny' was judged as sexually monogamous, while the 'fat' was considered promiscuous. Surrendering to fatty food automatically and immediately meant surrendering in the sexual realm." Social domination: we know indeed that obesity can be prognosticated according to the belonging to certain popular and immigrant social classes. The hatred of fat is thus a form of contempt of the powerful towards the weak, a form of class racism which would come to reinforce sexism and sometimes also racism. The *New York Times* headlined in 1992: "Rich lose weight, poor live on fries". Linda Murray-Berzok concludes: "The repulsion towards fat also has a class connotation. Just as thinness mania is an upper-class phenomenon and eating disorders occur primarily among upper-class women, so people gain weight as they move down the socioeconomic ladder."

Food aid or public food service?
The issue of food aid is becoming increasingly important with the programmed movement of "demoyennization" of society, with the rise of precariousness as a system and mass unemployment. The number of young people, elderly people and families going without food is exploding. It is estimated that more than 1 billion people worldwide are malnourished. According to a CRÉDOC survey, 5% of people surveyed said they had gone at least one day without a full meal in the last two weeks due to lack of money, with this proportion reaching 15% in poor households. According to the barometer of the French National Institute for Prevention and Health Education (INPES), 2.5% of French people aged 25 to 75 years

A political history of food. From the Pateolithic to our days

say they do not have enough to eat "often" or "sometimes". Nearly 40% of those surveyed say they have enough to eat but have to make do with undesirable foods, poor foods of poor nutritional quality. Although more than 7 million French people are entitled to food aid, only 2 million have access to it on a temporary or long-term basis, which proves once again that what prevails is not fraud, but the scandal of non-use of existing social rights[364]. This malnourished population is considered, like the impoverished in general, as a burden on a society that is tired of having to pay for a crowd of voluntary helpers.

I would like to show that another point of view is possible, one that would fundamentally transform the way we ask the question of food aid and the responses to the current crisis. Indeed, all the products described as *junk food are* included in food aid. Society makes little use of this sector, like the social catering sector, to question nutritional inequalities in addition to food inequalities linked to purchasing power alone. Low-income households have little or no right to the products recommended by nutritionists, those that appear in the official objectives of the National Nutrition and Health Plan (PNNS). Researchers from INRA and INSERM (National Institute for Health and Medical Research) have shown that at less than 3.50 euros per day it is very difficult to eat well.

I would like to draw a parallel with the situation of social catering (school, company, etc.), which has long been considered the poor relation of public policies, whereas with its economic weight (nearly one meal out of three) it could constitute a major political lever for transforming agricultural policies, thanks to new policies in public purchasing. It is obvious that if we have to re-municipalize school catering (and we have to), it is not to do the same thing as collective catering companies, but to move towards a food made on the spot, relocalized, reseasonalized, less water consuming, less meat consuming, ensuring biodiversity from organic farming and if possible from agroecology[365].

Why shouldn't this same reasoning also apply to food aid? Experiments prove that it is possible to provide food aid through short circuits, with seasonal products, favoring "do-it-yourself" rather than ready-made products. Other experiments, organized by social centers or communal social action centers (CCAS), show that it is possible to rely on popular know-how to relearn how to cook/eat differently. I therefore suggest that

---

364. [COLLECTIF Odenore], *Le scandale du non-recours aux droits sociaux,* Paris, "Cahiers libres", La Découverte, 2012.
365. Marie-Monique ROBIN, *Les moissons du futur. Comment l'agroécologie peut nourrir le monde*, Paris, La Découverte/Arte Éditions, 2012.

the most effective way of exercising the right to food should no longer be through food aid, but rather through a public food service. In order to do this, we must change the way we look at those who resort to food aid: they are not counterexamples of what should be done to make things better down here. The counterexamples are the food choices (naturally constrained by advertising and marketing) of a minority who starve the human race by destroying biodiversity and peasant agriculture. If so many people are hungry, undernourished, malnourished, it is not a problem of agricultural scarcity, because the planet is already rich enough to feed 7 to 12 billion people. The UN estimates that it would be enough to mobilize 30 billion additional dollars over 25 years so that no one would die of hunger and that 80 billion dollars would solve the problem of extreme poverty. These 40 or 80 billion dollars cannot be found, but the world military budget is 1,400 billion dollars, the advertising budget is 800 billion dollars and the "Criminal Industrial Product" (dirty money) is 1,000 billion dollars. The North American food waste alone reaches 100 billion dollars and the excess consumption of obese people represents 20 billion dollars per year. The equivalent of a single day's work worldwide could feed everyone! A public food service could free up territories to finally make something new. A free public food service? A feasible utopia or an illusion? With the average food consumption of the European Union of 28 countries at 1,600 euros per year, making food free for 60 million French people would cost 150 billion euros... that is, four times the budget of the army.

Eating "green"

Agricultural policies are widely debated but less so food policies. Yet this is the battle that must be waged against the delusions of productivism and hygiene. We will only be able to succeed in the transition to an ecologically and socially responsible diet if we know how to (re)symbolize and (re)ritualize our ways of eating. A life includes about 100,000 meals (not counting appetizers, cocktails, snacks and nibbles). Out-of-home food accounts for 50% of this. Social catering (school, company, hospital, prison, etc.) represents about half of this 50%: the public authorities therefore have a good lever. The choice is between this (re)politicization of the table and a techno-scientific headlong rush that will lead to an agriculture without livestock and then to a progressive separation of agriculture and food thanks to biotechnologies. The FAO estimates that we have gone from an average world consumption of 2,358 kilocalories per day and per person in 1965 to an average consumption of 2,803 kilocalories in 1998.

This caloric over-consumption concerns of course the rich countries and the rich of the poor countries while a significant fraction of the population risks to sink into a chronic malnutrition or will succumb to a new cycle of famines linked to global warming.

We cannot continue to sacrifice the future of mankind by maintaining our current diet. We can establish the maximum possible carbon expenditure per meal in a fairly reliable way. We know that the Earth cannot absorb more than 3 billion tons of carbon equivalent each year. Since food represents one third of the emissions, we can estimate that the effort to be made will be proportional. An ecologically responsible meal should therefore not exceed 3 billion tons of CO_2 equivalent (t CO_2 eq or t C eq) for 8 billion people, or 375 kilos of CO_2 eq (or C eq) per person per year. This means that these 375 kilos of CO_2 eq, calculated over 365 days at a rate of 3 food intakes per day, represent a maximum daily "food" CO_2 budget of 114 grams of CO_2 eq. These 114 grams of eq C represent 418 grams of CO_2[366]. This maximum is not respected by any form of commercial food. The annual "food" CO_2 budget should therefore not exceed: 0.418 x 365 x 3 (food intakes) = 458 kilos of CO_2.

Taking into account national disparities proves that we can act. An English person's diet represents 1,778 kilos of CO_2 per year, while that of a French person represents 1,444 kilos. However, a Western meal is equivalent to an average of 3 kilos of CO_2 eq. The western diet therefore represents on average more than seven times what the Earth can tolerate.

How do we calculate the greenhouse gases (GHG) in our food?

The expert Jean-Marc Jancovici reminds us that agriculture is also responsible for most of the emissions of greenhouse gases (GHG) other than CO_2 (such as methane or nitrous oxide). These last two gases cause one third of GHG emissions. Methodologies for calculating GHGs by food category must therefore take into account all gases and all phases of the agricultural and food process. Several organizations have put standard figures on GHGs in different plates. We can recall some calculations of Denis Delbecq:

Hungarian asparagus, 1 kg (truck): 500 g eq C
Peruvian asparagus, 1 kg (aircraft): 12.1 kg C
Bottle of Champagne wine (0.75 L): 2.2 kg C
Bottle of Bordeaux wine (0.75 L): 1 kg eq C
Plastic bottle (1 L): 129 g eq C
Cereal (honey popcorn balls - 350 g): 235 g eq C

---

366. We recall that, by convention, 1 kilo of CO_2 is worth 0.2727 kilo eq CO_2.

Grated Emmental cheese (200 g): 1.3 kg eq C
Spanish strawberries (500 g): 442 g eq C
Brick of orange juice (1 L): 1.7 kg C
Veal meat (100 g): 3.6 kg C
Strasbourg sausages (per 4): 1.025 kg eq C

You won't be surprised to learn that a *cheeseburger* represents, according to the calculations of the Brussels Institute for Environmental Management... 3 kilos of CO2! It is interesting to note that the European Environment Agency has calculated for two types of menus what they represent in carbon consumption:

Menu n° 1: 1 liter of city water; 1 chicken leg; 200 grams of fresh green beans; a quarter of fresh pineapple (from Ivory Coast, by boat), that is to say a total of 0,6 kg eq C.

Menu No. 2: 1 liter of mineral water; 150 grams of beef; 200 grams of frozen green beans; a quarter of fresh pineapple (from Ivory Coast, by air), for a total of 5.6 kg C eq.

Certainly, neither of these two menus is ecologically responsible even if the first one, with 600 grams of CO2, is not too far from the maximum quota of 418 grams of CO2. It would have been enough to replace the pineapple with a local fruit. Menu No. 2 represents 9.3 times the emissions of menu No. 1. The major challenge is therefore to invent an ecologically responsible food: first, agriculture should become an energy producer and no longer a consumer. Then, food policies should be implemented to reach eight major objectives.

A less meaty diet

Meat accounts for about 50% of our environmental impact from food, even though its nutrient content is much lower: the conversion rate of plant calories into animal calories is 4 to 1 for pork and chicken production and 11 to 1 for beef and mutton.

Not all meats have the same carbon footprint: on this criterion alone, we should prefer chicken to pork, pork to mutton, mutton to beef, beef to veal. However, the choice of the least harmful meats is not so simple with regard to other criteria. Thus, Jean-Claude Olivier (farmer and activist of the Confédération paysanne) explains that, against all odds, veal and beef should be preferred to pork and poultry[367]. Indeed, pork and poultry are omnivores and are therefore competitors of humans: 70% of cereals in France are used for animal feed! On the other hand, ruminants (cattle and

---

367. In *Les Zindigné(e)s*, December 2015.

　　　　A political history of food. From the Pateolithic to our days

sheep), thanks to their digestion system, transform coarse grass-based food into proteins that can be used by humans and this, most often, on surfaces (mountain plateaus, flood plains) where it would be impossible to grow market gardening or cereal crops. Beef is also much less contaminated with pesticide and chemical residues than other meats.

The expert Jean-Marc Jancovici specifies that the production of 1 kilo of veal rejects approximately the same quantity of GHG as a 220 kilometer car journey, 1 kilo of milk-fed lamb is equivalent to a journey of 1,800 kilometers, 1 kilo of beef to a journey of 70 kilometers, 1 kilo of pork to a journey of 30 kilometers. We also know that, for the same surface area, a diet based on vegetables, fruit and cereals can feed 30 people; that a diet based on meat, eggs and milk can feed 5 to 10 people; and, if the meal includes a lot of red meat, that only 2 to 3 people can be fed.

An ecologically responsible food should therefore have specifications that favor a less meaty diet, with a preferential option for less harmful meats (which are not, for sure, the "fake" meats from "biotech").

A relocalized food

Anglo-American countries use the concept of "food *miles*" officially recognized by the British government, but largely ignored in France. The principle is to measure the distance that food travels between the place where it comes from and the place where it is consumed. The problem is more complex with industrial products, as all the ingredients that make up the final product must be taken into account. Champagne manufacturers have decided to reduce the weight of the bottle to compensate for the mileage and to limit emissions as much as possible, given the technical constraints. The British government has decided to reduce food imports by 30% by 2020. The US administration has classified food as a national security issue since the CIA established that food products travel an average of 1,700 kilometers. The choices are often complex as it is better from an environmental perspective to eat local beef than imported chicken. It is estimated that if Canadians consumed local food products, they would save 40 kilograms of greenhouse gas production per year.

An ecologically responsible food should therefore have specifications that favor a relocalized food with mention of food miles...

A seasonal diet

Food represents about 30% of the ecological footprint of a European. One of the main levers available would therefore be a return to mainly seasonal foods. This effort could be developed in the institutional food sector because, with its 3.7 billion annual meals, it is a key factor in transforming industrial processes. A food imported out of season by plane consumes on average 10 to 20 times more oil for its transport than the same fruit produced locally and bought in season: 1 kilo of winter strawberries can require the equivalent of 5 liters of diesel to reach our tables.

An ecologically responsible food should therefore have specifications that favor seasonal products with an information system for those out of season.

A diet based on fresh products

Frozen products require a lot of energy for their production and preservation. Freezing consumes 40% more energy than preparing canned food. A frozen product is equivalent to consuming a product (fruit or vegetable) grown in a heated greenhouse and transported by plane over a distance of 4,000 to 8,000 kilometers. Ready-made meals also require a lot of energy to produce and preserve and are often over-packaged.

An ecologically responsible food should therefore have specifications that favor fresh products with a specific logo for each type of food.

Zero waste food

The United Nations Environment Programme (UNEP) has determined that more than one-third of the world's agriculture is wasted. Studies give much higher figures for the United States and England (45%). These losses occur during production, packaging, transportation, distribution and consumption. The available figures are indisputable: food waste in Belgium is 15 kilos per person and per year, and waste in school food is 6 kilos per person and per year. The Brussels Institute has established that wasting a loaf of bread is equivalent to driving a car for 2.24 kilometers, turning on a lamp (60 W) for 32.13 hours or running a dishwasher 1.93 times. Wasting a beef steak is equivalent to driving 4.89 kilometers, turning on a lamp (60 W) for 70.05 hours and using the dishwasher 4.20 times. One of the first issues would be not to follow the North American behavior in the bulimic evolution of portions. The use of plate setting has had a very positive effect in this respect as it represents a significant saving in this area.

An ecologically responsible food should therefore have specifications that favor a food without waste with reduced portions.

A political history of food. From the Pateolithic to our days

A less water-intensive diet

Fresh water will become the biggest problem for humanity in the 21st century as the amount available per human continues to fall. In 1950, there were 16,800 m³ per person, in 2000 only 6,800 m³, and in 2025, we will have to make do with 4,800 m³. The WHO estimates that 3 billion people will have less than 1,700 m³ (which corresponds to the alert threshold). This water crisis is the direct consequence of Western lifestyle choices: while the population has multiplied by 3 in 100 years, water consumption has multiplied by 7. A Westerner consumes 100 times his weight in water every day. A North American consumes twice as much water as a European... a sign that we can always do worse. Let's give some figures on the impact of food choices on water consumption.

Wheat: it takes 1,100 liters of water to produce 1 kilo.
Rainfed rice: it takes 1,400 liters of water to produce 1 kilo.
Flooded rice: it takes 5,000 liters of water to produce 1 kilo.
Soybeans: it takes 2,700 liters of water to produce 1 kilo.
Beef: it takes 13,500 liters of water to produce 1 kilo.
Pork: it takes 4,600 liters of water to produce 1 kilo.
Poultry: it takes 4,100 liters of water to produce 1 kilo.
Milk: it takes 3,000 liters of water to produce 1 liter.
Cheese: it takes 5,000 liters of water to produce 1 kilo.
Eggs: it takes 2,700 liters of water to produce 1 kilo.
(FAO, 1999)

A meat-eater consumes 4,000 liters of water per day. A vegetarian consumes 1,500 liters.

As a comparison, it takes 1,300 liters to manufacture a cotton T-shirt, the equivalent of 15 full bathtubs.

An ecologically responsible food should therefore have specifications that favor a low water consumption food with indication of the main measures by type of product.

Food from agroecology

Organic agriculture is fundamentally less CO2 emitting, but this "organic" must not be a bio-industry travelling thousands of kilometers or used in a de-seasonalized framework or with "ready-to-use" products. An ecologically responsible food should therefore be wary of "false-good" solutions, such as tofu (imported raw material and responsible for deforestation) or Quorn (food obtained by fermentation in order to industrially create a protein-rich mushroom, by adding sugar, vitamins and mineral salts), "food" resulting from an industrial process that emits more CO2 than meat.

An ecologically responsible food should therefore have specifications that favor "biolocal" type food, and even an agroecological approach with mention of the various existing labels.

A biodiverse diet

Biodiversity at the beginning of the 20th century was the result of tens of millions of years: experts estimate that by 2050, 15 to 37% of animal and plant species will have disappeared. We have entered the sixth great phase of species extinction, the fifth, 65 million years ago, involved the dinosaurs and 50% of the species then existing. What is serious is not that species are disappearing, but the abnormally rapid pace of this disappearance and the unprecedented engine of their extinction. Humanity today, having reached the stage of the Anthropocene, is directly responsible. The difficulty is first of all intellectual because the very notion of diversity is impoverished if we speak simply of the diversity of living things. The great danger is not the net loss of species but the homogenization of life in space and time since a few species dominate. It took more than 50,000 years after the last great crisis to find significant diversifications. This is why, rather than species diversity, it is better to speak of cultivated species diversity. Keeping extinct or endangered strains in the laboratory is not an adequate response.

Biodiversity not only allows us to eat better by enhancing organoleptic diversity, it is also a key element of global food security. It is estimated that there are between 300,000 and 500,000 species of plants, of which 30,000 are edible, but humanity only knows how to cultivate 7,000. Agriculture is constantly reducing the number of plants. The French industry uses only three large varieties of potatoes compared to 70 in Peru. Specialists estimate that 95% of cabbage varieties, 91% of corn varieties, 94% of pea varieties and 81% of tomato varieties have disappeared. The situation of livestock farming is just as catastrophic, since out of 500,000 species (birds/mammals), industrial agriculture uses only about thirty, of which half (cow, pig, sheep, chicken, duck, horse) provide 90% of the production. We have therefore lost 90% of animal diversity during the 20th century alone: 41% of the 1,500 remaining breeds are expected to disappear in the next twenty years because of our production choices. The countries of the South are much wiser: Asia continues to raise 150 different breeds of pigs, while the United States is satisfied with 40 different breeds. A local and seasonal diet should also be a biologically diversified diet.

                      A political history of food. From the Pateolithic to our days

An ecologically responsible food should therefore have specifications with quantifiable objectives for the use of plants and animals that ensure biodiversity.

A new eater is therefore being born. We have crossed paths with this new eater on various paths, those of globalization, industrialization and the endless artificialization of our food. I will be told that there are also byways that invite culinary adventure and guarantee food that is good to eat and to think about, and ecologically responsible. It is not for me to choose between these multiple possibilities, but I believe it is necessary to recall that the first objective must be to guarantee the right to food for all. This right encourages us to think of a solidarity that must no longer be only horizontal but vertical. Humanity's chance is that the impossible model of the "end of the eaters" linked to the "green revolution" only concerns a minority of human beings and that there is still the potential, not only in Africa, Asia and the Americas, but also in Europe, to build another food system to support the choice of a peasant agriculture. Only our children will be able to define the value of what we will have cooked in the 21st century. The reader now knows the menu. Can they be happy about it or should they reject it, disgusted?

Food utopias : The food utopias

Religious, philosophical and political currents are always prolix about food: about the table and on the table. Our era is no exception with its claim to feed 8 billion people with a few hundred thousand agronomists, using GMOs and nano-foods. Military academies, such as those in Canada and Great Britain, believe that we should do away with the agricultural origin of nutrients and develop a biotechnological food. Others dream of a relocalized, reseasonalized food, less water consuming, less meat, ensuring biodiversity, based on local agriculture, cooked on site and served at the table. I would like to conclude this long journey through the political history of food by leaving the spotlight on utopias - after having evoked the food counter-utopias. It is a good opportunity to come back before that, as we leave the table, to two diets that have never stopped being talked about, for lack, perhaps, of making us salivate... Wanting to eat like gods was often in history a way of not wanting to eat with humans.

Pythagoreanism to eat like the gods
We don't take food seriously enough anymore. Pythagoras (580-500 BC) died (unless he committed suicide) from refusing to share the *deipnon*. According to the legend, he refused to cross a field of beans, which would have allowed him to escape from his assassins, because destroying or eating beans is equivalent to eating one's parents, thus interrupting the cycle of reincarnations. Pythagoreanism remains, for many, the paragon of a society that knows what eating means and multiplies strict food regulations. Two prohibitions characterize its philosophical school: eating beans or the flesh of the ox. The ban on beans, inherited from the Egyptians, is logical since beans are similar to sexual organs - at the time the word "bean" was a slang term for testicles - and therefore to generation, and to

eat beans is to mix life and death[368]. Vegetarianism is more controversial. To eat meat is certainly to commit a murder, hence the refusal of any contact with cooks or hunters assimilated to criminals. The testimony of Aristoxenus on Pythagoras is however troubling. This founder of the first scientific approach to music shows a Pythagoras who loved meat, which he ate with barley bread, wheat bread, cooked and raw vegetables, accompanied by a good wine. Pythagoras fed on kids and suckling pigs, thus on animals fit for sacrifice, except for the womb and the heart of the animals. Plutarch, in his *Propositions de table* (or *Symposiaques*), presents him as a meat-eater, to the exclusion of beef... Pythagoras establishes, in fact, a clear-cut distinction between guilty victims and innocent animals: "The first animal victims who deserved death, the first animals sacrificed, are the pig and the goat: the pig, because he is the enemy of Demeter: he dug up the seeds, he ruined the crops. The goat, because he has offended Dionysus: he has eaten the vine and destroyed the grapes [...] "To these two guilty victims, Pythagoras contrasts two others, perfectly innocent, which should never have been offered in sacrifice: the sheep and the ox. The former offers wool and gives its milk with the same generosity that the earth shows in producing the harvest. The second is a fellow worker of the man: the closest relative of the plowman, his double, another himself. "To kill the ox, says Pythagoras, is to slaughter the ploughman"[369].

Marcel Detienne proposes to see in the contradictions of the Pythagoreans the echo of the opposition between their dimension as a religious sect and that of an open society with a political vocation: "On the one hand, the anti-city that takes shape in the behavior of the religious sect; on the other, the reformed city that takes shape through the action of the political group. This tension, the food system expresses and translates [...] by combining two models of food, the first of which emphasizes the maximum gap between meat and non-meat, in the opposition of aromatics and the bean, while the second marks the minimal gap between the same two terms by the difference between two types of sacrificial victims, the ox plow on one side, pigs and goats on the other."

---

368. There are other possible reasons for the dislike of beans. "The *Philosophumena* of the Christian bishop Hippolytus of Rome, written around 220 AD, contains some fascinating remarks on the subject. According to Hippolytus, chewed beans exposed to the sun emit the smell of semen. Worse, if one buries a flowering bean and then digs it up a few days later, one will see 'that it first has the shape of a woman's genitals,' and then 'a close examination will reveal the head of a child growing with them'" (Simon CRITCHLEY, *Les philosophes meurent aussi*, Paris, François Bourin Éditeur, 2010, p. 49.)
369. Marcel DETIENNE, "La cuisine de Pythagore" in *Archives de sociologie des religions*, vol. 29, n° 1, 1970, p. 141-162

The real secret of Pythagoras' conduct is here. The issue is to eat with and like the gods, including in the pure sacrifices performed every day. It is not only a question of making offerings with simple products, but with products that recall the primitive food, the communion with the forces of the golden age, without the intervention of techniques such as agriculture. Men must consume the foods they once ate on an equal footing with the gods. The perfect food, therefore, is mallow and asphodel, rather than wheat grown by man. The refusal to eat like and with men goes hand in hand with the desire to eat like the gods.

Catharism, the paragon of food virtue?

The difficulties encountered by the Catholic Church and the powers that be in overcoming the Cathar heresy in blood and fire are a sign that something important was at stake in this new religion. Catharism is indeed another Church, with its preachers, its temples, its dogmas, its sacraments, its two orders of faithful ("perfects" and "believers"). A strong characteristic of Cathar spirituality is the way in which the "good Christians" eat. The ex-weaver who became "perfect", Prades Tavernier, explains: "There are three kinds of flesh, one is that of men, the other that of beasts, the third is that of fish, which is done in the water. You others, my little children, eat only that which is made in water, for it is without corruption; but the others are made with corruption, and they make the flesh proud." So good Christians can only eat the flesh of fish, and even then, not much at a time and only three times a week at most. On the other days they are forbidden to eat fish and wine (always cut), in order to chastise their flesh lest it rebel and impose itself on them. Flesh is perverted by sexuality... therefore evil. The fish is then considered asexual, therefore pure. A "good Christian" must also abstain from anything fatty, except fish oil, and must not eat eggs, cheese, or drink milk. Breaking these prohibitions leads to the loss of the benefit of baptism and obliges one to undergo penance and to be "reconstituted". Moreover, one cannot eat alone, and it is not to share but to place oneself under the control of a companion. God created the spirit and the devil the matter... The refusal to eat meat or fat often goes hand in hand with the hatred of sexuality, and, more widely, of pleasure. The real utopias are in my eyes on the side of *eudemonia*, of the good life.

Politicizing the table

All those who, over the centuries, tried to lay the foundations of a better society necessarily came across the question of food. Anatole France wrote:

"Without the utopians of the past, men would still be living miserable and naked in caves. It is the utopians who drew the lines of the first city. It is necessary to pity the political party which does not have its utopians. From the generous dreams come the beneficial realities. Utopia is the principle of all progress and the outline of a better future. Plato had enacted, around 380 BC, the rules that would allow society to function like a healthy living organism. For Plato, the people can live as they please as long as they provide for the upper classes. The situations where the people feed the parasites are, in fact, the most common. This is why utopias commonly recycle the theme of the nourishing king, always with the same nuance that we find in the ideal society that Louis-Sébastien Mercier describes in his book *L'An 2440*: to make the king keep himself informed every day of the price of foodstuffs, and this in front of the people themselves... Only if the prince bypasses his bad advisors will Bon Temps be able to return.

The character of Bon Temps

The character of Bon Temps moves from one work to another between the 15th and 18th centuries. Bon Temps, Jean-Louis Roch tells us, is the one who makes the fruits of the earth ripen, he is the friend of Bacchus and the goddess Ceres, he lowers the prices of wheat and wine, he announces the end of dearth and famine, the return to abundance[370], etc. This theme is still found in the 19th century, since I found in the BnF a booklet from 1856: *Aux festins du bon temps on buvait en chantant*[371]. The opposite allegory is the disease of Faute d'Argent, "an eminently popular figure", says Roch, which can be found in Villon, Collerye and Rabelais. The people do not only complain about expensive bread, they look for those responsible; they curse the bakers and usurers, they attack the war and taxes. Jean-Louis Roch, analyzing these *sillinesses*, judges that they tell a story always similar: "Bon Temps has been on a journey, in prison, hidden under the ground, we thought he was dead, but he comes back and we would like him to stay." But Bon Temps, celebrated during the carnival, will return only "if justice does not fear force". It would be necessary for that to transform the impure joy of the revelers and the boasters into a more durable happiness: "The moralization would announce an exchange of good procedures in the negotiation with the power; if everyone is mad, all must amend, the people as much as the power, thus only one could reach the social concord

---

370. Jean-Louis Roch, "Le roi, le peuple et l'âge d'or : la figure de Bon Temps entre le théâtre, la fête et la politique (1450-1550)". In *Médiévales*, n° 22-23, 1992, thematic issue: *Pour l'image*, p. 187-206.
371. http://gallica.bnf.fr/ark:/12148/bpt6k5468335b.r

     A political history of food. From the Pateolithic to our days

and, who knows, with the golden age. The use of Bon Temps in the royal entries shows "the importance of the "folkloric" rooting of the elites, even of the mass, at a time when popular culture had not yet been repressed, before ancient mythology and "triumphs" invaded the festival, making it henceforth incomprehensible to a people confined to the role of spectator." The political discourse that accompanies the genesis of the modern state from the end of the 14th century to the beginning of the 17th century is therefore a discourse with a pastoral background, which makes the king a shepherd protecting the "poor people", this shepherd king is already no longer a nurturing king. One attends then, says Roch, the reversal of the figure of Bon Temps in Roger Bon Temps. This new character participates in the curse of the festival when it overflows into everyday life. Roger Bon Temps is the image of the incorrigible partygoer, and, I would add, the bad people. It is thus not only, as Jean-Louis Roch thinks, a popular culture centered on the festival which disappears, it is, according to me, also, the idea that the princes are responsible for the famines.

The City of the Sun by Tommaso Campanella
The City of the Sun (1602, published in 1604) is given by Tommaso Campanella as a simple appendix to a treatise entitled *Philosophia realis*. Tommaso Campanella (1568-1639), a Dominican monk and philosopher, proposed a pontifical theocracy that would be able to realize an ideal republic[372]. He was arrested twice for heresy, tortured, and spent twenty-seven years in prison before taking refuge in France. Noberto Nobbio noted that Campanella's opuscule was both the program of a failed insurrection and its philosophical idealization. Campanella is totally convinced of the realism of his prophecy. In *The City of the Sun,* women prepare the food and set the table, but service is provided by boys and girls under the age of 20. In the dining halls, women are separated from men. All produce is grown in abundance and only organic food is eaten. "They do not use manure or mud as fertilizer: these two so-called methods of fertilizing the soil, they say, corrupt the seeds and the products of the earth thus fertilized are harmful to human health. In this respect they compare the soil to a woman who beautifies herself with make-up and not with healthy exercise of the body, and who will produce, if not properly cared for, debilitated and unwelcome offspring. They repeat that the earth must not be made up, but cultivated with meticulous care. Jean Delumeau was able to show that this political philosophy of Campanella is nourished by an absolute

---

372. Jean Delumeau, *Le mystère Campanella*, Paris, Fayard, 2008.

"pansensism" concerning the whole universe which would have the capacity to feel by touch. Humans would have all naturally this same capacity since the taste would result from an interior touch, which, by the pores of the language, would make know the nature of a food to the "sensitive spirit". Smell is also touch because "smell is a subtle substance that everything exhales". The theme is ancient: did not Democritus live for three days on the simple smell of a warm loaf of bread? The table of the Solarians must be a table "good to the touch", i.e. suitable to satisfy all the senses.

Charles Fourier and the pleasures of the table

Charles Fourier (1772-1837), founder of the Sociétaire school, philosopher, considered as one of the fathers of utopian socialism, is the creator of gastrosophy, a theory proposing to transmit the culture of pleasure[373]. Gastrosophy offers to all the "refinements of good food that civilization reserves for the idle", without which "the Harmonians would soon be, like the French of 1822, miserable in the midst of abundance." The food satisfactions thus hold a very large part in the Fourierist system. It is advisable "to organize the general voracity", to promote greed, true "source of wisdom" and passions accessible to all ages, sexes and social circles. It is a question of raising "the appetite of the people to the sufficient degree to consume the immensity of the foodstuffs that the new order provides". What threatens, in the society of harmony, it is the overabundance of pleasures. There are five meals a day, each consisting of 40 dishes, which are eaten in huge refectories. Gastrosophy also reconciles the pleasures of cooking and health. Fourier proposes a hierarchy of foods that excludes unspeakable and indigestible foods, such as squash, badly cooked bread, the "rancid glue" contained in Italian vermicelli, English food and tea, "It is Anglomania that has led to the proscription of our country's good food at lunchtime, and to its replacement by a vile drug called "tea", a drug that the English are bound to accept, because they have neither good wine nor our good fruits, unless they spend a lot of money. They are reduced to tea like the sick, and to butter like children. Fourier advocates, on the other hand, coffee (even if he drinks little of it), small pastries, fine jams, sweet creams "puffed omelettes or even whipped, strawberries with cream"; "The excellence of the food and wine must have the aim of hastening digestion and accelerating the desire for the next meal rather than delaying it." Fourier is therefore clear: "Our moral doctrines are

---

373. Eddy Trèves, "Charles Fourier (1772-1837)" in *L'Homme et la société*, vol. 26, n° 1, 1972, thematic issue: *Art literature creativity*, p. 241-247.

     A political history of food. From the Pateolithic to our days

insults to God," for if God created the passions, it is because they are good. Therefore, we must not suppress them but create the conditions for them to flourish.

The forgotten banquets according to Jules Michelet and Jean Reynaud

The 19th century still believed in the political importance of the theme of the banquet. I would like to evoke two emblematic texts of this time, two texts not published during their author's lifetime... symptom of the difficulties of the subject.

The banquet of Jules Michelet

Jules Michelet (1798-1875) is one of the greatest historians, unjustly qualified as a populist, republican and free-thinker. His widow published in 1879 Michelet's unfinished manuscript, *Le Banquet*[374], which crossed the themes of Sacrifice and Revolution. This book is a reflection on the repression of the "Printemps des peuples" of 1848, with the conviction that only the unity of all the victims is the condition of a success of the revolution to come. Michelet is a supporter of the "sufficient life" for all the workers (according to the formula of Babeuf). He dreams of a huge table where all the peoples of Europe would be invited. He sketches the criticism of a socialism that will become ultraclerical, abandoning itself to religion and its false morality. He wants popular festivals, national and international festivals that "dilate the heart", he wants open-air concerts, theaters, banquets.

Jean Reynaud versus Pierre Leroux

The banquets are the occasion to make toasts and to open great debates like the one between Jean Reynaud and Pierre Leroux in the middle of the 19th century, about the general sense of the evolution of humanity, the place of religions and equality[375].

Jean Reynaud (1806-1863) is symptomatic of an era, initially a follower of the ideas of Saint-Simon and his disciples, he ended up as a good-natured radical, no longer hoping for a real reduction of wealth inequalities. A graduate of the Ecole Polytechnique, he was under-secretary of state for public instruction during the 1848 revolution. He was responsible for the creation of the School of Administration, which was to train the great

---

374. Éric Fauquet, "Les campagnes d'écriture du Banquet de Michelet" in *Littérature*, vol. 28, n° 4, 1977, p. 50-62.
375. Vincent Robert, "Le banquet selon Jean Reynaud", in *Romantisme*, n° 137, 3/2007, p. 37-47.

clerks of the State in the spirit of public service. He designed the program for the two classes recruited, before the change of regime led to the end of this experiment.

Pierre Leroux (1794-1871), a typographer and writer-philosopher, was one of the fathers of socialism, whose neologism he invented. He remained faithful to his convictions, even if he perceived the dangers of equality without freedom.

Reynaud and Leroux came together after their break with the Saint-Simonians and decided to write a *new Encyclopedia*, which would be, in the words of Heinrich Heine, to the socialist and republican thought of the 19th century, what *the Encyclopedia* was to that of the 18th century bourgeoisie[376]. This *new Encyclopedia* will never be published in its entirety because of their rupture. Reynaud was the author of the section "Banquets", where he strongly opposed the theses defended by Leroux in his own section "Equality". Leroux sees in banquets, from Antiquity to Christianity, both the expression of equality and the instrument of its realization. The equality would be in progress because the banquets would have been moreover widened to the former without-parts. The Greek banquets concerned certainly only the citizens of the cities, but they were an extension compared to the family and tribal banquets. The Christianity of Paul would have widened the banquet, therefore the equality, to the whole humanity. Equality, already liberated from "birth castes", will soon be liberated from "property castes". The banquet is a symbol and an instrument of equality. Jean Reynaud considers on the contrary that the time of banquets is over, that it belongs to the past, undoubtedly to the distant future, but not to the present. He refutes the idea of a deepening of the idea of equality through the enlargement of the banquet, because the Christian banquet is the antithesis of the Greek banquet: indeed, what can it mean to eat together when one has the body of God as food? Jean Reynaud recognizes that eating together does not only develop the mind (reason) but also the heart (feeling). He gives as an example the Dorian banquets (symbol of an egalitarian civilization). The unity of the State, for Aristotle, rests on the common education, on the common food and has for consequence the equality of the goods. The Christians precisely renounced the common life, after the primitive phase, because of their refusal of the community of goods. The Middle Ages could therefore not give any serious value to banquets, since they

---

376. Jacques Viard, "Pierre Leroux et les romantiques" in *Romantisme*, vol. 12, n° 36, 1982, thematic issue: *Traditions and novations*, p. 27-50.

---

were reduced to a mystical symbol of communion... Reynaud explains that under the empire of a religion, so detached from the earth, from matter, agapes can only become simple symbols. Even if, he continues, since the terrestrial side of life begins to reappear, one attends a resurrection of the old forms; but it is without danger because the taste of the celestial things is henceforth too much rooted in the world to run any risk of being smothered (*sic*). Logical with himself, Jean Reynaud proposes to reduce banquets to a function of civility: "Why should our villagers not give themselves the pleasure of conversation and society. Like our wealthier city dwellers, they would soon gain not only more cordiality, but more urbanity. Every Sunday would become a festival for the whole village in the countryside or for the workers' association in the city, as it is for the Church. It would be the time to make the famous "chicken in the pot" program a reality at last; and when we have reached a time when there is enough progress in morals for hearts to be disposed to such commitments, we may well believe that there will also be enough in the order of distribution of wealth for purses to make little resistance. In the future, therefore, I see each commune having its own banquet hall with its church, its school and its town hall. [...] The food may be simple, but the service is no less tasteful and every household will find lessons in it. I even imagine a laughing emulation between the families, which, in turn, were in charge of the arrangement of the feast. It is to the mayor that belong the presidency and the government of the toasts, not that his ministry of police is necessary here, the very authority of the company forms a magistracy in front of which no derangement could be tempted to occur; but it is the mayor who is the head of the family of the community, and it is at the common table, especially, that this character shows itself. A double choir of children, under the direction of the teacher, opens the banquet and an address by the spiritual leader of the souls ends it. There is no need for long periods of time here, everyone is half-heartedly disposed. The small enmities born during the week, and which time often aggravates, like small debts, are softened, jealousies are dissipated, even legitimate demands are tempered, and those who have come to join the banquet in sadness and discontent return with hearts that are free and full of hope and goodness.

Jean Reynaud's major work remains *Terre et Ciel*[377] in which he puts forward two theses: that of the plurality of worlds and the habitation of

---

377. Jean Reynaud, *Philosophie religieuse : Terre et Ciel*, Paris, Furne Éditeur, 1854, http://gallica.bnf.fr/ark:/12148/bpt6k627327.image.f3

the stars, and that of a progressive metempsychosis which he presents as an extension of Christianity. Of politics. There is not any more.

Let us leave, to end this journey, the word of the end (hunger?) to Pierre Leroux: "Down with the stars! Down with the stars! Politics and Champagne wine, that's my future life!"

THE BLASTER[378]

Western humanity has known since Adam and Eve that food can be dangerous. However, we have been able to establish throughout this political history of the table that what is at stake around food is as much a story of love as it is of loathing for humanity. Our most ancient ancestors were already fully human in terms of their food practices, their diet was much more diversified than we choose to believe: they seasoned food, they ate symbols, they already liked fat, they cooked their food long before they mastered fire, they knew how to store food in a skilful way, they organized meat or vegetable feasts according to the periods, funeral feasts, etc.

Everything began to go wrong when a minority claimed to be the only one able to communicate with the dead and appropriated the stocks, the beautiful pieces, the first intoxicating drinks, excluding the majority from the right to the banquet. This minority made the feasts as many occasions to challenge each other, to compete to prove who dominated the others. Our distant ancestors made the table a stake but also a political means.

Mankind, which has lived for most of its history by hunting and gathering, was not obliged to switch to agriculture and it took the colonization of hordes from the east of the continent for the natives to submit to this new way of life. The protohistoric societies that soon developed in the East did not invent the pleasure of the table, but much more banally the politics of cooking and the cooking of politics. The food separatism of the powerful will never cease to develop since the constitution of the first city-states, to the point that the table lent to the gods in legends is only a copy of the table practices of those who had managed to dominate the others.

---

378. Let's remember that the boute-hors (or boutehors) was the moment after the meal among the nobles of the Ancien Régime, reserved for a few intimates or initiates invited by their host to accompany him to his private apartments where wine and spices were served and where they sometimes discussed things more discreetly or more cheerfully than at mealtime.

The power and the wealth were said in a native way through banquets reserved to the powerful ones but also through the obligation, little by little admitted, to feed to its expenses the small people. One should not however have a miserable vision of the food of the people in Sumer, in Babylon, in Mesopotamia, which knew less chronic famines than modernity. This is why these civilizations invented a whole grammar of food which will remain with them, with the system of rations or food fields, with the duo bread/water then bread/beer, with the increasing opposition between the food of the rich and the poor.

Egypt was the first civilization to conceive its table as a real language, so much so that the same hieroglyph meant eating and speaking. We still owe it many of our food symbols. Greece will introduce the notion of sharing between equals, to the point that the same word meant eating and sharing and that participating in the banquet meant citizenship. The society that invented modern democracy was the one that pushed the art of the banquet as far as possible, inventing a cuisine of sacrifice and elaborating rituals. The ways of coming to the table, of sitting or lying down, of cutting the meat, of passing the word with the wine, of advocating the mixture of wine and water but also of other foodstuffs, constitute a language that serves to say that dividing and uniting the society is done in the same movement.

Ancient Rome of course inherited the food grammar of Egypt and Greece, but it brought an essential dimension by pushing the notion of pleasure further. The Republic and the Empire developed food policies alongside agricultural policies, through sumptuary laws limiting excesses at the table, and also through the principle of food distributions which were never reduced to the slogan *panem et circenses* ("bread and games"). The grammar of food, of which we are still largely the custodians, made a considerable leap throughout Roman civilization with its definition of the political status of food, vegetables, meat and pastries, with the practice of *prandium*, with the importance of the question of bread, with the opposi-tion, more political than culinary, between grilled, roasted and boiled. The Roman *convivium* certainly no longer displays the political dimension of the Greek *symposion* and the Romans replaced the discourse on frugality and simplicity with that on abundance and luxury, but the Roman food symbols are directly political.

The Gallic table will shock the Greek and Roman travelers so much its grammar was different. The political life of the various Gallic people was completely punctuated by the organization of great banquets which could last weeks and gather thousands of guests, so much the aristocracy had the duty not only to feed its customers (the people), but to waste. The

Gallic banquets thus have an essential political function although it is then interdict to speak politics during these agapes and that magistrates took care of this discipline. The Gauls will also surprise Greeks and Romans, not so much because they drink their wine pure, but because, although being recognized as the best breeders and farmers, they always chose to remain, in parallel, gatherers and hunters... The Romans will take support, at the time of the conquest of Gaules, on the rich Gauls which will adopt more or less their table manners against those which will preserve then the people of the countryside. The Gallic "collabos" like Ausone will become the propagandists of the Roman table thus creating a true cleavage between the food of the new elites and that of the people.

The collapse of the Roman Empire did not give rise to a "barbarian" table, quite the contrary. The Merovingian table was rich and diversified thanks to hunting and gathering, which complemented agriculture and animal husbandry in a pleasant and useful way. The Merovingians liked to eat and drink, but in a different way than the Gallo-Romans and the Franks, the new masters of the country, who brought with them quite singular culinary traditions. The table kept its political function as an identity marker but also by the organization of banquets by/for a king, at first itinerant, thus tracing his kingdom. However, the old and new masters very quickly made a political compromise on the back of the people, sending them back to the side of barbarism and reserving for themselves the status of civilized people. The barbarians were no longer those who ate meat and drank milk, but those who lived from the forests, marshes and moors, in short, also from gathering and hunting. Some powerful people belonging to the new Christian religion then wrote treatises on the right way to eat in order to fight what remained of the old Gallic paganism, but above all in order to defeat the Christian heresies, which were far from always being a minority in Gaul. The Church started to preach frugality to the people, reserving gluttony for the powerful. Sidonius Apollinaire and Anthymus even became advocates of meat-eating...

A Merovingian banquet will first be the sharing of a pig, a sign of national identity. The Carolingian tables will be characterized quite quickly by the abandonment of the principle of the nourishing king (God provides for everything thanks to the alms of the rich) and by the hatred of the flesh... This Christianization of the table will be done by the repression of popular food traditions: the "Christianized" people will have to stop eating four times a day, they will have to agree to give up desiring foods that the Church says are above their rank, they will soon have to accept the supremacy, against which they will rebel, of bread over meat. "Christian eating" is austere on the side of the powerful, but on the side of the people it is misery. The only exception will be the "Franc-Christian" drinking with the praise of the good French wine opposed to the bad English beer...

The table that follows the Carolingian era will be a clerical-feudal table based on an almost complete dualisation of the table justified by the Church and the doctors. The table will be used to express the power of the king and the Church and the smallness of the people of little. The invention of the French service was first conceived as a political device. The clerical-feudal table marks the passage from the nurturing prince to the new predatory prince.

The table of the absolute monarchy will be that of a state seeking to ensure its autonomy from the pope. The Gallican religion will soon be answered by the invention of a Gallican table based on the counter-models of the Spanish and British ways of eating and drinking. To the rigid respect of the precepts of the Church and its condemnation of the *gula* will be opposed the "natural eating" and the "rational eating" of the Renaissance and then the philosophy of the Enlightenment. The search for symmetry and aesthetics corresponds to a secularization. The absolute monarchy never ceased to invent the "absolute table" with new products, but above all with a new and skilful staging of the meal: service took precedence over cooking for a long time, despite the art of sauces and the "pastry-architecture". This "absolute" table had only one major flaw, that of totally abandoning the people, by deconstructing the mechanisms that ensured them a minimum of subsistence. The people will never stop revolting, not because they were hungry, but because they condemned the abandonment of food policies linked to the success of liberal theses.

The principle of taxing tariffs will never cease to be a popular demand. The French Revolution is also explained by this refusal to see this moral economy disappear. It will first try with/under Robespierre to recognize the right to existence of each person, that is to say to ensure politically, with the laws on the maximum, the food supply. One dreams of a structured food capable of structuring the thought, one adopts the ternary meal, one refuses the cooking of the lukewarm, that of the mixture because the table must be educational. Thermidor will mark the return to economic liberalism and the definitive victory of the so-called "republican" potato against the chestnut, emblem of a popular diet against which the good bourgeois society and the Catholic Church will rise. The people of the cities and the countryside had to work hard to be able to eat, not to celebrate.

The bourgeois table of the 19th century will be that of a people given over to the appetites of the fat. Economic liberalism coupled with the

A political history of food. From the Pateolithic to our days

blindness of the elites explains the food shortages that still hit France in the 19th century and the crisis of the French livestock, which was much worse than elsewhere. Of course, the 19th century was the golden age of the bourgeois table, but it was even more the age of dietary counter-utopias, when the intention was to make people eat bones, with the constant support of the highest scientific and moral authorities. The 19th century was the century of food falsifications that Paul Lafargue denounced. It was even advocated to make people vegetarians in order to reduce the cost of their food and to "moralize" them. The great cuisine flourishes, but as a language of revanchists, and it is not by chance that the great cooks and gastronomes that this century will give itself were all reactionaries and counter-revolutionaries.

The 20th century only really began in the agricultural and food sector with the "green revolution", that is, with the adoption of an industrial model. If it solves the food supply of those who will make up the "Trente Glorieuses" (but this does not mean that another agriculture would not have been possible), it will be at the price of the end of peasants, the destruction of ecosystems, the plundering of the Third World, the destruction of popular food cultures, and soon the return of the great food scares...

The 21st century will be born with the return of famines, which will be added to the malnutrition still affecting more than 1 billion people, not because of the climate, but because of Western political choices of agriculture and food based on extractivism, petroleum, speculation on agricultural raw materials, unfair competition of subsidized agriculture in the North against that of small abandoned farmers in the South...

Humanity is therefore at a crossroads: either it pursues the current trends towards ever more artificial foodstuffs and the destructuring of the table and invents an agriculture without livestock, thanks to meat substitutes, and a food without agriculture worthy of the name with the generalization of vertical farms, or it chooses to recognize the right to food sovereignty and develops a true agro-ecology based on the know-how of one and a half billion small farmers. The only way to ensure the ecological transition and therefore also social equality is to combine food policies that we will have to reinvent with agricultural policies that need to be revolutionized. We must indeed learn all the lessons of the political history of the table to compensate for the necessary decrease in energy waste (the folly of our time: we consume 10 calories to produce a single calorie of food) by an increase in culture. It is not by chance that the table of the economically poorest countries is often the richest in terms of culture, whereas the opulent nations have invented *junk food*. This choice is eminently political because it implies rethinking the hierarchy of legal norms to ensure that the right to food (officially recognized in the Universal Declaration of Human Rights) always takes precedence over the right to lucrative property. We must recognize that the popular cultures of the table, those that remain as well as those that will have to be reinvented, as well as the peasant cultures, those that come from the past as well as those that are emerging, are at the heart of the human fabric. The table is thus eminently political in its two aspects: what do we eat? how do we eat? because it always supposes both to say unity in division and to build commonalities. Bacchus and Comus must therefore become full citizens in order to be able to feed 10 billion people tomorrow.

TABLE OF CONTENTS

APPETIZERS

FIRST SERVICE
Prehistoric tables

SECOND SERVICE
The Mesopotamian table

THIRD SERVICE
The Egyptian table

FOURTH SERVICE
The Greek Table

FIFTH SERVICE
The Roman table

SIXTH SERVICE
The Gallic table

SEVENTH SERVICE
The Merovingian table

THE BLASTER

MÉMOIRES MILITAIRES

DE

JOSEPH GRABOWSKI

OFFICIER A L'ÉTAT-MAJOR IMPÉRIAL

DE NAPOLÉON Ier

1812-1813-1814

PUBLIÉS PAR M. WACLAW GASIOROWSKI

———

TRADUITS DU POLONAIS PAR MM. JAN V. CHELMINSKI
ET LE COMMANDANT A. MALIBRAN

PARIS

LIBRAIRIE PLON

PLON-NOURRIT ET Cie, IMPRIMEURS-ÉDITEURS

8, RUE GARANCIÈRE — 6^e

———

1907

MÉMOIRES MILITAIRES

DE

JOSEPH GRABOWSKI